PRESIDENTIAL
PERFORMANCE

PRESIDENTIAL PERFORMANCE

A Comprehensive Review

M AX J. S KIDMORE

McFarland & Company, Inc., Publishers
Jefferson, North Carolina, and London

Library of Congress Cataloguing-in-Publication Data

Skidmore, Max J. 1933–
    Presidential performance : a comprehensive review / Max J.
Skidmore.
        p.   cm.
    Includes bibliographical references and index.

    ISBN 0-7864-1820-6 (softcover : 50# alkaline paper)

    1. President — United States — Evaluation.   2. Political
leadership — United States — Evaluation.   I. Title.
E176.1.S6134   2004
973'.09'9 — dc22   2004008628

British Library cataloguing data are available

Manufactured in the United States of America

Cover photograph: ©2004 Comstock

McFarland & Company, Inc., Publishers
  Box 611, Jefferson, North Carolina 28640
    www.mcfarlandpub.com

For my wife, Charlene — may we experience
many more presidencies together

TABLE OF CONTENTS

INTRODUCTION

Are Presidential Rankings Meaningful?

Popular writers know that to attract the attention of Americans, a list is always helpful. An assertion of the "ten best," or "top one hundred," of anything is likely to attract immediate attention. Presidential rankings are no exception. They emerged in 1948 when one of the most popular journals in American history, *Life Magazine*, published what turned out to be the beginning of a booming enterprise. The prominent historian Arthur M. Schlesinger, Sr., had selected fifty-five experts on the presidency and asked them to rank the presidents. He then compiled his findings for *Life*.[1]

The result was interesting, and clearly it had some substance. Is it any wonder that Abraham Lincoln, George Washington, and Franklin D. Roosevelt ranked in the "Great" category, that Pierce, Harding, and Buchanan did not, or that study after study since has reflected the same finding? There is variation, of course. "The choice of best and worst presidents has remained relatively stable through the years," but there has been variety in the rankings of those in between. "Some presidents — particularly J. Q. Adams, Buchanan, Andrew Johnson, and Cleveland — have declined in the later polls."[2] For certain presidents the years have brought greater shifts, some of which have been quite dramatic.

One might question, though, whether it is necessary to undertake a formal ranking to recognize the most outstanding presidents, and whether it is meaningful — or even possible — to develop any kind of precision regarding the bulk of the incumbents, those who "rank" below the stars and above the failures. One value of such a study, of course, could be that it exposes the views of certain historians to the public — and that the views attract the

1

attention of a modern public that rarely pays any attention to historians (or, for that matter, to history).

Schlesinger conducted a follow-up study in 1962. The *New York Times Magazine* published his second report, which he had expanded to include seventy-five experts.[3] In both cases he asked his respondents to rank presidents into categories of "Great," "Near Great," "Average," "Below Average," and those at the bottom who fell into the category of "Failure." Schlesinger's work and similar studies have not escaped criticism. They are, however, interesting; they are even seductive — critics themselves have been known to publish their own lists.

Thomas Bailey is a prominent example of such a critic.[4] He developed more than one hundred initial criteria, which he distilled down to forty-three. He produced his list, applying his newly streamlined criteria, to determine whether he agreed with Schlesinger's results. To a considerable extent he did — even though he "regarded the Schlesinger polls as a Harvard-eastern elitist–Democratic plot."[5]

Additional scholars and others, following Schlesinger's lead, produced their own polls. Schlesinger noted that these came about when quantitative studies were "coming into vogue. Also," he said, "political scientists, with their faith in typologies and models, were joining the fun. Would not the results be more 'scientific' if presidents were given numerical scores against stated criteria?"[6]

Gary M. Maranell in 1968 classified presidents based upon a poll he conducted of more than 1,000 members of the Organization of American Historians, 571 of whom responded.[7] David L. Porter in 1981 published a similar study, although he based it upon a poll of only forty-one experts on the presidency.[8] The following year the *Chicago Tribune Magazine* polled forty-nine presidential scholars to come up with its own classification.[9] Dwarfing them all was the 1982 study by Robert Murray and Tim Blessing, which they based on 846 responses from some 2,000 questionnaires.[10] William Ridings, Jr., and Stuart McIver conducted another large project, beginning in 1989, that included a number of respondents other than scholars. They described their study somewhat vaguely in a 1997 book (revised in 2000), which even included a rating of William Henry Harrison. At least their study had the virtue of listing the participants; and a decidedly mixed group they were. The list — albeit admirably structured to represent women, minorities, regions, and the like — included a handful of outstanding scholars, but primarily its defining characteristic, at least insofar as it concerns presidential studies, was the obscurity of those responding.[11] Whatever their worth, these efforts in general certainly justified Arthur Schlesinger, Jr.'s, comment that the more recent studies have adopted "more pretentious methodologies."[12]

In 1996, the *New York Times Magazine* asked him, the other Schlesinger, to follow his father's example and produce yet a third ranking of presidents. Thirty-two historians, politicians, and scholars of government participated in the study, which appeared as "The Ultimate Approval Rating" on 15 December 1996. Schlesinger published an expanded version under the title "Rating the Presidents: Washington to Clinton" in the *Political Science Quarterly* in 1997.

A number of scholars have attempted to make some sense of presidential rankings on their own without referring to lists of experts. Many general works on the presidency have discussed presidential greatness and identified presidents who stood out for good or ill. They range from the excellent study by Clinton Rossiter[13]—a classic—to those adopting complicated, and often questionable, classification schemes. Probably the least satisfactory are the strained attempts to analyze (or psychoanalyze) presidents based on personality types. James David Barber's The *Presidential Character*[14] was the pioneering such effort. William Pederson and Ann McLaurin, in their *Rating Game in American Politics*, followed Barber's lead and attempted to expand his work. The result, if anything, was even more strained than his.

A recent such study—and one of the more interesting—was *The American Presidents Ranked by Performance*, by Charles and Richard Faber.[15] Judging all presidents by their performance on six separate categories, the Fabers provided each with an overall score. Wisely excluding Garfield and W. Harrison because of the brevity of their terms, they ranked thirty-nine presidents from Washington to Clinton in order from top to bottom. Their rankings, unsurprisingly, put Lincoln in first place. Washington comes in second. Tied for third place are Franklin Roosevelt and Wilson(!). At the bottom, the Fabers put Nixon, Arthur, Pierce, and—in last place—Grant.

Grover Norquist—who wants Reagan's face to be carved into Mount Rushmore, who conducted a successful campaign to change the name of Washington National Airport to "Ronald Reagan Washington National Airport," and who has vowed to see to it that every county in the United States has something substantial named for Reagan—no doubt was outraged by the Fabers' study (if, that is, he was made aware of it). The Fabers placed Reagan fifth from the bottom. Ironically, Reagan tied for that dubious honor with the president who, if press reports were correct, was his own favorite: Coolidge.

There are, as mentioned earlier, many criticisms of the entire ranking enterprise. Certainly a valid complaint regarding rankings is that they are inherently superficial. Occasionally they will be obviously so, such as those (not including the Schlesinger studies or the Fabers') that rank James A. Garfield, who was assassinated after only six months in office, or even William

Henry Harrison, whose presidency set a record for brevity: his time in office ended when he died a month following his inauguration. How can one take seriously the C-SPAN study in 2000 of "90 presidential experts rating ten qualities of presidential leadership," when it rated the unfortunate Harrison? (C-SPAN placed him fifth from the bottom, ahead only of Harding, Pierce, Andrew Johnson, and Buchanan in that order.)[16] At least that was "merely" a journalistic effort. Inexcusably, the often-cited Ridings and McIver study put Harrison even higher, immediately behind Garfield and ahead of Fillmore, Pierce, Grant, Andrew Johnson, Buchanan, and Harding![17]

Some presidencies also present special challenges, as a number of scholars have noted. Was Wilson great, as the Fabers have him; a failure; or both? What about LBJ, who both achieved and failed so enormously? Even assuming that it is possible to arrive at a useful quantitative measure for something so complicated and varied as a president's performance, could such a measure ever place in perspective the most extreme case: a record reflecting both such triumphs and such depths of disgrace as Nixon's?

Inadequacies therefore persist in all ranking schemes, and likely are unavoidable. This is true regardless of the complicated measures that many authors employ in their attempts to be "scientific" and to avoid what they perceive as the weaknesses of all previous studies: "none of them," as the Fabers put it, "specified in any meaningful detail the criteria to be used in the ratings."[18] The Fabers praised Bailey's forty-three measures, because "if we are going to make ratings with even a rough degree of plausibility, we must first set up measuring rods."[19] They did specify their criteria in advance, as they indicated was necessary. This enabled them, they believed, not only to know "the precise criteria on which to base" their ratings, "but also what evidence to look for to judge the extent to which each criterion was met."[20]

And there came the subjectivity — the "extent to which each criterion was met" was a matter of judgment. The use of a quantitative scale gives a veneer of precision, and numerous such scales combine to provide an aura of scientific validity. Despite that appearance, subjectivity dominates the fundamental placements on each scale, and the result says more about the notions of the evaluators than about actual presidential performance.

Consider, for example, one of the Fabers' highly rated presidents, Theodore Roosevelt. He would have been placed even higher than seventh, they said, but "we rated him no better than a tie for eighteenth in Foreign Relations, largely because of his cavalier attitude toward our Latin American neighbors."[21] They gave him this ranking despite his sterling record in diplomacy, despite his support for international arbitration, despite his generally better reputation at the time in Latin America (his attitudes and his actions in Panama notwithstanding) than most subsequent American presidents (better, certainly, than the Fabers' highly rated Wilson), and despite his receipt of the Nobel Peace Prize. He became the first American to win the prize — because, one should note, of his successful diplomacy.

The point is not that the Fabers were wrong (or that the Norwegian Nobel Committee's judgment was necessarily superior to theirs) but that their judgment was just that: judgment; it was not scientific fact. Is it really meaningful to say that Theodore Roosevelt ranked just below Truman, who tied for fifth place with Jefferson? What does it really tell us to say that he ranked just ahead of Kennedy (whose presidency did not even extend to three years), who placed eighth?

No two presidents have faced identical situations. In comparing the two Roosevelts, for example, one should recognize that FDR faced not one but two of the most severe crises in the history of the republic: the Great Depression and the Second World War. TR faced neither, yet nevertheless he also placed his mark indelibly upon the institution of the presidency and he also contributed mightily to the development of the American political system. How can one quantify such differences? Is it truly meaningful to classify the one as "great," and the other as not quite?

Perhaps to some extent it may be, considering that some sort of classification is inherent in any evaluation. A formal ranking, on the other hand, would appear to be worse than useless in that it provides a veneer of scientific precision that can only be spurious. To look at such an example, how meaningful could it possibly be to compare, say, the two popular, successful, and conservative Republicans William McKinley and Dwight Eisenhower — who served in two vastly different situations — and to conclude that one rates so many "points" higher than the other?

The argument here, of course, is critical of rankings. It also rejects the arguments of some of the critics that the trouble with rankings is that they are not sufficiently "scientific."

It rejects another criticism, as well: the charge that rankings are bad because they reflect a bias in favor of activist presidents. There can be little doubt that activist presidents fare better in the rankings, but this is not because of bias. Rather, it is because of the nature of the presidency. If rankings reflect anything, they reflect effectiveness. No president can be effective — however measured or evaluated — who fails to use the resources of the office, nor could any president be considered great (or effective) who worked to subvert or minimize the powers of the presidency. Rossiter put it forcefully: "We are not likely," he wrote, "to rate a President highly if he weakens the office through cowardice or neglect"; nor, I would argue, through ideology. "A place at the top of the ladder is reserved only," he noted perceptively, "for those Presidents who have added to the office by setting precedents for other Presidents to follow." [22]

If whiggishly oriented critics consider this to be a biased view, so be it.

No one, however — be it business leader, cleric, professor, or (especially) elected official — could legitimately be considered to have performed well unless that person had used the powers of the office wisely and effectively. Neither in politics nor in any other walk of life does one achieve greatness by constantly deferring to others, or by merely accomplishing routine tasks, however efficiently. An evaluation of good performance would seem to require that the office-holder used the full potential of the office to accomplish its stated goals. To discard ratings because they reflect an activist bias would be to discard them for the wrong reasons — it would be like disregarding the result of a horse race because determining winners reflects a bias in favor of horses with greater speed. The great presidents are the ones who use the office to accomplish the most in a positive sense.

Might it provide greater insight, therefore, to forego any attempt to be "scientific," and simply to evaluate each president based on the manner in which he handled the tasks he faced, and the way in which his performance in office had lasting effects? Such an evaluation would consider how the country fared as a result of a given president's actions, how those actions affected the quality of government, how they affected the presidency, what precedents they established, and whether they bequeathed to the nation a better government — and hence an improved quality of life however determined. The consideration must include both the immediate effects of an incumbent's presidency, and its broad effect upon the future. Of course, it is important to consider how successful a given president was in attaining his goals, but it is equally important to assess the goals themselves. Success in attaining destructive goals should not bring the mantle of greatness to a president.

Will the resulting evaluation be subjective? Of course, but it will be openly so. As an aside, it also would not commit the error of some scholarly studies — especially in political science — that ignore history, studies that treat the modern presidency as though it began with the New Deal. The approach suggested — and adopted — here provides information and an informed evaluation. It also avoids the spurious precision that is inherent in presumably "scientific" rankings.[23] By giving no pretense of absolute authority, it invites the reader to form his or her own conclusions — while providing sufficient information to do so. It thus stresses independent thought, and discourages reliance upon "authority" as a guide.

To accomplish this, of course, requires something lacking in too many readers — and often in authors as well: an understanding and an appreciation not only of politics, but also of American history. Too many studies of the presidency assume that the office as it exists today had its beginnings in the administration of Franklin D. Roosevelt. Such an approach loses historical insights, just as an overemphasis upon models and theory can cause one to lose sight of the subject matter itself.

One should keep in mind that it is the *subject* that is important; the subject is presidents and their administrations — not what conclusions others have drawn about them or what frameworks others apply to study them. Thus it is necessary to provide something that quantitative scales, capsule descriptions, and models do not. That something is a discussion — even a brief discussion, as long as it provides some depth, — of each president's administration. To their credit, the Fabers do provide at least a sketchy discussion of each president. This, rather than their multiplicity of scales, is what makes their effort one of the more interesting.

This study is, by the nature of its subject, one-sided. It concentrates almost entirely upon the president. Certainly no president acts in a vacuum, and no president's accomplishments are his alone. This is especially true in the modern, complex world. Many people are involved, and the very sources of presidential power involve circumstance. The Constitution, especially Article II, sets forth the basis for presidential power, as do statutes, court decisions, precedent, the nature of executive function itself, and the like.

There also are numerous informal sources. Public opinion is a major factor, as are the media, technology, the executive's near-monopoly of official information sources, and the like. Circumstance often is overwhelming, as when war inspires support for a president by creating a "rally-'round-the-flag" mentality. The extraordinary events of September 11, 2001 transformed virtually overnight the public image of a president from one who was somewhat bewildered and probably in over his head, to one who was a firm, committed, effective leader.

In the long run, however, and under normal circumstances, the most important determinants of presidential effectiveness come from the ability and personality of the president himself (or someday, one hopes soon, herself). Hence, this study concentrates upon presidents: how they have used whatever resources they have had at hand to deal with the circumstances in which the country found itself, and what the long-term consequences of those actions have been. It relies primarily upon existing knowledge, but does identify some factors that often go overlooked. Because of this, it often presents conclusions different from those that have become commonplace. It is worth repeating that no one should interpret this study as implying that presidents are solely responsible for what happens on their watch; but, as Harry Truman (if not George W. Bush) put it, it is with the president alone that the buck does stop.

$$\boxed{1}$$

GEORGE WASHINGTON
April 30, 1789–March 4, 1797

What can be said about George Washington that has not already been noted, and repeated frequently? He hardly had passed from the scene when Americans began to remember him less as a man than as a figure observed through the mists of myth. That myth grew throughout the next century to culminate in such presumably charming nonsense — but nonsense nonetheless — of the cherry tree story, as it sprang from the enthusiastic mind of "Parson" Mason Locke Weems. Both myth and solid history have commingled to produce an enormous outpouring of work dealing with America's first president.

Prominent among these are the massive biographies of Douglas Southall Freeman[1] and James Thomas Flexner.[2] Richard Harwell abridged Freeman's work to produce a more accessible one-volume study,[3] and Flexner himself wrote a separate Washington biography, also in a single volume.[4] On the Washington presidency itself, Forrest McDonald's excellent volume — although quite slim, and certainly somewhat ungenerous in its conclusions (e.g., "George Washington was indispensable, but only for what he was, not for what he did") — is arguably the best.[5]

Even during Washington's lifetime there was a mythical component in the aura that surrounded him — his commanding presence dominated a generation to an extent never since equaled. He headed the pantheon of America's great for decades. Now, though, the passage of more than two centuries since his administration has made him seem somewhat vague in the popular mind. Our memories have dimmed, encouraged by a weakened grasp of our own history. It is probable that we think today more frequently of two towering figures whom he had the wisdom to appoint to his

Cabinet—Jefferson and Hamilton—than of Washington himself. Recognizing this, according to press reports in April 2002, programs at Mount Vernon were revised to present Washington as an action figure in order to attract greater attention.

But to his contemporaries, no one among the Founders approached him in prestige or honor. "Light-Horse Harry" Lee's comment that the late president had been "First in war, first in peace, and first in the hearts of his countrymen" summed up his generation's attitude toward George Washington. What did they know that the American popular mind with its tenuous grasp of history appears to have forgotten?

They knew that he was steadfast, resolute, and honorable. They knew that he led the American forces during the Revolution and that he led them ultimately to victory—courageously and tenaciously—despite enormous hardships. They also knew that in 1783—before the country had a Constitution, let alone a president—he had suppressed the Newburgh Conspiracy, a cabal of army officers that seems to have sought to seize power. He could have encouraged the plan and possibly used it to set himself up as king, but instead he championed the principle of civilian control of the military. The people knew that he had chaired the convention that produced the U.S. Constitution. They may well have sensed that to some extent he had been responsible both directly and indirectly for the Constitution's creation of the presidency; directly because of his commanding role as presiding officer of the Constitutional Convention, and indirectly because of the assumption that he—the most trustworthy American to Americans—would no doubt be the first president.

It is tempting to assume, in common with many writers, that the Founders thus saw it as safe to create an independent executive with substantial power. The assumption finds support from a comment by a member of the Convention from South Carolina, Pierce Butler. Following the Convention, he wrote to Weedon Butler that presidential powers would not have been so great "had not many of the members cast their eyes toward General Washington as President."[6] Certainly Washington's presence was important, as was the expectation that he would be the first president. The historian Jack Rakove cautions, however, against reading too much into such an idea. He concedes that "historians should tread carefully when they challenge testimony like this," but argues that "Butler's casual judgment cannot be accepted uncritically. For the record of debate at the convention does not readily confirm his point."[7] He noted that historical circumstances, such as party competition for the presidency, caused the institution to develop in ways the Founders had not anticipated.

The important question here, of course, deals not with Washington's standing among his fellow Americans, but of the manner in which he handled the presidency once he assumed the office. Those Americans could hardly have known how important the presidency's creation would be to the future of the United States of America. Nor was it likely that they could have known how carefully and deliberately Washington crafted the institution by his conduct as president, and how important those actions would be to the development of the country, or to his successors in the presidential office. Washington did know, or sensed, the importance of those actions. He recognized that great consequences might flow from things that appear at the time to have little importance.[8]

As the first president, Washington's every action was precedent-setting. The Constitution made a powerful executive possible, but did not mandate one. That fundamental law at its very beginning, in Article I, deals with the powers of Congress, in which it vests "all legislative Powers herein granted." Section 8 of that Article sets forth a list of those powers; they are extensive, but they are specified and therefore limited to those enumerated (or inferred based upon a specific grant of authority).

In contrast, Article II — which deals with the presidency — merely indicates that "the executive Power shall be vested in a President of the United States of America." True, it does mention certain of the president's powers (along with Article I, Section 7 that grants to the president the veto power, without using the word "veto"), but it does not say that the list is exhaustive. It does not limit the "executive power" to the powers "herein granted," and nothing in its language implies that the list it provides constitutes the whole of "the executive power."

That list is considerably less broad than the first article's list of congressional powers, and in most cases it is less precise. The grant of military authority is clear: the president becomes commander-in-chief of the military. He can also "require the opinion in writing" of each Cabinet officer on matters within that officer's jurisdiction, but what did this imply? The extent of the authority that this provision gives to the president as the chief executive has had to be worked out in practice, as has the reach of his appointment authority.

The Senate must confirm appointments; does the president have the power to remove an official from office, or must the Senate approve that action as well? It is clear is that the president has (except in cases of impeachment) the absolute power to pardon. His power to "make treaties" with the "advice and consent" of two-thirds of the Senate, on the other hand, does not clearly specify what form the Senate's "advice" must take, or in fact what even constitutes advice.

He has the duty from time to time to provide Congress with information on "the State of the Union" and to suggest matters for its consideration. This implies a legislative role for the president apart from his authority to veto congressional acts but does not clearly spell out that role. Additionally, he has the power to "receive ambassadors." This provision could be entirely ceremonial. More likely, it implies — but again does not specifically spell out — the sole authority of the president to grant diplomatic recognition to other countries, thus to become the predominant force in foreign policy.

The president must see to it that the laws are "faithfully executed." This places him as chief executive. His power over appointments and his authority to request written opinions from the heads of the executive departments place him as head of the administration. The Constitution, however, does not provide a description of what the general limits to "the executive power" might be, or what it means to head the administration. It provides no definition of "chief executive," and in fact does not use the term. To a considerable extent, therefore, the executive power has emerged from the actions of presidents, and from their interactions with other parts of the political system.

There is broad consensus among scholars of the presidency regarding these points. The perceptive writers Milkis and Nelson, for example, in this instance are representative. They quote Charles Thatch as having written in 1922 that "the executive article fairly bristles with contentious matter." Not until it was "seen what decision was given to these contentions," would it be possible to say "just what the national executive meant," wrote Thatch. Milkis and Nelson proceeded to say that it is not possible "to determine from the words of the Constitution alone what were to be the appropriate relations of the chief executive to the chief officers of the executive departments, or those of Congress to the executive business. Similarly, the Constitution left unclear the extent of the powers that were implied by the executive's responsibilities in war and peace, as well as in diplomacy."[9] They noted that "in large measure, presidents have been able to fill the interpretive void, as 'presidentialists' at the Constitutional Convention such as James Wilson, Gouverneur Morris, and Alexander Hamilton had hoped," but that this "expansion of executive power did not come easily."[10]

Some writers conclude from all this that the Constitution established a rather weak office. It seems closer to the truth to say that the Founders, rather than creating a weak office, created a rather vague office, but one that nevertheless had enormous potential. Whether their vagueness was deliberate or not, they avoided specifying in great detail a position of awesome authority. Neither, however, did they specify rigid restrictions on executive power. To a considerable extent what they created was an open-ended position, one with limits that depended on the ability of presidents to take advantage of the very vagueness that they provided.

It was up to Washington, as the first president, to begin the process of determining what these powers, in practice, actually would mean. His fundamental task was to work within the constitutionally vague framework, and to function as an executive of a government with sufficient power to be effective, yet one that was sufficiently restrained as to be compatible with the principles of republicanism. His secondary task was to function with sufficient power to ensure the effectiveness of the executive within the government, without encroaching upon the legitimate powers of the other branches.

Washington, sharing the general disdain of the Founders for "faction," attempted to govern above party. The result of his attempt to establish precedent in this regard surely disappointed him. Two groups quickly emerged, loosely grouped around Hamilton and Jefferson. The Hamiltonian "Federalists" rallied to Washington's support. The Jeffersonian "Republicans" (or "Democratic Republicans") vigorously opposed the Federalists, and came often to oppose Washington as well.

Milkis and Nelson argue thoughtfully that Washington's attempt to be above party was not a complete failure. They write that his "extraordinary stature and popularity, combined with his commitment to the development of a strong and independent legislature," was successful in restraining "party strife for as long as he was president." They suggest, moreover, that "Washington's renunciation of party leadership left his successors a legacy of presidential impartiality that has never been completely eclipsed." Although a party system quickly emerged, "the Washingtonian precedent demanded that the chief executive lead the nation, not just the party that governs the nation."[11]

It would be difficult to overemphasize the importance of this precedent. It was in evidence to some extent — even if not always, and if never on the part of every player — in the venomously partisan Washington, DC, of the 1990s. It may well be that it had an influence in protecting the fundamentals of the American political system during that painful period.

Washington, as the first president, recognized the importance of symbolism. He therefore moved to establish a measure of dignity and status that would encourage respect for the office. This would require a certain degree of separation from the people, and it also would afford him time and space to attend to his duties — he discovered immediately that a certain amount of privacy was essential if he were going to get anything done. Such a separation could not, however, be permitted to isolate him because connection with the people was required for republican government. A title was in order, but not a grandiose one. He objected to flowery suggestions from Federalists such as Hamilton and John Adams and opted instead to become simply "The President of the United States," as James Madison and the House of Representatives had recommended. Washington's decision not only signaled to the people that the presidency was theirs as was proper for a republic, but it also saved us today from hearing the incumbent described as "His Majesty, the President," or as the "President of the United States and Defender of The Liberties of the Same."

Initially, Washington presided over a branch of government with no other members. He signed into law various acts creating executive branch positions, and those providing for Departments of State, Treasury, and War. He appointed Jefferson and Hamilton, respectively, as Secretaries of State and the Treasury, and Henry Knox as Secretary of War. Washington's ability to dominate an administration with two such powerful personalities as Jefferson and Hamilton — who were personally antagonistic and politically at odds with one another — and to make it function generally with effectiveness was remarkable, and important.

As Flexner put it, "Washington was neither a Hamiltonian nor a Jeffersonian. His point of view combined the attitudes of both men. It was his genius to reach, by recognizing the essence of a problem, the bedrock that underlay opposition."[12] This was especially impressive, considering the two figures involved. The gulf that divided them was social as well as theoretical. "As a Randolph of Virginia," Flexner remarked, Jefferson's blood was as blue as that of any man on the continent, and his livelihood was based on an inherited estate. Hamilton had been born in the West Indies, the illegitimate son of a woman jailed for sexual misbehavior; he had come to the United States as a pauper. Jefferson considered Hamilton a vulgar upstart and Hamilton considered Jefferson a snob who railed about equality.[13]

Washington also appointed Edmund Randolph as the first Attorney General, although not for some decades to come was there an act creating the Department of Justice. Washington's prestige was such that the Senate presented no difficulty in confirming these appointments, which helped establish the precedent that, in most instances, a president is given broad leeway in selecting his top advisors. When he took sides, as a rule it was to agree with Hamilton — which meant that it was to enhance governmental, and executive, authority.

He took special care, also, in selecting officials for other offices as legislation made those offices available. Leonard White has written of the personal care Washington took in applying a "rule of fitness" for the various positions.[14] Forrest McDonald noted that the first president resolutely refused to establish a patronage system, seeking loyalty to the Constitution rather than family connection or past support, for his appointees.[15] He therefore sought not only competence from those holding government positions, but — equally important — sought to appoint those whose actions in office would encourage respect for the new government.

Washington's chief ally in Congress as the new government got underway, was James Madison in the House. Madison had not yet evolved into a

Republican opponent. The president and Madison agreed that, despite the requirement for senatorial confirmation of appointments, the president in most circumstances should have the sole power to remove officials. Following Madison's lead, the House approved this principle, but in the Senate Vice President Adams had to cast a tie-breaking vote in order to secure congressional approval.[16] This provided an important foundation for the president's control of the executive branch, but the issue was not settled for all time. It re-emerged following the Civil War to cause considerable mischief before being laid to rest once more.

Washington moved to take the lead in diplomacy and foreign affairs. This leadership role had an effect regarding the requirement for "advice and consent" of the Senate on treaties that he had not anticipated. It also brought him to assert what came to be called executive privilege.

Regarding the former, in his first year in office Washington went in person to the Senate to seek its advice on a proposed treaty with the Creek Nation. After Vice President Adams read the document aloud to the chamber, there was confusion as to what to do, and it was moved to send the proposal to committee. Washington's formidable temper flared at having to waste his time, and he departed vowing never to repeat the attempt. He never did — nor has any other president gone to the Senate to request its advice. Henceforth, the Senate's role in treaty-making was limited to consent. Since that time, it is generally accepted that treaties are the president's to negotiate.[17] There may, of course, at times be considerable consultation between a president's aides and Senate committee members, but the principle remains.

In 1793, the new and not-yet-stable country was in danger of being drawn into a European war. France, which had assisted America during the Revolution, was opposing Great Britain and its allies. Jefferson and his supporters argued that Congress should determine U.S. policy — if Congress had the power to declare war, it followed that only the Congress had the power to declare that there would be no war. They argued also that America was obligated to assist France. Hamilton asserted that, contrary to the arguments of the Jeffersonians, foreign policy was the president's prerogative.

Washington accepted Hamilton's reasoning, but had Attorney General Randolph craft language that he hoped would be "moderate enough for Jefferson and forceful enough for Hamilton."[18] He issued a proclamation of neutrality indicating that the United States would be "friendly and impartial toward the belligerent powers." Although in deference to Jefferson he avoided the term "neutrality." Washington's proclamation asserted the president's primacy in foreign affairs, notwithstanding the Constitution's reservation to Congress of the power to declare war. His action prevailed, and also prevented the fledgling country from engaging in a potentially disastrous conflict.

Hamilton stayed in the Cabinet until 1795. By that time the last Republican member had departed from Washington's administration. Jefferson had resigned from the Cabinet in 1793. Randolph, who had joined the administration as Attorney General and had replaced Jefferson as Secretary of State was the remaining Republican. He resigned in 1794, after having been accused of attempted bribery and of divulging information to France. Historians even today disagree as to the extent of his guilt or innocence.

The Senate, dominated by Federalists, consented in 1796 to "Pinckney's Treaty" (the Treaty of San Lorenzo) with Spain that secured access for the Americans to the Port of New Orleans and to commerce along the length of the Mississippi. It also established the 31st parallel as the boundary between American territory and Spanish holdings in Florida.[19] The previous year it ratified Jay's Treaty. In neither case had Washington sought its advice.

Jay's Treaty occasioned great turmoil, when it seemed to Jefferson and the Francophile Republicans to defer too much to Britain at France's expense. Under its terms the British finally agreed to remove their troops from the Northwest — as they were supposed to have done more than a decade earlier. The British also granted some trading rights with their West Indian possessions. On the other hand, the United States acquiesced to British searches of American ships in international waters, and did not deal with the impressment by the British of American seamen. On the whole, however, as McDonald put it, "Jay's Treaty and Pinckney's Treaty, taken together, brought enormous advantages to the United States, three sets of gains that partisans in America generally had regarded as mutually exclusive: neutrality, commercial prosperity, and territorial expansion."[20]

In an effort to insert itself into the treaty process, the House, dominated by Republicans, demanded to see papers relating to the treaty. Its implementation would, they argued, require an appropriation, and appropriations very definitely involve approval by both houses of Congress. Washington pointedly refused (in McDonald's words, he issued a "thunderous refusal"). The House had no business concerning itself with foreign policy, he said, and the only legitimate aim for their request would be if they were considering impeachment.[21] The House backed down, the president's predominance in foreign policy prevailed, and Washington had asserted the principle of executive privilege.

Washington's precedent-setting actions were not limited to those involving foreign relations. On the domestic scene, if the new government were to be viable, he had to demonstrate that it could exercise authority. Hamilton provided him with an opportunity in his first term. The Secretary of the Treasury had encouraged Congress to levy an excise tax on whisky. Frontier farmers in western Pennsylvania resisted the tax as an unfair burden — as Hamilton may have anticipated. Transportation was difficult at best, and cash was scarce. They therefore had adopted the practice of generating income by converting their grain into whisky — which was compact and far easier than grain or other goods to transport over roads that were primitive or non-existent — and marketing it.

Hamilton eagerly urged Washington to respond vigorously. The president nevertheless remained cautious, even with growing threats of rebellion throughout 1792 and 1793. In 1794, following an attack upon a revenue agent, Washington federalized some militia units and rode with them to the area. He encountered little resistance, and the rebellion evaporated. Ultimately, he pardoned those involved, but as President of the United States he had made his point.[22] To Hamilton's pleasure, the national government had demonstrated that it had, and could effectively exercise, authority. The Federalists used the rebellion to great advantage in the elections of 1796, when even Washington criticized the influence of a number of "Democratic-Republican Clubs" as having instigated the turmoil.

In addition, the Washington administration pioneered the procedure for admitting new states. The Constitution in Article IV, Section 3, provided the authority — carried over from the Northwest Ordinance of 1787. The Union that consisted of thirteen states at the beginning of his presidency had grown to sixteen when he left office. Vermont, in 1791, was the first to join the original thirteen — it might have been among them but for opposition from New York occasioned by boundary disputes. Kentucky and Tennessee followed, in 1792 and 1796 respectively.

Certainly George Washington was the right person to be the first President of the United States. Certainly he performed his role not perfectly — as McDonald went to considerable length to point out — but nonetheless superbly. Elkins and McKitrick wrote that after Adams's election, "Washington and the new Vice-President, Thomas Jefferson, never saw each other again. Both of them were probably just as glad of it." Nevertheless, seventeen years later in a private letter, Jefferson would say of Washington that "his integrity was most pure, his justice the most inflexible I have ever known, no motives of interest or consanguinity, of friendship or hatred, being able to bias his decision. He was indeed, in every sense of the words, a wise, a good and a great man."[23]

One could hardly object to the use of the designation "Great" when applied to such a commanding figure. Without President Washington — as McDonald conceded — it is doubtful that the United States of America could have survived as it has. Does it add to our understanding, though, to compare him to other giants who followed? What does it mean to say that he "ranks" just behind Lincoln, and either just ahead of or just behind Franklin

D. Roosevelt (or in the Fabers' ranking just ahead of FDR — and, oddly enough, Wilson)?

Lincoln faced challenges even greater than those Washington faced. The challenges facing FDR were at least as great. Does this take anything away from Washington? Should it not be sufficient to say that each man was the right one to be president for his time?

2

JOHN ADAMS
March 4, 1797–March 4, 1801

John Adams — whose many strengths did not include charisma — had the misfortune as president to have succeeded George Washington, arguably the most charismatic person ever to hold the office. It was also to Adams's detriment that he attempted to govern with little or no attention to party. Remaining above party is a feat that no democratic executive anywhere has ever fully accomplished. Washington came closest to doing so, and even he was only partially successful. John Adams, with all his enormous talents, was no George Washington.

Adams served only one term, in all probability because the unique circumstances of that term nearly all worked against him. Richard Alan Ryerson has noted that he was never popular, and "has never been considered America's foremost founder," despite being "the most learned of the Founding Fathers in his chosen fields — law, political theory, and European history — the disciplines that formed the intellectual foundation of the new American nation."[1] His friend and contemporary, Dr. Benjamin Rush, said that Adams "possessed more learning probably, both ancient and modern, than any man who subscribed the Declaration of Independence." Theodore Parker, a generation later, remarked that "with the exception of Dr. Franklin … no American politician of the eighteenth century was Adams's intellectual superior."[2] More than failing to be popular, "he was at times decidedly unpopular," and was "perhaps the only prominent Founder who felt that he personally was fundamentally misunderstood by his countrymen."[3]

Despite everything, President John Adams had a record of substantial accomplishment. The greatest of his achievements was that he kept his country from an impending war for which it was ill prepared.

19

Even had he not followed Washington into office, he would have been at a disadvantage. His term "was absorbed, to a degree unequaled in any other American presidency, with a single problem, a crisis in foreign relations. The crisis had arisen out of hostile actions by the French Republic, ostensibly in retaliation for America's having reached an accommodation by treaty with France's enemy England."[4] The word "crisis" tends today to be overused — headlines, newscasters, and hence the public are likely to use the word to refer to any troublesome situation. The conditions resulting from the war between France and Britain that Adams faced throughout his time in office, coupled with the tension that partisan extremists generated domestically, could well have led to disaster for the newly formed United States. "Crisis" in this case seems appropriate.

National institutions had barely been established when Vice President Adams became President Adams. His rival for the presidency, Thomas Jefferson, had been anything but eager to run in 1796. Jefferson recognized that anyone succeeding Washington would be in for a difficult time. He also thought trouble was brewing. Writing to Madison, he said that Washington was "fortunate to get off just as the bubble is bursting, leaving others to hold the bag."[5] Nevertheless, Jefferson did become the Republican candidate and came in second to Adams in the Electoral College. This meant that throughout his presidency, Adams had his defeated opponent as his vice president.

No other president has been in Adams's position, nor after the Twelfth Amendment could another one ever again be.[6] His predecessor was the most honored of Americans, his entire term was devoted to an international crisis, and his own vice president was the leader of the opposition. How is it helpful, then, to develop a ranking? How useful is it to compare him to other presidents who faced entirely different conditions? What could it mean when historians placed him tenth, above Cleveland and below Truman, for example, in Schlesinger's 1962 poll[7] or when the Fabers[8] placed him twelfth, just below Madison and above Van Buren?

As one would expect in view of the circumstances, Adams had a troubled administration. Not only did he face fierce opposition from the Republicans and from his vice president, but elements of his own Federalists were working with equal diligence to undermine him. To be sure, many of his troubles he brought on himself. He came to office with an impressive background that included eight years as the nation's first vice president — but it was a background that did not include executive experience.

What he did bring to the office — in addition to solid integrity, a massive intellect, a commitment to "balance," an unblemished character, and a superb partnership with his wife, Abigail, whose extraordinary political judgment he valued highly[9] — was a volatile temperament, a stubborn disposition, and an abrasive tendency to blurt out whatever was on his mind. As if his challenges and personality were not enough, he also added to his difficulties by spending extended periods at home in Massachusetts — assuming, unrealistically, that he could run the executive as well from there as he could from the capital in Philadelphia — and he refused to try to make peace with those whose views were relatively close to his, such as Alexander Hamilton, who could have made considerable difference.

In fairness, Adams had no precedents to follow; no American president had ever succeeded another, and there was not yet a tradition that a new president should choose new heads of the executive departments. Any executive experience, however, might have taught him not to retain Washington's cabinet but, rather, to appoint his own. Cabinet officers who shared his principles and reflected loyalty to him could have made all the difference. Except for Attorney General Charles Lee, those in his cabinet — Timothy Pickering the Secretary of State, Oliver Woolcott the Secretary of the Treasury, and James McHenry the Secretary of War — did neither.

The Adams electoral victory had been a narrow one. Washington for both his elections had received a vote from every elector. Adams won by a majority of only three. The closeness of the election is an interesting story in itself.

Although Adams had been the Federalist candidate, and had had Washington's support, the powerful Federalist Alexander Hamilton worked behind the scenes against him. At that time, before adoption of the Twelfth Amendment, each elector cast two votes without designating one for president and the other for vice president. Hamilton recognized that he would have no influence over the strong-minded Adams, so he attempted to sabotage Adams in the Electoral College.

Hamilton worked to persuade southern electors to vote for Adams's running mate, the Federalist vice presidential candidate Thomas Pinckney, but to cast the other vote for anyone other than Adams. He anticipated that New England electors would vote for them both, which would give Pinckney more votes than Adams, thus making Pinckney — a Hamilton crony — president. To fend off this plot that they had discovered, New England electors voted for Adams, but cast few votes for his running-mate, Pinckney.

Hamilton's strategy reduced Adams's margin of victory to three votes, but of course did not succeed in denying him victory. It had the unintended consequence, however, of elevating Thomas Jefferson to the number two position rather than Pinckney, thus making Jefferson vice president. Hamilton must have been chagrined at the results of his scheme, since it led to the election of his archenemy as vice president.

On the other hand, Jefferson quickly became a strong enemy of Adams also, despite their former close friendship. He was in addition a devious enemy. The new President John Adams therefore came into office in March of 1797 with opponents on all sides. He had a disloyal cabinet — which he could have changed but did not — and he had a political opponent as his own vice president, about which he could do nothing. Such a situation was anything but a foundation for political success.

Two disturbing developments were to add to the difficulties. A venomous partisanship had developed, perhaps the most vehement in American history, characterized by vicious party newspapers on both sides, and by the first instance of a physical assault by one member against another on the floor of the U.S. House of Representatives.[10] Then, as cited above, there were the direct threats internationally. Jay's Treaty continued to incense the French, who perceived it to be pro–British. France therefore had begun interfering with American shipping — far more, in fact, than the British had done under Washington's administration. Moreover, French officials had refused to deal with the American minister sent by Washington, General Charles Cotesworth Pinckney, and expelled him from France.

In spite of the insult, and the "virtual war" with the French on the high seas that led to seizures of American ships, Adams sought to preserve the policy of neutrality that Washington had established. Jefferson and his Republican allies interpreted neutrality as favoring the Britain that they despised and as seeking deliberately to lead America to war with the France that they so admired. Adams sought protection for American shipping, and asked Congress in May 1797 to build up the country's virtually nonexistent naval strength. Just before adjourning in July, Congress responded, but only to authorize the mobilization of three frigates — the *Constitution*, the *Constellation*, and the *United States* — that had been constructed under Washington, but remained sitting unused.[11]

With his cabinet and vice president undercutting him at every turn, Adams determined to send a delegation to France to negotiate a reconciliation. He had reached out to the Republicans in hope that that Vice President Jefferson or former Republican James Madison would head the mission. Both had refused to work with his administration, and in any event the High Federalists were outraged at the suggestion and cabinet secretaries threatened resignation.

Adams therefore selected a three-person bipartisan team consisting of two Federalists, General Pinckney (who had remained in Amsterdam, where he had gone after France had expelled him) and John Marshall, with the addition of a Republican in whom he had confidence, Elbridge Gerry. By late summer the Senate had approved the appointments, and Adams had dispatched the mission to Paris.

The long-delayed outcome was so bizarre that the Republicans initially found it difficult to believe until Adams released all the relevant materials. Among other affronts, the French Foreign Minister, Tallyrand, humiliated the emissaries by meeting with them only briefly, then keeping them "dangling for three months in Paris" with no word.[12] Finally, he sent three agents, identified in the papers Adams released only as "X, Y, and Z," to inform them that any reconciliation would require not only a huge loan from America to France, but also a substantial payment to him personally — a bribe. He would meet with them, the Americans were informed, only if they agreed to these conditions.

When Americans received word in 1798 of what had happened in Paris, it strengthened nationalistic sentiment and caused widespread anger, even outrage, that another country could — let alone would — behave in that way toward the United States. Another reaction was befuddlement. The first thing that occurred to James Madison, for example, "on hearing the news was not so much the venality of the French Foreign Minister, Talleyrand, but rather how the Minister, acquainted as he was with America and the Americans, could have behaved so stupidly."[13] Madison was not alone. "The stupidity of Tallyrand's conduct, more than its depravity ... astonished Jefferson. He did not attempt to defend it, yet the consequences of accepting the administration's version of the XYZ Affair were too frightful to contemplate. So he offered excuses and mitigations for France."[14]

In line with their predisposition in favor of France, the Republicans had accused Adams of exaggerating the situation, of being pro–British and anti–French, and of seeking war with France. Any preparation for defense they perceived as reflecting a desire to go to war. When the administration released the relevant correspondence and the Republicans discovered that French conduct was actually much worse even than Adams had indicated, their solidarity weakened, as did their popular support. War fever swept the country.

Actually, most of the Federalist leaders, including Hamilton, had long agreed with Adams that it would be wise as well as prudent to avoid conflict. After the French actions in the XYZ affair, some of the High Federalists, including most members of his own cabinet, began urge a declaration of war. Treasury Secretary Woolcott seems to have been the only one who agreed with Adams that war would gain nothing.[15] Adams remained firm.

He did, however, ask for military preparation, a request that offended the Republicans. They thought it impossible to negotiate sincerely for peace while simultaneously preparing for war, and condemned his speeches as warmongering.

Finally, in the face of the evidence, Congress moved — although Jefferson would continue to believe that Marshall had pushed the French into an awkward position, or would blame Adams for past insults to the French,[16] or would contend that the demand for a bribe from Tallyrand did not truly reflect the position of the French government, The Directory. He did concede, however, that publication of the papers surrounding the incident "produced such a shock on the republican mind, as has never been seen since our independence."[17]

The Republicans, who had been on the attack leading a vitriolic campaign against Adams, found themselves suddenly on the defensive. Of course, Federalist invective was equally vitriolic toward the Republicans — and sometimes even toward their own president. It was a time of dangerously fierce partisanship. For a time, though, Adams was able to bask in the unaccustomed glow of popular acclaim.

He had long advocated military preparedness, especially naval measures. Ships, he believed, would constitute "wooden walls" to protect America. He found Congress accepting his call to create a Department of the Navy, a major accomplishment that would be of great significance to the future of the United States. He appointed as the first Secretary of the Navy the able Benjamin Stoddert of Maryland who conducted the new department with efficiency and who brought loyalty to Adams into his cabinet.

Congress, in fact, now was giving Adams "everything he asked for." It agreed to complete three frigates that had been started in the Washington administration, to permit merchant vessels to arm for their own protection, and to add protective measures for harbors. In addition, Congress "authorized the acquisition of twelve sloops of war of up to twenty-two guns each and ten galleys for the shallow coastal waters of the South. Twelve additional ships of war were authorized on June 30, and three more on July 16."[18]

The administration's actions for some time had been especially troubling to Vice President Jefferson. To him, "it was as though an evil spell had been cast over the capital. He called it a 'reign of witches,' and saw no difference between Adams and the 'war party.' The new navy, in Jefferson's view, was a colossal waste of money."[19] More than ever, Jefferson became the leader of the opposition, although he continued to prefer to operate behind the scenes, writing letters accusing Adams of warmongering, and fostering an opposition press. Dumas Malone, "his most distinguished biographer, has found the things Jefferson repeatedly said during this period ('unprovable assertions' and 'unwarranted suspicions') painfully disturbing, and some of them merit examination for the light they may cast on the extreme difficulty of forming a national policy toward France. His hatred of Great Britain, and the extent to which he imagined the corruptions of British influence penetrating to every corner of American life, now formed the themes of virtually all he said and thought'."[20]

Congress, by going further and proving more than Adams had sought, added both to Jefferson's unsettled state of mind and to Adams's troubles.

As Elkins and McKitrick put it, Adams's difficulties would increase in magnitude as the months passed because of "the things Congress gave him that he had not asked for. One was the Alien and Sedition Laws of June and July 1798; the other, the vastly expanded military establishment ... together with the taxes required for supporting it."[21]

The Alien and Sedition Laws were an enormous mistake. As bad as they were, they appeared even worse in contrast to the libertarian rhetoric of the Republicans. Adams always contended that he had not recommended them. He did, however, sign the measures into law — which delighted Abigail, whose ordinarily sound political judgment this time failed her. Of most concern was one of the three Alien Acts, that of 25 June 1798, and the Sedition Act of 14 July 1798. The Alien Act gave the president truly draconian powers, and as Jefferson put it, it "was in the teeth of the Constitution."[22] When it expired in June 1800, however, Adams had never invoked it.[23]

The Sedition Act was another matter. Peterson says that it was "generously enforced," but "generously" is in the eye of the beholder. "Twenty-five persons were arrested, fourteen indicted, and ten tried and convicted," he wrote, "all Republican printers and publicists." The Act provided for fines and imprisonment for those convicted of publishing "false, scandalous, and malicious writing" in opposition to the government, including that directed at Congress or the president. Peterson notes ominously that it did not include writing directed against the vice president.[24]

On the other hand, although to be sure Adams was not "on the side of the free speech angels," neither was he in 1798-1799 "the nation's greatest enemy to free speech."[25] In fact, "there were elements of the Sedition Act created under Adams's *aegis* that, as Professor [Leonard] Levy long ago pointed out, opened a path toward free speech as we have come to know it." When compared with Britain's common law of seditious libel, for example, "the United States's Sedition Act constituted an enlightened reform. The Federalist law empowered the jury, not the judge, to decide whether the words should be deemed libelous; and it also allowed the truth of the words to stand as a defense against the libel charge."[26]

In response to the acts, Jefferson "privately went beyond urging nullification and talked recklessly of secession or insurrection." As bad as they acts were, they cannot explain Jefferson's extreme reaction. "He saw them as only one sign of a vast conspiracy by the Federalists, under the evil inspiration of Alexander Hamilton, to impose a monarchy on the American people. As a matter of fact, though, Hamilton "seeing an earlier version of the [Alien] bill, thought his friends must be running wild."[27]

Jefferson's panic over the conspiracy was later neglected or downplayed by his admirers, who had to explain his own secret plot solely in terms of the Alien and Sedition Acts.[28] Garry Wills points out that although the laws clearly were unconstitutional, explaining them does not require assumption of a monarchist plot, nor were they the worst transgressions in American history — including some under Jefferson himself when he became president.[29]

The offensive acts were not long-lived, but they had long-lasting effects. One of these was salutary. The original interpretation of the Bill of Rights was far from the ringing defense of individual liberty that we tend to take for granted today. The reaction to the Sedition Act was so strong that it led to expanded interpretations of American liberties, especially those enshrined in the First Amendment.[30]

The other effect was troublesome. It brought about the Kentucky and Virginia Resolutions, which asserted the power of states to interpose their authority to shield citizens from the effects of federal laws. Vice President Jefferson, who characteristically kept his involvement secret, was the author of the two Kentucky Resolutions, and James Madison of the one from Virginia. As Wills describes it, "Jefferson became a secret nullifier in 1798, when John Adams was president and he was vice president."[31] In other words, he was working against the government of which he was a part.

Disappointing these two Republican giants and contrary to their hopes, other states did not rush to issue their own resolutions. The Resolutions asserted the power of states to judge federal laws, although even the more extreme Kentucky Resolutions were careful not to advocate independent state action. Madison's Virginia Resolution was the more moderate, but even so "in years to come elements in the South quoted him in defense of their moves" toward nullification, which he denied had ever been his intention.[32] Thus they had mischievous effects in years to come.

The second thing Congress forced upon Adams, the expansion of the army beyond what he had requested, put him in an uncomfortable situation. Adams had strongly favored a greatly enlarged navy. Along with the Republicans, however, he had grave reservation about a standing army. When faced with legislation creating it, he had little choice but to offer command of the new army, along with the responsibility of raising it, to the most distinguished soldier — in fact the most distinguished citizen — in the United States, George Washington.

Washington accepted, but forced Adams to name "the one man in the world he trusted less than any other, Alexander Hamilton,"[33] to be second in command. Effectively, that meant that it would be Hamilton truly in command, since no one expected the aged Washington actually to take to the field. Hamilton was clearly ambitious. Washington recognized that, but thought that his ambition would not lead him to act to the detriment of the country. Many others, including Adams, disagreed. Adams's enthusiastic biographer, David McCullough, for example, wrote of Hamilton as dreaming of "grand conquest with himself riding at the head of a new American army." His "idea was to 'liberate' Spanish Florida and Louisiana, possibly all of Spanish America, in a bold campaign combining a British fleet and American troops." McCullough noted that the idea had been around for years, and that Adams dismissed it summarily, but that the British had indeed shown some interest.[34]

Secretary of War McHenry had journeyed to Mount Vernon in person to deliver Washington's commission. Unknown to Adams, the secretary also — in a spectacular display of disloyalty to his president — carried a letter to Washington from Hamilton. The letter said that Adams cared more for the navy than for the army, and thus implied that Adams was unsuited to be in charge of preparations for the national defense. Washington therefore should organize the army according to his own judgment, regardless of any position that Adams might take. Secretary of State Pickering had previously indicated to Washington that Hamilton should be his second in command. Both secretaries supplied Hamilton with secret documents to use against Adams.[35]

The third congressional imposition upon Adams was a tax on land to finance the new army.[36] Unrest — inspired by genuine Federalist excesses, by Republican rhetoric exaggerating those excesses, and by a simple visceral reaction against taxes — swept the country. Armed action against collection of the taxes took place in Pennsylvania, the so-called Fries Rebellion. Captain John Fries was convicted of being the leader, found guilty of treason, and received a death sentence.[37] Adams deliberated carefully, and concluded that the offense had been to lead a riot, not to commit treason. Therefore, he pardoned Fries and the others convicted.

In the meantime, Adams resisted all pressures that he request a declaration of war against France. Among those close to him urging war was his wife, who previously had opposed such a move. His message to Congress said only that he would "never send another minister to France without assurances that he will be received, respected, and honored as the representative of a great, free, powerful, and independent nation."[38]

John Marshall had returned to the United States in June 1798, and had reported that he was confident that France was not seeking war. Moreover, Elbridge Gerry had stayed behind at the request of the French to continue negotiations to avoid war.[39] Gerry returned in October, reporting that Tallyrand assured him that the French sought peace, and were ready to negotiate seriously.

It was at this time that Adams received the letter from Washington threatening to resign as commander of the new army if he could not select Hamilton as his second in command. As he acquiesced, Adams had reason to believe that "now Hamilton and the army might not be needed at all."

He could not resist reminding Washington "a bit lamely" that the authority to determine the rank of officers remained with the president.[40] The threat of war subsided further when official word came in November that previous rumors had been correct: Admiral Horatio Nelson of the British Navy had destroyed the French fleet at Aboukir, in the Battle of the Nile off the coast of Egypt, on the first of August.

The president's forbearance, aided by fortunate developments in France, ultimately brought some success after what many contemporaries believed — supported in years to come by many historians — was a period in which a floundering Adams displayed a lack of vision.[41] In February 1799 he surprised everyone, including his cabinet, by nominating William Vans Murray, the current American minister at The Hague, to be America's representative to Paris. Murray would go, Adams assured the Senate, only with assurance from the French government that he would be received appropriately. Adams had hoped to send Patrick Henry and Chief Justice Oliver Ellsworth to join Murray, but Henry declined because of his health. Adams therefore nominated William Davie, the Governor of North Carolina, to accompany Ellsworth. The Senate confirmed Adams's nominations.

In August, Adams received word from Tallyrand that the French would receive the American envoys appropriately. The French government had become increasingly unstable, however, and in November it fell. Bonaparte had come to power, although Tallyrand continued to represent the foreign ministry (an Adams biographer remarked that Tallyrand "seemed always to be foreign minister regardless of who held executive power"[42]). In February 1800, France received word that Washington had died the previous December. Bonaparte declared ten days of official mourning, preparing the way for the reception of the American envoys. After months of negotiation, the envoys returned with a peace agreement, the Convention of 1800. Unfortunately for Adams, word of peace — which might have tipped the balance in his favor — arrived on the 11th of December, after he had lost the election. Ratification took place in parts throughout the remainder of the Adams administration and the beginning of Jefferson's.[43]

In May 1800, Adams had taken action that was long overdue — he fired two of the Hamilton spies from his cabinet, replacing Pickering as secretary of state with John Marshall, and McHenry as secretary of war with Samuel Dexter. Curiously, he permitted Wolcott to remain as secretary of the treasury. "For someone supposedly suspicious by nature, Adams had been inordinately slow to suspect the worst of his closest advisers, and to face the obvious truth that keeping Washington's cabinet had been a mistake." He had been required to avoid a war and to "keep Hamilton from gaining the upper hand with his 'mad' schemes." Abigail had warned him that Hamilton "would become a second Bonaparte."[44] He also moved to disband the expanded army, which Hamilton perceived as another strike at himself.

Smarting from this and from verbal abuse by Adams, Hamilton attacked. Despite nominally sharing with Adams a Federalist identity, the "driven" Hamilton circulated a pamphlet, *Letter from Alexander Hamilton, Concerning the Public Conduct and Character of John Adams, Esq., President of the United States*. In it he charged that Adams was unfit "for the office of Chief Magistrate," although he ended, oddly, by announcing that he was not urging that any elector withhold "a single vote" from the president. Ellis has concluded that "Hamilton was not only arguing against the election of Adams to a second term; he was also arguing that the long-standing weaknesses of Adams's character should disqualify him from admission into the pantheon reserved for America's founding heroes."[45]

The Federalists were dismayed, and the Republicans jubilant. The entire episode displayed much about the less attractive sides of both Adams and Hamilton. "The two hated each other to a degree exceeded by no comparable enmity in the early life of the republic." They were "two men who at their best had lived by the loftiest of civic humanist ideals, the pursuit of the public good as they had perceived and understood it." Now, they were "at their worst," and had "allowed the public good to become so intertwined with their own sulks, spites, and rages as to blind them to what might have been an intermediary loyalty, a loyalty to the joint venture they had seen into being in 1789."[46]

Shortly after seeing Hamilton's pamphlet, Adams moved to Washington, DC, into the new President's House. Abigail joined him soon thereafter. They were the first presidential couple to reside in what was later to be called the White House. Then came the election.

We think relatively little today of the Adams administration. We tend to assume that it was overwhelmed by the Jeffersonian "Revolution of 1800." Adams did better in the election, however, than we are likely to recognize. "Despite the malicious attacks on him, the furor over the Alien and Sedition Acts, unpopular taxes, betrayals by his own cabinet, the disarray of the Federalists, and the final treachery of Hamilton, he had, in fact, come very close to winning," wrote McCullough. He also pointed out that only 250 votes different in New York City would have thrown New York's electoral votes to Adams, giving him a clear majority of 71 to 61. As if this were not enough, he added that "were it not for the fact that in the South three-fifths of the slaves were counted in apportioning the electoral votes, Adams would have been reelected."[47]

After the election, John and Abigail invited Jefferson to dine with them at the President's House, and he accepted. Adams did not attend Jefferson's inauguration but left for Massachusetts before dawn. There is no record as to his motivation. Many observers conclude that he refused to attend because of bitterness at being defeated, but his having entertained Jefferson cordially after the election suggests that this may not be the case. Possibly he left when he did because of the scheduling of the coach, because he had not received an invitation, or for some completely obscure reason. Clearly he did not consider it vital that he attend, but we can never be certain why he left when he did.

Adams left office having achieved peace. He had averted a war that America, weak as it was at the time, would have discovered to be disastrous. He did little to strengthen office of the president, but he did strengthen the executive — and the country — by bringing about the creation of the Department of the Navy. Even with regard to civil liberties his record was favorable in relation to the standards of his day. In many specific instances, he did fall short, and certainly he could have performed better in many respects. Perhaps another person in office might have done so.

Overall, however, it is not an exaggeration to say that in a real sense, by avoiding war he saved the country. Ferling has quoted a number of favorable assessments of Adams's presidency, and wrote that they "err only in the faintness of their praise."[48] It would be difficult at best, and probably impossible, to "rank" with any meaningful precision his performance as president in comparison with the forty-one others. Clearly the country is better off because of what President John Adams accomplished. Is it really necessary to say anything else?

3

THOMAS JEFFERSON
March 4, 1801–March 4, 1809

Thomas Jefferson's election as the first Republican president ushered in, as he described it, the "Revolution of 1800." Faber and Faber gushed — with more enthusiasm than style — that he was "one of the greatest Americans who ever lived," and certainly this judgment today would find wide agreement. They conceded that "in his presidency he did not quite reach the heights that he attained outside that office," but they nonetheless placed him "in a tie for fifth among the 39 presidents rated. In the category of leadership and Decision Making," they wrote, "he scored twenty points, one of only three perfect scores attained."[1] Other rankings tend similarly to place him in an exalted position.

Jefferson's standing is reflected in more than formal rankings. He became one of the great quartet on Mount Rushmore with good reason. The Union expanded by admitting Ohio as a state in 1803. Even more important, his Louisiana Purchase doubled the size of the United States and helped secure its borders. This accomplishment alone justifies his presence in stone, carved in its lofty position alongside Washington who nurtured the infant country and enabled it to survive; beside Lincoln, who kept it from fragmenting into mutually antagonistic parts; and beside Theodore Roosevelt, who cemented national unity east and west at a time when the country still bore raw wounds north and south.

When John Kennedy quipped to a gathering of Nobel Prize winners that "this is the most extraordinary collection of talent, of human knowledge, that has ever been gathered together at the White House, with the possible exception of when Thomas Jefferson dined alone,"[2] his wit reflected today's common view of Jefferson. There is much to be said for that view.

31

Among American presidents, only Theodore Roosevelt can rival Jefferson in the breadth of his intellect and interests, and only a few can compare in intellectual depth. Landy and Milkis are correct when they point out that, "he was, along with Woodrow Wilson, Abraham Lincoln, and Teddy Roosevelt, one of the most cerebral and theoretical of all presidents."[3]

It certainly is understandable why anyone drawing up a ranking of presidents, glancing at Jefferson's presidency, and considering his popular image as the defender of liberty would place him high on the list. It remains possible to justify such a high ranking when considering his presidency's actual accomplishments. When considering his administration as a whole, however, although the greatness remains other factors intrude also. These other factors suggest that *any* ranking of Jefferson would have to be carefully qualified to avoid misrepresentation and oversimplification.

So pervasive is the awed view that it seems almost startling to come upon some of the rare reminders that Jefferson was a real person with his own imperfections — some of which, of course, were reflections of the age in which he lived. Landy and Milkis, for example, say that Madison's intellect and Albert Gallatin's equaled Jefferson's, perhaps even surpassing it. They go so far as to say that Madison "had the better theoretical intellect," and (quoting Henry Adams) that Gallatin was "perhaps the best informed man in the country."[4] An Italian visitor, Count Carlo Vidua, who had met both Jefferson and Madison and was impressed with them both, said that Jefferson's intellect seemed the more brilliant and Madison's the more profound.[5] Certainly Madison was less inclined than his predecessor to make impetuous — even rash — judgments.

Landy and Milkis also note the irony of Jefferson's having created "a democratic political party in the midst of a regime that proscribed popular leadership and opposed parties, and whose grounds for opposition he largely shared." In this regard, his personality made things even more difficult. "Jefferson, temperamentally speaking, was no democrat. His commitment to democratic principle was entirely cerebral. He was an aristocrat to the core, with the virtues and vices of that genre."[6] As Flexner has described it, "the true American aristocrats were, even if they spoke in the name of the common man, the Virginia Jeffersonians." Jefferson lived on inherited wealth and slave labor, and accepted the deference due him as a Randolph of Virginia.[7] He was a poor public speaker, was rather shy, valued his privacy, and lacked the ability to appeal in person to crowds. But he more than made up for these shortcomings by his "prodigious letter writing," which enabled him to accomplish with "his pen what he lacked in oratory," and he was "charming and persuasive in private conversation."[8]

Leonard Levy produced the classic study regarding civil liberties.[9] Today people tend to think of Jefferson only in relation to his ringing libertarian rhetoric in the Declaration of Independence and elsewhere. Levy identified another aspect — as he put it, a darker side — that emerges when Jeffersonian practices come under scrutiny.

Forrest McDonald, too, has painted a picture of Jefferson as a real person. "Even in his own time," he wrote, "Jefferson was regarded by friends and foes alike as a champion of liberty — whatever that elusive word may mean. Jefferson himself never wrote a systematic treatise on the subject, and he never thought it through as a concept." He added comments regarding Jefferson's understanding of liberty that today can only be considered startling:

> Its meaning to him can scarcely have been a conventional one, since Jefferson owned several hundred human beings during his lifetime and theirs, never made any serious effort to liberate them, purchased at least eight more while he was president, and once asked his friend Madison to acquire a black person for a visiting French lady who sought to be amused by breeding them — a request which the libertarian Madison cheerfully honored. Nor can liberty as Jefferson conceived of it have had much to do with such legal and constitutional rights ... as the writ of habeas corpus, freedom of the press, freedom from unlawful search and seizures, and judicial review of the acts of legislatures and law enforcers. Regarding some of these, Jefferson wrote strong words of support; but equally often he denounced the abuse of these "rights," and when he exercised executive authority he was capable of running roughshod over them.

In short, McDonald said, Jefferson "saw broadly, but only from where he stood."[10]

His view of women was hardly less limited. When "Treasury Secretary Albert Gallatin ... suggested naming women to certain posts," his proposal "elicited Jefferson's curt reply: 'the appointment of a woman to office is an innovation for which the public is not prepared, nor am I'."[11] Worse, on a related subject, was an opinion he expressed after he left the presidency. In a letter to Samuel Kercheval on 5th September 1816, he wrote that "women could not mix promiscuously in the public meetings with men." Were they to do so, he believed, it would lead to "deprivation of morals and ambiguity of issue." It may have been unexceptional in Jefferson's day to believe that the parentage of a women's children, her "issue," would inevitably be suspect if she went out unchaperoned, but such an idea should have been no less outrageous then than it would be today.[12]

Jefferson's one outstanding achievement prior to his presidency — and truly it was outstanding — was his authorship of one of the great political documents in history, the Declaration of Independence. Before the Constitution's adoption he had served in legislative and diplomatic posts without any special distinction. During the Revolution he was governor of Virginia for two years, and accomplished little — in fairness, the governorship at the time was extraordinarily weak, and thus there was little that he could have done in the post. As governor, he faced accusations of cowardice because he fled when the British attacked Virginia's capital after having urged Washington — who understandably was preoccupied — to drop what he was doing and rush home to defend his state.

He was "hardly a combative man." He avoided face-to-fact controversy whenever possible. "True, he could be callous and even bloodthirsty on paper or at a distance, but not directly. He held the most advanced ideas, as Richard Hofstadter has remarked, 'but he was not in the habit of breaking lances to fulfill them.' ... But because of his essential optimism Jefferson seldom felt it necessary to break lances."[13] Again in fairness, it would have done neither the state of Virginia nor anyone else in America any good for him to have remained to be captured.

As secretary of state under Washington, he became disheartened when he believed himself unable to counter Hamilton's influence. Jefferson then worked covertly against the administration. For example, he and Madison persuaded Philip Freneau to establish a Republican newspaper to oppose administration policy. Jefferson even provided Freneau with a job at the State Department to help his financial difficulties. Thus, Jefferson arranged that "government money would be spent to undermine government policies."[14] Sensing that he was losing his battle with Hamilton, Jefferson ultimately resigned. Similarly, as vice president under Adams, working largely in secret, he led the opposition against the administration in which he held the number two position.

As McDonald noted, this hardly is the background that one would anticipate could lead to presidential greatness, "but so to think is to regard the man as narrowly as critical libertarians regard him," he said. Regardless of the honor Jefferson received as the author of the Declaration of Independence, he was until 1801 a failure in his own mind as a public man. "But," McDonald wrote with keen insight, "that failure derived from the fact that in public life he had never been in a position to be master of his own responsibilities. For Jefferson, in order to function well, required complete authority that was based on habit and consent. Far more than the Father of His Country, George Washington, Jefferson in real life was the ultimate paternalist. He took care of people," all walks of people, "and managed their lives gently, kindly, tactfully, and totally. All he asked in return was their absolute devotion, and he got it. He was quite inept at dealing with his peers, but when he was master of his circumstances he had no peers."[15]

McDonald's insight provides the key to understanding Jefferson's presidency. It helps explain his achievements and failures by revealing strengths, weaknesses, and in fact an approach to life. Only with such an explanation do reasons emerge for the contradictions that are so glaring in his administration.

Whatever the assessment of Jefferson's mind and talents, it is clear that they were extraordinary, and that many of his attitudes were far advanced for his day. It also is clear that an accurate assessment of his presidency must center not upon abstract qualities of his intellect but upon what he actually accomplished. As important as Jefferson's ideas are to American political thought, they should not influence judgment of his performance as president, except of course as they relate to what he did in office.

His first term — although it left a number of legacies that haunted him later and went on to haunt his successor — in most respects was a splendid success. If he had left office following that term, the "rankers" undoubtedly would agree to place him among the "greats."

> Had history ended with the adjournment of the first session of the Eighth Congress on March 31, 1804, it could have been written that the Revolution of 1800 had been completed as thoroughly and successfully in foreign affairs as in domestic. The achievements of the Jefferson administration during its first three years rivaled those of Washington's first three; they would never be matched again, not by Jackson, by Lincoln, or by either Roosevelt. Popular approval of the president was very nearly unanimous west of the Hudson River, and even in New England those who faulted him were a narrow and privileged minority.[16]

Even under the kindest interpretation, the second Jeffersonian term, in contrast, came close to being a disaster. Ironically, many of the same factors that brought him such triumph initially led to his troubles later. Also ironically, it should give those developing rankings pause, just as it might when they try to rank his spiritual descendent, Woodrow Wilson. Each was a great president who also could be judged a great failure.

Jefferson began his presidency more skillfully than Adams had begun his. The Republican victory was no landslide. If Jefferson had lost New York — which he likely carried only because New Yorker Aaron Burr was his running mate — Adams would have won a second term. Likewise, Jefferson clearly would have lost had he not had the advantage of "the margin given his southern supporters by the inclusion of three-fifths of the slave population in the weighting of electoral votes." Moreover, it is highly doubtful that he would have won if he had not hidden his role in the Kentucky Resolution.[17]

Jefferson began with a brilliant inaugural address, his "greatest presidential utterance,"[18] in which he called for unity. His "we are all Republicans — we are all Federalists" statement foreshadowed many similar assertions (including probably the most famous of them all, Mohandas Gandhi's comment to the public of India more than a century later: "we are all Hindus — we are all Muslims"). He would pay down and eliminate the national debt, respect the states, preserve the Union, and would ensure "absolute acquiescence in the decisions of the majority."[19]

Although disdainful of "party," Jefferson surrounded himself with Republicans of like mind with himself, including appointing a loyal cabinet. He did not see this as giving into party; rather, he was confident that the Republicans represented the people, and any party organization was to be temporary until it succeeded in banishing the vestiges of Federalism. As much as he could he countered the "midnight appointments" of the Adams administration by refusing to deliver commissions to those Adams appointed who had not already received them before Adams ended his term. Also as much as possible, he attempted to place Republicans into office.

Jefferson did not attempt a wholesale removal of Federalist appointees. In fact, he professed opposition to what under Jackson came to be known as the spoils system, and asserted his belief that appointments should represent merit. He saw no inconsistency in trying to weed out "those whom he regarded as irreconcilable monarchists, namely the devout Hamiltonians," or those who were corrupt or incompetent.[20] By so doing he was merely attempting to redress what he saw as Federalist partisanship.

Nevertheless, as Landy and Milkis have noted, "it is fair to say, as Merrill Peterson does, that Jefferson, not Jackson, invented the spoils system. Characteristically, Jefferson allowed himself to be 'forced' into adopting partisan patronage policies." He had written to New York Governor George Clinton in May of 1801 that although he was reluctant to hire and fire on a partisan basis, "circumstances ... require something more" than nonpartisanship. "By July, he was advocating Federalist dismissals sufficient to bring Republicans a *proportionate share* of federal offices," by which he meant some three-fourths of the positions. Within the first two years of his administration, he had replaced more than half of the Federalist office-holders with Republicans.[21]

Jefferson showed great deference to Congress, and succeeded in winning members over by charm. "Jefferson and his party rose to power preaching the Whiggish doctrine of legislative supremacy against the allegedly monarchical tendencies of the Federalist administrations." He "honored the theory," but at the same time "he devised a subtle language of indirection with Congress in which recommendations were suggestions and demands were veiled in obscurity."[22]

Consistent with his attempt to demonstrate deference — a decision that came easy to him because he was a poor speaker and was uncomfortable speaking in public — Jefferson began sending his messages to Congress in writing instead of delivering them in person. Although both Washington and Adams had addressed Congress directly, the practice still generated comparison with the practice of monarchs addressing their parliaments. Following Jefferson, every president until Woodrow Wilson continued his practice of submitting messages, including State of the Union Addresses, to Congress in writing.

Both Washington and Adams during their presidencies, while rejecting the trappings of monarchy, had presented themselves as privileged gentlemen. Eliminating the pomp of their administrations — he regularly rode
horseback, for example, rather than riding in a fine coach — Jefferson entertained members of Congress at small dinner parties, overwhelming them by
his personality. In a calculated display of republican simplicity, although he
served the finest French food and wine, he dressed casually and often met
with his guests while wearing slippers. Jefferson's tactics succeeded. He was
enormously effective in leading Congress.

His primary subordinates, James Madison as secretary of state and
Albert Gallatin as secretary of the treasury, were two of the most brilliant
and able figures of the age. Gallatin became his legislative liaison, but
Jefferson himself also worked closely — and carefully — with party leaders.
Their goal was to dismantle as much as possible of what Hamilton and the
Federalists had established. The Sedition Act had expired the day before he
assumed office, but he pardoned the ten persons — all Republican editors —
convicted under its provisions. He even persuaded Congress to repay with
interest all fines imposed under its provisions.[23]

Republicans found the judiciary troubling. Jefferson did not dispute the
power of the courts to judge the constitutionality of issues, but he and his
followers insisted that each branch — and the states as well — shared in that
power. They sought to repeal the Federalists' Judiciary Act of 1801, only to
fail when Vice President Burr cast a tie-breaking vote in the Senate against
their effort. They then succeeded in passing an amended version of repeal,
passing also the Judiciary Act of 1802 — which continued those features of
the 1801 act "that were consistent with the Republicans' partisan and personal interests," and passing yet a third act that delayed the next sitting of
the Supreme Court for a year. "President Jefferson signed all three bills into
law."[24]

James Monroe had argued that even the act establishing the entire federal judiciary below the Supreme Court, the Judiciary Act of 1789, should
be repealed. When Marshall's Court handed down *Marbury v. Madison* in
1803, among the Republicans "such voices became a majority." In March of
that year, "they took a first step in a trial run." The Republican majority in
the House voted to impeach U.S. District Judge John Pickering of New
Hampshire. He had committed no "high crime or misdemeanor" but was
insane and an alcoholic. "If these reprehensible but quite non-constitutional
defects should result in conviction and removal from office, the entire federal court system could be picked clean."[25]

As a matter of fact, Pickering's impeachment probably began with good
intentions — he was, after all, clearly an unfit judge by virtually any standard. But the Constitution provided no way to remove a judge for reasons

of mere unsuitability. Whatever its beginnings, it degenerated into "a partisan brawl." The Republican leadership sought to trap a judge, to declare an insane man guilty of "high crimes and misdemeanors." For their part, the Federalists were no better. They were "perfectly willing to keep an obviously deranged and thoroughly incompetent man on the federal bench indefinitely to foil Republican designs."[26] They proceeded to accuse the administration of "launching a reign of terror in the judiciary."[27]

They were more than ever convinced when on 12 March 1804 — the same day that the Senate convicted Pickering and removed him from office — House Republicans impeached the venomously partisan Supreme Court Justice Samuel Chase, a Federalist. The Senate, however, failed to convict Chase. Although Jefferson had courted Vice President Burr assiduously, the vice president conducted the trial fairly, and it became clear that Chase's conduct failed to the meet the Constitution's standards for removal.[28] This, added to Burr's indiscretion in having voted against repeal of the Judiciary Act of 1801, eliminated any future that he might still have had in the Republican Party. The Republican concern for the courts, though, no doubt was less systematic than the Federalists perceived it to be and certainly less effective; it appears not to have been a preoccupation. Peterson has remarked that "if Jefferson pursued a grand strategy against the judiciary, he left no record of it. The Chase impeachment," he said, was simply "a piece of improvisation, like every other encounter in the so-called 'war on the judiciary'."[29] Its failure did, however, convince Jefferson that impeachment was not an effective method of re-forming the courts.

Jefferson secured from Congress an abolition of internal taxes, leaving duties on imports as the major source of funding the government. He reduced the army to almost nothing — in the Republican ideology, militias should be adequate for national defense — and he almost eliminated the navy. Navies generate an elitist officer caste, which violated Republicans' sensibilities. Moreover, they feared that it could lead the country into war. Therefore, they substituted what McDonald called a naval equivalent of militias: gunboats. These were little more than floating platforms with one or two guns, which were cheap to produce and maintain. The theory was that gunboats would be an effective and inexpensive way to secure coasts and harbors. The Federalists had left America with the best fighting ships of their class in the world, McDonald said, but the Jefferson administration was prepared to let them "rot at the wharves."[30] Jefferson and his administration managed to pay much of the national debt, but they left the new country with virtually no military capacity for its own protection.

For a time, it mattered little. Jefferson was highly successful in foreign affairs, dealing with leaders of other countries as skillfully as he dealt with members of Congress. His "style was uniquely his own," using Madison in international affairs in a manner similar to that of Gallatin in the domestic sphere. Madison "was all propriety, reserve, caution, and protocol, and he worked himself to the emaciation point into the bargain. The president assumed a manner that seemingly clashed with but in fact complemented the secretary of state's stiff formality, treating diplomats with calculated casualness, with a threadbare and homey simplicity" that somehow conveyed a "New World innocence" that at the same time seemed elegant, sophisticated, and cosmopolitan.[31] McDonald credits him, moreover, with being the "only head of state around who was still even partly motivated by ideals in the conduct of foreign relations."[32]

Despite the cutback in the navy, however, naval expenditures stayed high. The Barbary states had long harassed shipping in the Mediterranean, and the Pasha of Tripoli declared war upon the United States in the first year of the new Jefferson administration. The Pasha's declaration was a protest over what he considered to be inadequate payments of tribute — tribute that from the American point of view amounted to piracy. The war was a minor irritant, but it dragged on for four years and kept costs from declining as Jefferson had hoped they would. Ultimately America prevailed, and the tributes ended.

Jefferson's greatest accomplishment as president was the Louisiana Purchase. It fulfilled the Republican desire for expansion, it provided hope for slaveholders who wished to extend their "Peculiar Institution," and it was a step toward Jefferson's dream of a vast inland empire that might be peopled by independent yeoman farmers.

In addition, it secured the country's western flank while giving it unquestioned rights to navigate the Mississippi River. Moreover, the cost was absurdly low, merely a few cents an acre for a huge expanse that doubled the land area of the United States. It was a triumph.

Still, as his biographer, Merrill Peterson, concedes, "the Louisiana Purchase was made in France, not in America, and it owed more to the vagaries of Bonaparte's ambition than to Jefferson's cautious diplomacy."[33] Wills goes even further to remark that "Napoleon almost forced the territory on him."[34] Certainly Jefferson's patience and skill were significant elements of the complicated circumstances that brought Louisiana to America, but good fortune was at least equally important. Whether Jefferson engineered the acquisition, or whether the Purchase should be dismissed as mere luck, Jefferson saw its importance and seized the opportunity. Regardless of his restricted view of the central government's powers under the Constitution, he recognized the good of the country and acted accordingly. It happened on his watch. The triumph was Jefferson's.

An accomplishment that without question was all Jefferson's was the resulting Lewis and Clark Expedition. In 1804, he dispatched the Corps of

Discovery to explore the route of the Missouri in the new territory, and to continue on to the Pacific Ocean. The co-commanders, Meriwether Lewis and William Clark, were splendid choices, and the results would be all that could have been hoped. Jefferson's scientific curiosity dictated their charge to acquire as much geographic and scientific information as possible. The new knowledge it generated more than justified the exploratory journey into lands not yet America's own.

In 1804, Jefferson received re-election with only token opposition. The Federalists were in disarray, and in the process of dissolving as a party. The Republicans gleefully contrasted Jefferson's four years in office with those of Adams. They contrasted taxes added under Adams, versus taxes eliminated under Jefferson; rising national debt versus debt elimination; added governmental officers versus reduction; alien and sedition laws versus freedom; large and expensive military versus small, inexpensive, defensive forces only.[35] Moreover, there was the Louisiana Purchase.

Peterson characterized Jefferson's two administrations as revolving around geography: the Mississippi River and the Atlantic Ocean. The Mississippi loomed large in his first administration. As he sought to secure American navigation on the mighty waterway, he was led to the Louisiana Purchase. In the second, Jefferson's greatest effort sought to secure "America's seafaring frontier with Europe," and it "met with crushing defeat. The two frontiers, of land and of ocean, westward and eastward, had divided American energies from the beginning." The addition of huge territories beyond the Mississippi seemed to redirect American destiny westward. "So fabulous was the triumph of Jefferson's western vision that it greatly mitigated the costs of defeat in the Atlantic."[36]

But costs there were. Jefferson shared the romantic optimism common among Republicans that produced an astonishing amount of wishful thinking. Were navies expensive and perhaps dangerous? Were armies? The answer was to rely on gunboats in the one case and on citizen militias — which had demonstrated little military effectiveness — in the other. Did the renewed outbreak of war between Britain and France threaten American interests? Simply deny them the American goods upon which they had become dependent, and they would quickly surrender. America thus could have a vigorous and aggressive foreign policy with little in the way of military expenditure. Any differences could be resolved rationally. "Like FDR and Ronald Reagan, Jefferson radiated a sunny optimism."[37]

Optimism, however, could not protect American shipping. An 1805 change of government in Britain brought re-imposition of the Rule of 1756, which had not been enforced since Washington's administration. The rule asserted Britain's right to prevent the passage of goods from the West Indies to France. Within a period of months, the British Navy had seized dozens of American ships. Jefferson responded slowly, but ultimately decided upon a policy of embargo. If no American ships left for Europe, there would be no further outrages on American shipping. If Britain were denied American goods, it soon would relax its policies. In December 1807, Congress passed the first of a series of embargo acts. Neither it nor the president could foresee the troubles that would result.

American ships no longer could transport goods abroad legally, nor could foreign ships load American cargo. Jefferson personally oversaw enforcement, and directed ever more harsh penalties in attempting to secure compliance. With regard to citizens of towns that had been "tainted with a general spirit of disobedience," Jefferson substituted presumption of guilt for presumption of innocence. He ordered that there would have to be "positive proof" of their innocence — proof that a citizen had "never said or done anything himself to countenance that spirit." He lamented that there were too many who were guilty for them all to be hanged, and said that "the most guilty may be marked as examples, and the less suffer long imprisonments." The Apostle of Liberty "had set up a state terrorism that made the Alien and Sedition prosecutions under Adams look minor by comparison."[38]

The result was less to prevent goods from leaving the country than it was to throw seamen, merchants, and others out of work, damage manufacturing, ruin American shipping, and crush civil liberties. Under Jefferson's orders, even ships sailing from one American port to another were at risk. Ships could be detained without warrant. Jefferson told Gallatin to be suspicious of any ship carrying certain cargoes. If there were doubt, he said, "consider me in favor of detention." Nothing under the Alien and Sedition Acts had been so repressive as the policies of the Republicans (whose party, one should remember, was also the party of slavery) — and still those policies remained ineffective and unable to halt completely the flow of goods.[39]

In the west, former Vice President Burr had been making headlines. He had dealt with Gen. James Wilkinson, Jefferson's territorial governor in Louisiana, with regard to various schemes that involved both England and Spain. Burr's schemes apparently ranged from the treasonous — seeking to sever western territory from the United States — to a "more honorable plan of leading an American force against Spain in the event of war."[40] Despite having no real force of his own, Burr became Wilkinson's target.

Whatever doubt there may be regarding Burr and his intentions, Wilkinson clearly was duplicitous and unscrupulous. McDonald termed him the "arch conspirator and traitor," and graphically described his actions from December, 1806, through the next February. He trampled "the Constitution and the Bill of Rights into dust," McDonald said. "In New Orleans, Wilkinson arrested without warrants and held incommunicado three of Burr's couriers and lieutenants." He refused to permit them to have counsel, and "clapped them in irons and sent them by sea to Washington" when he received writs of *habeas corpus* on their behalf. "He also jailed their attorney, the judge, the judge's closest friend, the editor of the *Orleans Gazette*, former Senator Adair, and some sixty other citizens. None was specifically charged." All were denied constitutional rights; all were sent in chains secretly to Washington. Jefferson "privately approved all Wilkinson's actions, his only reservation being that Wilkinson must remain within the limits, not of the Constitution, but of what public opinion would bear."[41]

Ultimately, Burr stood trial for treason. He won acquittal "in the Virginia circuit court, John Marshall presiding."[42] Jefferson had taken an active role in the case, quite beyond his constitutional duties.[43] In the course of the proceeding, Marshall issued a subpoena requiring the president to appear in court and testify. Jefferson cooperated, and supplied the court with necessary documents, but he refused to appear, or to "dignify the subpoena with a formal answer and would resist any effort to enforce it."[44] No such effort was forthcoming, thus avoiding a clash between the branches.

The administration lost, and the entire episode surrounding Burr's prosecution did nothing to strengthen Jefferson's reputation. On the other hand, although Jefferson clearly pursued Burr "with a vengeance that ignored basic civil liberties," the situation was complicated. "Before condemning Jefferson, one must ask whether any other president would have stood idly by while his former vice president met with representatives of the nation's major adversaries, openly condemned the administration, and traversed the Western states twice to make plans for a mysterious expedition down the Mississippi."[45] Presidents in later centuries — including the twenty-first — have imprisoned people on the basis of much less evidence, and seemingly with considerable public approval.

About the only real achievements of the second Jefferson administration were the triumphant return of the highly successful Lewis and Clark Expedition in 1806, and the abolition of the importation of slaves as soon as the Constitution permitted, in 1808. Jefferson's practices regarding slavery were mixed, but in principle he always opposed it. As for the policy itself, slaveholders were divided. Many, especially in the upper South, favored banning importation. There were large numbers of slaves in the country already.

In New England there were threats of secession because of the economic effects of the embargo and the severity of its enforcement. Nationally, the embargo had another pernicious effect. It encouraged a belief that the country could adopt an aggressive foreign policy, yet not back it up with military force. Thus, it laid the groundwork for a persistent American myth that taxation — or sometimes even that adequate government — is unnecessary; that citizens can have the services and policies they need or desire without paying for them.

Jefferson and his Republicans were bound by their ideology. They were remarkably successful in some respects. They expanded the country immensely, they undid much of Hamilton's financial structure, and they relocated the country's social base "from that of an Anglican gentry to that of southern slaveholders, Celtic-American back-country men, and evangelical Protestants."[46] Above all, they performed the exceedingly valuable service of connecting the presidency with the people, rather than leaving it set apart from them.

They did not, however, succeed in the long run; they could not halt the rush of history. They failed in the long run because their ideology was not adequate to deal with an increasingly complex world — elimination of the debt and restricted government, after all, can go only so far before it becomes apparent that something more is needed to prevent stagnation and even chaos — and because they were powerless to resist their ideology.

They generally were unable to bring themselves to accept an alliance with Britain, even when it clearly was in the national interest to do so, because they hated Britain. They veered toward France, even when it was proto-totalitarian. They let wishful thinking create a situation that led to disaster for their next president. They let their practices violate their libertarian principles in order to protect those principles.

Jefferson established a presidency that at its best functioned superbly. He worked carefully with Congress, but by an indirection that preserved congressional dignity and confidence, and without cajoling or bribery. "One of the open secrets to Jefferson's enormous success during his first term was his ability to impose his will on Congress without leaving a presidential fingerprint."[47] He did not find it necessary to veto a single bill during his eight years as president. The force of "his intellect, his character, and his personality" was key — but it also was a weakness in his system. "The system could be made to work only with a Thomas Jefferson at the helm," and there has been only one Thomas Jefferson. When he "faltered, as he did on several occasions during his presidency, the government almost stopped functioning" except in routine matters.[48]

Jefferson had faltered most severely at the end of his presidency. For months Secretary of State Madison and Secretary of the Treasury Gallatin had tried to arouse him, but Jefferson had "lapsed into a weird torpor through the whole last third of his last year in office." Wills quoted many who have tried to "explain this paralysis," Henry Adams, he wrote, thought it resulted from losing popularity; Leonard White thought that it came from loss of self-confidence; "the resolutely admiring Dumas Malone" thought he was merely tired (Wills, though, pointed out that other presidents used no such excuse and that the presidency gave Jefferson enough free time to retreat to Monticello for three months every year); Robert Johnston thought that it displayed an inability to resolve conflict, and that Jefferson had been "horrified at what he was doing" in violating civil liberties and expanding the executive."[49]

Wills pointed out that the explanations ignore a pattern throughout Jefferson's career. As governor, Jefferson had urged Washington to come with his army to take over Virginia, and then left without doing anything. As Washington's secretary of state, he resigned when he thought Hamilton had greater influence than he, and "left the cabinet "with no strong Republican voice." Similarly, he left for home, rather than presiding over the Senate when it was to pass the Sedition Act. Jefferson, in short, had a tendency to walk away from difficult situations, but his "worst defection occurred when he gave up governing the nation for four crucial months, passing on a stalled executive to his successor, Madison." Wills believes that Jefferson in 1808 "faced a situation where he could find no rationale," and that his "great theorizing capacity … just shut down."[50]

Although he remained popular, Jefferson's time in office ended in drift. He surrendered policy to a turbulent Congress. Tragically, "not until Andrew Jackson would a President regain control of the reins of government."[51] Any ranking, therefore, that considers only Jefferson's achievements would place him among the top few presidents. On the other hand, any ranking that relied primarily upon his failures would place him far down the scale. Thus, any ranking that comes up with one final placement — that is, any ranking of presidents at all — obscures more than it reveals. Jefferson's legacy to his country involves much of what makes it great, but it also involves some of what has troubled that country through the years.

4

JAMES MADISON
March 4, 1809–March 4, 1817

Of all the vast material written about James Madison, relatively little pertains to his presidency. Like Jefferson, his predecessor and Republican ally, Madison had an extensive career of public service. His presidency, though, "is semi-forgotten. When Madison expert Jack N. Rakove published a selection of his writings in 1999, only 40 of its 864 pages came from the presidential years." A brief biography Rakove wrote in 1990 devoted thirty-five pages "to the two years in which Madison shepherded the Constitution to ratification, while only 24 pages are devoted to his eight years as president." A compilation in 1840 of Madison's papers included nothing at all from his time as chief executive. ""The disproportion reflects a consensus that Madison, though one of the nation's greatest founders, is not one of its greatest presidents."[1]

One scholar of the presidency, Michael Genovese, has concluded that Madison, "Like Jefferson, had a republican and limited view of executive power. Unlike Jefferson," he said, "Madison was reluctant to abandon this view when necessity warranted." Had he exerted more forceful leadership, Genovese thinks, Madison might have averted the War of 1812. In any case, he charged Madison with having managed the war badly. He did say, however, that the fourth president was "a man of principle and honor."[2]

The Fabers recycled their awed and simplistically enthusiastic line about Jefferson into their comment on Madison. He was, they assured their readers, "like his friend Jefferson … one of the greatest Americans who ever lived." They conceded, nevertheless, that, "like Jefferson, he, too, made perhaps his greatest contributions outside the presidency."[3] Although hardly anyone could disagree that his greatest contributions came elsewhere, President John Kennedy found his presidency to be impressive. "James Madison is our most underrated president," he once remarked."[4]

Some of the disdain directed at Madison's presidency results no doubt from the influence of a descendent of John Adams, the Federalist president who fell victim to the Republican "Revolution of 1800." The historian Henry Adams, John's great grandson, between 1889 and 1891 produced a magisterial multivolume history of the United States during the administrations of Jefferson and Madison. Springing from the bastion of New England Federalism, Adams took on the Virginia Dynasty of presidents with such caustic brilliance that for decades few historians saw fit to challenge his interpretation.

The 2001 attacks that destroyed the World Trade Center, damaged the Pentagon, and annihilated airliners full of passengers shocked and horrified Americans. Symbolically, not even 9/11 humiliated the country as did the spectacle of its capital city in flames. Yet none of these events had great military significance, none destroyed American morale, and quite the contrary all of them inspired American purpose and determination. Madison's reputation bore the disgrace of the country's great embarrassment in the War of 1812 — Henry Adams made certain of that — whereas that of the second President Bush improved, rather than suffered, for more than a year after the attacks on America.

Taking a "New England view," though, does not necessarily mean hostility toward Madison. Kennedy, who re-assessed Madison's presidency favorably, like Henry Adams was a New Englander (though one who hardly had been a Federalist). Adams's great ancestor John Adams himself, moreover, viewed Madison much more favorably than did his great-grandson. Shortly before Madison left office, Adams wrote to Jefferson — part of the legacy of correspondence that the two former presidents and outstanding figures of the Revolution left to their country — that he and Jefferson found their children, grandchildren, and great-grandchildren "cheering." He said he believed they kept him and Jefferson alive, and therefore he had "pitty" for "our good Brother Madison," all "the more, because, notwithstanding a thousand Faults and blunders, his Administration has acquired more glory, and established more Union, than all his three predecessors, Washington Adams and Jefferson, put together."[5]

Madison had no difficulty getting elected. He did have two rivals within his party, the ill and elderly Vice President George Clinton, former governor of New York, and James Monroe who had allied himself with Madison's vitriolic and bitter enemy, the erratic John Randolph of Roanoke. Monroe, though, did not contest the election vigorously, probably because he did not wish to offend his other ally, Jefferson, who supported Madison. Oddly, Clinton was re-elected vice president, but he did receive six presidential electoral votes as well. He died in office, during the final year of Madison's first term.

The Federalists by this time presented little threat. The party had little support outside New England. The "Embargo Act had devastated the economy; moreover Madison was a principal architect of the ruinous policy." Madison's victory thus in all probability was more a reflection of Federalist weakness and disorganization than a statement regarding issues or candidates.[6]

Timing also worked on behalf of the Republicans. "Had the Embargo become law a year earlier, the backlash against it might have hurt Madison's chances within the party or against his Federalist opponent, Charles C. Pinckney." But many states had voted before the full effects of the embargo had become apparent. The congressional tally of electoral votes in December 1808 showed that Madison trounced Pinckney by 122 to 47.[7]

The government that Madison inherited had suffered from the largely successful Republican zeal that he shared — a determination to eliminate taxes, restrict the military, and in fact if their rhetoric was any guide to minimize government itself, all the while retaining an aggressive foreign policy. The only way sober statesmen could adhere to such a position was to engage in extraordinarily wishful thinking. Madison frequently heard what he wanted to hear,[8] and frequently he "leaped at what he thought *should* be true before he could verify that it was true."[9]

Pressuring the great European powers by restricting commerce had not worked, and Jefferson's "administration had never seriously considered what it would do if economic coercion failed. The Republican majority still looked to the White House for leadership. But at that crucial time — his final four months in office — a dispirited Jefferson, pining for Monticello, insisted that he was only 'a spectator,' and that the initiative for revising policy should come from his successor."[10] The embargo clearly either had to be eliminated or made all-inclusive, but Madison did not — in fairness, possibly he could not — act while his predecessor still held the presidency.

Thus, not only had Republican policies under President Jefferson and Secretary of State Madison made President Madison's task incomparably more difficult, the virtual crippling of the administration in the months before he took office made the new president's challenges almost insurmountable. Adding to his woes were his weak appointments. Madison wisely was determined to have Albert Gallatin's extraordinary abilities in the cabinet. To name him to the top post, however, secretary of state, would cause a furor. Several leading Republicans despised Gallatin, and Madison sought to smooth over party difficulties. He kept Gallatin on as secretary of the treasury. Since he already held the post, he did not require Senate confirmation, and Madison avoided a party fight.

For State, Madison nominated Robert Smith, Jefferson's incompetent secretary of the navy but a brother of the powerful Republican Senator Samuel Smith. "The appointment was less than brilliant." Worse, Smith would prove to be an enemy of Madison within the cabinet. The acid-tongued John Randolph summed up Smith's abilities: "at least," Randolph quipped, "he could spell."[11] Paul Hamilton of South Carolina went to Navy, and Dr. William Eustis of Massachusetts to War. Republican ideology deemed neither post important, and the level of competence of the appointees reflected that disdain. Gallatin was the only effective member of the cabinet. Madison knew, therefore, that he would have to act as his own secretary of state[12] — at least.

Appointing a disloyal secretary of state, whatever the political justification, was a great error. Another disloyal member of the administration, however, was beyond Madison's control. His opponent for the presidency, George Clinton, as mentioned above also ran for the vice presidency; that office he won. He therefore was in a position to cast tie-breaking votes in the Senate against Madison's policies. For example, Madison's administration (primarily Secretary of the Treasury Gallatin) had come to recognize the necessity of a bank of the United States. In 1811, the administration supported its re-establishment, but Clinton cast the defeating vote. Madison found himself facing the "kind of disloyalty Jefferson had shown to Washington as his secretary of state ... and had shown to Adams as his vice president."[13]

Even more detrimental than his cabinet appointments, some biographers believe, was Madison's retention of the "badly tainted James Wilkinson," the general whom Jefferson had protected. Madison's secretary of war was unqualified for the position, but he was a physician. He noticed that Wilkinson's troops in New Orleans were dying at an alarming rate from disease, and ordered him to move them away from malarial areas. Wilkinson disregarded the order, and he lost one thousand of the two thousand men under his command. A court-martial "left the decision on Wilkinson's future career up to Madison," who continued the "whitewash" of the inept and corrupt general that Jefferson had begun.[14] Wills remarked caustically that one could "imagine the quick work George Washington would have made of a general who willfully destroyed a thousand of his own troops. Madison's weak response to this problem," he said, "retained a man in command who would be responsible for more needless deaths in the War of 1812." He noted that the difficulty resulted from Madison's refusal "to treat war as a real possibility."[15]

Not all of Madison's appointments were unfortunate. He named Joseph Story to the Supreme Court, and Story went on to perform with distinction. Sadly for Madison, however, Story's rulings frequently were contrary to Republican preferences.

Just as Madison's administration began, the embargo expired. Replacing it was a Nonintercourse Act designed to allow the president to resume trade with France, Britain, or both if they would only agree to leave American ships alone. As that would imply, the new act was ineffective, but in any case, "whatever the United States did, both belligerents were likely to persist in their illegal and oppressive edicts. In that case, Madison faced the grim alternatives of a disgraceful withdrawal of American commerce from the high seas or measures of self-defense almost certain to mean war."[16]

Still, not all was unfavorable at the start of the new administration. It is easy to underestimate the value of social matters to a president, and Madison was extremely fortunate in that regard; Mrs. Madison was perfectly suited for her responsibilities as first lady. "Clearly, under Dolley's presiding genius, and with her husband's entire approval, both in Washington and at Montpelier the years of Madison's presidency were a social triumph." Jefferson had adopted informality as a policy, but Madison considered "the honor and dignity of the republic ... to require some elegance and style in its social life," and to reflect "the success of the experiment in republican government."[17]

It also appeared for a time as though the new president might have the same kind of good fortune that Jefferson had had with the Louisiana Purchase. Madison heard that Britain was revising its policy, so — acting under the optimistic assumption that the embargo had worked — he lifted the restrictions against British commerce, as the Nonintercourse Act had authorized. The country was jubilant, and Madison left Washington's summer heat to return to Monpelier.[18]

His optimism was misplaced. Gallatin, in fact, had been skeptical. "Madison," however, "was hearing only what he wanted to hear."[19]

Although any impressment by the British was a humiliation to the United States, it was not realistic to expect American policy to end it completely. "The British navy could not survive if it let its seamen escape to American ships, where they were better paid and flogged less often."[20] The British could not reasonably have been expected to avoid impressing even American citizens, at least while they were at war with France. Not only was service on American vessels more pleasant than in the British Navy, American citizenship at the time could be acquired so casually that British "desertions were sometimes wholesale, and would have unmanned the fleet if not opposed resolutely. No British ministry that gave up the power of impressment could last a day."[21]

Of course, America could have settled the issue itself, but it refused to do so. If American ships employed no British subjects (or recent British subjects), the trouble could have evaporated. To some extent, the Americans found themselves in the same situation as the British. "The government could have issued certificates allowing employment only to American seamen. British deserters could have been confined in ports. But American merchants did not want any of these steps taken. They depended too heavily on British seamen. When Gallatin surveyed the overseas commercial trade in 1807, he found that roughly nine thousand British seamen were engaged in it — over a third of the overseas crews working under the American flag." As Wills put if, "the merchants whose vessels were being stopped preferred that invasion of their rights to the drying up of their work pool."[22]

News that Britain would not lift its restrictive policy brought the jubilation to an end. Outrage swept the land. Madison returned to Washington as his secretary of state declared that the president had no authority to reimpose the restrictions against trade with Britain that he had lifted. Madison nevertheless did restore the restrictions, and returned to Montpelier. As for the embargo's influence on Madison, it "made him not only inherit but prolong Jefferson's period of drift"[23] throughout his first two years in office.

By 1811, Madison finally demanded the resignation of his secretary of state, and replaced him with James Monroe. With Jefferson's encouragement, he and Monroe had resolved their differences that had stemmed from Monroe's challenge to him in vying for the presidency in 1808. Both recognized "that political reconciliation would also serve their interests. Madison gained a competent secretary of state, while Monroe ended his self-imposed political exile and rejoined the Republican leadership."[24] The political benefits were manifest. Madison brought off Smith's dismissal "in a way that strengthened his cabinet and his standing in the country." On a personal basis, too, the change was welcome. Although relations between Madison and Monroe for a time had been awkward, there had been a thirty-year friendship between the two men.[25]

The cabinet change, along with other developments — such as congressional pressure from the "War Hawks," led by Henry Clay in the House — ultimately brought a shift in position regarding war. With the failure of the policies with which he had sought peace, Madison became the first president to ask Congress for a declaration of war. His request came on June 1812.

The president and his Republican followers had convinced themselves that Canada would be theirs for the taking. Seizing Canada would expand the great Republican empire. It also would eliminate the possibility that Canada's booming economy and ample land might attract the loyalty of northern farmers away from the United States. Finally, an American Canada would halt a huge flow of goods to Great Britain that had begun to shake "Madison's confidence in the efficacy of economic coercion."[26] Jefferson thought Canada would fall to the Americans before the end of the year; it would "be a mere matter of marching," he had indicated. Unfortunately for Madison and the Americans, the "war euphoria paired a vast overestimation of American military ability with a vast underestimation of Canada's."[27]

The election of 1812 came in the midst of war fever. Vice President George Clinton had died in office. His nephew, New York Governor De Witt Clinton, became the Federalist candidate to oppose Madison for president. Madison won clearly, although not overwhelmingly, with an electoral vote of 128 to 89. The loss of Pennsylvania, which had twenty-five electoral votes, would have thrown the election to Clinton. Madison's new vice president, Elbridge Gerry from Massachusetts — whom the Republicans had selected in the vain hope that a New Englander on the ticket would encourage New England to support the war — ironically also died in office. In any case, it was unrealistic to expect New England in general to favor the conflict.

The entire war, when it came, was largely a military disaster for the Americans. Major exceptions were naval engagements — on the Great Lakes and Lake Champlain as well as on the ocean — and the great Battle of New Orleans that, unknown to the participants, took place after the declaration of peace. America had been unprepared. Republican ideology had kept taxes unrealistically low while paying down the national debt, and had opposed the maintenance of an effective military. Neither Secretary of War William Eustis nor the few top military leaders that existed were competent. Madison replaced Eustis with John Armstrong, who proved little if any better. His replacement of the alcoholic secretary of the navy, Paul Hamilton, with William Jones was considerably better, and brought ability to the top of the Navy Department.

It is ironic that the greatest successes came from naval engagements, because the British navy was the world's largest and most powerful. Just as the Republicans had relied primarily on militias for their land forces, so too did they conclude that they could provide naval defense with substantially no naval vessels. "Gunboats" were their answer, floating platforms with a gun, which the Republicans believed could provide ample defense. Not being seaworthy, they could not be used offensively. For offense, they turned to their "*real* weapon, commercial blackmail." Gunboats and commercial pressure were "clever shortcuts. They were the "magic solution."[28] Neither worked. Nor, as a rule, did militias. Regular troops, on the contrary, in the rare instances in which they were available performed quite well. Several times General Jacob Brown and his subordinate Winfield Scott, with regular troops, repelled or defeated larger British forces from Canada in New York.

If gunboats were worse than useless, frigates, sloops, and privateer ships "all performed gloriously." Madison's best weapons were George Washington's original six frigates. A Quaker, Joshua Humphreys, designed them, and they were "technological marvels, the most advanced fighting ships of their time." Moreover, while Madison's generals "found excuses for not fighting" — Wilkinson was especially troublesome — naval commanders "ran ahead of orders into the fight."[29]

Madison would not have had even these six if his arguments earlier in his career had prevailed. During Washington's administration, as a member of the House he had attempted to reduce the Federalists' request for the six to two or three. Jefferson, when he was president, "tried to put the obnoxious frigates in drydock; but by then their use in the Mediterranean had become effective and popular."[30]

During the attack on Washington, Madison demonstrated great physical courage. His reputation had "hit rock bottom," but his valor when the British pillaged the executive mansion and burned the capitol on 24 August 1814 "won back some public esteem."[31] Then, early in 1815, when news of Andrew Jackson's great victory in New Orleans arrived followed closely by official dispatches telling of a peace treaty, "peace struck the country like a thunderbolt.... In terms of a renovated national pride, the change was enormous."[32]

Madison had led the country into a war for which it was completely unprepared. Wills has cited his weak points as "a certain provincialism with regard to the rest of the world and a certain naivete with regard to the rest of his fellow human beings."[33] As for management of the war, Wills identified "four main causes of failure:" there was no provision for intelligence, there was no clear command structure, politics — rather than ability — determined military appointments, and the country continued to rely primarily on militia rather than regular troops.[34]

The outcome was hardly conclusive. Britain had not changed its policies on the high seas, and the Republicans had been forced to abandon some of their key principles, especially those relating to commercial policies. Despite Madison's desire for authority over the Floridas — he had issued a secret proclamation on 27 October 1810 sending occupation troops to West Florida — U.S. control over West Florida remained questionable, and was completely nonexistent over East Florida. On the other hand, European powers no longer retained power in the West. America controlled New Orleans and the length of the Mississippi.[35]

Historians have tended not to look with great favor on Madison's presidency. Deliberately leading the country into war with inadequate resources, an incompetent cabinet and military staff, and exercising little effort to improve any of these weaknesses hardly inspires praise. Nevertheless, "they do not count him a failure — and they cannot. He was too popular at the end of his second term." Wills has concluded that "he must have been doing something right."[36]

What were these things? He did not panic. At the darkest times, he was coolest. He did not attempt to coerce the reluctant New England governors to support the war. Even in the face of harsh criticisms from the cabinet members he ultimately let go, "he did not let himself get trapped in a cycle of recriminations." Above all, "despite what Andrew Jackson did in the truly desperate New Orleans situation, he did not himself violate the civil rights of a citizenry at war." His record in that regard was much better than subsequent presidents.[37] It was far better, also, than those of his immediate predecessors, Adams and Jefferson. Just as John Adams demonstrated the great principle that limited constitutional government can survive, that a leader can relinquish power to the opposition, so too did James Madison demonstrate an equally great principle. Madison made it clear that it is possible to conduct a war while remaining true to the principles of a republican constitution; that civil liberties need not fall victim to a war effort. Perhaps this is what President Kennedy meant when he praised Madison. Perhaps ultimately it will serve as an example to presidents and attorneys general after 9/11.

Former President Adams listed five major accomplishments of the Madison Administration. It demonstrated that the Constitution established a political system under which it was possible first to declare war, and second to make peace. Third, regardless of funds or government, it made it clear that Britain could never conquer the United States. Fourth and fifth, Madison had shown that America's land forces were equal to those of Britain and Europe, and its naval forces the equal of "any that ever floated on the ocean."[38] In addition, the Union expanded by the admission of two states, Louisiana in 1812, and Indiana four years later, in 1816.

Wills has brilliantly assessed Madison's accomplishments. As he noted, war's centralizing force can — in fact usually does — bring authoritarianism. Madison, however, stood firm against "any such tendency," and his "scrupulous constitutionalism served the nation." The Federalists had favored centralization, but thought that it involved concentrating "all power in the hands of a few wise leaders, excluding others." Madison's centralization, on the other hand, was inclusive. "It incorporated the energies and informality of the western territories. It made citizens more aware of the different parts of the nation. Psychologically, it shrank America," while dogmatism lessened and tolerance increased. Contrary to some interpretations, Madison's evolution was not a shift from Republicanism to Federalism; rather "what Madison was forced unconsciously to adopt was not an ideology but a historic phenomenon — modernity."[39]

No longer were the forces of modernization associated with an inherited class or with religion as the Federalists had assumed. Madison's presidency set the stage for a political and military leadership based on merit, populism, and pragmatism. Technology and secularism would dominate. No longer would social class determine military leadership; it would come rather from such leaders as engineers from West Point. "The manufacturing complexes that built cannon during the war were soon turning out steam-

boats." When the New England clergy had opposed the War of 1812 as "god-
less," they became discredited. "Madison reflected modern values when he
refused to institute the customary day of prayer and fasting during time of
war." Congress asked him to issue a proclamation, but he responded that
people could pray "if so disposed." Thus, "it makes little sense to ask whether
Federalism or Republicanism won in 1815. Neither of them won. Nationalism did."[40]

Even in this regard, though, Madison's record is mixed. Although he
strongly favored internal improvements and recognized that they were vital
to the future of the country, his constitutional scruples led him — two days
before he left office — to cast a veto that shocked Washington, DC. This
veto turned down the "Bonus Bill" that the young Representative John C.
Calhoun (who at the time was still a nationalist, and not yet a nullifier) had
carefully led through the House. The legislation would have reserved for the
construction of roads and canals the substantial bonus that the Second Bank
of the United States had paid to the government, and all future revenues
from the Bank. A stunned Henry Clay had announced that it would have
been no more a surprise if an earthquake had swallowed up half the city.[41]

McCoy has argued that no one should have been surprised; that Madison clearly had set forth his opinion that the Constitution forbade federal
support for internal improvement in a number of his messages to Congress.[42]
The question that arises here is a president's responsibility both to uphold
the Constitution, and to act for the good of the country. Madison thought
that the Constitution did not confer the necessary authority upon the
national government to support internal improvements. He did come, however, to conclude that the government could, constitutionally, charter a
national bank, and he provided his signature to the act that chartered the
Second Bank of the United States — and the Constitution no more mentions
a power to charter banks than it does a power to finance roads and canals.

What, then, was the president's obligation? He thought that improvements were so important that he favored a constitutional amendment to
empower the government to support them. One could argue that by so doing
he was upholding both his responsibility to act in the public interest, and
his obligation to preserve constitutional principles. Certainly that would be
the case if the language of the Constitution had been forthright on the issue.
But one could argue the contrary case as well.

The Constitution's language on the issue was not so clear. Nor was the
question one of a fundamental human right. On the contrary — and at the
risk of giving offense to many (including to some members of the current
U.S. Supreme Court) — however emotionally charged it was, it was essentially a legalistic quibble. The issue was not the potentially vital one: "does
government have the authority?" Rather it was simply, "which level of gov-

ernment is it that has the authority?" Admittedly, as time went on the question did come to take on an added dimension when expansionist policies came to dominance in the South, as Calhoun's opportunistic shift away from nationalism demonstrated. Slaveholders then came to fear that power at the national level could come to mean interference with their cherished goal of expanding slavery without impediment.

There was disagreement regarding the Constitution's grant of authority. On the other hand, there was hardly any disagreement that the country needed internal improvements. One therefore could argue the opposite of the position above: that Madison's action in this regard reflected what might be called political fundamentalism — a view that, if it had continued to prevail indefinitely, would have prevented the development of the United States into a modern nation-state and endangered its survival in a world that was to become ever more hostile.

So how would one "rank" a president such as James Madison? He blundered, he deferred excessively to Congress, and he took the United States deliberately into a war that could have been disastrous — and was in fact disastrous to the extent that it led to destruction of the national capitol. Some of his actions reflected a view incompatible with continued development of a modern nation state. Nevertheless, other of his actions strengthened the constitutional system. Additionally, he prepared the country — perhaps unconsciously — truly to enter the new century, and in many ways he conducted himself in a manner that could serve as a model for presidents even today.

As with Adams and especially with Jefferson, one could look only at the accomplishments and conclude that Madison's presidency was "great," or by considering only his failures of leadership could conclude that it was weak and bumbling. To look at a ranking of Madison in relation with other presidents could only obscure true understanding of his presidency. To conclude that "on balance" he did well or ill is oversimplification enough. To attempt a precise ranking — in the case of both the Fabers and Genovese, eleventh (the Fabers place him just above Adams and just below Monroe and Jackson, while Genovese puts him just below Adams and above Eisenhower) — would appear to offer something concrete while in reality it is meaningless.

5

JAMES MONROE
March 4, 1817–March 4, 1825

James Monroe, the fifth president, was the final one to have been a member of the revolutionary generation. Appropriately, he also was the final president to dress the part by powdering his hair, and wearing "small clothes" (the tight knee breeches of earlier days). Monroe was in fact more than a mere member of that generation; he was a legitimate hero of the Revolution, having been wounded with Washington's forces after the well-known winter trip across the Delaware to attack the Hessian mercenaries at Trenton. Additionally, he was the fourth Virginian to hold the office, and was the final member of the "Virginia Dynasty"—that triumvirate of Jefferson, Madison, and Monroe. What opposition there was to his nomination arose from questions about whether yet another Virginian should be elevated to the country's top office. Once he received the nomination from the congressional caucus, his election in 1816 was assured.

The Federalists had discredited themselves as a party. Their actions during the War of 1812 created a widespread perception of disloyalty, which the abortive Hartford Convention—called to consider secession—underscored. They did not even bother to go through the nominating process, although there was a general understanding that Rufus King of New York was their candidate. He carried only three states.

With the disintegration of an opposition party, there was no chance that Monroe's candidacy would suffer from his vote against the Constitution a quarter-century or so before in Virginia's ratifying convention. There similarly was no adverse comment regarding his diplomatic experience during Washington's administration. As minister to France, Monroe's Jeffersonian orientation was so openly pro-French that Washington had to recall him in order to maintain his administration's strict neutrality policy in the French-British conflict.

By 1816, however, foreign policy had become Monroe's major strength. President Jefferson had sent him again to France, where he helped negotiate the Louisiana Purchase. Moreover, despite briefly having been Madison's rival for the presidency in 1808, there was no resistance to Monroe's candidacy from the Madison administration. There had been strained relations between the two after the 1808 election, but Jefferson had stepped in as a mediator, and succeeded in smoothing over their differences.

Just how well Jefferson succeeded is indicated by Madison's cabinet appointments. In 1811 he made Monroe his secretary of state. For a time Monroe also served Madison as secretary of war, thus holding two cabinet positions at once in Madison's administration.

With the Republicans ascendant, Monroe's partisan contributions to Philadelphia's *National Gazette* during Washington's administration also would not have been held against him — if they had even known or remembered. The *Gazette* was the opposition newspaper that Representative James Madison and Secretary of State Thomas Jefferson established in 1791. So it was that James Monroe was elected handily in 1816. In 1820, running unopposed for re-election, he carried every state, receiving every elector's vote except for one, that of William Plumer of New Hampshire.

Plumer cast his vote for John Quincy Adams, who was not a candidate. Folklore has it that he did so in order to maintain Washington's record as the only president to receive a vote from every presidential elector. In reality, however, he simply did not like Monroe. Ironically, the elderly former President John Adams was an elector that year, and after having left the presidency he had moved steadily toward the Republicans; he headed the Massachusetts slate of electors, and joined the others in casting a Monroe vote.[1]

In his inaugural address, Monroe spoke largely in general terms. He mentioned the importance of internal improvements, sincerely recognizing the country's great need for roads, bridges, canals, and the like. His rigid Republican interpretation of the Constitution, though, was not evident in his address. It became clear later when he vetoed an appropriation for internal improvements as unconstitutional. He thus followed Madison in vetoing a bill that would have provided for development he recognized as vital. He, like Madison, called for an amendment to the Constitution that would sanction federal support for such improvements. Also like Madison, he was unsuccessful.

Despite the objection to internal improvements, the Republicans in response to developing conditions had shorn themselves of some of the more rigid Jeffersonian principles. Monroe sought Madison's advice on a number of matters. The two had come to agree not only with regard to internal improvements, but each had come to accept the need for a national bank and for a tariff. Each in addition had come to recognize the need for greater national defense.

Also on the positive side, Monroe's commitment to republican principles led him to do something that no president since Washington — not even the dedicated Republicans, Jefferson and Madison — had done. Washington had understood the immense importance — especially for the first president — to forge connection with the people. Monroe followed Washington's example, and set out on an extensive tour through the United States. Later, he toured yet again.

During the New England portion of the first trip, Monroe paid a courtesy call on John and Abigail Adams. The visit meant much to the former president who tended to think that he had been forgotten.[2] Adams also took great pride in the appointment of his son, John Quincy, to the cabinet as secretary of state.

Monroe used the occasion as well to visit military installations, and build support for strengthening the country's defenses. Nicholas Biddle, former secretary to Monroe when he was minister to England and future director of the Bank of the United States, perceptively recognized the symbolic importance of Monroe's tour. Too often, he told Monroe, the president seemed "to the nation too much like the Chief Clerk of Congress."[3]

That was correct, and Monroe's initiative was important. His presidency, however, did little to change the impression that the president was a mere appendage to Congress. Such an impression had been developing ever since Jefferson had left office. Even after Monroe had carried every state in his re-election, Speaker of the House Henry Clay taunted the president by saying that "Mr. Monroe has just been re-elected with apparent unanimity, but he has not the slightest influence on Congress. His career is closed."[4] This, of course, was an exaggeration, since the president's authority still included that most powerful legislative tool, the veto. Nevertheless, power had shifted from the executive to the legislative branch.

Because the Federalist Party had dissolved, and Monroe appeared to be presiding over a unified government since it was devoid of parties, the *Columbian Centinel* in Boston heralded his visit as reflecting an "Era of Good Feelings."[5] The title stuck. Despite the dissolution of party, however, trouble was brewing as Southern politicians began campaigning for an expansion of slavery into the territories. The question of Missouri's entrance into the Union — slave or free — frightened the elderly Jefferson as though it were, as he put it, "A Fire Bell in the Night." The Missouri Compromise in 1820 postponed the issue for a time by admitting Missouri as a slave state, Maine a free state, and declaring that slavery in the Louisiana Territory would be permitted south of the southern border of Missouri, but (except in Missouri) not north of the 36° 30' line.

One important function of the president and first lady is one that seems trivial and is easy to overlook. To a large extent, they set the social tone of Washington — and more political developments than outsiders recognize take place during social occasions. Elizabeth Kortright Monroe, the first lady, presided over the re-decoration of the President's House. Congress appropriated funds to help restore it after the serious damage it incurred during the War of 1812. Her efforts brought comments from foreign and domestic visitors upon the mansion's elegance.[6]

The funds appropriated were insufficient for the job, and the Monroes used some of their own funds for the decoration and restoration. In addition, they needed to supply much of their own furniture to fill the huge mansion. Questions arose regarding Monroe's own tangled finances. They were complicated by his choice of Samuel Lane, the superintendent of public buildings, not only to disburse public funds for the executive mansion, but to manage his own accounts as well.[7]

The Monroes, however, caused resentment by declining invitations to private or diplomatic residences. "Few social customs aroused more controversy and ill feelings then the etiquette of making calls. By the time Monroe took office, the convention had been fixed in the minds of many senators that heads of departments should make first calls on them, while members of the House were to initiate calls on the secretaries." Secretary of State Adams and the Monroes themselves found such expectations to be time-consuming and impractical.[8]

Monroe's presidency is best known for advances in foreign relations. John Quincy Adams was a superb secretary of state, and Monroe gave him the support that he required. Many of Spain's possessions in Latin America were restive, and Madison — reflecting the most healthy aspect of the republican spirit — recommended that he support the emerging revolutionary movements whenever possible. "The ex-President urged his successor to give 'every lawful manifestation' of United States approval of the revolutionaries, 'whatever may be the consequences'." Madison suggested that Monroe seek the help of the British — who would have been happy to eliminate Spain from this part of the world — in supporting independence of the colonies. Adams, however, recommended a unilateral declaration against European colonization in the Western Hemisphere.[9]

The resulting "Monroe Doctrine" became enshrined as a key principle of American foreign policy. Monroe elected to announce it in his seventh annual message to Congress on 2 December 1823. He had assumed as a principle, he asserted, that the "American continents, by the free and independent condition which they have assumed and maintain, are henceforth not to be considered as subjects for future colonization by any European powers."[10]

Monroe's republican principles dictated deference to Congress. Nevertheless, regarding foreign policy he felt more independence. He acted on his own to declare the doctrine. By seeking no congressional support, he reinforced "a president's power to take the initiative and make policy in foreign affairs."[11] Monroe had sought advice from Jefferson and Madison, but went beyond their recommendations and followed Adams's advice to act unilaterally in defense of the hemisphere. Adams provided the major content of the message, but it was "Monroe who decided to announce the policy in his message to Congress, thus proclaiming it to the world."[12]

During Monroe's presidency the Union expanded to include twenty-four states. Mississippi (1817), Illinois (1818), Alabama (1819), Maine (1820), and Missouri (1821) achieved statehood while he was in office. At least equally important, he finally secured Florida from Spain and successfully extended U.S. territorial claims to the Pacific.

Florida had been a thorn in the America's side since the founding. Monroe had been unsuccessful in his attempts to purchase the area, when late in 1818 and into 1819, General Andrew Jackson entered the territory under controversial circumstances. The extent of his orders has remained in dispute. Regardless of formal orders, though, it is clear that Jackson thought he had the authority, that Monroe wanted Florida and at least implied to Jackson that he might seize the territory, and that Secretary of State Adams thought he had acted appropriately.[13]

Jackson was to have led a punitive expedition against Seminole Indians who had conducted attacks across the border. He did not stop there, though, but continued on to attack Spanish installations. He ordered two British nationals executed as troublemakers. The Spanish, recognizing their weakness, finally agreed to sell Florida to the United States.

Monroe appointed Jackson governor of the Florida Territory when the United States assumed control on 17 July 1821. He served only briefly, and then resigned. As a result of his Florida campaign, there was a strong censure movement against him. The movement failed, and certainly failed to dent Jackson's formidable popularity, but it outraged the old general. He did not know until considerably later that Secretary of War John C. Calhoun was secretly behind the censure effort.

The tendency is to see Monroe's presidency as a transition; to see him as "more caretaker than leader."[14] He did not seek to lead Congress. As a political figure, he "aroused neither the adulation nor the detestation that Jefferson stirred in his admirers or detractors." He aroused fewer strong feelings than any of his predecessors. He appeared plain, despite having restored formality to the executive office, "reversing Jefferson's casualness."[15] He had neither the learning nor the brilliance of his three immediate predecessors. The visiting Italian Count Carlo Vidua, for example, met with them all and also with Monroe after he left the presidency. Vidua found John Adams, despite his age, still to be impressive. Jefferson he thought to be the most brilliant but Madison to be the most profound. John Quincy Adams was the most cultivated, while Monroe's mind he found to be "the least keen."[16]

Nevertheless, Monroe appointed a strong cabinet, and had the good judgment to support his superb secretary of state, John Quincy Adams. He listened to advice, and pursued his chosen course with determination. He was a mediator, and presided over the Missouri Compromise — delaying the most intense party of the slavery controversy until the nation was strong enough to weather the enormous storm that it brought. His foreign policy accomplishments were outstanding, as were his contributions to the territorial integrity of the United States. He may not have attempted to be a legislative leader, but he nonetheless asserted executive authority in foreign affairs and was responsible for the Monroe Doctrine. Legislatures of many of the states passed resolutions of appreciation for his service when he left office. As Garry Wills said about Madison, Monroe must have done something right.

From this brief description alone, it is apparent that the circumstances of Monroe's presidency were unique. He took office at a time of national pride resulting from the end of the War of 1812. Other presidents — Lincoln comes to mind — served when parties were fragmented and confused, but only Monroe held office at a time when parties appeared more or less to have vanished. All the while, sectional controversy was building. The legislative branch had come to overshadow the presidency. Monroe's strong cabinet contained several rivals to succeed him as president, and for the first time a populist leader from outside the established elites — Andrew Jackson — was building support for a presidential bid. Jackson's bid came just as states were eliminating property requirements for voting, and were shifting to the popular vote to select presidential electors.

Can Monroe thus be "ranked" meaningfully? His example demonstrates the added difficulty of attempting to rank those presidents who are neither truly outstanding nor outright failures. Genovese called Monroe "above average," and placed him fourteenth of the thirty-nine rated — just below Eisenhower and Kennedy, and just ahead of McKinley and LBJ, in that order.[17] The 1962 Schlesinger poll puts him the lowest, at eighteenth out of thirty-one, and in the "average" category[18] — although Landy and Milkis remark harshly that Monroe (along with Madison and John Quincy Adams) was "among the most ineffectual presidents in all of American history."[19]

As the Fabers noted, he tends to range in various rankings from twelfth to eighteenth. They, on the contrary, say that he is "the most underrated of all U.S. presidents. His administration," they wrote, "was marked by some of the most brilliant diplomacy in American history." They speculate that times were too good under Monroe, and that historians might rate him higher, "had there been more crises for him to face. They place him in a tie with Jackson for ninth of thirty-one, just behind Kennedy, whose tenure in office — despite being limited to two years and ten months — greatly impressed them, and ahead of his predecessor, Madison.[20]

Placing the patrician Monroe in the same ranked position as the frontier populist Jackson reflects the shortcomings of rankings. The two did share some similarities. Both were in the republican tradition of limited government. Jackson, however, was a vigorous and active executive. Both had significant accomplishments to their credit, but Jackson established traditions that strengthened the executive, while Monroe did little to rescue it from the shadow of legislative authority — at least in domestic matters. The situation was similar regarding the authority of the states. Both Jackson and Monroe favored protecting it, but Monroe did little to counterbalance that authority by asserting national authority, and thus encouraged the centrifugal forces that Jackson, and later Lincoln, had to counter.

This is not to question which ranking of Monroe is correct. Rather it is to ask whether any ranking can add to understanding. Is it possible to learn anything about such different figures as Monroe or Jackson, for example, to see them placed together in a ranking?

6

JOHN QUINCY ADAMS
March 4, 1825–March 4, 1829

John Quincy Adams came to the presidency after a tumultuous election that failed to choose a winner in the electoral college. Of all the presidential elections in American history, only two have had to be decided by the House of Representatives: Jefferson's in 1800, and J.Q. Adams's in 1824. For Adams, the consequences of his election were considerably more serious than Jefferson's had been for him. As the first president who failed to obtain a plurality either of the popular or the electoral vote,[1] Adams might have been apprehensive regarding the course of his presidency; if so, he was justified in his concern.[2] Moreover, he began his term by making the same mistake his father had made: wishing to be above party and personal interest, he retained all cabinet members from the previous administration who wished to stay in office.

Monroe's cabinet had included three rivals to succeed him as president. Secretary of State Adams was the favorite, but Secretary of War John C. Calhoun was a serious contender as was Secretary of the Treasury William H. Crawford. Crawford, however, was in very poor health as the result of a recent stroke. He continued to be accepted as a candidate primarily as a matter of courtesy to him. The ambitious and formidable Henry Clay also was in the race, making it the largest group of candidates since the government's beginning.

The race was unusual in several other respects as well. For the first time there was an outsider: the people's favorite, the war hero General Andrew Jackson. Never before had there been a presidential challenger from outside the elite circles that had ruled the country since its beginning. Jackson's candidacy was a harbinger of things to come, and it brought turmoil.

For another first, states had moved to eliminate property requirements for voting, thus expanding the electorate considerably. For yet another, by 1824 most states had begun to choose their presidential electors by popular vote.[3] The 1824 election thus was the first in which the popular vote weighed heavily. Andrew Jackson received more popular votes, and more electoral votes, than any other candidate, followed by Adams in both categories. Clay came in third in the popular vote, but was almost tied with Crawford, who came in third in the electoral college, leaving Clay fourth in electoral votes. Calhoun, who was only forty-one years of age, had decided in March to drop out of the race and try later. He ran for the vice presidency with both Jackson and Adams, and won easily.[4] He based his decision on simple practicality. He had counted on support from Pennsylvania, which, when added to support from the South, he believed would boost him to victory. Pennsylvania's delegates at their convention on 4 March dashed his hopes by rallying instead to Jackson and giving Calhoun their support only for the vice presidency. With no support outside the South, "Calhoun was simply another southern candidate without the slightest chance of winning the general election."[5] Under the circumstances, his choice to accept the vice presidency was an easy one.

For the presidential contenders though, things were not so simple. No candidate had a majority in the electoral college, which meant that the choice fell to the House of Representatives. It also meant that Clay was out of the running, because the Constitution requires the House to select from the three who received the most electoral votes. Effectively, therefore, because of Crawford's disability the choice had to be between Adams the secretary of state, and Jackson the outsider. After considerable wrangling, Speaker of the House Clay threw his support to Adams, who won. Clay agreed with Adams that "the Union must be strengthened by higher tariffs and federal support for roads, canals, and manufacturing."[6] Whatever Clay's motives, it is likely that his own ambition made him unenthusiastic about building up the power of a fellow Westerner who later would compete with him for support from the West.

Initially, Jackson "accepted the House's vote with equanimity, and even greeted Adams cordially at a reception held the night of the House vote." Three days later, however, the situation changed abruptly. When Adams became president, it caused a vacancy in the position of secretary of state. Adams named Clay, causing Jackson to erupt in rage. He was convinced that there had been a "corrupt bargain," a promise to make Clay secretary of state as payment for his support for Adams's presidency. This was a serious issue, because the post of secretary of state gave its holder an advantage as a presidential contender. No evidence has ever supported Jackson's dark suspicions of a secret deal. In fact John Quincy Adams's integrity argues against the existence of one, as does his diary in which he wrote that he had heard about his support in the House a week before he "had any conversation with Clay upon the subject."[7] Regardless, the "corrupt bargain" charge tainted both his career and that of Clay.[8]

Adams thus began his presidency under a cloud. Moreover, he faced a bitter and extremely popular enemy. Andrew Jackson began to conduct a systematic campaign to win the presidential election of 1828 and to undermine the Adams administration. All this was made worse by Adams's retention of a cabinet that bore him no loyalty and in fact included some members who worked against him.

Madison is best known as Father of the Constitution, and Jefferson as author of the Declaration of Independence. In both cases, their pre-presidential careers have somewhat overshadowed their presidencies. In contrast, although enormous accomplishments marked his career before the presidency, the most distinguished part of John Quincy Adams's career arguably came after he left that office (when he served with great honor in the U.S. House of Representatives). All three, though, do share something in common. For none of them was the presidency the most outstanding part of their careers.

For Adams, in fact, one of his biographers had to explain why his book devoted "only a single chapter to [Adams's] administration." He wrote that "his four years in the White House were misery for him and for his wife. All that he hoped to accomplish was thwarted by a hostile Congress. His opponents continually assailed him."[9] This biographer, Paul Nagel, spoke of a failed administration. In the sense that Adams failed to get Congress to enact a single part of his ambitious agenda, this judgment is correct. Ironically, although Madison and Monroe had each vetoed acts supporting internal improvements, Adams could not prevail upon Congress to pass one.

Adams did, though, set forth a vision for the country that was ahead of its time. The late historian Richard Hofstadter wrote that "his first annual message to Congress was one of the most wholly impolitic documents in the history of government,"[10] because it went so far beyond what the citizenry of the day expected, or what most of them assumed the Constitution would allow. Another historian noted that the message "nearly blew the dome off the Capitol building." It was a clear "assertion of the doctrine of affirmative government."[11]

Adams, though, despite warnings from his cabinet had decided to direct his message not to his closed-minded contemporaries, but to future generations. He called not only for an ambitious program of roads and canals, but asserted that the federal government had an even more important responsibility, that of advancing scientific knowledge. Even more important than roads and canals, he said, were geographical explorations, improved patent laws, a system for uniform weights and measures, and a national university. "Finally, Adams offered the proposal that drew him the greatest ridicule. He urged the establishment of a national astronomical observatory." He referred to such observatories as "light-houses of the sky."[12]

Impolitic his message may have been, but it also was prophetic. It was not long before canals connected the Ohio and Delaware Rivers to the Chesapeake Bay. National roads emerged that tied many portions of the country together. Military academies began to train bright youth for national service. "More significant, the prescience of Adams's overall project was underscored by his awareness that the future of America depended on the development of the nation's intellect."[13]

Adams continued to govern as though there were no parties. Vice President Calhoun, the wily Senator Martin Van Buren, and some of his cabinet were working against him to form a new party, the Democratic-Republicans, or simply Democrats.[14] With no party support from the president, the National Republicans, as the anti–Jacksonians were coming to be called, were far too weak to overcome Jackson's rising Democrats.

Added to the mix was the fear among some Southern leaders, such as John Randolph, that a government sufficiently powerful to build public works would be powerful enough someday to abolish the institution that they had come to cherish: slavery. Supplementing fears of Adams's domestic agenda was an extremely high tariff — the "tariff of abominations — that he signed reluctantly in 1828. "Not until the inauguration of Abraham Lincoln in 1861, would another president strike such terror into the heart of the South."[15] Tragically, "with the rejection of Adams's domestic agenda, Congress lost one of the few institutional mechanisms that could conceivably have abolished slavery peacefully in the United States, just as Parliament would abolish it in the British West Indies in 1833."[16]

The election of 1828 was one of the most irresponsible in American history. Bitter and unfair charges — including overt lies and sexual allegations —filled the air from both sides. So uncivil was the atmosphere, that Jackson, after his victory, failed to call upon the president. That president, John Quincy Adams, likewise left town quietly as his term ended — becoming, along with his father and Andrew Johnson — one of only three departing presidents who failed to attend the inaugurations of their successors.

John Patrick Diggins has noted that we frequently pay little attention to politicians who serve during good times. Stability and comfort were more in evidence during the Adams administration than severe crises that demand great leaders. He wrote poignantly that "under less bland circumstances, this great man might well have made a great president."[17] The Historian Robert Remini commented more pointedly, that "what happened to John Quincy

Adams is tragic. He could have been a great President, but like his father before him he was ruined by politics."[18]

So what are we to make of President John Quincy Adams? Has any other president ever served under such a combination of circumstances? Without a doubt, his presidential achievements fail to place him among the most outstanding chief executives, but is it possible to derive any insights by comparing him with others whose situations were entirely different? Does the 1962 Schlesinger poll that placed him thirteenth (just below Madison and above Hayes)[19] demand more or less respect than the Fabers' study, in which he tied with Bill Clinton for eighteenth?[20] That pairing, alone, should give pause to those who think that rankings of presidents can enhance understanding.

7

ANDREW JACKSON
March 4, 1829–March 4, 1837

Andrew Jackson — the tall, thin, quick-tempered, and imperious general known affectionately as "Old Hickory" — without a doubt changed the presidency. He lessened the elitism within Jeffersonian republicanism and brought it closer to the people. His movement fostered new methods of popular campaigning. He strengthened the Union. His infusion of energy into the presidency inspired the creation of an opposition Whig Party, the short-lived anti–Jacksonian effort that attempted paradoxically to combine a minimized executive authority with an activist and expanded national government. Sometimes for the better and sometimes for the worse, Andrew Jackson acted. There can be no doubt that he left his mark.

Except for George Washington, whose military heroism was only part of the reason he was popular among all Americans, Jackson was the first president who achieved the office because he was a popular war hero. He was the first president who came from outside the elite, the "national gentry" that had controlled politics since the beginning. He was the first whose emergence grew from the sentiment of the people.

This is not to say that his popular image as the "man of the people" presents a completely accurate picture. Despite John Quincy Adams's disdain for the old hero as an illiterate, Jackson was not a rough, poorly dressed, ignorant, frontiersman. He was a lawyer, well educated by the frontier standards of his day. However ill-versed in grammar and spelling, he was articulate and thoughtful. He lived an aristocratic life as a plantation owner and very wealthy slaveholder. Early in his legal career, he had become "one of the most important landowners in Tennessee."[1] To be sure, he was a military man, but as a general he certainly was no foot soldier. In no way was he a "common man," nor did he consider himself to be one. Nevertheless, symbolism is as important as reality to a presidency, and Jackson carried with him an abundance of symbolism.

As a consequence of that symbolism, the seventh president has had his legions of fervent admirers and equally fervent detractors. His skillful use of power and its effects upon the presidency ensure that those who rank presidents must give him due consideration. In Schlesinger's pioneer ranking, he was among the six presidents classified as "great."[2] Subsequent rankings usually place him as a "near great," as in Schlesinger's 1962 follow-up poll, which ranked him sixth,[3] (Lincoln, Washington, FDR, Wilson, and Jefferson were "great) and Schlesinger, Jr.'s, 1996 poll, which placed him fifth[4] (that poll designated only three — Lincoln, Washington, and FDR — as "great").

The complications in dealing with Jackson are apparent in his evaluation by the Fabers. They could not help but note his many contradictions. They praised his accomplishments in foreign relations, yet they were highly critical of him as well. They placed him in a tie for ninth place with the vastly different James Monroe.[5] One would be hard-pressed to find a clearer example of the oversimplification of rankings than this most unlikely of pairings.

Jackson, the man of extremes, has always presented a difficult case. It is especially so today. As Landy and Milkis so graphically put it, "of all the great presidents, Andrew Jackson grates hardest against contemporary sensibilities." He was, they said, a duelist, a slaveholder, and a slayer of Indians. "But," they noted, "greatness is not goodness. One need not forgive Jackson for his racism or his murderous temper to appreciate his extraordinary contribution to American politics. What Jefferson had begun, he completed. He democratized the presidency, but not in the manner of a demagogue." Jackson continued what Washington had begun, and preserved the Union that was facing a serious threat. He succeeded in bringing the people closer to the government "in a way that empowered it and reinforced its republican character."[6]

After his bitter loss to John Quincy Adams in the election of 1824 when no candidate had a majority in the electoral college, Jackson worked diligently for victory in 1828. The Tennessee legislature obligingly nominated him again as it had done in 1824. As an outsider, he was insulated from the unseemly squabbling that took place in Congress regarding nomination of presidential candidates. Some members thought that since there now were only Republicans with no opposition party, the nominating caucus should choose only one nominee. Others — and many potential candidates — shouted that this would be despotism. Jackson's mode of nomination not only added to his insulation from the turmoil but also killed the practice of choosing presidential candidates by congressional caucus.

He accepted Adams as president, and initially "took his defeat with dignity and grace." When Adams appointed Speaker of the House Henry Clay as secretary of state, however, "the Hero poured out his wrath at them, cursing them for their villainy." Clay, of course, had thrown his support to Adams rather than to Jackson when the election was thrown into the House. But Jackson's "public frenzy was carefully staged in order to create political capital, for the General's public outbursts were never impulsive or uncontrolled (and it did make extraordinarily effective propaganda); even so he sincerely believed that a monumental fraud had been perpetrated against the people and against himself."[7]

He also believed that elitist institutions were part of the trouble. "The electoral college was a prime target. He considered it unthinkable that such an institution should be empowered to contradict the voice of the people. Later, in his first message to Congress, he called for its elimination but on this issue he found no substantial support. Almost two centuries later, the electoral college exists unmolested, having remained unshaken as well as unstirred, even after its manifest failures in the election of 2000.

Jackson smarted from the "corrupt bargain" that he was convinced must have caused his defeat, and saw further corruption throughout society and government. By corruption, he meant manipulation of power to subvert republican equality — to perpetuate rule by a privileged elite, an "aristocracy" of financiers and politicians. The equality that concerned him, of course, was equality among white men. He had personally suffered during the panic of 1819, and blamed the troubles on banks, and "the credit system," that worked to benefit an elite at the expense of the people.

Despite his reputation for impetuosity, Jackson worked cautiously and professionally to move toward election. He "corresponded solemnly with inquiring committees, propounding moderate views on the tariff, internal improvements, and related issues of the day, and advocating an old-fashioned set of republican values with dignity and restraint."[8] New York's Senator Martin Van Buren worked shrewdly to weld Jackson's supporters into a new party, the Democratic Republicans. To distinguish themselves, the supporters of President Adams became the National Republicans.

The Founders generally had opposed parties, and preferred governing for the good of the republic, without regard to the demands of special interests. Experience, however, had suggested that expecting to maintain a republic without parties was unrealistic. Jefferson's comment regarding "a fire bell in the night" may have been the most graphic, but he was not the only one alarmed by the prospect of sectional discord.

That prospect arose when the Missouri question in 1819 introduced the subject of slavery's expansion into national politics. Van Buren, who had built a powerful party organization in New York, put forth a perceptive and powerful defense of parties as an alternative to sectional conflict. He designed his plan not to defend slavery, but to "substitute *party principle* for *personal preference* as one of the leading points" in a political contest. He argued for "political combinations between the inhabitants of the different states," and especially for one "between the planters of the South and the plain Republicans of the North."[9] Jackson also was well aware of the threat of sectionalism to Union, and throughout his presidency he worked to keep the question of slavery out of political discourse, and also to preserve party. As a reflection of his recognition of the importance of party, in 1829 Jackson added the postmaster general — in this case, William T. Barry — to the cabinet.[10] The party connection here is clear: the postmaster general had become a major political adviser because the position controlled such a huge number of patronage positions. That status continued for more than a century.

Some scholars have argued that party also served the republic well by restraining Jackson's impetuosity. Landy and Milkis remarked that one can only speculate what kind of president Jackson would have been if party loyalty had not served to restrain his more violent impulses.[11] There may be some truth in this, although one should note as mentioned above that Jackson's outbursts often reflected a deliberate political tactic. His actions in seeking the presidency were careful and controlled. There is evidence to indicate, for example, that he was aware of Calhoun's duplicity, yet he allied himself with the South Carolinian to oppose Adams and to campaign for president. Moreover, as president he tended to be more cautious in action than in rhetoric.

Jackson's victory was substantial in the presidential election of 1828. With 178 electoral votes to 83 for Adams, his total was more than twice that of his opponent. His popular vote of nearly 56 percent was the highest any presidential candidate received until Theodore Roosevelt in 1904. Turnout also was high, with some 56 percent of the potential electorate casting votes.[12]

Unfortunately, the 1828 election was one of the most vicious in American history. Both sides hurled reckless and outrageous charges at the other. Some of the worst — especially considering the sensitivities of the age — dealt with sexual improprieties. The Democratic Republicans accused Adams of having secured prostitutes for visiting dignitaries when he was minister to England. The National Republicans accused the Jacksons of adultery, and jeered that Jackson's wife had been a "loose woman" and worse.

Jackson as a young lawyer had boarded near Nashville in the home of the widow of Col. John Donelson and her family, which included her vivacious daughter Rachel and Rachel's jealous husband, Lewis Robards. Lewis and Rachel had been separated for a time because of his suspicions, but had reconciled. With Jackson living under the same roof, Robards's suspicions flared again. Robards ordered Jackson from the house. "Demonstrating caution and good sense, which he could summon when necessary, Jackson left the house shortly afterward" to live elsewhere.[13] Robards then stormed off to Kentucky, but missed Rachel so much that he persuaded her to join him. When she did, he renewed his abusive behavior.

She pleaded with her brothers to come rescue her, but instead it was Jackson — in an act that his most distinguished biographer said "surely was absolute folly or absolute calculation" — who arrived. Jackson took her to the home of her sister, but he had laid the groundwork for divorce. Hearing that Robards intended to come for her, Rachel fled to Natchez, accompanied — again not by her brothers — by Jackson. Soon, when Jackson heard that Robards had secured a divorce in Virginia, he returned to Natchez, where he and Rachel in 1791 were married. "Slightly more than two years later the Jacksons learned the awful truth, that not until September 27, 1793 did Robards receive a divorce. Undoubtedly, both had believed they were legally married. They repeated their vows on 17 January 1794.[14]

The Jacksons were close, and their marriage was happy. They had no children of their own, but raised as their own several children who had lost their parents. They undeniably had deep affection for one another, but their relationship had a practical side as well. Rachel was a talented manager, and took good care of his estates during his absences.

Despite their lengthy and comfortable companionship, Jackson remained sensitive to the plausible charge that he had stolen another man's wife, while Rachel became ever more pious and withdrawn from the public. After his election, but before he took office, Rachel died. The bereaved Jackson blamed the venomous campaign by his political enemies for her death. Jackson, an accomplished hater, was not one to forget and forgive.

The inauguration was a fearsome spectacle to those who valued decorum and who were accustomed to the rather tame affairs of the past. Thousands of people — many of whom traveled for hundreds of miles — thronged to Washington to see the new president. They mobbed the president's house and provided fodder for later historians by standing on tables and chairs, and by ruining satin cushions with their muddy boots. Daniel Webster marveled at the crowd, and remarked that they seemed to think the republic had been rescued from some fearful danger. "Indeed they did," wrote Jackson's biographer Robert Remini, who quoted Webster, "from the tripleheaded danger of aristocracy, privilege, and corruption."[15]

Jackson's new cabinet, except for Secretary of State Van Buren, was weak. At least this avoided "the situation that had plagued Monroe, whose ambitious cabinet officers elbowed each other to become the next president."[16] It did not help the new president to get his administration underway. Nor did it help when a divisive issue arose that may sound petty today, but was very serious at the time. That issue was the infamous Peggy Eaton affair.

Margaret (Peggy) O'Neale was the vivacious daughter of a Washington innkeeper. She had married a U.S. Navy purser, John Timberlake, who was at sea for extended periods. John Eaton, a political ally of Jackson's from Tennessee, boarded at O'Neale's, and the rumor spread that he and Peggy were romantically involved.

When word came that Timberlake had died, possibly as a suicide, Eaton decided to marry Peggy, but sought Jackson's advice. Jackson knew all those involved, and was fond of Peggy. "Marry her by all means," he replied. Eaton then admitted that Peggy's reputation in Washington "had not escaped reproach. 'Well,' Jackson fired back, 'your marrying her will disprove these charges, and restore Peg's good name.' And so, on January 1, 1829, two months prior to the inauguration, the restoration took place. But the wedding did not disprove the charges; in fact, in the minds of some, it proved them."[17]

It was not until Jackson appointed Eaton secretary of war that the real trouble began — as Van Buren called it, the "Eaton malaria." Vice President Calhoun's wife, Floride, initially had been friendly to the new Mrs. Eaton, but refused to associate with her after Major Eaton joined the cabinet. Even Emily Donelson, the wife of Jackson's secretary and nephew, refused to meet the Eatons socially. Remini argued that both Calhoun and Donelson were jealous of Eaton's influence with Jackson, and that their wives were simply serving their husbands' ambitions, seeking Eaton's disgrace "through the vulnerable and pathetic little figure of his wife."[18] Other cabinet wives and prominent Washington hostesses followed this unfortunate example.

Jackson likely saw some similarities to the poisonous charges that had been directed against him and his beloved Rachel. He looked into the situation carefully, and concluded that Peggy was blameless. He took the position that if she had not been guilty of misconduct, then clearly she should not be ostracized. If she and Eaton had acted improperly, however, they now had done the right thing. He roared his displeasure, resigned from his church because the minister had made reckless allegations regarding Peggy, and ordered Emily Donelson back home to Tennessee. Her husband accompanied her, but returned after six months.[19]

Through it all, Secretary of State Martin Van Buren, long a widower, stood by Jackson, and was pointedly friendly toward the Eatons, inviting them to parties and accepting them as social equals. He became Jackson's most trusted adviser and chosen successor. Calhoun's influence, already weak, vanished. Jackson's "moral understanding of the situation was far subtler and deeper than that of [the Eatons'] critics. The 'high minded independence and virtue' that Calhoun ascribed to 'the ladies of Washington' for snubbing Peggy Eaton was neither independent nor virtuous."[20]

It is perhaps difficult for modern Americans to recognize how serious this issue was, and the extent to which Jackson based his response to it on deeply felt principle. "During the first two years of his presidency, close to half of Jackson's letters were devoted either to the affair itself or to the growing hostility toward Calhoun that it fueled."[21] It was apparent that Jackson could not work with his cabinet — in fact, he had been dealing instead with a group of informal advisers, his "kitchen cabinet." Van Buren offered to resign to give Jackson an excuse to ask for the resignations of the others. When he and Eaton did so, Jackson had a plausible reason to seek the additional resignations. They all came in together and balanced various sections and interests, he argued. Since two members were gone, the others must go also to permit him to rebuild and keep the balance. Jackson appointed Van Buren minister to Great Britain, and rebuilt his cabinet to be free of Calhoun's influence. Ironically, the Senate ultimately failed to confirm Van Buren's appointment. The vote was tied, and Vice President Calhoun relished the opportunity to cast the tie-breaking vote, which would — he thought — kill Van Buren politically. In this, as in so many things, Calhoun's judgment was badly flawed; Van Buren was hardly dead. He came back stronger than ever.

Partly as a result of the Eaton matter, Jackson came quickly to recognize the benefit of party, and to value Van Buren's contributions to a party structure. Loyalty, he concluded, was more likely to come through party than through disinterested statesmanship. No doubt this contributed to his removal of public officials, and the charges that he implemented the spoils system. In his first annual message to Congress, he had called for "rotation in office" as fundamental to republican principles. Terms that were too lengthy led to corruption. His critics exaggerated what he had done. He was debauching the government, they said, but he responded with figures demonstrating that he had removed fewer than 10 percent of the officials, and there never has been a serious challenge to his figures.[22] It did not help that an ally, William L. Marcy, made his famous statement, "to the victor belong the spoils of the enemy," but current thought tends to discount the notion of a Jackson spoils system.[23]

Reflecting his new interest in the party, Jackson encouraged the use of the nominating convention when he decided to run for re-election in 1832. The Democrats were not the first party to use a convention, but they were the first major party to do so, and the first to make it a lasting tradition. The convention consisted of delegates representing the party from all sections of the country. It was much more democratic than earlier nominating methods, and was completely consistent with Jackson's professed republican principles.

Jackson without question would be its presidential nominee, but he wanted to be certain that Van Buren would be nominated as the party's candidate for vice president. He not only made his preference known, but encouraged the convention to adopt the "two-thirds rule," requiring two-thirds to select either nominee. None of Van Buren's rivals could hope to achieve two-thirds, leaving him as the convention's choice. The rule survived until 1936, when candidate Franklin D. Roosevelt was sufficiently strong to persuade the convention to eliminate it.

Jackson assumed office with a commitment to Jeffersonian principles, but he was less an ideologue, more a pragmatist, and considerably more prudent in his actions than his reckless image would suggest. He had developed keen political skills, and frequently sought compromise. He recognized the importance of internal improvements, but his Jeffersonian heritage caused him to hesitate in throwing the support of the federal government behind them. The National Republicans, led by Clay, favored a comprehensive national program, which he could not accept. When Congress passed the Maysville Road bill in May 1830, Jackson vetoed it, causing a furor. He argued that it would be inappropriate to support a road that was solely in one state. The fact that it was in Clay's home state of Kentucky did not work in its favor.

Jackson vetoed other projects as well, but some he approved. He rejected some major programs, but his actions did not signify complete opposition to the idea of federal support for improvements.[24] They did, though, signify an attack upon his political enemies — those who, in Van Buren's terms, were the "Internal Improvement party." Jackson reacted much more favorably to initiatives from Democrats. The first time his party won both houses of Congress, in fact, he said explicitly that he was "not hostile to internal improvements," and that he wished "to see them extended to every part of the country."[25]

His vetoes were more frequent than those from any of his predecessors, and they were more clearly related to policy. He was the first president to use the veto as a "carefully calculated political move."[26] His opponents of course condemned his use of the veto power — there were even calls for a constitutional amendment to restrict or eliminate it — but Jackson had energized a presidential authority that clearly was constitutional, and left the presidency stronger as a result. Despite his development of the power of the veto, by modern standards Jackson used it very sparingly. It is remarkable today, in view of the furor that they caused, that he cast only twelve vetoes.

Surely the most disastrous of Jackson's policies was Indian removal. He seemed genuinely to believe, however, that removal was the most humane approach possible, and that it would be better for Indians as well as for whites. He was well aware that Americans' hunger for expansion and profit was destroying Indian culture and causing Native Americans to lose their land. It seems apparent, despite some interpretations, that Jackson did not pursue removal because of a hatred of Indians. Not only had he had Indian allies in battle, but he had adopted an orphaned Indian boy.

When Georgia sought to expel its Cherokees — a civilized tribe that had adopted settled ways, had its own constitution, and had produced a written language — the tribe appealed to the Supreme Court. The case was *Worcester* v. *Georgia*. Chief Justice Marshall handed down the Court's decision supporting the Cherokees. Folklore has it (and countless writers have repeated) that Jackson dismissed the judgment, saying "John Marshall has made his decision — now let him enforce it." Remini has pointed out that this was highly unlikely. Jackson did not like Marshall, and criticized many of the Court's decisions. Nevertheless, "he would never advocate or encourage annulling the federal authority, even that portion of it held by the judicial branch." The decision remained unenforced "because, as the realistic President knew full well, the people in the West and the South would not tolerate its enforcement. They wanted the Indians removed — right now. Therefore, in 1830, Congress passed the Indian Removal Act," exchanging Indian-held lands east of the Mississippi for lands in the trans-Mississippi West.[27]

The fact that Jackson did not seek to decimate tribal peoples did not lessen the horror that resulted. The removal policies that began under his administration and continued after he left office produced one of history's great tragedies. In common with most Americans, Jackson did consider Indians to be inferior, and did believe that they could not live together with whites in peace — or with justice. He deserves to share the blame for his policies, but he should not bear it alone. Sharing its prejudices, he was acting on behalf of a nation which, along with its president, was responsible for a holocaust that caused mass death and destruction of cultures. To be fair to that generation, one should note that all along there was protest against, and strong opposition to, the harsh Indian policies. Majority sentiment, though, overwhelmed that opposition.

Probably the most often cited of Jackson's actions as president was his war against the Bank of the United States. There is no doubt that the Bank's director, Nicholas Biddle, used bank resources to affect public policy and to try to undercut Jackson. This intensified the president's long-standing prejudice against banks. There is also no doubt that the bank, which was a private institution with huge deposits from the U.S. government, caused wealthy private interests to profit from public funds. It was an obvious example of the kind of "aristocratic" institutions that Jackson had campaigned against. On the other hand, there is little doubt that the BUS helped restrain reckless banking practices, and did perform valuable functions for the economy. Most analysts believe that the lengthy depression that began as Jackson's term in office ended resulted at least in part from his shattering of the Bank's power.

Although the Bank's charter was not to expire until 1836, Congress passed an act in 1832 renewing its charter. Henry Clay, who was running against Jackson, led the re-charter movement. Jackson vetoed the renewal with a powerful message damning the Bank as unconstitutional, and as undermining equality. Many of the more settled members of the community were outraged, but the people loved it. Jackson then ordered Secretary of the Treasury William Duane to remove government deposits. Under the law, the decision was the secretary's. Duane refused, and Jackson fired him. He moved Attorney General Roger Taney to the Treasury post, and Taney withdrew the deposits, placing them in selected state banks which Jackson's opponents quickly dubbed "pet banks."

Meanwhile, South Carolina's leaders had become increasingly radical. Vice President Calhoun — anonymously — had written an inflammatory "South Carolina Exposition and Protest" in 1828 in response to the tariff that President Adams had signed into law that year. In 1832, President Jackson had signed into law a reduction in that tariff, but it failed to suit the South Carolinians. The state was the most reactionary in the Union. In 1832, it was the only state that had not begun choosing its presidential electors by popular vote. The legislature selected them, and also selected the governor. Accordingly, there were no statewide elections in South Carolina. "Out of this setting emerged a group of South Carolinians who considered themselves culturally special. They believed themselves more aristocratic ... and in general superior to planters and merchants in other parts of the South." They also were more sensitive than most other southerners.[28] Their national spokesman was John C. Calhoun, who busied himself attempting to spread South Carolina's doctrines to the rest of the South, holding his state up as a model.

Calhoun's "Exposition" argued that the Constitution was a compact among the states. A state could declare a national law to be unenforceable within its borders. Since conventions within each state ratified the Constitution, a similar convention could nullify acts of Congress within a state. A vocal group began advocating nullification. In 1830, at a dinner honoring the late Thomas Jefferson, Jackson stated his position forcefully and challenged the nullifiers directly. Looking straight at Vice President Calhoun, he proposed the after-dinner toast, ending with "Our Federal Union, It Must Be Preserved." Calhoun's response began: "The Union — next to our liberties most dear" but then rambled on and lost its effect.

Rejecting the 1832 tariff revision as inadequate, South Carolina's leaders called a convention that promptly nullified it. Jackson moved quickly to alert military forces, but he did not bluster in public, although there was little doubt that he would invade the state if required. On the softer side, he arranged to have duties collected on ships outside the harbor, and he worked to compromise on the tariff. On the firm side, in December he issued his Nullification Proclamation, asserting that it was his duty to support the supremacy of the nation. The Constitution, he pointed out, formed a government, not a league. The people in conventions, not states, ratified the Constitution, and the House of Representatives and the presidency were the people's — not the states' — institutions. It would be absurd to permit a political subdivision to nullify a general law. Union, he argued, existed before states had come into being. Lincoln later adopted the idea of a perpetual union in his arguments against secession.[29]

A wave of approval came to the president from around the country. Much support came from within the South as well. When Jackson then asked Congress to pass legislation authorizing him to take all necessary measures to enforce the tariff laws, Congress complied with support from all sections and all parties, and passed the Force Bill. Faced both with the prospect of force and the achievement of some of their goals, the South Carolinians backed down, elected a more moderate governor, and sent Calhoun to the Senate to represent their interests.

That meant that Calhoun resigned the vice presidency. He was the only vice president ever to do so until Spiro Agnew, Nixon's vice president, resigned in disgrace considerably more than a century later. Any influence that Calhoun may have wielded as vice president had, in any case, long since vanished. Moreover, his term would have ended anyway the following March, and Martin Van Buren — whom he had not killed, after all — had already been elected to succeed him as vice president.

In foreign policy, Jackson's presidency generally was quite successful. For the first time since independence, trade resumed with the British West Indies. A number of trade agreements developed around the world, and the United States was looking outward to the international community. One of the more impressive was with Russia, where Jackson had sent future president James Buchanan as minister (after being required to correct his initial, potentially disastrous, appointment of the brilliant but unstable John Randolph of Roanoke). Most impressive, the administration's firm and persistent diplomacy resulted in payment of claims against the French that dated to the Napoleonic wars.

Jackson's forceful presidency led his opponents to coalesce into a new political party. The Whigs took their name from British opponents of arbitrary actions by the monarch. To the Whigs, Jackson's attack on the Bank, his casting of more vetoes than all his predecessors, and his assertion that the president represented the people as fully as Congress did led them to think of him as "King Andrew the First." Led by Henry Clay, the Senate censured him in 1834. Smarting from the insult, Jackson defended himself and the Senate expunged the censure from the record in 1837.

During his presidency the Union grew by two. Arkansas became a state in 1836. Michigan followed closely, achieving statehood in 1837.

For better or worse, any attempt to categorize Andrew Jackson as president would have to recognize his greatness. He energized the executive branch and made it more effective than it had been since the days of Washington and Jefferson. "He was as much a conservative revolutionary as were his two great predecessors. He presided over a democratic revolution in political and governmental practice, but one that he kept within constitutional bounds."[30] He retained the Jeffersonian commitment to limited government, but brought that government closer to the people. He strongly protected and preserved the Union, and despite respecting the position of the states moved away from a destructive emphasis on states' rights. He solidified party development. He attacked economic privilege, albeit likely causing or at least adding to economic turmoil. His record on human rights is the most troublesome part of his presidency, but he moved the country in the direction of a national cohesion—a cohesion that would be required before it could deal in any way with those rights.

Arthur Schlesinger, Jr., pointed out that presidential greatness generally comes only in times of crisis. "Still," he said, "two of the immortals, it should be noted, made their mark without benefit of first-order crisis. Jackson and Theodore Roosevelt forced the nation through sheer power of personality to recognize incipient problems."[31] One need not equate Jackson with Roosevelt to recognize that their forceful personalities and manifest abilities did, indeed, enable them to "make their marks" on their own initiative, rather than being forced to react.

The challenges that Jackson faced were unlike those of any other president. The conditions existing when he met those challenges existed only at that time. It is one thing to chart his accomplishments and his failures—even perhaps to label him, "great," or "near great." It is another entirely to attempt a ranking. Andrew Jackson, like so many of those who have held the presidency—like each of them, in fact—was unique.

MARTIN VAN BUREN
March 4, 1837–March 4, 1841

In common with some of his predecessors, Van Buren's accomplishments during his presidency were not the major achievements of his career. He should be heralded for his role prior to his presidency in laying the groundwork for America's system of political parties. Moreover, it was Van Buren who developed a theoretical justification for parties, countering the antiparty bias that motivated the Founders and much of the official thought of the early republic.[1]

In his view, parties could provide national political competition that could reduce the likelihood of sectional strife.[2] Parties obviously did not succeed completely — because of the poisonous effect of slavery, a party system could not prevent the Civil War. Nevertheless, it assisted in bringing cohesion back to national politics following slavery's elimination, and continues to maintain that cohesion. This, of course, has little to do with the Van Buren presidency.

Martin Van Buren stepped into the presidential office with a handicap similar to that which had burdened John Adams. He followed a charismatic leader whose personal flair he could not hope to match. Moreover, the Red Fox had to contend with the anti–Jacksonian factions that had coalesced into a well-organized opposition, the Whig Party. The new party used its power in every way possible to undercut him, making it difficult for him to exercise the political skills that had caused him to be called the "Little Magician."

As though this were not enough, just after he began his presidency, the Panic of 1837 hit. The Whigs charged that Jackson's policies, especially his attack on the Bank of the United States, had been responsible. As Jackson's vice president, Van Buren bore the brunt of the attacks. He and the Democrats retorted that the panic instead was a local reflection of worldwide economic troubles.

Whichever was the case — and very likely there was some truth to both assertions — economic panic set the tone for Van Buren's entire term. He could do little about the depressed conditions for two reasons. Not only was he in a weak position in any case, but as a good Jacksonian he adhered to the traditional republican ideology, according to which it was unacceptable for the central government to intervene directly in the economy. He was unable to prevent the diminution of the executive, as Congress reasserted its prerogatives in response to the energy that Jackson had infused into the presidency.

The Van Buren administration nevertheless did have some accomplishments. The 1962 Schlesinger poll placed him squarely in the middle — seventeenth of thirty-one rated — as an average president.[3] The Fabers evaluate him somewhat more favorably, and place him thirteenth of thirty-nine,[4] whereas Genovese is more critical, rating him twenty-fourth of thirty-nine and calling him "below average."[5] There is inconsistency here, but nothing dramatic. Yet what does it mean to place him just above Reagan and below Taft, as Genovese does, or just below Adams and above Hayes, as the Fabers would have it? Genovese certainly is correct in saying that Van Buren demonstrated weakness in political skills, the very qualities in which he previously had excelled,[6] but did any other president face the same combination of circumstances that rendered Van Buren's political abilities impotent? It would seem more meaningful to evaluate him on his own merits, rather than to compare him to others whose challenges were vastly different.

Van Buren's administration faced several crises in addition to the persistent economic panic. In his first year in office he had to deal with the "Caroline Affair." A citizen of Ontario, William Mackenzie, had led a rebellion against the British government in Canada. The Canadian rebels retreated to Navy Island, in the Niagara River, after having failed in an attempt to seize Toronto. Anti-British Americans set out on the *Caroline* to deliver supplies to the rebels, but while it was in American waters Canadian militia seized the ship, burned it, and sent the blazing vessel over Niagara Falls. One American died in the skirmish.

Van Buren, of course, protested vigorously. He dispatched troops to the region but rejected demands that he call for war with Britain. Instead, he issued a proclamation of neutrality in the Canadian civil strife.

There were other reflections of American hostility to the British in Canada. Residents of Maine had been demanding that America seize disputed territory between their state and New Brunswick, which both countries claimed. The area involved several thousand miles along the Aroostook

River. In 1839, a Mainer, Rufus McIntire who had a commission from his state government, journeyed into the region and attempted to expel Canadians. Canadian officials seized him. In response, militias from Maine and New Brunswick faced one another. State and provincial authorities each demanded military backing from their countries. Van Buren did send General Winfield Scott to the area, but only as a negotiator. Scott succeeded. The "Aroostook War" ended with no casualties, and Van Buren again had secured peace.

American-Canadian tensions nevertheless remained. In 1840, New York authorities arrested Alexander McLeod, a Canadian who was in the state, for murder in connection with the death of the American in the *Caroline* Affair. Tension subsided somewhat when the trial court found McLeod not guilty.

In 1838, Van Buren had succeeded in countering the sentiment against a standing army enough to persuade Congress to increase its size from some eight thousand men to around twelve thousand. Other changes involved streamlining organization, equipment, and procedures and improving teaching at the U.S. Military Academy at West Point. Even so — and this helped reinforce his commitment to peace — the disastrous potential that the Aroostook War had threatened led him to recognize that the United States was still inadequately prepared for military action.

He endorsed a plan that his secretary of war, Joel R. Poinsett, proposed to reform the archaic militia system that had plagued the country since its beginning. Poinsett, who is best remembered (at least indirectly) for his botanical work — especially at Christmastime — saw his name immortalized in the plant that he introduced into the United States, the poinsettia. His plan would perhaps have immortalized Poinsett in other ways as well, had he and Van Buren been able to secure congressional approval.

Half of the army was in Florida, and much of the rest was in the West. Any attempt to have mobilized the army in New England for the Aroostook War, Poinsett warned Van Buren, would have been "a very silly exposure of our weakness."[7] Recognizing the complete incompetence of the militias in both discipline and military skills, his proposal would have created an "active" force of one hundred thousand troops with a reserve force of equal size. The active force would receive annual training to develop military skills. After four years of service, members would go into the reserve force where they would remain on call for another four years. Thus, a potential of two hundred thousand, men could be rapidly mobilized as needed to supplement the twelve thousand-man regular army.

Immediately, the plan encountered vigorous opposition. The republican ideology had historically rejected any contention that national defense required the military to be professional. Added to the republican bias was "the force of local interests and of politics identified with the old militia organization. Most of all, the ingenuity of Whig foes, particularly in the South," succeeded in arguing that the plan reflected executive despotism. It would "break down the barriers of States' rights."[8] This, of course, could affect the predominant concern of Southern politicians, the expansion and perpetuation of slavery.

Richmond newspaper editor, Thomas Ritchie, told Van Buren in 1840 that opposition to Poinsett's plan was the only reason Whigs had won spring elections in Virginia. Fears of the proposal, he warned the president, would undercut his chances for re-election later that year. So potent was the issue, that Van Buren backed away from his own administration's plan.

He wrote a long statement claiming that his earlier endorsement was premature. When his administration had submitted the proposal in March of 1840, he explained, he had not had time to study the issue sufficiently to recognize how dubious was its constitutionality. With the tortuous logic that frequently had infused republican positions in attempting to reconcile their strict construction views with national needs, he said that Congress could "organize, arm, and discipline" the militia. The Poinsett proposal thus far was acceptable. On the other hand, he argued, the Constitution reserved to the states the power of "training" the militia. The entire plan was therefore unacceptable. As his biographer, Major L. Wilson, has noted, "clearly, the 'politician' in Van Buren here overrode statesmanlike considerations."[9]

Poinsett did not mention the proposal again, even in his extensive reports to the president after the 1840 elections. He listed his achievements as the removal of more Indians than had been accomplished under any previous war secretary, improvements of the army along with reductions in cost, and maintenance of peace along the frontiers, including the Canadian border. Wilson concluded that Poinsett's reports were good summaries of Van Buren's administration. Jackson's policies had laid out the essential goals, while the economic troubles had limited the way in which Van Buren could pursue them.[10]

The president was well aware of the huge number of bank failures, the worsening economic conditions, and even of food riots. The credit system was collapsing. Consistent with his Jacksonian values, he could not propose a new bank. Instead, he called for an "Independent Treasury" that would separate government deposits from private banking. The government would operate subtreasuries around the country, where it would deposit its funds. The subtreasuries could provide loans to help ease the shortage of credit. This would avoid both a national bank, and the continuation of Jackson's "pet banks."

In the ensuing struggle in Congress, Van Buren attempted to curry favor with Calhoun. The South Carolinian — who had broken with Jackson and joined the Whigs — abandoned the Whigs and rejoined the Democrats. At first he supported the independent treasury but ultimately changed sides once more and voted against it. The bill went down to defeat in the House after the Senate had passed it, and emerged in several incarnations during the next few years. Congress finally approved it in the last year of Van Buren's term, in July 1840.[11] The Whigs repealed the act a year later, after he had left office.

An acute student of Van Buren, historian Donald Cole, asked — and answered — an intriguing question. Why was it that such an able politician as Van Buren spent three years of his presidency on the independent treasury? His answer was that Van Buren, upon becoming president, sought to unite the party by choosing to deal with the old Jacksonian banking issues, rather than the new divisive issues of slavery and expansionism. When the sudden economic panic hit, "it was only natural that Van Buren should respond by shaping a compromise banking policy designed to hold the party together." Then, the issue trapped him. He thought he had to achieve success "in order to prove his administration a success." His once keen political sense had failed him. In vain, "he hoped that the bill would demonstrate that he, like Andrew Jackson, was fighting for the common people."[12]

In a sense, however, Van Buren succeeded after all. Although the Whigs soon repealed the measure, they were unable to restore a national bank. The Polk administration restored Van Buren's system in 1846. As a scholar favorable to Van Buren put it, "the Independent Treasury remained in operation until the Federal Reserve System was created in 1913. Thus, Van Buren's central domestic measure, which had been put forth in order to save the Jacksonian heritage, survived his defeat for reelection."[13]

By far the thorniest question facing Van Buren or any other president from his administration until the Civil War was the expansion of slavery. Shortly before he took office, Texas won its independence from Mexico. As vice president, Van Buren had encouraged Jackson, who normally was eager for expansion, to take a cautious position. Jackson therefore had sent a message to Congress saying that since recognition of the Texas Republic might lead to war with Mexico, he would defer to congressional guidance on the matter. As president, Van Buren continued to pursue a course of moderation.

There were enormous pressures from those favoring annexation, as well as some provocative actions on the part of the Mexicans. Van Buren nevertheless resisted the pressures, and in his message to Congress in December of 1837, echoed Jackson's request for congressional guidance. Representative John Quincy Adams roared that it was Jacksonianism with "a new coat of varnish." Anti-slavery interests feared that it was a covert ploy for annexation, while Southerners demanded it. Van Buren kept attempting to steer a neutral course between the diametrically opposed interests.[14]

That same month, 115 women from New Jersey submitted to the Senate a petition calling for elimination of slavery in the District of Columbia. The Senate tabled the petition, and Calhoun "offered a series of six resolutions designed to force the Senate to commit itself in defense of slavery."[15] The Senate passed five of the six; the votes were almost three to one, including most Democrats. The votes clearly reflected the administration's pro-slavery position. Even when Ohio Democratic senator William Allen introduced a measure to ensure that "nothing in Calhoun's resolutions should be interpreted as an abridgement of speech, the administration senators voted for slavery and against freedom," laying the resolution on the table.[16]

His policies, however increasingly pro–Southern, failed to placate the South. Van Buren lost the election in 1840 to the Whig, William Henry Harrison, who claimed to be a war hero. Demonstrating the disarray of the Democrats, Van Buren did not have a running mate. Vice President Richard M. Johnson had — and still has — a unique distinction. The electoral college had chosen Van Buren as president in 1836, but defecting electors who refused to vote for Johnson as Van Buren's running mate that year caused him to lack an electoral-college majority. This caused the election to be thrown into the Senate (in such circumstances, according to the Constitution, the House would choose a president, but it is the Senate that would choose a vice president). He is the only vice president in history to have been selected by the Senate rather than by the electoral college. Despite the failure of the electoral college to choose presidents in 1800 and 1824, Aaron Burr had sufficient electoral votes in 1800 and John C. Calhoun in 1824, to be the winners.

In 1840, there was fierce Southern opposition to Johnson. He had a black common-law wife with whom he raised a family. Having a liaison with a black woman may have been one thing, but living openly with her greatly offending Southern sensibilities. Johnson remained popular in the West, however, and was a legitimate war hero who might have offset some of the Harrison propaganda. Jackson urged Van Buren to support a young James K. Polk for the nomination, but Van Buren refused to take a position. The Democratic convention simply refused to select a vice presidential nominee when it nominated Van Buren for a second term as president.[17]

So what does one make of President Martin Van Buren? Wilson's favorable assessment is that he consistently "remained a champion of the Union as the highest good," and that he "contributed more perhaps than another other public figure in his age to the political formula that secured the Union throughout the decade of the 1850s. By grafting new party organization onto the older Jeffersonian ideology, he helped to provide a means for holding together a nation of such diverse elements."[18] This is correct, as far as it goes, but it is inadequate to evaluate the Van Buren presidency.

More critically, Cole has written that Van Buren "was neither a successful nor a great President." He failed to grow in office, and "if anything showed signs of losing some of his native strength and ability."[19] This, too, is correct. The fact that such disparate assessments can both be accurate is a demonstration of how oversimplified presidential rankings — rankings that must give each president a precise placement on a scale in relation to others whose challenges were completely different — must inevitably be.

Van Buren's shortcomings are evident. His successes, although undeniable, are less so. Nevertheless, they were genuine.

9

WILLIAM HENRY HARRISON
March 4, 1841–April 4, 1841

General William Henry Harrison, the triumphant Whig victor over Martin Van Buren, was by far the oldest president ever inaugurated until Ronald Reagan, almost a century and a half later. He also was the first president to die in office. Hs death took place just a few hours less than one month after his inauguration, making his quite the shortest presidential term in American history.

Because of the brevity of his term, the more thoughtful rankings of course leave Harrison out. None of the studies by either Schlesinger includes him, nor does that of the Fabers, nor do studies resulting from most leading presidential scholars. Not all producers of rankings, though, have the good sense to exclude the unfortunate Harrison.

One wonders what he could have done, or not done, in one month to warrant comparison with any other president. Despite the obvious lack of time to develop a record, Harrison sometimes finds his way into listings. In the year 2000, for example, a C-SPAN study of "90 presidential experts rating ten qualities of presidential leadership" placed Harrison fifth from the bottom, ahead of Harding, Pierce, Andrew Johnson, and Buchanan in that order.[1] Other rankings, such as the Reuters 2000 poll[2] and the oft-cited Ridings and McIver study,[3] include Harrison as well. One can only wonder, also, which "experts" might have thought it warranted to include a one-month presidency in their rankings.

It was not Harrison's first presidential race; he had run four years previously. In 1836, he had been one of three Whig candidates for the presidency. The party that year — despairing of defeating Jackson's choice, the Democrat Van Buren, in an open vote — nominated three candidates, each of whom ran in a different region. Their hope was to produce such a diversity of votes that the electoral college would fail to give any candidate a majority, making it necessary for the House to decide. They failed, and Van Buren won a close race.

Harrison had been a general, heralded as a war hero. In 1811, by winning the battle of Tippecanoe he ended Indian resistance in the Indiana Territory. By most accounts he fought bravely and well. In the War of 1812 there had been sufficient questions about his leadership to warrant a congressional investigation, but he received complete exoneration. He had also been secretary of the Northwest Territory, territorial delegate to the U.S. House of Representatives, governor of the Indiana Territory, member of the Ohio Senate, member of both the U.S. House and the Senate, and U.S. minister to Colombia. His background was therefore impressive, but when he received the Whig nomination in 1836, he held a relatively trivial position as clerk of the Cincinnati Court of Common Pleas.[4]

The 1840 election paired Harrison as the Whig candidate with John Tyler, running with him for the vice presidency. Tyler was a firm advocate of states' rights from Virginia. He was principled and forthright, but rigid, stubborn, narrow-minded, and impolitic. The Whigs had chosen him as a gamble, hoping for support from the South. It was a dangerous way to balance the ticket, and came later to haunt them.

The campaign was one in which there were few if any issues presented or discussed. The Whigs did not even adopt a party platform. They portrayed Harrison, despite his privileged background in Virginia, as having been born in a log cabin. Moreover, they said, he drank the common man's drink: hard cider. All the while they jeered at the Democratic candidate, Martin Van Buren, as an effete dandy.

The "log cabin and hard cider" campaign saw Harrison fighting vigorously for office, the first presidential candidate to do so openly. The Whigs won on the slogan, "Tippecanoe and Tyler Too!" Over 80 percent of the eligible electorate cast ballots. Although Harrison won handily in the electoral college, his popular vote margin, although comfortable, was not overwhelming; he received 52.9 percent.[5]

Harrison arrived early in Washington, to begin to deal with the massive number of requests for appointments. He attended parties and balls, and visited with leading Democrats as well as Whigs. He graciously declined Van Buren's equally gracious offer to depart early from the executive mansion for the new president's convenience.

Harrison had announced that he would serve only one term, and that there would be no wholesale turnover of federal employees. He clearly favored a nonpartisan civil service, rather than the spoils system, for federal appointment. He also agreed for the most part with the Whig position against the use of the veto. He said that he would use it only in extraordinary circumstances, but he refused to renounce it entirely. He agreed, also, with the Whig position that Congress should be the dominant force, and that the president should present matters to the cabinet. The cabinet would decide matters by vote, with the president's single vote counting no more than any other.

Harrison appointed a strong cabinet, with Daniel Webster as secretary of state. Clay's Whig rival, Henry Clay, had turned down the position hoping to direct matters from Congress. "But Harrison increasingly was sensitive to any hint of his being someone's dupe." In one argument with Clay, he dismissed the Kentuckian with a curt, "Mr. Clay, you forget that *I* am the president."[6] At another time he sent Clay into a rage, telling him that he was too impetuous on matters of appointment.[7]

Despite the Whig ideology that Harrison accepted, there is nothing in the Constitution that requires cabinet approval for a presidential decision. In fact, the Constitution does not even use the word "cabinet." Even in his short time in office, Harrison became "restive" under the arrangement that provided him with only a vote in dealing with his cabinet. Secretary of State Webster in one meeting informed him that the cabinet had selected James Wilson of New Hampshire to be governor of the Iowa Territory. Harrison stood and blasted his cabinet. He said, "William Henry Harrison, President of the United States, tells you, gentlemen, that by _____, John Chambers shall be Governor of Iowa."[8]

Thus, in spite of Whig ideology, there were some indications that Harrison might have become an effective chief executive had he lived. As the historian Norman Lois Peterson put it, "even in the short month of Harrison's administration, there were decided indications that all was not well with the Whig concept of a powerless president."[9] But it was not to be. Harrison attended a round of balls on the cold night of his inauguration, and earlier he had delivered an inaugural address that lasted more than an hour and a half. He delivered it outside, with no hat, gloves, or overcoat to ward off the early March wind. Some days later, he became ill. His death occurred on 4 April 1841.

Representative and former President John Quincy Adams had never been among Harrison's admirers, although as president Adams had appointed him to be minister to Colombia. Yet he expressed profound sympathy to Anna Harrison, the late president's widow and his family. He remarked that Harrison had been "amiable and benevolent."[10] These, in fact, may be the qualities most prominent in the Harrison presidency — hardly ones that could provide a basis for evaluation, let alone ranking.

10

JOHN TYLER
April 4, 1841–March 4, 1845

John Tyler had been William Henry Harrison's vice president for one month when the president died. It was the first time a president had died in office, and Tyler became the first vice president to fill a presidential vacancy. It had not been a foregone conclusion that the vice president would do so in such a situation.

Upon receiving a message from the cabinet that President Harrison was dead, Tyler rushed to Washington. The cabinet message had addressed him as vice president, and there were reports that its discussions had led to the conclusion that Tyler should bear the title: "Vice President Acting as President." The young Tyler — at fifty-one he was the youngest person until that time to be president — would have none of it. He insisted on being called "President," and he refused to open mail addressed to him as "Vice President."[1]

He met with the cabinet on 6 April. When he took the oath that day in the cabinet's presence he swore faithfully to execute the office of President of the United States. Secretary of State Daniel Webster agreed that this was the correct course, and the other members concurred. Shortly thereafter, each house of Congress recognized Tyler as president.[2]

There were those, including Representative and former President John Quincy Adams, who disagreed. To them, Tyler became "his Accidency." Scholars throughout the years similarly have disagreed as to the meaning of the Constitution's ambiguous wording on succession. Article II, section I provides that in case of the "Removal of the President from Office, or of his Death, Resignation, or Inability to discharge the Powers and Duties of the said Office, the Same shall devolve upon the Vice President...." The argument regards whether the Constitution meant that only the powers and duties of the office would "devolve" on the vice president, or whether it was the office itself that did so. Regardless of the merits of the arguments, two facts are clear.

First, Tyler's bold assertion that he was president, not a mere acting president, established a precedent that quickly became secure. Hardly five years later it happened again when President Zachary Taylor died in office, and then yet again some fifteen years after that when President Abraham Lincoln was assassinated. There was no question that Vice President Millard Fillmore actually became president, or that Andrew Johnson was the legitimate successor to the slain war leader. Moreover, should any constitutional question linger, the ratification of the Twenty-Fifth Amendment in 1967 laid it to rest. The Amendment made it plain that a vice president filling a presidential vacancy actually becomes president.

Second, despite the opinions of some then and later, Tyler did the right thing in stubbornly insisting that he was fully the president. A special election would certainly be more disruptive than an orderly succession, and it would take time — possibly quite a long time. An acting president likely would lack the full authority or the respect due the office, and such an acting official would probably be unable to provide the strong leadership that would be especially needed after such a traumatic event. The Twenty-Fifth Amendment's ratification was also a confirmation by the political system of this view.

In an additional bold move, when Tyler met with the cabinet he made it clear that its members would not dictate to him. President Harrison had announced that he would adhere to the Whig view that the cabinet would decide policy with each member, and the president, having one vote. Harrison had begun to recognize that this was unsatisfactory, even in his short month in office.

Tyler from the start made no pretense of accepting cabinet dominance. Whig ideology may have demanded it, but nothing in the Constitution — which does not even use the term "cabinet" — did. Tyler had inherited Harrison's cabinet, which he had not had a voice in selecting, and to avoid controversy he decided to keep them. He knew well, though, that they bore no loyalty to him. Henry Clay, lurking in the senatorial wings, would attempt to dominate.

He stood up to their pressures and announced in blunt terms exactly where he stood. "I am very glad to have in my cabinet such able statesmen as you have proven yourselves to be," he said, "and I shall be pleased to avail myself of your counsel and advice, but I can never consent to being dictated to as to what I shall or shall not do." Making the point that he had inherited the entire office of the presidency, he continued, "I, as President, will be responsible for my administration. I hope to have your co-operation in carrying out its measures; so long as you see fit to do this, I shall be glad to have you with me — when you think otherwise," he said making his point absolutely clear, "your resignations will be accepted."[3]

So Tyler, whose presidency began with a tragedy, embarked strongly upon his duties with two wise decisions. In some ways, it was the high point of his time in office. He was stubborn and headstrong, honorable and principled. Yet his principles at their best were inadequate to the country's needs, and at their worst were detrimental to the values of a humane and civilized society. As William Lee Miller put it, "The ambiguities of Harrison on the slavery issue were succeeded abruptly by the unambiguities of Tyler — no hope, to put it mildly, for any antislavery impulse."[4] Tyler had successes in foreign policy, but his pro–Southern and pro-slavery domestic policies were in stark contradiction to his desire to preserve the Union.

Tyler had accepted the vice-presidential nomination as a Whig, but until he broke with Jackson he had been a Democrat. He had been president only a few months when his entire cabinet resigned, except for Secretary of State Webster who was busy negotiating the Webster-Ashburton Treaty settling the Canadian border dispute. Webster, too, resigned the next year, in 1842. Tyler rejected Whig policies, and in turn the Whigs, responding to Clay's leadership, expelled him. He became a president without a party. Gridlock is a modern term, but it well fits much of Tyler's time in office.

He does not fare to good advantage, of course, in rankings. Schlesinger's 1962 poll placed him twenty-fifth of thirty-one.[5] Genovese puts him thirty-first of thirty-nine ranked, as did the Fabers.[6] These tell us almost nothing, however. To understand what kind of president Tyler was, it is necessary to look at his accomplishments and failures. Rather than comparing him with another, it is more productive to consider whether he made the most of the circumstances in which he found himself, and whether he may himself have created some of his own troubles.

Tyler quickly moved to occupy the executive mansion, and by the middle of April he, his wife Letitia, and five of their eight children had settled into Washington. In those days executive branch employees were few, and our recent aversion to nepotism had yet to develop. He placed one son, Robert, in the United States Land Office and another, John, Jr., became his private secretary.[7] Letitia could not function as First Lady. She had suffered a severe stroke in 1839, and was a complete invalid. Performing social functions in her place was Tyler's daughter-in-law, Robert's wife Priscilla Cooper. Former First Lady Dolley Madison, despite her advanced age, assisted her with regard to Washington etiquette, "and Daniel Webster often was on hand to guide her in the choice of food and wine."[8] Letitia immediately upon moving into the executive mansion retired to the living quarters on the second floor, and apparently descended only one time; over a year later, in 1842, she attended a daughter's wedding. Shortly thereafter, she died. She was only fifty-one.[9]

Politically, Tyler's stubbornness — or, depending upon perspective, his adherence to principle — was to cause considerable difficulty both to him and to the government that he headed — not to mention to his country. As Miller remarked, the Whigs had put him on their ticket simply as an attraction to "Southern states'-rights voters," and he was a man "whose views were sharply at odds, as events would prove, with the Whiggery of the free states. He was the Virginia states'-rights advocate who in the Senate had almost matched Calhoun in the clashing antlers of absurdly high principles."[10]

On the other hand, at least his gracious Southern manners served the new president well. Social life in the capital faced none of the gridlock that characterized politics during his administration, and Tyler waited no longer than the official period of mourning after his wife's death before it resumed.

When balls and parties did resume, in no time at all he met Julia Gardiner, the twenty-two-year-old daughter of prominent New Yorker David Gardiner, who previously had served in the state's Senate. Margaret Truman reported that she was a "smashingly attractive brunette" who "mesmerized" the considerably older Tyler. If Truman's account is accurate, Tyler managed to kiss her on her second visit, and two weeks later he proposed. For a time, she resisted flirtatiously while making known her interest in a member of Congress and a Supreme Court justice. Her behavior was enticingly unconventional. In 1839 at the age of nineteen, "proper New Yorkers had been shocked to open their newspapers and discover" her picture in an ad for a department store. "She told her mortified parents she had posed for the ad 'for the fun of it'."[11]

Her resistance faded after another tragedy struck the executive branch — and struck her personally as well. On 28 February 1844 she and her father, along with a large number of dignitaries of the highest rank, boarded the navy's steam frigate *Princeton* for a cruise down the Potomac commanded by Captain Robert Stockton. The state-of-the-art ship was the pride of one of the party, Secretary of State Abel P. Upshur. Until the previous year, Upshur had been secretary of the navy, and the *Princeton* had been one of his pet projects. It was iron, and boasted an innovative screw propeller rather than a paddle wheel. It also boasted, along with other armament, two new giant cannon, the "Peacemaker" at the bow, and the "Oregon" at the stern. For several days the ship had been impressing VIP passengers on brief excursions, and amazing them with the firing of its guns.

The "Peacemaker" could fire projectiles exceeding two hundred pounds through its fifteen-foot barrel for a distance of more than three miles. As the largest wrought-iron cannon ever made, it was designed to use up to fifty pounds of powder. No ship then afloat could withstand it. As the delighted party watched, the crew fired the "Peacemaker" twice.

Later that afternoon, after a sumptuous meal and a series of champagne toasts, the ship approached a deserted stretch of the river. Some of the guests requested another firing of the "Peacemaker," and Captain Stockton agreed. The passengers poured up to the deck to witness the spectacle. To the cannon's left were two cabinet members, Upshur and the new Secretary of the Navy, Thomas Gilmer, who had been in position for less than two weeks. Standing with them was Senator Thomas Hart Benton. Benton moved to the right to get a better view. Tyler was still below. After a quick demonstration of the gun's maneuverability, the crew pointed it down river and fired.

The gun itself exploded, shooting metal fragments into the crowd and blasting apart some twenty feet of the ship's hull. Several people lay dead, including the two cabinet members, and David Gardiner. Benton lay unconscious from the concussion, but he survived.[12]

Tyler comforted the distraught Julia, and in June they were married. The new Mrs. Tyler stepped quickly and effectively into the role of First Lady. She charmed the press and politicians alike. Contributing a light touch to the otherwise grim Washington atmosphere, the merriment of the social functions over which she presided was in stark contrast to the political scene of Tyler's administration.[13]

The president had much to preoccupy him in addition to courtship. Most important among presidential responsibilities was the urgent need to reconstitute his cabinet. He appointed John Y. Mason of Virginia to head the Navy Department. For his new secretary of state he chose the belligerent defender of slavery who had militantly championed nullification and was the major spokesman of the Southern sectionalists, John C. Calhoun.

Students of Tyler's administration disagree as to how he came to select Calhoun. Did he desire to add him to the cabinet, or was it political pressure from those such as Virginia Representative Henry Wise (who did claim the credit) that "forced" him to designate the South Carolinian to keep the State Department in "safe Southern hands?" He may well have been reluctant to have added so prominent a sectional spokesman, because he needed national support for the annexation of Texas. Still, although Tyler had not joined Calhoun in praising slavery as a "positive good," at least not in public, he was no less concerned than Calhoun to maintain Southern influence in the Union.[14]

The mass resignation of Tyler's cabinet in his first year in office came after he vetoed two congressional acts that would have created a third bank of the United States. Support for a bank was a cornerstone of Whig policy, but the president considered it to be unconstitutional. For the Whigs, this was unforgivable. They expelled him, leaving John Tyler as the president without a party. As such, he was unable to get support for his own proposals, and in turn he cast veto after veto, turning down Whig policies. The Whigs then played the censure card against him as they had against Jackson. The result was the same. Tyler scorned their assertion that the use of the veto as a policy matter was unconstitutional, and dared them to impeach him. It was censure, he said, that had no constitutional sanction, not his veto power.[15] Although some Whig leaders railed against the veto and suggested a constitutional amendment to restrict it, they failed to secure either an amendment or impeachment. They did succeed in blocking so many of Tyler's Supreme Court nominations — five out of six — that he holds the record for the number Senate rejections. He managed to place only one justice on the Court.[16]

Tyler did sign one important act, a Land Act or Preemption Act, that made permanent a temporary law of 1830 that had permitted squatters on certain public lands to purchase up to 160 acres. The new law also provided for distribution to each new state of one-half-million acres of public land within its borders. Ten percent of the proceeds from the sale of that land would be assigned to the state, with the rest distributed to other states based on their population.[17] This was a purely Jacksonian measure which catered both to settlers and to the states. Some Southern Democrats nevertheless opposed it as an indirect funding of internal improvements. They also feared that it would lead to higher tariffs to replace funds that otherwise would have gone to the federal government from land sales.

With his domestic policy stalled, Tyler found more success in foreign policy. The Webster-Ashburton Treaty of 1842 with Great Britain finally settled the Canadian boundary dispute which had been especially bitter between Maine and New Brunswick. But the treaty went beyond the concerns of Mainers and secured the boundary as it exists today from the Atlantic to the Rocky Mountains. Tyler's administration in 1844 also secured the Treaty of Wanghia with China which established trading rights with that vast country. That same year, his administration negotiated a treaty of annexation with the Republic of Texas.

Texas had declared its independence from Mexico in 1836, and had sought annexation to the United States. Jackson and Van Buren had been cautious on the issue, wishing to avoid both a war with Mexico and an increase in the sectional tension regarding slavery. Tyler, however — always sympathetic to Southern demands for slavery's expansion — pursued the issue.

James K. Polk, then a contender for the vice presidency, announced his support for immediate "re-annexation," arguing that the Texas Territory legally belonged to the United States already. On the other hand, former President Martin Van Buren, who sought to regain the presidency, opposed immediate action. Van Buren's position infuriated his mentor, former President Andrew Jackson, who had come to believe the popular, but inaccurate, notion that it was necessary to obtain Texas in order to block British influence in the area. He therefore withdrew his support from Van Buren's presidential candidacy. Polk therefore became the dark horse Democratic nominee, and won the election as president to succeed Tyler.

Complicating matters were communications from Secretary of State Calhoun to the British Minister in Washington, Richard Pakenham. Calhoun defended slavery as "essential to the peace, safety, and prosperity of the South, and argued that blacks were inferior beings who were better off as slaves. He argued explicitly that the United States needed to annex Texas in order to preserve its "domestic institutions."

Calhoun's statements served to inflame opinion outside the South, and to undercut Tyler's efforts to present annexation as meeting the interests of the entire nation. Tyler's own secretary of state had made it seem clear that the purpose of Southern support for annexation was merely a way to extend slavery. Tyler then saw his treaty with Texas meet defeat in the Senate.[18]

Thereupon the president tried another strategy, and this time he succeeded. Treaties require ratification only by the Senate, not the House, but they must have a two-thirds vote. Tyler recognized that although it had been impossible to secure approval of two-thirds of the senators, he might be able to obtain a majority in each house. Thus, he abandoned the attempt to produce a treaty — ignoring his own generally rigid views regarding constitutionality — and called for Congress to annex the territory of Texas by a joint resolution. Tyler reportedly hesitated in signing the resolution, thinking that it might be preferable to leave the matter up to his successor — who obviously shared his expansionist views. Just before leaving office, however, Tyler's cabinet agreed unanimously with Secretary of State Calhoun that the president should act with no further delay, and Tyler signed the annexation measure. He considered it his crowning achievement.

An evaluation of Tyler's administration must give him mixed marks that could not be reflected in a ranking. To his great credit, he moved quickly and firmly to establish himself as president when he stepped — without precedent to guide him — into the vacant office. Marcus Cunliffe made an excellent point when he said that by so doing, Tyler "went a long way toward establishing the Presidency as an institution independent of death." Because of Tyler's precedent, he said, "there would never be an automatic diminution of executive prestige, either at home or abroad," when it became necessary for a vice president to take over.[19]

Moreover, Tyler did not hesitate to use the powers of the presidency, including the veto to which Jackson had supplied a new importance. He demonstrated that the executive could remain powerful even when Congress opposed it — that the executive could even restrain a Congress determined to impose policy directions that he disapproved. Florida became a state during his administration, in 1845.

On the other hand, he demonstrated no ability whatsoever to work *with* Congress or to exercise leadership. He was the first president to face an impeachment resolution, he faced a congressional censure, and he was read out of the party that should have been his own, the one that had placed him in the vice presidency. He was strongly biased toward the pro-slavery policies that not only were inexcusable in themselves, but that came close to tearing the country apart. It was his policies, as presidential scholar Richard Pious remarked, that had done "so much during the 1840s to exacerbate tensions between the regions."[20]

Even Tyler's rather friendly biographer, Norma Lois Peterson, titled her summary chapter "A Flawed Presidency." She noted that he left office with a sense of pride and a feeling of success, but that he erred in assuming that history would vindicate his administration. His "stubborn pride" had been his undoing. Although clearly flawed, though, Tyler's accomplishments were such that no one should consider his presidency to have been a failure.

Departing from Washington, the Tylers returned to his plantation, "Sherwood Forest." There, they had seven children to add to the eight that Tyler already had when he became president. Along with other records that he set — first vice president to succeed to a presidential vacancy, the youngest president to date, the only president to be expelled by his party, the first president to face an impeachment resolution, the first president to be married while in office, etc.— Tyler's fatherhood of fifteen children set another that stands to this day.

However one evaluates Tyler's presidency, he apparently did have a sense of humor. Immediately before leaving office, he and Julia threw an enormous ball at the executive mansion, thrilling all but the most jaundiced of official Washington. During the lavish entertainment Tyler remarked wryly that no longer could it be said of him that he had been a President Without a Party!

11

JAMES K. POLK
March 4, 1845–March 4, 1849

James Knox Polk's election in 1844 made him, at the age of forty-nine the youngest president to date, and also the first "dark horse president"; that is, the first whose nomination had been completely unanticipated until well into the convention. It took nine ballots for the Democratic National Convention to nominate him. Polk had, in fact, not received a single vote until the eighth ballot. After it became obvious on the seventh ballot that there was a deadlock, Gideon Pillow of the Tennessee delegation, historian George Bancroft (whom Polk would appoint secretary of the navy), and Massachusetts delegate Benjamin F. Butler suggested Polk.[1] This came after some behind the scenes maneuvering by Polk's friend Cave Johnson (another Tennessean whom he was to appoint postmaster general).

Polk initially had been hoping to secure the Democratic Party's vice presidential nomination, but a visit with former President Andrew Jackson who had become disappointed with former President Martin Van Buren's lack of enthusiasm on the Texas question, convinced him that he might try for the top of the ticket. The Van Buren forces had attempted to persuade the convention to drop the two-thirds requirement, and to nominate by a simple majority. They failed because of opposition from Southern expansionists such as Senator Robert Walker of Mississippi.[2] Van Buren had a majority of the delegates, but not the required two-thirds that the Democratic Party's rules mandated (and in fact, continued to mandate until 1936). The very requirement that had enabled Van Buren to be chosen as the Democrats' vice presidential candidate in 1832 killed his chances to regain the presidential nomination in 1844. Polk's vice-presidential running mate was George M. Dallas of Pennsylvania.

Polk came to office relatively unknown, but his administration, many scholars believe, was "the one bright spot in the dull void between Jackson and Lincoln."[3] Both Genovese and the 1962 Schlesinger poll place him as a "near great," and rank him number eight. Genovese's very brief, but quite perceptive, assessment succeeds in presenting the diverse views of this complex president.[4] The Fabers, on the other hand, demonstrate their independence. They conclude that Polk was the most overrated of all American presidents. "Having the foremost historian of his era as his press agent perhaps had an effect," they speculate.[5] They noted that historians tend to rank him favorably because of his territorial acquisitions. They conceded that these accomplishments were significant, but they nonetheless said they believed "that his actions leading us into war with Mexico were unjustified."[6]

Overrated or not, there is no doubt that Polk's presidency stands out in that quarter century elapsing between the Old Hero and the Great Emancipator. There is a word of caution here, though. One should remember that while it may be appropriate to use "dull void" to apply to the presidents of that period, it certainly does not describe the politics of the time. The tumult of those years made them anything but dull.

The eleventh president did not attract attention because he had a magnetic personality — quite the contrary. Comments by historian Sam Haynes are consistent with the overwhelming consensus. "Polk was as stiffly formal in his personal relations as he was dogmatic in his political views," Haynes wrote. "The grim, humorless president had few close acquaintances and seemed most content when working alone at his desk, attending to official business. He had no hobbies or pastimes, no interests beyond the duties of his office. His reading material consisted entirely of government documents and the scriptures." He was "provincial in outlook and tastes," he knew little of the world beyond Tennessee "and showed no particular inclination to learn." He reminded one observer, Haynes said, of a "penny postman" who "had little to converse about," except for politics. He knew nothing of the arts and cared less. "To the puritanical Polk," remarked Haynes, "even the most innocent diversions seemed a frivolous waste of time."[7] Except for daily walks, his "only other recreational activity was horseback and carriage rides."[8] Polk did take time for church, and piously refused to accept visitors on Sundays.

His wife Sarah Childress Polk, on the other hand, was a tremendous asset. She functioned well in social settings, compensating for her "socially maladroit husband," and was popular with Polk's opponents as well as with his supporters — despite her ban of dancing in the executive mansion.[9] She was thoughtful and well-informed, and discussed policy with other leaders as well as with her husband. They valued her advice. She even read newspapers for Polk, who "was averse to wasting time" with them, marked important passages, and "stacked them beside his chair in his office."[10]

Polk was methodical and well-organized, and meticulously kept a diary — one that has been of enormous value to historians. He was careful to appoint a cabinet that balanced sectional interests — and was careful also to require a pledge from each appointee not to use the cabinet post to seek the presidency.

The ambitious James Buchanan of Pennsylvania became secretary of state, although he appeared to be less than forthright in response to Polk's request for assurance that he would not use the most prominent post in the cabinet as a springboard to higher office. The president selected Buchanan despite this, and despite opposition to the appointment from Vice President Dallas who also was a Pennsylvanian but who was a member of a competing political faction.[11]

Robert J. Walker of Mississippi accepted the Treasury post, and helped Polk achieve his Jacksonian economic policies. Responding to urging from the president and the treasury secretary, Congress approved sharply lowered rates by passing the "Walker Tariff" in July 1846 — although passage in the Senate required a tie-breaking vote by Vice President Dallas. The same month Congress, again at Walker's urging, passed the administration's independent treasury act. Polk reported in his diary, on the other hand, that Walker — along with the secretaries from the departments of the navy, state, and war — probably would have urged him to sign another bill that July that he vetoed. In ringing Jacksonian terms, Polk turned down legislation that would have funded improvements to rivers and harbors: the projects were local, he said; government should be limited; the improvements were constitutionally suspect; they might engender sectional discord.[12]

New Yorker William L. Marcy became secretary of war. Marcy was a Jacksonian and one-time Van Buren supporter. He was famous for having boasted after Jackson's election that "to the victors belong the spoils."

As attorney general, Polk appointed John Y. Mason of Virginia, who had been secretary of the navy in the Tyler administration. As indicated earlier, George Bancroft of Massachusetts and Cave Johnson of Tennessee accepted the top positions in the Navy and Post Office Departments. Bancroft in late 1846 left the Department of the Navy to represent the Polk administration as minister to London, and Mason then became secretary of the navy once again.

Polk's schedule reflected his "passion for efficiency," and his "rather inflexible personality" influenced his managerial style, under which "the policy-making process became systematized as never before."[13] He also exercised rigid control over federal spending. No president before him, and probably none afterwards until well into the twentieth century, managed the federal budget so carefully. One example of the efficiency of his administration came in the Post Office Department. Postmaster General Cave Johnson introduced postage stamps, replacing the previous system that required the recipient of a letter to pay the fees.[14]

The day before Polk took office, outgoing President John Tyler signed a joint resolution calling for the annexation of Texas. There was considerable maneuvering before the new president could accomplish annexation, however. When the Texas legislature voted in June to accept, Polk ordered General Zachary Taylor to move his troops to the border to defend the Texans against possible action from the outraged Mexicans. Hoping to secure their approval, Polk sent John Slidell on a diplomatic mission, instructing him to persuade the Mexicans to approve US annexation of Texas, and to sell the extensive New Mexico and California territories. The Mexicans refused to receive Slidell.

In the meantime, Polk negotiated with Great Britain regarding the disputed boundary of the Oregon Territory. Ultimately, despite jingoistic cries from Americans in the West of "Fifty-Four Forty or Fight!" Polk and the British came to a more moderate agreement. The forty-ninth parallel became the U.S.–Canadian boundary, and remains so today.

The friction with Mexico, however, was another matter. American arrogance and open belligerence offended Mexican pride. Although they had not been able to establish effective government in the area in question, the Mexicans' national honor prevented them from accepting the loss of some half of their land without a fight. On 11 May 1846, Polk requested that Congress issue a declaration of war against Mexico, and the next day Congress complied.

Unfortunately for Polk, the army's two senior generals, Winfield Scott and Zachary Taylor, were Whigs. The intensively partisan president was wary of them both, and had no desire to position either one as a hero who might become a presidential contender, but he had no alternative. Taylor led the assault on Mexico, and his exploits did carry him to the presidency. In 1848, the Senate ratified the Treaty of Guadalupe Hidalgo. The Mexican Congress approved it on 25 May, and the United States grew greatly with the addition of the enormous territories of California and New Mexico in addition to Texas.

In his final state of the Union message, 5 December 1848, Polk pointed proudly to the annexation of Texas, the settling of conflicts regarding the Oregon Territory, and the acquisition of New Mexico and Upper California. He noted the importance of these additions to "future progress" and added that they would "preserve us from foreign collisions."[15] These territories that his administration added included all or parts of what came to be the states of Arizona, California, Colorado, Nevada, New Mexico, Oregon, Texas, Utah, Washington, and Wyoming.

Iowa, Texas, and Wisconsin actually did become states during the Polk administration. California, however, did not make it into the Union under Polk. The slavery issue prevented agreement on California until 1850. On his last day in office, Polk signed legislation creating the Department of the Interior.

This was undoubtedly a great list of accomplishments, especially from a man who had assumed the presidency with "limited experiences, a narrow vision, and a stubborn determination to have things his own way." He shared with his mentor, Andrew Jackson, a commitment not only to strict constitutional interpretation, and also to the notion that the president was "more representative of the people than any other federal official." Such conviction gave him the confidence to lead, rather than to defer to Congress. This brought him his success, and he took pride in what he had done. Politically, though, he was upset that the Whigs at the end of his term won the presidency. They also had won control of Congress two years earlier in the midterm elections of 1846, which meant that Polk's greatest accomplishments came in the first part of his presidency — a circumstance that this strong president had in common with many others who have held the office.

Polk stood out because he laid out an agenda — reduction of the tariff, creation of an independent treasury, acquisition of California, and settlement of the Oregon boundary — and said that he would accomplish it and would serve only one term. He did accomplish that agenda, and did retire as promised after completing only four years in office. In that single term he had added more territory to the United States than any president since Jefferson purchased the Louisiana Territory.

Nevertheless, the Polk legacy also contained troublesome elements. His policies left a deep bitterness in Mexico toward the United States. Within the United States itself, he "failed to appreciate the socioeconomic changes that had occurred."[16] Accordingly, he failed to anticipate the tensions that would come close to tearing the country apart. In fact, he contributed significantly to them.

Thus, any meaningful assessment of the presidency of James K. Polk must acknowledge his great accomplishments — accomplishments that contributed so much to his country. At the same time it also must take note of the troubles that he left to his successors — troubles that so damaged his country. As with nearly all who have held the presidency of the United States, an evaluation of the man and his administration must reflect enormous complexity. No ranking can reflect, or even take note of, that complexity. On the contrary, any ranking must, of necessity, obscure it and by so doing will impede understanding.

12

ZACHARY TAYLOR
March 4, 1849–July 9, 1850

General Zachary Taylor, "Old Rough and Ready" and hero of the Mexican War, was the second and final Whig elected president. Both he and his sole elected Whig predecessor died in office. Each had a successor who changed the course of his administration — neither for the better.

The election of 1848 was the first occasion upon which American voters cast their ballots on the same day throughout the country.[1] Taylor almost assuredly would not have won sufficient votes that year to be the victor, had it not been for former president Martin Van Buren's attempt to regain the office. Van Buren was the first former president to attempt a comeback. His positions had changed considerably after he left the presidency — so much so that when the Free Soil Party, which opposed slavery in the territories, offered him its nomination, Van Buren accepted.

The former president received much support also from "conscience Whigs," those Whigs who opposed slavery, and from "Barnburners," those Democrats who would "burn the barn to rid it of rats" (that is, who allegedly would do anything to eliminate slavery). Although he carried no state, Van Buren took some ten percent of the popular vote nationwide, and ran ahead of his Democratic opponent in Massachusetts, Vermont, and New York. He thus denied the Democrats electoral votes in a close election. Van Buren was the only candidate in the race who spoke forcefully against slavery's expansion into the territories.[2]

The Whigs had been successful in 1840 by running a general and adopting no platform. Their candidate, General William Henry Harrison, had stayed carefully away from the issues. In 1848, they reverted to the formula that had brought them their sole victory. Taylor, too, was a general — a most prominent one, in fact — and he had no political record to attack. As it had done eight years previously, "the Whig ticket found geographical balance with a running mate." This time it was a New Yorker, Millard Fillmore, who had served in the U.S. House, but who "had never opposed slavery."[3] Taylor was a Southerner, a Louisiana slaveowner.

That alone was enough to endear him to many in the South without any need for him to mention the burning issue of the day: slavery in the territories. The Democratic candidate, Lewis Cass of Ohio, argued for "squatter sovereignty" — for letting the inhabitants of a territory determine whether it should to be slave or free. Both candidates dissatisfied the anti-slavery wings of their parties. Taylor in office may to an extent have been a pleasant surprise to that wing of his own Whigs, but the slave interests soon discovered that they, too, had misjudged the new president — and they were furious.

Some historians have drawn the conclusion that Taylor was ignorant of politics, pointing to his own statement that he had never even voted. Taylor's failure to vote, though, could reflect something quite apart from ignorance; it could simply have been a principled application of the professional military officer's duty to remain free from partisanship. Regardless, as his biographer Elbert Smith has noted, "Zachary Taylor was accustomed to making hard decisions and standing by them. He was highly intelligent and was better informed on various important issues than a great many people, including James K. Polk, realized."[4]

Polk's antipathy toward his successor may have influenced attitudes toward Taylor, including the attitudes of some scholars. Polk and the general had feuded throughout the Mexican War, and Polk, a Democratic partisan, was none too happy to be succeeded in office by a Whig — especially by a popular Whig. Although the two were civil when they met and rode together in a carriage to and from Taylor's inauguration, "a very critical and somewhat arrogant Polk" — as one of his biographers put it[5] — "could find nothing to laud in Taylor's Inaugural Address," which was quite brief. Polk wrote that he had no doubt Taylor was a "well-meaning old man," but that the new president was "uneducated, exceedingly ignorant of public affairs," and was of "very ordinary capacity." This meant, Polk felt certain, that Taylor would be a tool in the hands of others, including his cabinet.[6]

Polk's opinion was hardly the only thing at work regarding views of Taylor, though. It was common for each party to have its own semi-official, overtly partisan, newspaper. The Democrats throughout the years of Jackson, Van Buren, and Tyler had the *Globe* under the editorship of Francis P. Blair who had "honed the art of colorful but reasonably polite insult to a fine art." Succeeding him as spokesman for the Democratic Party was Thomas Ritchie of the *Union,* who "eschewed all courtesy as well as Blair's wit and humor; he attacked with a blunderbuss. Almost from the first day of Taylor's presidency, the *Union* pictured him as a senile fool with no principles," who had appointed a corrupt cabinet that was filled with traitors. The Whigs had their own editors, but none to match Ritchie, "even in their influence on future historians."[7]

Those historians in Schlesinger's 1962 poll placed Taylor among the "below average" presidents.[8] They did, though, at least make him the best of the six in that category. He was twenty-fourth of the thirty-one on their list.

Genovese more or less dismissed Taylor in a few sentences, among which he included those from Polk's pessimistic assessment. He did note correctly that Taylor's "election was the last gasp of a dying Whig party," and that his performance suffered because of his "Whig view of a limited presidency." Still, for Genovese to say flatly that Taylor made no attempt to exercise leadership requires more support than he provided — he bolstered his conclusion with nothing more than a brief quotation from Taylor on executive-legislative relations. Even more unwarranted is the conclusion that, although "Taylor, a southerner, was appalled by talk of secession," he "felt helpless in the face of fast-moving events."[9] Genovese rated him well down in his list of twelve "below-average" presidents, which gave him the position overall of thirtieth among the thirty-nine that he rated.[10]

The Fabers reminded their readers of the obvious. "Where Taylor would have ranked had his administration not been cut short by his untimely death will never be known," they cautioned. They did know something, though, which made it clear that they actually had examined the record, rather than being content to rely on superficial comments from others. Taylor, they wrote, "achieved enough in his 16 months in office to deserve a higher ranking than presidential polls usually give him."[11] The Fabers' ranking placed him twentieth among thirty-nine.[12]

Thus, the more presidential rankings one sees, the more flimsy the entire ranking enterprise becomes. It is one thing to conclude that a president is "great," "poor," or even a failure. It is another thing altogether to attempt the precision of a ranking. We should care enough for meaning to be more than suspicious of efforts to provide precision where it cannot exist.

No presidential record presents this more clearly than does Taylor's. His circumstances were unique (as were those of all presidents). He served only sixteen months — not the two years that Genovese mentioned[13] — the third shortest time in office of any president. He represented a party that was dissolving, and that held a diminished view of executive authority. He faced an impending sectional crisis.

All presidents attempt sincerely to do their best, but Taylor seemed more than most to be able to withstand political pressure. In any case, he likely would have cared little for the subsequent judgment of historians. Almost assuredly, he would have had no patience for those who attempt to compare the incomparable.

Despite his brief period as president, Taylor did have some substantial accomplishments to his credit. His acceptance of Whig doctrine regarding presidential limitations did not prevent him from exerting leadership. As a career military officer he had become accustomed to exercising command, and certainly had not earned his nickname, "Old Rough and Ready," by failing to take action. Nor did he do so as president.

Relations with Indian tribes were a prominent concern of presidents throughout much of the nineteenth century, and Taylor's administration was no exception. As a general, Taylor had long experience in Indian affairs, and according to his biographer Elbert Smith, he "had always tried to be both realistic and fair."[14] This is especially noteworthy in view of the prevailing attitudes, the racial views, and the political climate of the mid-nineteenth century. His experience served the country well when several incidents took place during his presidency that caused residents in both Florida and the Southwest to demand war against various tribes.

Taylor handled such situations with discretion, making certain to ascertain the true circumstances and not to be swayed by hysterical calls for action. "In every case," says Smith, "the actual battles were held to a minimum, the Indians were given every chance to make a face-saving peace, and hostilities were stopped when the Indians agreed to do so." Smith noted further that "the *Washington Union* charged that Taylor had started two Indian wars," when in fact he had reflected a "sense of justice" and a policy of trying to keep the peace even at the risk of infuriating the local citizenry." Such an approach, Smith believed, "probably prevented Indian wars of a far more serious nature."[15]

In foreign affairs, Taylor approached matters with candor and strength. He succeeded in maintaining neutrality in a dispute between Germany and Denmark despite pressures from the antagonists. Similarly, he took vigorous action to observe neutrality when revolutionary sentiments developed in Canada, and some American groups sought to interfere with British rule there. He moved toward settlement of a long-standing controversy with Portugal that had resulted from two incidents; one during the War of 1812 and another during John Quincy Adams's administration—his policy enabled the Fillmore administration to bring matters to a satisfactory conclusion. Most important, he secured the Clayton-Bulwer Treaty with Great Britain. The treaty dealt with a proposed canal across Nicaragua, and generated criticism from Taylor's opponents. The controversy resulted from more from partisanship than from the treaty's effects. Those effects included reducing friction with the British — possibly heading off a war — while blocking further colonization in Central America. Smith credited Taylor's "stubborn stand against the claims of a powerful Britain" for these successes.[16]

By far the most significant illustration of Taylor's strength came from his policy regarding the expansion of slavery into the territories. Southern leaders had been pleased to welcome a Louisiana slaveholder into office. Many of them saw their pleasure evaporate when they recognized that he would not support their demands for slavery's expansion. They found it appalling that, rather than commit himself to slavery, Taylor's commitment was to the Union.

Originally, the prevailing opinion among the South's slaveholding leaders recognized that human chattel slavery was an evil that ultimately should disappear. Nevertheless, there had been pressure even before the Constitution to expand the system beyond the boundaries of the existing states. When Jefferson attempted in 1787 to incorporate a ban on territorial slavery in the Northwest Ordinance, he failed. The Ordinance prohibited slavery only in what at that time was the Northwest Territory, not in the southwest (which included such future states as Alabama and Mississippi). Acquisition of the Louisiana Territory opened the question once more. The result was similar. Southern leaders were content to accept the Missouri Compromise, which permitted slavery only in the southern part of the Louisiana Purchase and in Missouri. They insisted on expansion, but agreed to limitations.

By the time Taylor was in office, however, many Southern leaders had come to reject the Missouri Compromise. Led by John C. Calhoun, they demanded the unlimited right to expand what they had come to call their "peculiar institution." In January 1849, while Polk still held office, Calhoun called a caucus of Southern members of Congress. He did not invite the strong unionists, Missouri Senator Thomas Hart Benton or Texas Senator Sam Houston, but Houston attended anyway. By a vote of forty-eight to forty-one the caucus approved Calhoun's "Address of the Southern Delegates in Congress to their Constituents."

Calhoun's "Address" charged that every national policy that had affected slavery had been an "aggression against the South." These included not only the Northwest Ordinance and the Missouri Compromise, but even the 1848 incorporation without slavery of the Oregon Territory. There could be no further encroachments, and the "tyranny" must halt or secession would follow. "Calhoun conveniently ignored the recent annexation of Texas with its legal right to subdivide into five slave states and the recent election" as president of a "rich slaveholding planter," Taylor. His two predecessors, Tyler and Polk, also were Southern slaveholders. "Indeed, of all the previously elected presidents since 1789, only John Adams and John Quincy Adams could not be classified as Southern or pro–Southern presidents in their attitudes toward the constitutional rights of slaveholders."[17] Calhoun also ignored the fact the he had voted for the Missouri Compromise himself.

Prior to assuming office, Taylor sent word, secretly, to California and New Mexico "that he would support their admission regardless of the provisions on slavery in their constitutions."[18] As president, he told Southern secessionists that he would "not hesitate to use the army to preserve the Union."[19] He was equally forceful with Texans, who thought their state entitled to New Mexican territory and who threatened to march all the way to Santa Fe to seize it for Texas.

In 1850, that was a more immediate threat of civil war than of secession. "A civil war to defend slavery against a slaveholding president would have been impossible," Taylor's biographer Elbert Smith contended. This may or may not be correct, but surely he was right to argue that the real threat of war at the time was that Texas might invade New Mexico. Texans could have been encouraged to mount a campaign if they had entertained the unrealistic thought that they would have only New Mexicans to fight. The South would likely have rushed to Texas's defense when the Texans found themselves confronting the U.S. Army. Taylor headed off the conflict. He "minced no words. When he announced that he would defend New Mexico, in person if necessary, no one doubted it." Smith classed this as a major contribution to sectional peace.[20]

Taylor opposed what he called the Omnibus Bill. Henry Clay had introduced it as a compromise measure relating the admission of California to numerous other issues. Taylor favored California's admission without contingencies. After his sudden death, the provisions of the measure became law as five separate bills grouped together as the "Compromise of 1850."

There was one major scandal during his administration. Before Taylor became president, a Georgia family named Galphin had received a partial settlement of a long-standing claim against the United States. The payment was the amount that had been in dispute for more than seventy years. George Crawford had represented the family, and had received half of the amount awarded. After Taylor appointed Crawford secretary of war, the family continued to seek payment of the interest, which amounted to many times the principal that had been paid. The secretary of the treasury, William Meredith, paid the amount on the advice of Attorney General Reverdy Johnson. Secretary of War Crawford then received half the interest payment as well — a payment that resulted from a decision of two of his cabinet colleagues.

Whatever the legalities of the situation, it clearly was improper for a cabinet officer to profit in such a manner. A political furor resulted. Taylor's opponents, of course, gleefully exploited the issue to the full extent possible. Taylor determined to restructure the cabinet, but fate intervened.

After sitting in the hot sun on the 4th of July, eating what usually is reported to have been sour cherries and cold milk, the president developed severe gastrointestinal distress. On the evening of 9 July, he died. In 1991, in response to pressure from some historians who took seriously the rumor that disgruntled Southerners may have poisoned Taylor, one of the most bizarre episodes in presidential history took place. A forensic anthropologist directed the exhumation of Taylor's remains, and subjected them to analysis.

The result was to have been expected. There was no evidence that Zachary Taylor, the twelfth President of the United States, had died of anything other than natural causes. The only surprising thing was that the project got as far as it did.

Taylor certainly has had a bad press. Note, for example, his treatment in the companion volume to the public television series on the presidency. It presented him as being less well-prepared for the job than any other president, it implied that Taylor's "healthy temper" caused him to antagonize one faction after another, and it said that as president, he "dug in his heels and refused to cooperate with anyone." The implication was that he stood in the way of Congress's noble efforts to compromise with demands from such figures as Calhoun, and thus assured a civil war.[21] Such interpretations surely reflect the Southern vindication that dominated American history for more than half a century. It is equally certain that much of the bad press has been unwarranted. Smith, on the other hand, wrote approvingly of Taylor's policies, and mentioned his "willingness to cultivate personal friendships with outspoken opponents of slavery," as indication of "an unusual breadth of vision." He proceeded to say that while there "is no evidence that Taylor was looking to the demise of slavery," he did respect its opponents and their views, "and he tried to promote personal tolerance and understanding between the opposing groups."[22]

How, then, may one rank Zachary Taylor? To paraphrase the remark from the Fabers, quoted above, no one can know what sort of presidency his would have been had he lived. One thing is certain: the impossibility of a valid ranking of such a figure.

13

MILLARD FILLMORE
July 9, 1850–March 4, 1853

Millard Fillmore was the second vice president to replace a president who died in office. The country had operated under the Constitution for more than half a century before such an event occurred, and then it had happened once again within a decade. Fillmore benefited from Tyler's precedent; there was no attempt to portray him as "vice president acting as president," and whether or not his circumstances affected his effectiveness, there was no significant question of his legitimacy.

The new president needed more than mere legitimacy, however, to deal with the situation in which he found himself. By most estimates, he came up short. He is one of those nineteenth-century presidents who, justly or not, have tended to fade into obscurity. Historian Jean Harvey Baker, who believes that he deserves better, has mentioned that his "anonymity [is] such a joke to members of the Millard Fillmore Society that they meet annually on his birthday to celebrate his invisibility."[1]

To be sure, some biographers have praised him and have sought to improve his reputation. Historians in general, though, have not thought highly of Fillmore and those who indulge in rankings tend to be reasonably consistent in putting him far down their lists. Schlesinger's 1962 poll placed him in the middle of six presidents it classed as below average, putting him twenty-sixth of thirty-one.[2] Genovese listed him as thirty-second of thirty-nine (tenth of the twelve he rated below average).[3] The Fabers put him at twenty-sixth overall of the thirty-nine they rated.[4] Harry Truman — himself well read in history — said that the country needed a strong man at the time, but in Millard Fillmore "what we got was a man that swayed with the slightest breeze."[5] Truman called Fillmore "colorless," and criticized Rayback's biography[6] as "trying to make a great man out of him."[7] Horace Greeley said, "Fillmore lacks pluck ... he means well, but he is timid, irresolute, uncertain, and loves to lean."[8]

Being irresolute, however, or swaying with the slightest breeze seems not to have been the source of Fillmore's trouble. For example, he quickly asked for, and received, the resignations of all members of Taylor's cabinet so that he could appoint his own. He also did not rescind Taylor's order for troops to defend New Mexico against Texas; on the contrary, he "ordered an additional 750 soldiers to New Mexico.... Aside from the fact that Fillmore, unlike Taylor, did not threaten to lead the army in person, there was no discernible difference between Fillmore's Texas policy and that of Taylor."[9] The source of his trouble, rather, was his judgment.

He had begun his political career as an Anti-Mason. To be sure, membership in such a party did not carry the stigma in his day than it would in ours. No less honorable a figure than John Quincy Adams had associated with the Anti-Masons for a time, the presumed kidnapping and murder of a man allegedly for betraying Masonic secrets encouraged an anti–Mason reaction, and there was a democratic suspicion of secret groups, especially a group that had members strategically placed throughout society and politics. Moreover, Andrew Jackson was a Mason, and his opponents could justify their opposition to masonry on that score as well.

Nevertheless, it was not the Anti-Masonic Party that was to be the strongest counter to Jacksonian Democracy. Fillmore's poor judgment led him to choose a losing movement. The effective counter to Jacksonianism was not even to be Fillmore's own Whig Party, which also proved to be short-lived. The most effective opposition turned out, ultimately, to be the new Republican Party, but Fillmore never accepted the Republicans. Rather, his judgment of the new party came to be that they presented more of a danger than did his own long-time opponents, the Democrats. Accordingly, after his presidency he threw his support first to the nativist and anti–Semitic and anti–Catholic Know-Nothing Party — and was even its candidate for president in 1856 — and finally supported the Democratic candidate George McClellan against Lincoln in 1864. McClellan's platform favored a halt to the war, and accommodation — that is, surrender — to the demands of Southern slaveholders.

His judgment led Fillmore to affiliate with one losing group after another, including those whose principles seemed to be most in contradiction to his own. As president, his judgment was that peace and continuation of the Union depended, for the most part, upon accepting demands from the South. He thought of his policies as presenting the best hope for the future. Numerous of his contemporaries hailed them, and agreed. Similar policies nearly a century later, however, and under different circumstances, came to be called "appeasement." In neither case did they work.

Although the major issue of Fillmore's presidency revolved around slavery and led to the Compromise of 1850, he did have successes in foreign policy. In the seventeenth century, Japan closed itself off from the outside world. Recognizing the commercial potential, Fillmore dispatched a mission to Japan. Commodore Matthew Perry led the expedition, which in addition to a letter of friendship to the Emperor carried "gifts, including one hundred gallons of Kentucky bourbon whiskey, wines, two telegraph transmitters with several hundred feet of wire, a quarter-scale railroad with 370 feet of track, four volumes of Audubon's *Birds of America*; and an excellent interpreter."[10] Although the success of Perry's mission came after Fillmore left office, the "combination of military threat and peaceful assurances" worked. It opened Japan, and the credit should go to Fillmore and to his secretaries of state, first Daniel Webster and then Edward Everett.[11]

In June 1852 a controversy arose with Peru, which claimed ownership of the Lobos Islands, a few miles off its coast. The islands contained a treasure of rich fertilizer, guano, deposited there over the centuries by birds. Peru had announced that it would attack foreign ships that sought to remove guano without paying for it, but a group of American merchants received assurance from Secretary of State Webster that the U.S. Navy would protect them if they did so. They planned to send a fleet of ships and harvest thousands of tons of guano. When Fillmore examined the situation, he concluded that the order was unjust to Peru, and countermanded it. Because ships already were enroute with an assurance of protection, however, the president agreed that the United States would pay Peru for the guano that they harvested. Any future American ships that violated Peru's sovereignty, though, would do so at their peril. His policy brought praise from Peru,[12] and political criticism at home. It was perhaps most important, as Elbert Smith noted, that "Fillmore had refused to bully a weaker neighbor."[13] He also should receive credit for having adhered to his policy in the face of political pressure. Fillmore followed Taylor's lead in moving against those who led "filibustering" expeditions attempting to seize Cuba, and he held to a policy of neutrality with regard to disputes in other areas such as Canada and Austria-Hungary.[14]

It was Fillmore's response to Southern demands to expand slavery, however, that produced the hallmark of his administration. Despite Taylor's objections to the "Omnibus Bill," indications are that Fillmore would have voted for it while he was vice president, if he had been called upon to break a tie in the Senate. As president, he encouraged Congress to come up with what came to be called the "Compromise of 1850," and signed it into law. Indicating that facts do not speak for themselves, and that sound scholars can read the record to mean different things, there is disagreement regarding Fillmore's effectiveness in the struggle over the Compromise. Michael

Holt has written that through the use of patronage and other means he "played an indispensable role" in its passage.[15] Baker, on the other hand, said that he lacked "the forcefulness of presidents who have advanced their policies through judicious patronage and alliances with powerful congressmen. Fillmore also seemed to lack the personality," Baker wrote, "to forward the policies he supported."[16] There is evidence to support both interpretations. As Smith pointed out, Fillmore lacked what modern Americans call "fire in the belly"—he did not thirst for power. Accordingly, he likely could have been nominated in 1852 if he had used his power over patronage to do so. He was capable of using that power effectively, but he did so "only in selected cases." One of those cases was the Compromise of 1850, and in that instance he did use patronage to build support for the proposals in New York.[17]

The legislation making up the Compromise actually was a group of measures that supposedly balanced Southern interests and those of the rest of the country. Stephen Douglas had separated the Omnibus Bill into five parts in a successful attempt to put together different majorities for each. California would enter the Union as a free state (and it did so in 1850), slavery would continue in the District of Columbia but there would be no more slave trade there, and Utah and New Mexico would become territories with no restriction regarding slavery. Additionally, a bill established the boundaries of Texas, which included its Mexican claims but not its claim to a large portion of New Mexico. Finally, and of vast importance, a fifth bill provided for a new Fugitive Slave Law. Oddly, it was not the border states, from which slaves might more readily escape, that demanded such a law. It was states in the Deep South, from which escape was almost impossible. The law provided for no civil liberties and no judicial review. The only gesture toward due process was a provision for a commissioner to determine the facts of a case, but even this rudimentary protection reflected a bias against the accused, who could not testify. Moreover, the commissioner received a fee of $10 for every person he sent south, but ruling against a slaveholder's claim brought him a mere $5 fee.[18] The law obligated state authorities—and in fact all citizens—to assist federal officers in capturing and sending south any person of African descent whom a Southerner claimed was a slave. Thus, free blacks were fair game for "slave catchers," and none had any recourse.

In response, several northern states passed personal liberty laws forbidding their authorities from cooperating with federal officers to capture alleged runaways. Such laws offended the South still further—although it was the South that had stressed "states' rights" and asserted that states had the authority to nullify federal laws within their borders. In this instance, the firm advocates of state rights demanded national supremacy.

Controversy remains. Whitney, for example, called the Compromise of 1850 "more a capitulation to Southern slave interests than a compromise."[19]

The Kunhardts, on the other hand, while conceding that Northerners were infuriated by the draconian Fugitive Slave Law said that "Southerners came to regret the many concessions they had made" in the Compromise.[20] What is beyond controversy is that, Compromise of 1850 or no, a Civil War resulted — a war that was one of the bloodiest in all of history.

There is little doubt that two factors — only one directly under his control — made Fillmore's task considerably more difficult. The first was that he announced shortly after assuming the presidency that he would not run for a term in his own right. This ensured that some who exercised political power would view him as a lame duck (he did, apparently with some reluctance, permit his supporters to submit his name as a candidate in 1852, but the convention rejected him in favor of Franklin Pierce).

The other factor was one for which he bore at least some responsibility indirectly; it was a response to the Fugitive Slave Act. This was the appearance in 1852 of Harriet Beecher Stowe's electrifying novel, *Uncle Tom's Cabin*. Along with Thomas Paine's *Common Sense*, Stowe's novel is one of the most forceful pieces of political propaganda in American history (Lincoln allegedly remarked upon meeting her a decade or so later, "So you are the little lady who started this big war"). Her book caused opinion outside the South to harden against slavery. Inside the South, reaction was hysterical, irrational, and — by that time, as a result of Calhoun's legacy — typical. Although the South was then prosperous along with the rest of the country, although at the South's urging the tariff had been lowered substantially, and although the South had since the beginning almost always dominated national policy, Southern leaders saw Stowe's criticism of slavery as "Northern aggression." For some time Southern officials had banned anti-slavery material — including censoring the mail — and they, with the assistance of mobs, violently suppressed her book.[21] For Fillmore's efforts to smooth over the sectional tension, *Uncle Tom's Cabin* could not have come at a worse time.

Surely, it would be expecting too much of Fillmore, or of any other president at the middle of the nineteenth century, to insist that he should have prevented the war. It is not too much, though, to criticize his judgment in accepting a Fugitive Slave Law that demanded that every American citizen become an agent to protect Southern slavery, and one that provided no protection for the accused. His own wife, Abigail — an astute political observer who was a major adviser to the president — urged him not to sign the law, saying (correctly) that it would cause enormous difficulties.[22] She told him that signing the law would be political suicide.[23] "Although he expressed some doubts, he proceeded to sign it nonetheless.[24] The law was a final blow to an already fragmented Whig Party. Although in General Scott the Whigs fielded a candidate in 1852, he was their last. The Democrats overwhelmed him, electing Franklin Pierce, and the Whigs evaporated as a party.

Millard Fillmore, by all accounts, was a strong partisan, but also a man of integrity who adhered to principle. In general he supported civil liberties and religious freedom, but these did not seem uppermost among his considerations. He did move to counter those whom he considered to be extremists, but in his view this category included not only those leading illegal filibustering expeditions against Cuba but also those who advocated slavery's abolition. It seems that he did attempt to do what he considered to be right, but his judgment as to what constituted right and wrong at times was seriously flawed.

Historian David Jacobs wrote the Fillmore might have been judged a good president if he had led the country at a different time — say twenty years later or a decade earlier. "He was a selfless public servant and a good administrator who accomplished much in a term of less than three years." But the time was not right. "Fillmore became president in 1850, and history in its judgment cannot divorce his achievements from the needs of the times. He is counted among the presidential mediocrities because of his lack of vision." One could say also because of his lack of judgment. "He knew that slavery had to go, but he did nothing to hasten its end."[25]

The war did not result from Fillmore's actions, but however well-intentioned his efforts, they did not reduce its likelihood. He thought he had done well. Most historians now disagree. That much is clear. But it also seems clear that it is not possible to place him in a ranking that compares him precisely with other presidents — and that also is in any substantial manner meaningful.

14

FRANKLIN PIERCE
March 4, 1853–March 4, 1857

Presidential biographers, with notable exceptions of course, tend to present their subjects in a favorable light whenever possible. Scarry, for example, was merely being more forthright than most when (with rather more enthusiasm than style) he ended his biography of Millard Fillmore with the comment that, "if this writer has been able to give readers a more favorable and complete impression of the thirteenth president, this work was not in vain and may help make Millard Fillmore no longer so obscure."[1] Scarry made a substantial effort, but he set a difficult task for himself; Fillmore likely will retain his obscurity.

Franklin Pierce presents an even more difficult case — so difficult, in fact, that it is a rare writer who would even try to polish his tarnished image as a president. Biographies of Pierce tend, understandably, to be sparse. When a writer does offer praise, in most instances it is only to compliment him for his appearance and his sociability, not his performance. James Rawley, for instance, described Pierce as affable, as "an effective orator, and a boon barroom companion, possessing both personal magnetism and a desire to please others." Pierce had "strong features," he said, "and opaque gray eyes." He dressed well, was "erect in bearing," and "contributed greatly to Washington society." He sought to please everyone, however, and "proved unequal to the extraordinary stresses of his presidency."[2] Martin Luray wrote that "on paper, Pierce looked good; and in person he looked even better." Pierce, he said, was "a handsome man" who was "a sight to see in his sparkling uniform" (a brigadier general's uniform from the Mexican War). But even though Luray's commentary is more kind than most, he conceded that Pierce was one of those presidents who had "become part of the dustheap of history."[3]

Larry Gara in his excellent study of the Pierce administration noted that "those who play the presidential ratings game have always assigned to Franklin Pierce a below-average score. Thomas A. Bailey," he said, "rated Pierce 'less a success, not wholly a failure.' That is about the best one can say about his presidency," Gara concluded.[4] Schlesinger's 1962 poll not only placed Pierce in the below-average category, but put him far down on the overall list: twenty-eighth on a roster of thirty-one.[5] Genovese put him thirty-fourth of thirty-nine, a mere one notch above "failure."[6] Harshest of all, the Fabers place him "next to last among the 39 presidents rated."[7] As Gara put it, "Franklin Pierce was no genius. Indeed, the ordinary demands of the office were often beyond his ability. He was a politician of limited ability, and instead of growing in his job, he was overwhelmed by it."[8]

Misfortune seemed to follow Pierce. In the Mexican War he was injured when his horse threw him. Although he attempted to continue to lead troops, he could not. Throughout much of his life, he drank heavily. His wife, Jane Means Appleton, was frail both physically and mentally. She was a stern, judgmental, Calvinist who "despised politics and politicians,"[9] and resented his political career. After Pierce's election but before he took office, the Pierces along with their eleven-year-old son, Bennie, were riding on a train when it went off the rails. Pierce and his wife were unharmed physically, but watched in horror as the wreckage mangled and killed Bennie. Jane Pierce never recovered from the shock, or from the resentment against her husband.

For secretary of state, Pierce chose a New Yorker, William ("To the victors belong the spoils") Marcy who had served Polk as secretary of war. Treasury went to a Kentuckian, James Guthrie. For secretary of war, Pierce named Jefferson Davis from Mississippi.

Davis, who had been a military hero in the Mexican War, in contrast to most Southerners had opposed the Compromise of 1850. He believed that slavery should be forced into the territories and that federal force should maintain the "peculiar institution" there. He had failed to win his state's governorship in 1850, proving too radical even for Mississippi politics of the time. The appointment resuscitated Davis's political career. He became a very strong figure in a largely weak group, and exerted a pernicious influence on a weak president — reinforcing Pierce's already biased views that politically were in favor of all things Southern, including slavery. Ironically, Davis did much to modernize the military that ultimately crushed the Southern rebellion that he headed.

Caleb Cushing of Massachusetts became attorney general. He was an efficient administrator who proposed reform and expansion of the judicial branch. Recognizing that Pierce would simply have packed an expanded judiciary with supporters of slavery, Congress rejected Cushing's proposals. Following the Civil War, however, his suggestions became the basis for revamping the judicial branch. In another ironic twist, Cushing, who strongly supported Pierce's pro-slavery policies, later became a Republican. The Department of the Navy went to James Dobbin, a North Carolinian; the Post Office to a Pennsylvanian, James Campbell; and the new secretary of the interior, Robert McClelland, was from Michigan.

Pierce's inaugural address suggested what was to come.[10] He strongly expressed his view that slavery was constitutional and had to be protected.

> I believe that involuntary servitude, as it exists in different States of this Confederacy, is recognized by the Constitution. I believe that it stands like any other admitted right, and that the States where it exists are entitled to efficient remedies to enforce the constitutional provisions. I hold that the laws of 1850, commonly called the "compromise measures," are strictly constitutional and to be unhesitatingly carried into effect. I believe that the constituted authorities of this Republic are bound to regard the rights of the South in this respect as they would view any other legal and constitutional right, and that the laws to enforce them should be respected and obeyed, not with a reluctance encouraged by abstract opinions as to their propriety in a different state of society, but cheerfully and according to the decisions of the tribunal to which their exposition belongs. Such have been, and are, my convictions, and upon them I shall act. I fervently hope that the question is at rest, and that no sectional or ambitious or fanatical excitement may again threaten the durability of our institutions or obscure the light of our prosperity.

It was to prove a vain hope. Pierce clothed his unqualified support for the South's position on slavery in the language of constitutionalism. Not only should the rest of the country support the South's position on slavery, it should do so "cheerfully." He was adamant that no interpretation of the Constitution other than his own could have merit.

Pierce also promised effective and honest management. In general, the departments did operate smoothly. Under his administration, there even was "the introduction of a limited civil service examination system."[11]

The United States expanded only slightly under Pierce's administration, which paid Mexico $10 million in 1853 for the Gadsden Purchase. It took the name of the minister to Mexico who negotiated the purchase, James Gadsden. The land involved was a strip along the border between Mexico and what now are the states of Arizona and New Mexico. The hope was to secure a southern route for a transcontinental railroad. Also, in 1856 Pierce signed into law an act providing that "any U.S. citizen who discovered an unoccupied and unclaimed island containing guano deposits could claim it for the United States." About seventy islands became U.S. property under the terms of this act over the next thirty years, including the later-familiar Christmas Island and Midway. "While guano diplomacy provided one of the few successes of the Pierce foreign policy, Cuba provided its most significant failure."[12]

Pierce was both a Jacksonian expansionist and a believer in slavery's expansion. He therefore authorized Secretary of State Marcy to pursue negations with Spain to acquire Cuba — which would have led to an immediate expansion of America's slave territory. He made it clear that if Spain were not to agree to sell Cuba, Marcy should seek ways to seize it.[13] Marcy accordingly dispatched instructions to the Pierce administration's erratic minister to Spain, Pierre Soulé, to meet with John Y. Mason and James Buchanan, ministers to France and Great Britain respectively. The meeting took place in Ostend, Belgium, and produced the infamous "Ostend Manifesto," calling for seizure of Cuba if Spain refused to sell.

Pierce, shocked at the public outcry, characteristically waffled. Unfortunately for him, the news came just in time to affect the mid-term congressional elections. The results were disastrous for the Democrats, and Pierce dropped the Ostend Manifesto. The administration also suffered from its midadventures in Latin America, but it faced its major crisis in the Kansas-Nebraska Act, a measure that Pierce had supported.

The 1854 measure explicitly repealed the Missouri Compromise, and adopted "popular sovereignty," which provided that statehood for Nebraska and Kansas could include slavery or not, depending upon the expressed wishes of the white residents. The South, of course, originally had supported the Missouri Compromise, but its increasing demand for slavery's expansion led Southern leaders to change their position, and to argue that the Compromise had been unconstitutional — that under the Constitution, Congress had no authority to exclude slavery from any territory. The Kansas-Nebraska Bill thus came to characterize the Pierce administration — and to tear the country apart.

Stephen A. Douglas introduced the Kansas-Nebraska Bill into the Senate to facilitate a Chicago-based transcontinental railroad, but Missouri Senator David Atchison spoke for other senators representing slaveholding interests to demand that any territorial bill repeal the Missouri Compromise. Senator Douglas gave in to their demands to open the northern part of the Louisiana Purchase to slavery, and President Pierce — whose weakness made it difficult for him to resist pressure and who in any case was sympathetic to slaveholding interests — signed the measure.[14] The legislation laid the basis for civil strife, as free-soil and pro-slavery forces flooded into Kansas in attempts to determine its policy on slavery. Pro-slavery Missouri voters crossed the state line in waves to vote in Kansas elections and elect a pro-slavery legislature and congressional delegate.

Despite charges that it was fraudulent, Pierce recognized the legislature which proceeded to pass draconian legislation. Pierce's own appointee, Kansas Territorial Governor Andrew Reeder, vetoed laws that provided jail for Kansans who were discovered reading Free-Soil newspapers, or who declared slavery to be illegal in the territory. He vetoed laws disenfranchising voters who refused to take an oath supporting the Fugitive Slave Law, or mandating that only those advocating slavery could hold office. He vetoed an act providing the death penalty for anyone who circulated any publication that, in the eyes of the pro-slavery forces, might incite a slave revolt. The legislature overturned all of these vetoes. Reeder appealed to Pierce for support, and Pierce's response was first to offer him another position, which he refused, and then to fire him. Pierce preferred a governor who did not reflect an "anti-slavery bias."[15]

A fanatical John Brown and his sons, who had moved to Kansas, took up arms to murder slaveholders. A pro-slavery mob, largely from Missouri, attacked the town of Lawrence, burning the Free State Hotel. Violence erupted throughout the territory. "Bleeding Kansas" was a mini-beginning of the Civil War.

The year 1856 saw numerous tragedies for the United States, and for Pierce. The violence in Kansas escalated. In the United States Senate, Charles Sumner of Massachusetts gave an inflammatory speech condemning slavery. Two days later, Representative Preston Brooks of South Carolina stormed into the Senate chamber, and beat Sumner repeatedly with a walking stick. Sumner's speech, Brooks said, was a libel on South Carolina. Sumner received permanent injuries. Massachusetts re-elected him, but he could not return to the Senate until 1859. South Carolinians hailed Brooks as a hero. The Democratic National Convention, meeting in Cincinnati, denied Pierce renomination for another term as president. The convention chose James Buchanan, instead, with John C. Breckenridge as his vice presidential running mate. "Buchanan's nomination was one more bitter pill for Free Soil Democrats, who saw him as the quintessential 'Doughface,' a northerner with southern sympathies."[16] That he was. The Democrats at the time at least could defend themselves against any charges of inconsistency.

Pierce considered himself to be a unionist. His view of Union, however, was conditioned by his acceptance of Southern attitudes. Secretary of War Jefferson Davis became his closest associate, and reinforced his already prejudiced views. "I can scarcely bear the parting from you," he wrote to Davis at the end of his term, saying that Davis had "been strength and solace to me for four anxious years and never failed me." Gara noted that this was not mere flattery. "As another national crisis loomed in 1860," he said, "Pierce proposed Davis as the best Democratic candidate for president."[17] No better reflection of his views — or of his judgment — is possible.

Pierce would not concede that different interpretations of the Constitution could be valid. If it sanctioned slavery in certain states — as clearly it did — then it must also prevent Congress from regulating slavery in the territories. His administration's actions were so biased that they encouraged the momentum already present among its opponents to form a new political party. That new Republican Party fielded its first presidential candidate in 1856, having emerged a mere two years earlier. It "formulated an ideology for the North that included deep resentment of the South's power, attachment to the American Union, both pragmatic antislavery and a moral revulsion against the institution, and a strong commitment to the economic and social order of the North." As Gara has noted, "never before had a major political organization openly pitted one section against the other."[18] When Pierce threw his support behind the South's effort to repeal the Missouri Compromise, this professed Unionist could not more surely have increased the likelihood — if not even the inevitability — of a sectional split if he had done it deliberately. Can one rank such a president? The question arises whether even if possible it would be worth the bother.

15

JAMES BUCHANAN
March 4, 1857–March 4, 1861

James Buchanan of Pennsylvania was the third ante-bellum president in a row who was from outside the South, yet who devoted himself to Southern interests. Each of these presidents has regularly appeared far down the lists of presidential rankings. Buchanan could do no better than twenty-ninth of thirty-one in the 1962 Schlesinger poll.[1] Genovese placed him thirty-sixth of thirty-nine,[2] although the Fabers viewed him more favorably, twenty-fifth of thirty-nine.[3] In fact, their impression was that Buchanan had tried hard to prevent the Civil War, and that in spite of his efforts, "he is still underrated by many historians, at least partly," they concluded, "because of his bad press."[4]

Bad press he certainly had, and in abundance, but that is hardly the reason for historians' disdain. Rather, it was Buchanan's record of vacillation, insensitivity, and disastrous policies. Baker has noted that Buchanan's own character and personality were as much the cause of his failure as were the obviously intractable national issues. "Despite his caution and prudence," she wrote, "James Buchanan was an erratic trimmer who twisted this way and that, and once he made up his mind, he stubbornly adhered to his positions."[5]

One of his biographers, Philip Klein, noted an "oddity of Buchanan's life." His travels in the United States were quite limited. "He saw more of the continent of Europe during his Russian Mission than he saw of the United States in his whole lifetime."[6] Perhaps this helps explain why he understood so little of his own country, and misjudged it so greatly. Another biographer, the thoughtful and moderate Elbert Smith, said that in the 1850s there was a desperate need in the United States for presidents who were strong and eloquent, who could understand each section and communicate that understanding to the other.[7] Buchanan's commitment to the values of the South's slaveholders clearly disqualified him to fill such a role. Smith did concede that the war was for the preservation of slavery.[8] More to the point, however, is his assumption — reflecting the Revisionist School's belief that a "blundering generation" stumbled into conflict when, with proper leaders, they might have been able to work things out amicably — that the trouble arose because "each section was slowly but inexorably developing a highly inaccurate image of the other's objectives and intentions, and only the president had the national platform from which a more balanced and realistic appraisal could emanate."[9]

On the contrary, the trouble arose because the South changed its position, and became so aggressive that the rest of the country no longer could harbor any illusion about Southern "objectives and intentions." The South's insistence upon the spread of slavery made its "objectives and intentions" crystal clear. It became difficult if not impossible to misunderstand them when Southern spokesmen rejected the view that the South had once held in common with the rest of the country: the view that slavery was an evil and ultimately should vanish. The South's new insistence that its "peculiar institution" was a "positive good" would seem to have been a clear signal of those "objectives and intentions," especially when its spokesmen threatened disunion unless they were free to take slavery anywhere in the country.

Buchanan understood the Southern position quite well, but assumed that slavery's spread was of little importance. It was the position of the rest of the country — presumably his own part of the country — that he failed adequately to understand. Whether the most skillful president could have dealt successfully with the South following Pierce's disastrous presidency is doubtful, but regardless of that, Buchanan's skills turned out to be minimal, at best.

Any glance at any randomly selected commentary on Buchanan will likely uncover a statement that rarely has a president come to office with such a strong background as Buchanan, or left it so discredited. He had been elected to the Pennsylvania legislature at the age of twenty-three, had served in both houses of Congress, had been U.S. Minister to Russia and to Great Britain, and had been Polk's secretary of state. Polk, however, had been unimpressed. He concluded — foreshadowing the Buchanan administration — that Buchanan was too timid and too erratic, and wrote in his diary that although he was able, in small matters he acted "without judgment and sometimes acts like an old maid."[10] Buchanan was to demonstrate in his presidency that his lack of judgment extended to large matters as well. An indication of that, prior to his presidency, had been his association with the Ostend Manifesto. The Manifesto had emerged from the Pierce administration, and Buchanan had been one of its major instigators. It demanded that the United States attempt to purchase Cuba from Spain. If Spain would not sell, it said, the United States should use force to seize its island neighbor. Public protest forced the Pierce administration to back away from the Manifesto, which had been a reflection of Southern desire to acquire more territory into which to expand slavery.

Buchanan was fortunate in having been in Britain as minister to the Court of St. James's during the furor over the Kansas-Nebraska Act. He had taken no position on the controversy, and had thus avoided making enemies. His absence thus strengthened his chance of receiving the Democratic presidential nomination in 1856. When the convention rejected Pierce, it turned to Buchanan. Although he did not win a majority of the popular vote — the Know-Nothing and Republican candidates polled approximately 55 percent of the vote between them — he won easily in the electoral college. At last, he had achieved his lifelong ambition. In another sense, though, Buchanan's absence during the Kansas-Nebraska chaos may have made his task even more difficult — it may have prevented him from recognizing just how serious the situation was.

In his inaugural address in March 1857, the fifteenth president said that he would serve only one term. He was sixty-five at the time, quite old to be embarking upon the office. He also condemned anti-slavery activists. The Supreme Court, he said, soon would rule regarding slavery in the territories. "I shall cheerfully submit, whatever this may be," he said of the impending ruling.

Although he pretended not to know what the decision would be, he knew very well. He had in fact, and with great impropriety, conspired with a member of the Court to influence its ruling. Buchanan's friend, Justice Catron (who was from Tennessee) had revealed to him that the decision would uphold the Missouri Supreme Court's ruling against the petitioner, Dred Scott (Scott was a slave who sought his freedom on the ground that his owner had lived with him for some years in free territory) but that it was likely to be a simple decision, unless Buchanan were to become involved.

Catron urged the president to write to a wavering Justice (James Grier of his own state of Pennsylvania) to say "how necessary it is — & how good the opportunity is, to settle the agitation by an affirmative decision." Buchanan did so, and with Grier's support, Chief Justice Taney handed down the infamous majority decision in *Dred Scott* v. *Sanford*, arguably the most outrageous ruling in the history of the Supreme Court. No Negro, Taney wrote, slave or free, could ever be a citizen. All were "unfit to associate with the White race," and all were "so far inferior that they had no rights which the white man was bound to respect." The U.S. government could not bar slavery from a territory, nor could the territory's own legislature do so. Although only three justices supported Taney's conclusion denying citizenship to blacks, "it quickly became the official law of the land."[11]

Buchanan's reaction to the *Dred Scott* decision reflects just how incredibly deficient was his understanding of the entire situation — of the South's aggressiveness, and also of the reaction to it. He considered all the sectional trouble to have resulted from anti-slavery agitation. Moreover, he was confident that the Court, in *Dred Scott*, had settled the issue. There would be no more controversy regarding slavery in the territories.

For his cabinet, rather than selecting officials to balance various interests in his party, he selected men, mainly Southerners or Southern sympathizers, with whom he was comfortable. For secretary of state he chose the elderly Lewis Cass who had lost the presidential race in 1848 to Zachary Taylor. Two Southerners, Howell Cobb of Georgia and John B. Floyd of Virginia, became secretaries of the treasury and war respectively. He chose his friend Jeremiah Black from Pennsylvania for attorney general. He selected Isaac Toucey from Connecticut for secretary of the navy, and Aaron Brown of Tennessee for postmaster general (Brown died in office; his replacement was Joseph Holt of Kentucky). Jacob Thompson of Mississippi became his secretary of the interior. Because of his hatred for Sen. Stephen A. Douglas, he chose no representative of the Douglas faction. The makeup of his cabinet almost assured that the president would receive little conflicting advice.

Buchanan may have been able to avoid commitment on the Kansas question before he became president, but he could not ignore it afterward. As Kansas's territorial governor, he appointed Robert Walker of Mississippi. During his governorship, pro-slavery forces met in Lecompton to hold a constitutional convention. Walker urged that the people should approve any constitution, but the Lecompton document provided that they could vote only to admit, or not admit, *additional* slaves into Kansas. Over Walker's objections, Buchanan urged that Congress admit Kansas under the Lecompton Constitution. Congress rejected the measure, however, with Senator Stephen Douglas vigorously leading the opposition. It violated his principle of popular sovereignty. Ultimately, the Lecompton Constitution was the subject of first one and then another referendum. Both times it failed, overwhelmingly. When Kansas finally did become a state, in 1861 before Buchanan left office, it was without slavery. Minnesota also entered the Union during his administration, in 1858.

Other matters added to Buchanan's woes. Buchanan was well known for being meticulous in his own financial dealings, but a congressional investigation concluded that government money funded Democratic candidates, that there had been "public printing contracts" involving "kickbacks and bribes," and that there also had been offers of bribes to members of Congress in return for votes favorable to the Lecompton Constitution." Buchanan fired Secretary of War Floyd, partly as a result of the scandals. Postmaster General Joseph Holt (who had been responsible for the famed Pony Express) moved over to replace Floyd in the War Department. The Republicans, of course, gleefully printed these charges in their campaign literature in 1860. Fairly or not, Gienapp has written that "Buchanan presided over the most corrupt administration in American history before the Civil War."[12] In 1857, the country entered a severe economic depression — a panic. After the Republican victory in 1860, South Carolina seceded. Others states followed, so that the entire Deep South was gone shortly after the new year began.

Buchanan said that secession was unconstitutional, but also that he had no power to do anything about it. The elderly and changeable Secretary of State Cass had urged the president to reinforce U.S. forts in the South, and resigned when Buchanan refused. Attorney General Black then moved over to the State Department, and Buchanan appointed Edwin Stanton of Ohio as attorney general in his place. Secretary of the Treasury Howell Cobb had been Buchanan's closest confidant, but both he and Secretary of the Interior Jacob Thompson of Mississippi resigned from the cabinet to join the Confederacy.

Buchanan had always been a Unionist, and thus opposed secession. Whether it was the effect of a new and non–Southern cabinet, or simply that he had finally had enough, Buchanan did ultimately request that Congress provide for military preparedness. Congress refused.

Buchanan's Southern friends, one by one, shunned him as a traitor. Outside the South, his more extreme detractors charged him with treason in the other direction. He was a Judas; he fostered secession; he sold his country to the South. In his defense, he hardly caused the war — it had been long in coming. He had, however, played a part in the *Dred Scott* case, that dreadful case. He had fanned the flames by observing in public that Kansas "was as much a slave state as Georgia or South Carolina." "When Republicans and Northern Democrats passed legislation designed for economic progress, Buchanan contributed vetoes based upon obsolete principles directly attributable to the South." Even after secession, his message to Congress "echoed the Southern complaints and further alienated Northerners."[13]

Although he clearly had indicated that he would serve only one term, accounts frequently say that the convention in 1860 refused to renominate him. To be sure, some of his friends did foster the idea that he sought to be re-elected, but the evidence is to the contrary. Klein quoted not only Buchanan's own statement that he "positively would not accept a renomination," but similar comments from numerous letters to friends "expressing his 'final and irrevocable' determination to retire." Buchanan wrote to Mrs. Polk that he was sixty-nine and tired of being president, said Klein, concluding that there is "no reason to believe he was not sincere."[14] Apparently, therefore, he did leave office voluntarily. His comment when he rode with Lincoln to the new president's inaugural has been repeated over and over. "My dear sir," he said, "if you are as happy in entering the White House as I shall feel on returning to Wheatland, you are a happy man indeed."[15]

Buchanan meant well, and he tried. His abilities were unequal to the challenge. Worse, his principles were shocking, especially by today's standards. Even by the standards of his day they were so outmoded as to be inexcusable.

He thought, though, that he had done well, and spent the rest of his life defending his administration. In 1866 he published his memoirs, *Mr. Buchanan's Administration on the Eve of the Rebellion.* He was not responsible for the troubles; rather, he asserted, they had come from anti-slavery agitation. To his credit — and in contrast to his predecessor, Franklin Pierce — he did support President Lincoln's war effort, and rejected the Democratic Party's appeasement plank of 1864. To his discredit, he opposed emancipation, and could never reconcile himself to black suffrage.[16]

James Buchanan died at the age of seventy-seven, on 1 June, 1868. Shortly before his death, he expressed confidence that history would vindicate him and his administration. It has not. Nor is it clear that comparing this sad and disastrous president with others enhances our understanding.

16

ABRAHAM LINCOLN
March 4, 1861–April 15, 1865

In 1860, Abraham Lincoln won election as the first Republican president. The party had only been in existence since 1854. In bringing it to the forefront of American politics, Lincoln defeated three other candidates. He received less than a majority of the popular vote (just under 40 percent of the total), but won an easy victory in the electoral college. He has come to be recognized quite widely not only as his party's greatest president, but as the greatest in America's history — it is not an exaggeration to say that many Americans and others would rate him the greatest *American* in history.[1] Even a brief survey of his accomplishments is enough for objective and perceptive observers to establish this; no formal ranking is necessary. Lincoln saved America — it is as simple as that. Less simply, but almost as assuredly, he saved the possibility of government by the people as well.

By the time of Lincoln's inauguration on 4 March 1861, South Carolina had already led a series of states to secede. That was only the beginning. As Lincoln scholar James G. Randall put it, "secession grew state by state till it quickly engulfed the lower South. Well before Lincoln's inauguration seven states had gone out of the Union...."[2] Together they had formed the Confederate States of America — quickly to include eleven states — and elected Jefferson Davis president.

Shortly thereafter, on 12 April, the Confederates fired on Fort Sumter. His response should have come as no surprise, because "as president-elect, Lincoln had made it known that if President James Buchanan gave up the forts, he would retake them."[3] In the absence of aggression from the South, however, he presented no military threat. In fact, the Republicans as a party had not called for abolition, and by no means was it an abolitionist party.

Lincoln personally had assured the South that he could not constitutionally interfere with their "peculiar institution," and therefore would not do so.

Because he already interpreted the Constitution to forbid federal interference with the domestic institutions of any state, he even said in his Inaugural Address that he would have no objection to an amendment that made explicit such a limitation on federal authority. With a clarity unavailable to many observers in later generations, Lincoln went on to explain the disagreement. There was only one issue in substantial dispute between the sections, he said. One believed that slavery was right and should be extended, while the other believed that it was wrong and should not be. "In *your* hands, my dissatisfied fellow-countrymen," he proceeded to say in his Address, " and not in *mine*, is the momentous issue of civil war. The government will not assail *you*. You can have no conflict, without being yourselves the aggressors. *You* have no oath registered in Heaven to destroy the government, while *I* shall have the most solemn one to 'preserve, protect and defend' it."[4]

The assurances did not matter. Southern leaders had come to insist not only that slavery prevail in the South, not only that it be permitted to expand through the territories, not only that the rest of the country accept bondage, but that the rest of the country also cease its criticism and declare that it had accepted slavery as a moral institution. This, the nation refused to do. This, President Abraham Lincoln would not, and could not, do. And, as he said, the war came.

A later president, Theodore Roosevelt, who also was an accomplished historian, took issue with a friend who said that every quarrel has two sides. At a time early in the twentieth century when Southern vindicators were rewriting history and coming close to saying that virtue and right were completely on the side of the South, Roosevelt said that "as regards the actual act of secession, the actual opening of the Civil War, I think the right was exclusively with the Union people and the wrong exclusively with the secessionists; and indeed," he said, "I do not know of another struggle in history in which the sharp division between right and wrong can be made in quite so clear-cut a manner."[5] Roosevelt's mother was from the South and had sympathized with the Confederacy, and all his life he had taken pride in the heroic deeds of his maternal uncles who fought for the South. He was too keen an observer, however, to ignore the facts. Slavery and secession were indefensible.

A mini-war already had taken place in Kansas. The true war began when Southern states seceded to form the Confederate States of America, took military action against American installations, and, on 6 May 1861, declared war upon the United States. Congress was in adjournment. Rather than call a special session, Lincoln acted on his own initiative. He issued a call for troops, he expended funds for arms and military preparations, he ordered a blockade of the Southern coast, and he suspended the writ of *habeas corpus* in certain areas. Later, however, he did call a special session, and Congress approved his actions.

War dominated the whole of Lincoln's presidency, a circumstance that no other president has had to face. Despite this, during his administration — freed from the obstructive votes of representatives and senators from the South — there were significant domestic accomplishments.[6] In 1862 Lincoln signed into law four significant pieces of legislation. The Homestead Act greatly encouraged settlement in the plains states after the war. Earlier, the South had blocked such a program because of fears that it would encourage westward migration without slavery. The Pacific Railroad Act was the first national inducement for a transcontinental railroad. The Morrill Act granted public lands to the states to sell and create agricultural and mechanical colleges. It was this farseeing legislation — named for its sponsor, Representative Justin Morrill of Vermont — that made possible a vast democratization of American higher education and led to the creation of the great land-grant universities. The third act provided for the first income tax in U.S. history. Congress repealed the law after the war, but it had "established what until then was considered a revolutionary principle: the idea of taxing rich people at a higher rate compared to the rate for people less well off." It was to become "a permanent feature of the American political and economic landscape."[7] Those of the "anarcho-capitalist-libertarian" school have never forgiven him for thus encouraging the emergence of a modern nation-state, nor for playing a significant role in 1863 in securing the National Banking Act. It sought to "eliminate the chaos of a national system dominated by state banks," and provided federal inspection for national banks "overseen by a new position called Comptroller of the Currency."[8] Additionally, two states, Nevada and West Virginia, joined the Union during the Lincoln administration.

Once the war did come, it created new possibilities for the president. As a democratic leader within a constitutional structure, Lincoln's domestic authority was limited. However much he was opposed personally to slavery, he had no power to move against it. But with the military emergency came new presidential powers. As LaWanda Cox, one of the most perceptive Lincoln scholars, wrote, "war, and the participation of blacks as soldiers, made it possible to 'do better.' And Lincoln did. Keeping political support intact, he moved from his prewar advocacy of restricting slavery's spread to a foremost responsibility for slavery's total, immediate, uncompensated destruction by constitutional amendment."[9]

The care that he took to keep political support made his progress seem slow and reluctant to frustrated observers in his day and to unperceptive ones in ours. Had he attempted to move quickly, however, he would have failed.

It would have taken little to frighten the slaveholding border states into secession. Keeping them from the Confederacy meant, in the case of Kentucky alone, some four hundred miles of buffer to protect the Union. In the case of Maryland, it meant preventing the national capital from being surrounded by hostile territory. Modern critics nevertheless occasionally fault Lincoln for not doing more to implement what we would call "affirmative action."

Such criticism reflects complete ignorance of what was possible at the time, and it fails also to recognize just how much Lincoln accomplished. In contrast to many interpretations, Lincoln's Emancipation Proclamation was an immensely bold step. It went much further than anything Congress had done regarding slavery. Instead of requiring slaves to seek their freedom on a case-by-case basis, it was "a sweeping blow against bondage as an institution in the rebel states, a blow that would free all the slaves there — those of secessionists and Unionists alike."[10] Rather than being of minor importance, as J. G. Randall had alleged, "it was the most revolutionary measure ever to come from an American president up to that time. This 'momentous decree,' as Martin Luther King, Jr., rightly described it, was an unprecedented use of federal military power against a state institution. It was an unprecedented federal assault against the very foundation of the South's planter class and economic and social order."[11] Nor was Lincoln's own generation under any illusion as to the significance of the Proclamation. Oates remarked that the wonder is "that Lincoln stuck by a measure that aroused such public indignation."[12]

It is common to hear that Lincoln has been the subject of more words written in the English language than any person other than Jesus. The Civil War, similarly, has been the subject of countless accounts, and it was the war that consumed Lincoln's attention during his presidency. The war's details are familiar. Evaluating the Lincoln presidency thus does not require minute scrutiny of Lincoln's actions, or a repetition of the many existing accounts of the Civil War. It is sufficient simply to consider what Lincoln accomplished, and to recognize that the challenges he faced far exceeded those of any other president, including even Washington.

Through the exercise of enormous political skill and constant effort, the president turned a war for Union into a war for equality — in a country not sympathetic to equality. He certainly saved the United States of America, and quite possibly he preserved the principle of constitutionally restrained democratic government that now characterizes much of the world. He did this with determination, with consummate political skill, with a sensitivity to the minds of his fellow citizens, and with an unparalleled ability to craft the English language and imbue it with a persuasive and poetic appeal.[13]

His genius at rhetoric was one of the major keys to Lincoln's success.

Because of his commitment, his growth, and his skill the war that began as a defense of Union, ended as a moral crusade for political equality — and Abraham Lincoln was its leader. Garry Wills, in his brilliant *Lincoln at Gettysburg*, has documented the shift.[14] His subtitle, *The Words that Remade America*, captured Lincoln's achievement. He did remake America's view of itself, and he did so with words, especially in two of the greatest political utterances in history, the Gettysburg Address and his Second Inaugural.[15] Despite the myth that he prepared his speech at Gettysburg hurriedly, Wills made it clear that Lincoln crafted it with extraordinary care, and that he knew precisely what he was doing. He was skilled at speaking and acting, his "text was polished, his delivery emphatic, he was interrupted by applause five times. Read in a slow, clear way to the farthest listeners, the speech would take about three minutes." He did exactly what he intended to do, and "we are still trying to weigh the consequences of that amazing performance."[16] He knew what he had accomplished.

Lincoln had used "the power of his rhetoric to define war aims." He had searched for "occasions to use his words outside the normal round of proclamations and reports to Congress," and this was his prime opportunity. He had been determined "not only to be present," at Gettysburg, "but to speak."[17] He did so, and his words still resonate. He did not mention slavery. Rather, said Wills, he drove the discussion "back and back, beyond the historical particulars, to great ideals that are made to grapple naked in an airy battle of the mind." He derived a "new, a transcendental, significance from this bloody episode." He won the Civil War "in ideological terms as well as in military ones." And, against all odds, he succeeded. "The Civil War *is*, to most Americans, what Lincoln wanted it to *mean*. Words had to complete the work of the guns."[18]

Of course there were those then and later who recognized what Lincoln had done — that, as Wills put it, he had performed a "giant (if benign) swindle." The old *Chicago Times*, a Democratic paper, blasted the president as having betrayed the Constitution. It said that the Founders had "too much self-respect to declare that negroes were their equals, or were entitled to equal privileges." Wills noted that heirs to that "outrage still attack Lincoln for subverting the Constitution at Gettysburg — suicidally frank conservatives," he called them in a delicious phrase, "like M. E. Bradford or the late Willmoore Kendall." Most conservatives, though, Wills noted, have been too prudent to challenge Lincoln's "clever assault on the constitutional past" that now has become so hallowed.[19]

Certainly the average Confederate soldier fought to defend his home, rather then to defend slavery. It nevertheless is important to recognize that however he viewed it his leaders had sent him to war to defend their Peculiar Institution. It is important also, even though the average Union soldier certainly did not go to war to defend equal rights for blacks, that America today views the Civil War as the great struggle for political equality and democracy which, because of Lincoln, it became.

Few of those today who fault Lincoln for one thing or another have given thought to what might have happened had there been no Lincoln in the presidency, or what the consequences might have been had he failed. Arthur Schlesinger, Jr., is an exception. He remarked upon the Civil War's terrible toll, but noted approvingly how one "amateur historian of impeccable Confederate ancestry justified the war," a century later.[20] That "amateur historian" had written a commentary on an article by MacKinlay Kantor in *Look* Magazine, "If the South Had Won the Civil War." That writer speculated on what would have happened if Lee had won at Gettysburg:

> England would have recognized the Confederacy, and France would have stayed in Mexico with a French Empire from Panama to the Rio Grande.... The Northwest would have seceded from the Northeast and taken over 54/40. Russia would have kept Alaska and in all probability have taken all Northwest Canada.
>
> There would have been the Northwest Republic, the Northeast Republic, the Confederate Republic, the Mexican Empire in the Southwest, with California, Utah, Arizona and New Mexico as part of that Empire.
>
> And the Bolsheviks would have had the whole Northwest, and what then? Maybe the Northeast and the Southeast could have created an alliance and held the Russians at the Mississippi. Isn't it great to contemplate?
>
> My sympathies and my family were on the side of the South. But I think the organization of the greatest republic in the history of the world was worth all the sacrifices made to save it.
>
> Harry S Truman
> Independence, Mo.

And one thing that President Truman did not mention is that the Confederate Republic, assuming that it survived as a republic, would have maintained a system of human slavery. Because of Abraham Lincoln, there no longer was a likelihood of an extensive system of human slavery existing in the western world throughout the twentieth century and on in to the twenty-first.

For Lincoln to have accomplished what he did required superb political skills as well as steeled determination. The historian John Hope Franklin summed up those skills. Lincoln, he said:

> successfully urged the admission of Republican-dominated Nevada in time for its electoral votes to be counted. He ordered the furlough of many soldiers who wanted to go to their homes to vote, confident that the majority of them would vote for their Commander-in-Chief. He had been responsible for the disintegration of the opposition within the party and for undermining the arguments and proposals advanced by the Democrats. The political victory of 1864 was therefore in a real sense a Lincoln victory.[21]

The early years of his administration, moreover, had brought defeat after defeat, but Lincoln slowly and carefully managed to pull things together. For a time, he assumed he could not be re-elected. The historian Bruce Catton wrote of the "little slip of paper he filed away in a pigeonhole"—a note expressing his doubts and promising cooperation with the victor in 1864—and expressed his awe at Lincoln's strength of will. "There have been few bitter-end fighters in all history quite as tenacious as Abraham Lincoln," he said.[22]

Stephen Oates has pointed out, along with LaWanda Cox, that it is necessary to consider what was possible in the 1860s when evaluating Lincoln and the later Republicans. It was, he noted, "a white-supremacist era in which a vast number of Northern whites were hostile to black freedom." Nevertheless, Lincoln issued the Emancipation Proclamation, and he "used all the powers and prestige of his office to get the present Thirteenth Amendment through a recalcitrant House of Representatives." The Senate already had passed it. The Amendment, which Lincoln signed personally (even though no presidential action is required on an amendment) ended slavery throughout the country. Oates quoted Frederick Douglass as perhaps the best at summing up Lincoln and emancipation. "From the genuine abolition view, Mr. Lincoln seemed tardy, cold, dull, and indifferent, but measuring him by the sentiment of his country—a sentiment that he was bound as a statesman to consult—he was swift, zealous, radical, and determined."[23]

It was Abraham Lincoln who grounded America's political thought in the Declaration of Independence. It was he who set in motion the "Lincoln Myth" that continues to help cement Americans' sense of cohesion. It was he who, more than any other single figure, directed America toward a biracial democracy—or more broadly toward the fundamental goal of political democracy. It was Abraham Lincoln who made possible the standards that have become the aspiration of self-governing countries around the world.[24]

We could ask no more of any president. We could expect so much of no president. But he accomplished it, sacrificing his life as a result.

17

ANDREW JOHNSON
April 15, 1865–March 4, 1869

Abraham Lincoln died on the morning of April 15, 1865. A crazed assassin, obsessed with outrage that the president might bring about equality for blacks, shot him during a performance at Ford's Theater the evening before. The attack had taken place on Good Friday. Vice President Andrew Johnson was the new President of the United States.

Lincoln's assassination "removed from the political scene a master politician who tried to balance conciliation with justice and understood how to frame policy in accordance with circumstances." But the course of reconstruction between 1865 and 1869 reflects more than his absence. "Just as important was the man who became president" succeeding him. "No other single individual contributed more to the shaping of the contours of reconstruction policy" than Andrew Johnson.[1]

The fallen President Lincoln had recognized that the defeated South must be integrated back into the United States; it had to be reconstructed. The Republican Party, unfortunately, had chosen in 1864 to rely on a Union ticket, rather than to re-nominate Vice President Hannibal Hamlin to run for a second term as a Republican with Lincoln. It replaced Hamlin with a former Democrat, Andrew Johnson. Johnson was from Tennessee, where Lincoln had appointed him military governor with the rank of brigadier general. He was a loyal Unionist, angered at secession and at the economic elites of the South who had imposed it upon the region's common people — its common white people.

Historians in recent years have tended to be rather harsh regarding Andrew Johnson, just as his enemies in Congress had been — and with good reason. His contemporaries, and those who wrote of Johnson in the years

135

following his presidency, were under no illusion about the damage that he inflicted. That he rated better in the first part of the twentieth century reflected the Southern bias that dominated American history in that period. That he rates even as well as he does today reflects the continuing influence — now often unconscious — of that bias.

Johnson was a man whose considerable political skills had been effective in the rough and tumble world of Tennessee politics, but who did not adapt well to the world of Washington. He was an old Jacksonian, but without Jackson's broad view and with none of Jackson's ability to grow — at least to some degree — with the times. In addition to being a strong Unionist, he was a man of energy and determination who fought for his principles — among which were education and religious freedom. Some writers understandably have admired him for these reasons. Unfortunately, not all of his principles were so laudable; many of those that he defended so avidly — especially in the early days of Reconstruction — were destructive in the extreme.

The Fabers placed Johnson twenty-second of the thirty-nine presidents they rated; their comments regarding the seventeenth president were gentle, if not especially perceptive.[2] Clinton Rossiter grouped presidents with eight as great, and six who "turned in creditable or at least unusual performances." Among these he included "Andrew Johnson, a man of few talents but much courage, whose protests against the ravages of the Radicals in Congress," he said, "were a high rather than a low point in the progress of the presidency."[3] The 1962 Schlesinger poll placed him twenty-third on its list of thirty-one. That was at the bottom of the "average" category,[4] but Genovese put him thirty-fifth of thirty-nine, the top of his list of failures.[5] There thus is more variation regarding Johnson than with many presidents. This is understandable because he presents a great mixture of qualities, but it also reflects how a single ranking cannot capture him or produce a good picture of his performance.

Johnson was a self-made man with no formal education whatever. His devotion to the Union and his concern for the Constitution, for the common people, and for states' rights would have been unexceptional in the early days of Jackson's Democratic Party. An ideology that might have been able to bring him triumph at that earlier time had become wholly unsuited for the period in which he occupied the presidential office. He was at least as stubborn as Jackson, and considerably less able than Jackson to recognize that changed conditions required changed policies.

As his foremost biographer, Hans Trefousse, put it, Johnson's accession to the presidency had "fateful consequences — for the freedmen, for their former masters, and for the country." Nothing could be further from the truth, he said, than the common statement that Johnson merely carried Lincoln's plans for reconstruction into effect — although Johnson always purported to be doing just that. Lincoln's proposals had been wartime measures designed as much to further the war effort as to restore the seceded states. "When Johnson became president, however, the war was virtually over, and what Lincoln might have done in times of peace is a largely unanswered question."[6] There is one thing, though, said Trefousse, that is clear. Whatever Lincoln would have done regarding reconstruction would have been different from what Johnson did.

Lincoln "openly advocated limited black suffrage in Louisiana" in his last public address. Moreover, there were radical differences in the two men's views on freedmen's rights. "To be sure, Johnson had belatedly endorsed emancipation — he even promised to be the black man's Moses — but his deep-seated racial antipathies never faded away. Lincoln, on the other hand, had gradually come to realize the possibility of black development in the United States, a change of outlook he made so abundantly clear in his last speech."[7]

Two additional differences also were obvious. The first was a difference in abilities. "Lincoln with his sense of timing was a supreme pragmatist. While adhering firmly to certain fundamental principles, he knew how to yield when it was necessary to do so. Johnson, too, was capable of making political compromises, but his manner of dealing with adversaries was much less subtle" than Lincoln's. The second was political philosophy. Lincoln was a former Whig who continued always to concede "some concurrent powers to Congress. Johnson, a good Jacksonian, firmly believed in the power of the executive to direct Reconstruction policies."[8]

Regardless of his administration's ultimate fate, Johnson began his presidency cautiously. He "had adopted a policy of letting people think what they wanted to think."[9] Initially, he spoke less forthrightly and more soothingly than he had done at times earlier in his career. There was "no controversial airing of his views." He sought to reassure the country that "he would carry on the government as before."[10] He also used Lincoln's legacy for his own purposes. Because much of Lincoln's plan for the defeated South had remained ill-defined, it was a "malleable tool for Johnson to manipulate." He could pick and choose from Lincoln's comments, and sometimes even fabricate or misrepresent Lincoln's position.[11]

He also avoided giving any credence to the widespread rumor that he was an alcoholic. During his inauguration as vice president hardly more than a month previously, Johnson had been ill and had fortified himself with several substantial belts of whiskey. He left no doubt that he was drunk on that ceremonial occasion, but there is no evidence that this was typical or that he was a heavy drinker. Nothing of the sort marred his inauguration as president, but he had given his opponents ammunition to use against him.

He chose to keep Lincoln's cabinet, which helped to reassure the public. Also, as a gesture of courtesy to Mary Lincoln, he offered to let her stay in the executive mansion until she could get her affairs in order. Several weeks passed before he actually took up residence in the president's house. He also asserted, without providing details, that he wished to prosecute Confederate leaders. Johnson made a favorable impression, but it was not to last.

On the 29th of May 1865 he issued two proclamations. One dealt with the manner in which North Carolina would structure its government. The other extended a pardon that included nearly all the former Confederates. Those not included could apply for pardon on an individual basis.

Excluded were hose who had been officials of the U. S. government or the U. S. military, and those who had held high positions in the Confederate government. Additionally, the proclamation also withheld pardons from all those owning property worth over $20,000. This latter provision raised the prospect of confiscation and redistribution of land, as Johnson had discussed before becoming president. Such a move could have been consistent with his commitment to the "common people," and his hostility toward wealthy secessionists, but any distribution would have been limited to white farmers. In any case, he soon dispelled any thought of confiscation and redistribution. He ordered restoration of all confiscated lands to the previous owners, and began to issue individual pardons liberally.

Moreover, he refused to order the enfranchisement of blacks. At times, he had suggested that states consider granting the vote to certain freedmen, those who were literate and relatively affluent. No state, however, followed his suggestion and he took no action to force — or even to encourage — them to do so.

Johnson's view was that secession is unconstitutional; therefore no state had ever been out of the Union. His conclusion from that was that no state had to be "reconstructed." His Jacksonian states-rights philosophy convinced him that states knew best what was best for them. It also led him to oppose federal funding for internal improvements or for education. As governor of Tennessee, he strongly supported public schools. As president, he refused to do so because of his restricted view of what the Constitution permitted.

Moreover, he believed that it was Southern whites who knew what was best for the black population. His lenient policies led to the election in state after state of former Confederates to head their new governments, and to represent them in Congress. Under his policies the states also were free to enact "black codes," that placed restrictions upon the civil rights of black citizens so severe that many observers charged that the South was systematically re-enslaving blacks. Northern opinion did not appear to be inflamed by denial of suffrage to blacks, but the rash of violence and the arrogance of Southern leaders led many to question whether the war had been in vain, and whether Johnson would do anything about it. He did not. He did not even act to counter the Ku Klux Klan when it emerged as a terrorist guerilla army to intimidate black citizens. Its clear purpose, was to negate — to the extent possible — the effect of the Thirteenth Amendment that abolished slavery. One historian remarked that Johnson knew full well "what was going on; he simply did not deem it important or unexpected."[12]

His troubles reached a crisis point when Congress passed, over his veto, a series of measures that he forcefully opposed. These included, among others, a Civil Rights Act, an act continuing the Freedmen's Bureau, and a Reconstruction Act. It was not enough to veto the acts — he condemned them with intemperate language, and attempted to appeal directly to the people. Nor did he attempt to exploit differences among Republicans that he might have used to his advantage. Rather, he belligerently made enemies of congressional Republicans as a whole. Johnson told the *New York Post*'s Charles Nordhoff, that "the people of the South, poor, quiet, unoffending, harmless, are to be trodden under foot to protect niggers."[13]

Violating 19th-century standards of propriety, he embarked upon an extensive speaking tour, his "Swing Around the Circle," to harangue audiences seeking their support. He continued to use intemperate language, and permitted himself to become engaged in shouting matches with hecklers. Even his supporters were disturbed. Johnson also lobbied state governments to oppose the Fourteenth Amendment, but they ratified it nonetheless, as they had ratified the Thirteenth.

There were numerous other vetoes as well. One involved an act enfranchising black residents of the District of Columbia. He did not dispute Congress's authority to pass the act, but local residents in a December, 1865, special election, had overwhelmingly rejected black suffrage. Congress overturned that veto as well. All told, in his one term of office President Andrew Johnson vetoed twenty-nine acts of Congress, more than twice the number of any president before him — though far from a record. He does hold the record, however, for the number of his vetoes that Congress overrode: fifteen.[14]

He refused to be influenced by a delegation of freedmen that included Frederick Douglass, imploring him to support suffrage. Johnson told the delegation that "the people" would have to decide, and that while Negroes had gained a great deal from the war, the poor whites were the losers. His private secretary told Philip Ripley of the *New York World* that "the President no more expected that darkey delegation yesterday than he did the cholera." Ripley reported that the president had said: "Those d____d sons of b____s thought they had me in a trap. I know that d____d Douglass; he's just like any nigger, & he would sooner cut a white man's throat than not."[15] As historian Brooks Simpson remarked, "the contrast with Lincoln's favorable impression of Douglass could not have been more marked."[16]

Fearing to add Republican votes in Congress, Johnson also vetoed legislation providing for statehood for Nebraska and Colorado. Congress overrode the Nebraska veto, and Nebraska became a state during his administration. The Colorado veto, however, stood.[17] Colorado did not become a state until 1876, during Grant's second term.

In response to Johnson's forceful opposition, Congress passed the Tenure of Office Act, again over his veto. The law — itself of doubtful constitutionality — limited the president's power to remove appointed officials without the Senate's consent. Johnson defied the law and removed Secretary of War Stanton. Before it was all over, Stanton, in a bizarre move, refused to go, and barricaded himself in his office.

The House impeached Johnson, but the Senate — by merely a single vote — failed to provide the two-thirds majority required to convict. Despite the serious issues, the impeachment and trial were obviously political. Johnson's defense team was skillful, but other factors were also important. Foremost among them was a sense of duty on the part of some of the seven Republicans who voted for acquittal.

Edmund G. Ross of Kansas, for example — later immortalized for his action in John F. Kennedy's book on the Senate, *Profiles in Courage* — wrote that "the impeachment of the President, was an assault upon the principle of coordination that underlies our political system," and thus would be a menace that would lead to the destruction of the "Executive Department." Another Republican voting for acquittal was Lyman Trumbull of Illinois. He said, perceptively, that if the removal of a president because of the "excitement of the hour" had succeeded, "no future President will be safe who happens to differ with a majority of the House and two-thirds of the Senate on any measure deemed by them important." This would be particularly true, he said, if the issue were political. The checks and balances of the Constitution, he continued, "so carefully devised and so vital to its perpetuity" would be gone.[18] Almost any reasoned observer who understands the importance of the presidency in the American political system would have to agree.

President Johnson had less than a year remaining in his term when the Senate voted, in May of 1868, to acquit him. His influence for the rest of his presidency was even less than it had been. Impeachment and acquittal, however, had little effect on reconstruction. "He had already done his damage several years earlier, especially in the first twenty months of his presidency."[19]

On Christmas Day in the year of his impeachment he issued a general amnesty for all who had rebelled against the United States. He had hoped that the Democrats would turn to him as their candidate, but they chose Horatio Seymour of New York instead. The Republicans selected the extremely popular hero of the Civil War, Ulysses S. Grant — whom Johnson, in a clumsy and unsuccessful attempt to undermine, had made a bitter enemy — as their candidate. Grant won substantially in the popular vote, and overwhelmingly in the electoral college.

On the day of Grant's inauguration, the newly elected president rode up in his carriage to the gate of the executive mansion, only to be told that President Johnson was too busy to come out. "Whether Grant rebuffed Johnson by declining to invite him earlier, or whether Johnson snubbed Grant by refusing to attend remains in dispute. But for the third and last time in American history an outgoing president did not accompany his successor on the ceremonial trip to take the oath of office."[20]

Johnson returned to his home in Greeneville, Tennessee. Grateful citizens had strung a banner across the street lauding Andrew Johnson, as a patriot. When he had been military governor of the state, the citizens had displayed a different banner entirely, one condemning him as a traitor.

Trefousse has observed that Johnson achieved what he sought, at least in the long run. There were viable governments in the Southern states within the Union, and white supremacy prevailed. "His boost to Southern conservatives by undermining Reconstruction was his legacy to the nation," Trefousse said, "one that would trouble the country for generations to come."[21]

Could things have been different? A number of observers in Johnson's own day and later — before the contamination of historical understanding by the Southern vindicators — were convinced that they could have been. One newspaper reporter in the North, John T. Trowbridge of the *New York Herald*, said of Johnson's policies that the more lenient the government became, the more arrogant were the Southern leaders. "Now," he said, "they do not plead for mercy, but demand their rights."[22] This was not a unique conclusion, nor was it limited to the North. Initially, the South was broken, and stunned by defeat. But with Johnson in control, everything had changed. Southerners had been "ready for almost anything. As the editor of the *Raleigh Press* told the newspaperman Whitlaw Reid in the summer of 1865, they were 'willing to acquiesce in whatever basis of reorganization the President would prescribe.' Even black suffrage 'would be preferable to remaining unorganized and would be accepted by the people.' Johnson missed this opportunity to inaugurate a policy that would at least have protected the minimum rights of the freedmen."[23] At the very minimum he could have encouraged the development of a Republican Party, and thus a two-party system, providing viable political alternatives in the South. Instead, he feuded with the Republicans and threw his lot in with the Democrats, the segregationists, and — ultimately — with the Southern elites whom he had hated.

Johnson's personal success in upholding states' rights and white supremacy was the nation's failure, and the South's. It ushered in a century of bitterness, backwardness, and violence against the South's black citizens.

It left a legacy that troubles the country to this day, after nearly a century and a half. Things could have been different.

Andrew Johnson was, and remained, a classic Jacksonian Democrat, without, unfortunately, Jackson's capacity for growth. He became President of the United States — a disastrous president, whose stubbornness brought him impeachment and near removal from office. Oddly, however, although he failed to wrest the South from the control of its economic elites, in one very real sense he had been a successful president. He achieved one of his primary goals: expansion of the United States. In 1867 Secretary of State Seward negotiated the sale of Alaska from Russia to the United States. The purchase was at first ridiculed as "Seward's folly," but it soon became clear that ownership of the vast territory was a great boon to the United States. He achieved another goal to which he was equally devoted: a white man's South. His success in this instance was America's tragedy — and also that of the South.

18

ULYSSES S. GRANT
March 4, 1869–March 4, 1877

Historians, beginning in the early twentieth century, have tended to look askance at the Grant presidency. Those who produce rankings have been almost unanimous in placing Grant near or even at the bottom. The Fabers, for example, went to great lengths to condemn his record — naming not a single source — and ranked him "in last place by a large margin."[1] The historians in the 1962 Schlesinger poll[2] rated him only marginally better, next to last, as did Genovese.[3] President Warren G. Harding occupied the one position below him in each of these rankings. Schlesinger, Jr.'s, 1996 poll put him sixth from the bottom, but still in the group of "failures"[4]— though less harsh than most he pointed out that neither Grant nor Harding was "villainous," and asked whether each really deserved his customarily low ranking.[5] Genovese's comments were a good summary of the conventional wisdom: "Grant is considered a failure as president. His limited view of the office, limited experience, and limited abilities all contributed to this failure, as did the rise of congressional assertiveness. He is most remembered for the scandals that took place during his tenure."[6] One suspects that even in Colorado, which became a state during his administration, few citizens could find anything good to say about the eighteenth president.

Recently, however, scholars have decided to look at Grant's record for themselves, rather than accepting the "conventional wisdom" without question. That is, some of them have decided to do their job rather than relying upon others to form their conclusions for them. The result has been new opinion regarding Grant's presidency, and revelations regarding the basis for his unfavorable reputation — the reason that he indeed is remembered as president most for the scandals during his administration.

The tendency has been to assume that Grant's presidency lacked accomplishment. On the contrary, his accomplishments were substantial. In view of the conditions existing at the time he held office, they were remarkable.

First, there is the allegation of Grant's political naiveté. It is true that the new president frequently made decisions with little or no consultation, but this was a habit that carried over from his enormously successful military career. He was far from a political innocent. "During the Civil War and the early years of Reconstruction he had displayed an awareness of the larger political issues connected with the war and its resolution; he had usually played politics skillfully in his relationships with his civil superiors and fellow officers."[7] During Andrew Johnson's presidency he had to serve as a buffer between the Radical Republicans in Congress who sought retribution against the South, and a president who had no intention of seeing it happen, or of seeing rights granted to the newly freed slaves.

It was a role that he performed with skill. After Lincoln's assassination, "Grant," said his biographer Jean Edward Smith, "had carried the burden of reconstruction. He had demobilized the world's largest army, maintained order in the West, assisted in the overthrow of the Archduke Maximilian in Mexico, and ushered the freedmen of the South into a new era. He had steered adroitly," Smith said, between the radicals in Congress and an obstructionist president, "and when Johnson chose to do battle," Grant routed him thoroughly. "Grant," he said, "was not an instinctive politician, but his familiarity with the ways of Washington had been finely honed by three years of vicious infighting."[8] As a matter of fact, his political instincts awed George William Childs, the Republican editor of the *Philadelphia Public Ledger,* during the election of 1872. He had journeyed to Washington to urge Grant to concentrate more on the campaign, but Grant merely spread out a map, he said, and pointed with a pencil to state after state, saying that the Republicans would carry this and that state. "When the election came," Childs reported, "the result was that Grant carried every state that he had said he would."[9]

Congress had proposed the Fifteenth Amendment barring race as a criterion for voting, shortly before Grant's inauguration. He worked diligently for ratification, which he considered necessary to give blacks a way to defend themselves at the polls. It came on 30 of March 1870, just over one year after he took office. He then "took the unusual step of commemorating" ratification by issuing a proclamation to the effect that the Amendment totally repudiated the *Dred Scott* decision.[10] Perhaps it is a "forest and trees" phenomenon, but it requires enormous effort to find among the writings of those who disdain Grant's presidency the barest recognition that ratification was in any manner a Grant accomplishment — or in fact that the amendment itself was important. None of his critics has considered how a population predominantly holding ideas favoring white supremacy and opposing black suffrage could have been induced to ratify a measure that was so radical for the time — one affecting Northern states as well as those in the South.

Typical accounts tend to conclude that Grant began his presidency with a show of weakness by failing to secure repeal of the Tenure of Office Act. Even such usually perceptive presidential analysts as Milkis and Nelson say that instead of insisting on full repeal, the president "not realizing the implications of his decision" capitulated to the Senate and accepted a so-called compromise that "essentially preserved its role in the removal of executive officials." They argue that Grant was so popular at the time that he "probably" would have prevailed had he insisted. His failure to do so, they concluded, was a "strategic error" that "set the tone for his entire two terms as president."[11]

A look at what really happened suggests that this is far from the only interpretation, and may in fact not be a reasonable one. Moreover, second-guessing — more than a century and a quarter after the fact — Grant's judgment as to what would have been likely under the circumstances would seem to require more confidence than to say merely that he "probably" could have prevailed. Grant, one should remember, actually was on the scene, and "he was scarcely the political babe in the woods sometimes depicted."[12] The House had passed repeal, but the Senate jealously guarded its patronage powers and refused to concur.

Grant thereupon announced that he would obey the letter of the law, and would fill no offices — thus leaving Johnson's appointees in place — as long as the Act remained in effect. Senators discovered that Grant's actions had denied them the spoils that they anticipated — no new postmasters, customs collectors, or the like. "By halting patronage appointments the president was using the one weapon the senators understood. Even Roscoe Conkling now suggested compromise." The compromise that rapidly emerged gave the president "complete control over removals from his cabinet. Grant was satisfied. Rather than fight a protracted struggle for total repeal of the Tenure of Office Act, he signed the new measure on April 6."[13] This is hardly the picture of a subservient president, or one ignorant of the political realities, regardless of interpretations as to whether his decision might have been better.

Milkis and Nelson return to solid ground when they examine Grant's presidency in more detail. Despite being president during a period of congressional dominance, they wrote, "Grant did not abdicate presidential responsibilities entirely in the face of this legislative onslaught. Indeed, he restored the most important power of the nineteenth-century executive: the veto." Johnson, they said, "wielded the veto aggressively, but most of his vetoes were overturned. [Actually he vetoed twenty-nine bills of which fifteen were overridden.] Grant used the veto ninety-three times — more than all his predecessors combined — and only four of his vetoes were overturned."[14] One of his vetoes turned back the 1874 Inflation Bill that would have printed greenbacks in an effort to combat the Panic of 1873. Most analysts agree that the bill would have been disastrous. Milkis and Nelson quote a Grant biographer, Frank Scaturro, to the effect that more than any other president, Grant was responsible "for putting the country on the gold standard." They concede that "Grant was thus a stronger president than most scholars have recognized."[15] Exactly.

For another example, Grant enjoyed the company of wealthy men, and was not always wise in his choice of companions. He associated socially with two of the classic robber barons, Jay Gould and Jim Fisk. They took advantage of their association with him, and misrepresented its character to enhance their credibility on Wall Street. This was a circumstance that Grant should have avoided in the first place, and apparently took too long to recognize.

When the two attempted to corner the gold market, however, Grant and Secretary of the Treasury George Boutwell discovered the plot — and incidentally that Grant's own brother-in-law was implicated — and Grant acted with dispatch. "The secretary suggested that the government sell $3 million in gold from the New York subtreasury to break the corner. 'I think you should make it $5 million,' said Grant." Ultimately, they settled on $4 million, a huge sum at the time. "The news hit the Gold Room like an avalanche. Gold, which had been hovering between $160 and $162, plummeted to $133 within minutes. The Gold Ring had been broken. Grant's role had been decisive."[16] For the first time in American history, the government "had intervened massively to bring order to the marketplace. It was a watershed in the history of the American economy."[17] Gould and Fisk attempted to implicate Grant in the plot, saying that he had ordered Secretary Boutwell to withhold gold sales. Some historians and biographers — with absolutely no evidence — believed them and rushed to blame Grant. They overlooked or ignored Boutwell's explicit denial of the charges.[18]

Even some of Grant's critics concede that the Treaty of Washington was a landmark in American diplomacy. It led finally to the long-awaited settlement of the *Alabama* claims against Great Britain resulting from British aid to the Confederacy, and was a "landmark of international conciliation."[19] It incorporated precedent-setting requirements for binding arbitration, and also established the basis for international law on the subject of maritime neutrality.[20]

Grant deserves credit for keeping the United States from a war with Spain. In June of 1870, Congress came close to passing a resolution recognizing a state of belligerency in Cuba, where rebels were resisting the Spanish government. The resolution — regardless of constitutional questions — would have undercut administration policy, and would likely have led to war. Grant sent a message to Congress expressing sympathy for their cause, but pointing out that the rebels held no town or city, had no prize courts, had no organization for collecting revenue, and had no seat of government. The resolution failed. "Grant's intervention proved decisive," and his message has drawn praise from diplomatic historians.[21]

Grant's diplomatic record was strong. He prevented a likely war with Spain, he brought lasting peace with Great Britain, he settled the *Alabama* claims, and he introduced the principle of arbitration in disputes among countries. As Smith put it, "under his leadership"— note the use of the word "leadership"— the United States crept onto the world stage, almost unnoticed."[22]

Grant's Indian policy stressed assimilation and humanitarian treatment. Although he strongly favored separation of church and state, in one respect he anticipated a later administration's "faith-based" initiative. Recognizing the vast corruption among Indian agents that subverted policy, he specified church groups — Quaker and others — to take over certain policies on reservations, including education and health.

Certainly his approach would fail to pass muster today. Regardless of the church-state implications, it reflected no awareness of the value of preserving Indian cultures. Nevertheless, by nineteenth-century standards it was enormously enlightened, and he should receive credit for his appointment of Eli S. Parker, a Seneca Indian, as commissioner of Indian affairs. Grant also was the first to adopt a policy that Indians were to be dealt with as individuals, not solely as tribes. This was a first step toward incorporating them into the United States as full citizens.

In 1870, Grant sought unsuccessfully to annex Santo Domingo (now the Dominican Republic). This was not the usual imperial grab for territory. First, the Dominican government had requested the annexation. Second, Grant saw it as a means of providing the newly freed slaves with bargaining power in the South. Instead of being an effort to colonize blacks, Grant recognized the vital nature of black labor to the South, and hoped — naïvely — that a threat to emigrate would cause the white South to offer its black citizens inducements to stay. He sent a commission, consisting largely of figures who publicly supported black rights, to Santo Domingo to study the situation. Among its members was Frederick Douglass, who endorsed annexation. The judgment of naïveté in this instance seems clear in hindsight, but the fact that Frederick Douglass, a longtime foe of colonization, endorsed it suggests that reasonable people at the time could have had a different view.

Although a biographer such as William McFeely can criticize Grant for having done too little for the rights of the freed slaves,[23] it is difficult to see how anyone else in his position could have accomplished much more than he did under the circumstances. Grant should indeed have moved sooner. Violence against blacks swept the South. But Andrew Johnson had already sabotaged effective efforts at reconstruction. Democrats opposed Grant, and Republicans did not have overwhelming congressional majorities. Even among Republicans, some opposed him, citing constitutional issues. Additionally, a faction of reformers — reformers, that is, on matters other than black rights — broke away to form a Liberal Republican Party. In 1872 this group allied themselves with the Democrats. Together they ran Horace Greeley for president in 1872, opposing Grant — who nevertheless won handily.

In 1870, Congress passed three Enforcement Acts, and established a new Department of Justice. No longer was the attorney general merely the legal adviser to the president. Grant appointed a "powerful team," and U.S. attorneys during the early 1870s brought nearly one thousand indictments in northern Mississippi alone, and secured convictions in fully 55 percent of the cases. Reconstruction histories during the early twentieth century vastly understated the rate of convictions of Klan members.[24]

In 1871 Grant called for action. Some Republicans joined Democrats in arguing that the federal government had no constitutional authority to intervene in state matters, even to suppress violence. Seeing that his proposed Ku Klux Klan bill was headed for defeat, Grant personally "made a rare visit to Capitol Hill to rally his forces." Although reconstruction had lost its electoral appeal, they told him, he nevertheless prevailed. On 20 April he signed the Ku Klux Klan Act authorizing him to use force. He had hoped that other methods would be effective, but ultimately had to send troops.

Attorney General Amos Akerman and the Department of Justice quickly put the Klan on the defensive. "By 1872 Grant's willingness to bring the full legal and military authority of the government to bear had broken the Klan's back and produced a dramatic decline in violence throughout the South. Akerman gave full credit to the president." The following election, with blacks voting freely, has been called the fairest and most democratic in the South until 1968."[25] Similarly, Grant strongly put down an attempt by Democrats in Louisiana to oust Republicans and seize the state's government by force. Grant paid a high price for his success. Outraged Northern voters had had enough of armed protection of democratic government and equal rights.[26] In any case, there were vast limits as to what the federal government could do. The Department of Justice had inadequate resources, as did the courts. Ultimately, "even avid supporters of enforcement came to admit that public support for prolonged intervention was frail."[27]

One may reasonably ask just how much more could have been expected of Grant. One thing perhaps might have been his reaction to corruption. The Crédit Mobilier scandal broke during his administration, but it had taken place earlier and had nothing to do with Grant, or even with the executive branch. It had to do with corruption in the financing of the Union Pacific Railroad, with bribes to members of Congress and misuse of federal funds. More significant to Grant was the "Whiskey Ring," which diverted tax money into the pockets of distillers. Grant called for quick action, and said "let no guilty man escape." Unfortunately for his reputation, when the scandal touched his own secretary, Orville Babcock, Grant believed in his innocence and helped secure his acquittal. Despite the judgment of hostile historians, there was little evidence against Babcock, and there were more than one hundred convictions. Also significant was a bribery scheme in which Secretary of War William Belknap received illegal payments. He resigned to avoid impeachment. Such scandals were of course serious, but they hardly distinguished Grant's administration from many others. His misplaced loyalty to friends was his greatest fault.

Accounts that the Republicans denied Grant nomination for a third term are incorrect. There was in fact a strong third-term movement. Grant, however, long before the convention, wrote a letter to the *New York Times* taking himself out of the race. He declined to run for a third term.[28]

Grant behaved in an exemplary manner in the disputed election of 1876. Republicans controlled only the Senate; Democrats controlled the House. Grant assured the Democrats that he would remain impartial, and would not attempt to interfere with the choice of Democrat Samuel Tilden or Republican Rutherford Hayes. Ultimately Hayes did become president, but despite earlier rumors that Democratic Rifle Clubs and Confederate organizations would march on Washington and install Tilden by force, the Democrats accepted the decision with good grace, partly because "Grant's unflinching resolve steadied the nation."[29]

Why have historians often portrayed Grant as a weak president, why have they ignored his accomplishments, and why has corruption been the foremost theme in so many works on Grant's administration? Grant's own statements following his first election have brought some confusion into interpretations of his presidency. The president, he said, is "a purely Administrative officer"—thus leading many analysts to conclude that he considered the president to be hardly more than a clerk. Such a conclusion fails to consider his next statement—one that Simpson said "sounded Jacksonian (and almost Johnsonian) in its statement of independence"—the president, Grant said, was an administrative officer "who should always be left free to execute the will of the people." As Simpson put it, "this statement deceived listeners at the time and historians every since."[30] As for why historians have been so quick to condemn Grant, there is another explanation, more sub-

tle, and more sinister. To dismiss Grant, it has helped to have no appreciation for the importance of equality for the newly freed slaves. More important was the development of a Southern counterpart to the Lincoln Myth.

This counterpart myth did not deal with the Southern president, but
with Grant's Civil War antagonist, General Robert E. Lee. When Lee died
in 1870 his death "brought an outpouring of grief from Southerners," but
it brought more as well. It "crystallized the efforts of individuals who would
fashion the 'Lost Cause' interpretation. Jubal Early, William Nelson Pendleton, and Rev. John William Jones led the refashioning of history and along
with others, mostly fellow Virginians, would dominate the forthcoming histories of the war."[31] Early and his followers gained control of the Southern
Historical Society and used it to disseminate their views widely. Lee's reputation was central to their argument. As they shaped his image, Lee surpassed Stonewall Jackson, rose above criticism, and became the flawless
general. The apex of the Lee cult came in the 1930s with Douglas Southall
Freeman's influential and widely read four-volume biography.[32]

This corresponding myth found broad acceptance in the North. Much
like the Lincoln myth, which is even stronger, it has achieved a pervasive
quality that elevates its subject to the status of a folk image — oddly, it is a
national folk image.

The historian Joan Waugh — with a conclusion startling enough even
to reach into newspapers — pointed out the subtle, effect of the dual myth:
"with the rise of Robert E. Lee and the 'Lost Cause' came the diminution
of the Union cause."[33] The South lost the war but for a time conquered in
the interpretation of that war. Their writers "put the best possible spin" on
the conflict, and "characterized the South's shattering defeat as an honorable effort against impossible odds," historian Gary Gallagher has remarked.
"And to distance the Confederacy from the taint of slavery, those so-called
Lost Cause writers suggested that the war itself was not about slavery but
about constitutional issues."[34] They created the myth of the "South as a land
and a culture apart," a land that in the words of one of the Confederate
romantics had developed a way of life that had been "the most glorious in
the history of the world."[35] Thus, they set about weaving the emperor's new
clothes.

The apotheosis of Lee along with Lincoln brought a denigration of
Ulysses S. Grant. It was necessary for the pro–Confederate school to prove
that Grant could not have been superior in any way to the object of their
worship, Robert E. Lee.[36] "For the better part of the last century the images
of two of the greatest icons of the Civil War remained fixed in the American imagination: Robert E. Lee as the noble and tragic leader of the Confederate forces, the brilliant tactician fighting against overwhelming odds,
and Ulysses S. Grant as the heavy-drinking butcher who used the North's

superior resources to grind down the South, then became one of the worst presidents in the nation's history."[37] Thus, as Grant biographer Smith has noted, "Lee as the exemplar of slave-owning aristocracy was romanticized by three generations of Southern historians," while Grant's reputation suffered under "this same school of historiography which really dominated American thought through World War II."[38] Ironically, Lee himself would have been among the first to condemn this interpretation of Grant. He remarked that having searched military records of both ancient and modern history, he could find no superior to Grant as a general.[39]

Reconsideration of Grant now is well underway. Brooks D. Simpson has pointed out that none of the historians who have been so critical have been able "to suggest how he could have forged a policy that would have achieved both sectional reconciliation and justice for black Americans," in view of the conditions existing at the time and the obstacle presented by the courts. He mused that the failure perhaps was not Grant's after all.[40]

It is remarkable that such pro Confederate views were so successful for so long. National glorification of the rebel military leader and of the "Lost Cause" clearly must appear odd to any thoughtful observer in an age that condemns racism and strives for civil rights — as must any interpretation of the Civil War that minimizes slavery. Although there had been caveats from a number of writers along the way after the controversies culminating in the 1950s, it was not until the year 2000 that the reaction again became sufficient to attract much in the way of popular attention. That attention, as noted above, came forcefully in the form of an article in the *New York Times*.[41] The article quoted the historian James McPherson, who neatly summed up the situation: "The kind of romanticized sympathy-with-the-underdog attitude to the Confederacy has been increasingly outweighed by the recognition that what the Confederacy was fighting for was a society based on slavery. And what the North was fighting for, if not initially and always enthusiastically, was a society moving toward biracial democracy."

So what may we make of the administration of Ulysses S. Grant? One need not think of him as a great president to recognize that the popular image of him as a weak, naïve, leader who led the nation's most corrupt and chaotic administration is nonsense. Ranking presidents is meaningless; putting President Ulysses S. Grant at or near the bottom of a ranking is worse.

Grant may not have been among the best, but he is the most underrated president in the history of the United States. It is inexcusable that this came about by design and even more so that generations of historians failed to recognize what was taking place.

19

RUTHERFORD B. HAYES
March 4, 1877–March 4, 1881

The tangled election that brought Rutherford B. Hayes to office may not be the only interesting thing about his presidency, but it certainly is the thing that stands out the most. Only two elections in American history truly reflect failures of the American electoral system: the election of 1876 that ultimately placed Hayes in office, and that of 2000 that led to a second Bush presidency.

In 1888, the system rejected the winner of the popular vote and chose Benjamin Harrison instead of Grover Cleveland, but the system nevertheless functioned more or less as the Founders intended. The electoral college in 1800 and 1824 failed to choose the winner at all, but in those cases, too, the system met the Founders' expectations. In 1876 and 2000, however, the system broke down.

In the first case an extra-constitutional commission in effect made the decision on a partisan basis, while in the latter it was the Supreme Court, acting in a hardly less partisan manner. The Founders had anticipated neither such circumstance. That the political system survived both is a testimony to its durability; that both presidents functioned with a minimum of question regarding their legitimacy is a testimony to its strength. Democrats in 1878 did, however, conduct an investigation into the Hayes victory. They were unable to find dishonesty in the Republican victory — despite gibes at "RutherFRAUD" Hayes, and the belief of some that he should be called "your fraudulency" — but were embarrassed to discover evidence that Tilden supporters had attempted to bribe electors.

In 1876, the Republican presidential candidate Rutherford B. Hayes faced a reform Democrat, Samuel J. Tilden, of New York. Trailing in the popular vote, Hayes initially thought he had lost. He and his wife Lucy each feared that the South would in effect nullify the Civil War amendments, that "disorder will continue," and that "prosperity to both whites and colored people will be pushed off for years."[1] The result in the electoral college certainly suggested trouble for the Republican ticket.

Victory required a majority, 185 votes. Tilden had 184 clear votes while Hayes had 165, but 20 additional votes were in dispute. The states of South Carolina, Louisiana, and Florida turned in two slates of electors each, one Republican and one Democratic. These three states were the only remaining states that had Republican reconstruction governments kept in place by federal troops. One of Oregon's votes also was among the twenty in dispute. A Hayes victory would require that all twenty of those votes go Republican.[2]

Months dragged by without a decision. Ultimately the parties agreed upon an electoral commission of fifteen members. As it happened, the commission consisted of eight Republicans and seven Democrats. In every case, it rendered a decision — on a strict party-line vote — accepting the Republican slate. The election remained undecided until two days before the constitutionally-mandated beginning of the new presidential term. On 2 March 1877 the commission arrived at its decision, and Hayes became the nineteenth President of the United States. His formal inauguration took place on the 5th.

It will never be clear who actually should have been named the winner of that election. Various writers have condemned the Republicans "on the grounds that the popular verdict was clearly in favor of Tilden," but others disagree. "As early as 1906, Paul L. Haworth came to the conclusion that the exclusion of the black vote in various Southern states rendered Hayes's victory legitimate."[3] President Grant at first thought that Tilden had won, but later concluded that the systematic exclusion of blacks from the polls in Southern states with Democrats in charge of their governments had prevented a fair election. In any case, the president firmly established that he would maintain order, and that in no way would he use federal authority to influence the result of the election. His action calmed a potentially dangerous situation.

Since the Hayes victory, there have been consistent references to the "Compromise of 1877," by which Democrats agreed not to stand in the way of the Hayes victory and Hayes would agree to withdraw the remaining troops of occupation from the South. The reality is somewhat more complicated than that. There certainly had been negotiations between Republicans and Southern Democrats. But public support for continued occupation had in any case all but vanished already. Moreover, there were implicit promises of federal aid for internal improvements for the South that had had its economy devastated by years of total warfare. Regardless of the details, however, the result was the same. The new Republican administration withdrew troops, relying upon the pledges of Southern leaders to ensure black equality and civil rights.

There can be little doubt that Hayes had the interests of black citizens at heart, but his judgment was badly flawed. "Grant had grown to distrust the sincerity of most southern whites; Hayes still took them at their word and hoped to cultivate reconciliation by abandoning coercion."[4] In 1877, for example, he addressed a mixed audience of Democrats and Republicans, blacks and whites, in Atlanta. The crowd cheered him when he told them that the "rights and interests" of the South's black citizens "would be safer if this great mass of intelligent white men were let alone by the federal government."[5] Andrew Johnson could have made the same statement — and in fact did make similar statements. Hayes, however, actually believed that his policy would be the best for everyone. Senator L. Q. C. Lamar of Mississippi remarked that the new president was "well-meaning," but that, although he was "full of the idea of being a great Pacificator," it was obvious that he was "very ignorant of the South."[6] Yet it tends to be Grant, rather than Hayes, whom writers call naïve.

Writers have varied in their assessments of Hayes. Clinton Rossiter thought highly of him. He identified eight presidents who in his opinion were "great," and six who followed closely behind those eight. He rated Hayes among those six. Certainly there was more to Hayes than his failed Southern policy. He insisted upon having the men he wanted for his cabinet, and despite Senate opposition, he persisted until he succeeded. Rossiter made no direct mention of Hayes's policy toward the South, but gave him deserved praise for vetoing seven appropriations bills to which Congress had attached riders preventing supervision of federal elections. Hayes defeated Congress on those issues as well. Rossiter described Hayes as a "vastly underrated president."[7] He also approved of Hayes's dispatch of troops during the railroad strike of 1877. Hayes sent troops not to run the railroads, but to protect federal property from violence.[8]

The Fabers place Hayes fourteenth in their list of thirty-nine. One poll, they say, (unidentified) puts him higher, at thirteenth, but "the other polls all rank him between twentieth the twenty-fifth."[9] Rossiter's, of course, was not a "poll," nor was Genovese's ranking which placed Hayes at twenty-sixth, "below average."[10] Genovese made the interesting comment that the controversial election involved "one of the dirtiest campaigns in history," but that it featured "two of the cleanest candidates ever." He, too, credited Hayes with standing "firm in asserting the rights of the executive in the face of Congressional pressure," although his "accomplishments were few."[11]

Hayes was devoted to honest government, to education, and to a merit-based civil service. He did issue an executive order forbidding employees of the federal government from partisan activities, which angered some members of Congress. He angered key senators still more by removing Chester Arthur (the future president) from the New York Customshouse, which placed it out of control of the Republican "Stalwarts." He did not, however, succeed in replacing Arthur with the reform-minded Theodore Roosevelt, Sr., the father of the future president. Although sentiment had been building for some years, the time was not quite right for civil service reform.

In addition, as important as education was and always is, education alone was not sufficient to deal with the ills of the South. As Amos T. Akerman of Georgia, who had been Grant's attorney general, observed, "Hayes's course amounted to combating 'lawlessness by letting the lawless have their own way'."[12] It took time for Hayes to recognize that his Southern policy had failed, but on balance he was supremely self-confident, and was convinced that his administration had been highly successful. It had, he maintained, restored national unity.

Republican professionals, though, would likely have disagreed. Hayes had challenged the Stalwarts of his own party, and alienated other factions as well. Hardly any Republican considered his Southern policy a success. It is doubtful that he could have been re-elected had he tried.[13] On the other hand, since Andrew Johnson had effectively destroyed any serious likelihood for generations to come for a two-party South, and in view of the popular resistance nationwide to military rule there, it may not have been possible in fact for him to have done much more than he did.

One of Hayes's appointments to the Supreme Court, John Marshall Harlan, came to rank among the greatest justices in the Court's history. Harlan became known as the "Great Dissenter," because of his numerous sound and thoughtful opinions that took issue with the Court's majority. Many of these became the bases for majority decisions in years to come.

The greatest was his ringing 1896 dissent in *Plessy v. Ferguson*— the outrageous decision ranking second only to *Dred Scott* in sanctioning racial injustice— that approved racial segregation. Sadly, he was the only dissenter in that case. The Court reversed itself in 1954 with *Brown v. Board of Education*, and Harlan's reasoning figured prominently in the reversal. He had argued that state laws mandating racial segregation fomented race hatred by branding one race inherently inferior. Harlan served until his death in 1911, his term of nearly 34 years making him one of the Court's longest serving justices.

Hayes had one other opportunity to appoint a member of the Court. In his effort to be even-handed, late in his term (December 1880) he appointed William Woods, the first justice since the Civil War from a Confederate state. Actually, although Woods had stayed in the South following the Civil War, he had been born in Ohio and had fought with the Union army. The result nevertheless was similar to the rest of Hayes's Southern policy. Woods sided with the majority in 1883 to overturn the Civil Rights Act of 1875 — after Hayes left office. In 1886 he sided with extreme states'-rights advocates in holding that the Bill of Rights limited only the federal government, not the states, the Fourteenth Amendment to the contrary notwithstanding. He died in 1887.

One undeniable success of the Hayes administration was the popularity of Hayes's wife, Lucy. She was a strict Methodist who banned alcohol from the executive mansion, and persuaded her husband also to abstain completely. The President of the United States, after all, should set an example. It was an age with many emerging reform movements, and both Lucy and Rutherford Hayes were committed to reforms of various sorts. In spite of the reformist zeal at the White House — and the dryness of its entertainments and banquets that brought her the name of "Lemonade Lucy" — she was a gracious hostess. During the Hayes presidency Washington's social life was lively.

An amusing example of his sincerity and his simplicity is the memorandum that Hayes left for incoming President James A. Garfield. He feared that Garfield would restore alcohol to the executive mansion, saying in his diary that it would be an indication that the new president "lacks the grit to face fashionable ridicule." The memorandum urged Garfield to continue the ban. "Whatever may be true of Europeans, the Hayes note declared, 'the American who drinks wine is in danger of becoming the victim of drunkenness, licentiousness and gambling'," and that return of liquor would greatly damage Garfield's chance for re-election. One may note that "Garfield was unimpressed with Hayes's argument."[14]

From the beginning, Hayes had pledged to serve only one term. He honored that pledge, and made no attempt to be re-nominated. He and Lucy attended Garfield's inauguration, and retired happily back to Ohio. The rest of their lives they spent in reformist activities. Hayes was committed especially to education and to prison reform. He acted upon his concern for humane conditions in prisons, and became president of the National Prison Association. He continued his interest in politics, and remained an active supporter of Republican candidates. Lucy died in June of 1889, and he lived on until 17 January 1893. They are buried at their home, Spiegel Grove Estate in Fremont, Ohio.

Rutherford B. Hayes was a decent, honest, well-meaning, stubborn man who was rather simple, moderately conservative, and quite able. His biographer Ari Hoogenboom called Hayes "both a good man and an able president."[15] He defended the executive, and expected better from the South than he received. Essentially, however, his policies there under the circumstances were merely bowing to the inevitable. Can it reveal more to compare him to other presidents, none of whom faced the same conditions?

20

JAMES A. GARFIELD
March 4, 1881–September 19, 1881

James A. Garfield, the twentieth President of the United States of America, served barely more than six months as America's chief executive. This was the second shortest time in office of any president. For more than two months of this of this brief term he could barely function as he wasted away. A deranged assassin had struck the president on 2 July. He died on 19 September.

After the shooting, "the nation lacked a leader. Fortunately, Congress was not in session, and the president had only to sign one paper. Temporarily, all went smoothly. As Robert Todd Lincoln wrote, the government was 'running along — every man running his own Department and thinking he is doing so well that he may be President some day."[1] Lincoln, the son of Abraham Lincoln, was Garfield's secretary of war.

To their credit, those who produce rankings of presidents usually exclude Garfield along with William Henry Harrison because of the brevity of their time in office. There is reason to believe that he might have become an effective president. Although he made some missteps, he engaged in an early battle over patronage with Senator Roscoe Conkling, of New York, who had dominated patronage matters for many years, and he won decisively.

Conkling was eager to regain control of the New York Customhouse, the most lucrative position in the government, for his "Stalwart" faction of the party. President Hayes had removed Chester Arthur from the position, and Garfield nominated William H. Robertson to be the collector. Ironically, Arthur had become Garfield's vice president, chosen to provide a Stalwart to balance the ticket with Garfield. Arthur pleaded with Garfield to withdraw Robertson's name, but Garfield refused. The basic question,

Garfield boldly asserted, was "whether America's principal port of entry would be under the administration's direction or 'under the local control of a factional senator.' Robertson may be carried out of the Senate head first or feet first,' he commented, 'I shall never withdraw him'."[2]

Garfield recognized that Conkling might simply delay confirmation of Robertson while accepting the nominees that he had recommended, and let the session end. The president therefore withdrew all nominations, and submitted only Robertson's. The senator then made a rash move: he resigned from the Senate, confident that New York's legislature would return him, and he thus would have renewed power. His plan backfired. The legislature would not return him, and Garfield had won the fight to choose his own officials. The *Chicago Tribune* commented that "Gen. Garfield has determined to be President of the United States."[3]

Garfield, like Hayes, had great confidence in education. His plans for the South probably revolved around providing education, but he did not live to deal with the issue. Similarly, when the "Star Route" scandal broke, he ordered a full investigation that would shield no party official, but could not follow through.

After the shooting, he appeared to rally a few times but otherwise steadily declined. Doctors had probed the wounds with unsterilized fingers and instruments, and infection had set in. The infection probably was the cause of death. His body was returned to Ohio, and was buried in Cleveland at Lake View Cemetery.

21

CHESTER ALAN ARTHUR
September 20, 1881–March 4, 1885

Chester Alan Arthur was the fourth accidental president in American history, and all of these first four had come within roughly forty years. Except for his vice presidency, Arthur had never before held elective office. Reformers were dismayed at the accession to the presidency of a "Stalwart," a spoilsman, an associate of former Senator Roscoe Conkling.

Polls tend to place Arthur rather low in their rankings, although in the 1962 Schlesinger study he managed to make it into the average category — twenty-first of thirty-one.[1] In Schlesinger, Jr.'s, 1996 poll he also was low among the averages, twenty-sixth of thirty-nine.[2] The Fabers placed him far down their list, thirty-seventh of thirty-nine,[3] while Genovese rated him better, but still below-average, twenty-seventh, also of thirty-nine.[4] Some of the jaundiced views of Arthur, it appears, may have little to do with his performance as president. As the Fabers put it, "although Arthur exhibited a satisfactory level of morality as president, the prestige of his presidency was diminished somewhat by the low standards he had exhibited earlier"— so much for scientific precision in rankings — but they did concede that he "did not turn out to be as bad a president as reformers feared."[5]

When the nominating convention selected Garfield, from the "Half-Breed" wing of the party it chose Arthur as his running mate to balance the ticket and placate the more conservative "Stalwart" segment. When he heard about the overtures to Arthur, fellow Stalwart and fellow New Yorker, Roscoe Conkling, urged him to reject any thought of the nomination. He told Arthur that he should "drop it as you would a red hot shoe from the forge," assuring him that Garfield would go down to defeat. Arthur, however, said

159

that the vice presidency was a "greater honor" than any he had "ever dreamed of attaining," and accepted it happily.[6]

Arthur's nomination occasioned little concern among reformers, his ties to the "spoilsmen" notwithstanding. As vice president he would have little or no influence, they assumed, on policy. Their nonchalance turned to dread at Garfield's death when Arthur suddenly became President of the United States. Immediately they assumed that Conkling would be the power behind the throne. During the weeks that Garfield lay dying, however, the vice president had behaved in an exemplary manner, and had explicitly refused any suggestion that he attempt to attain power.

When he did become president, Arthur did not act immediately to restructure the cabinet. He moved cautiously, perhaps to offset public nervousness regarding the new and inexperienced chief executive. He did have some advantages: "he was bright, he was a good administrator, and his conduct during the assassination crisis had won him public sympathy."[7]

Before long, he did begin to replace cabinet members. The first to go was Attorney General Wayne MacVeigh, a staunch reformer, in October. Arthur replaced him with Benjamin Brewster of Pennsylvania, another reformer. In November Secretary of the Treasury William Windom resigned to run for the Senate. Arthur replaced him with Judge Charles Folger of New York. In December Arthur replaced the postmaster general. The most controversial member of the cabinet was Secretary of State James G. Blaine. Blaine resigned, and the new secretary was a well-respected former senator from New Jersey, Frederick Frelinghuysen. Interior and Navy received new secretaries the following year. The only member of the Garfield cabinet to stay in office throughout Arthur's presidency was Secretary of War Robert Todd Lincoln, son of the former president.[8]

Chet Arthur, machine politician, changed when he became president. Cynical analysts say he saw the handwriting on the wall, and recognized public support for civil service reform. Whether this is correct no one can say — nor is it necessary, or even profitable, to speculate as regards motives — one can say with assurance only that he left his past as a spoilsman far behind. "Once he became president, Arthur ceased to act like a 'Gentleman Boss.' While he still welcomed Stalwart cronies to sumptuous feasts, he refrained from doing favors to such a degree that one Conkling follower complained, 'He has done less for us than Garfield, or even Hayes'." Most telling, as one of his old Customhouse associates explained it, "He isn't 'Chet' Arthur anymore; he's the President."[9]

As the president, Arthur had a Congress that was closely divided. He showed due deference to the legislature, but did suggest some startling measures in his annual messages. He requested an amendment to provide the president with an item veto, he urged a government for Alaska and a new building for the Library of Congress, and in view of the surplus, he asked that all internal taxes be repealed except those on liquor and tobacco. Moreover, he called for regulation of interstate commerce, including rate regulation. "Congress felt little compunction about ignoring such suggestions and others as well."[10]

In his first annual message to Congress, Arthur astonished everyone by calling for civil service reform. After the elections of 1882, although the Republicans picked up a seat in the Senate that gave them the majority (the Senate previously had been divided equally), they lost the House and the Democrats took control. Arthur that year requested passage of the Pendleton Act that would lead ultimately to a merit-based civil service. Arthur signed it into law in 1883. Although the initial act "was of limited application," it nevertheless was a quantum leap forward. In addition to providing the basis for merit-hiring by examination, it established a Civil Service Commission, and banned solicitation of campaign funds from federal workers. "Finally, the president was authorized to expand the bounds of civil service coverage by executive order. However limited its initial application, the Pendleton Act laid a solid foundation on which to build the civil service in succeeding decades."[11]

Arthur did not hesitate to use his veto. In July of 1882, he vetoed a steamboat safety bill, citing technical errors. Congress corrected them, and he signed the new legislation. He turned down a rivers and harbors bill as a raid on the U.S. Treasury. Earlier, in what some have termed his most significant veto, Arthur blocked a measure restricting Chinese immigration and citizenship. Both parties supported restriction, as did labor. Arthur cited its harsh terms, and ultimately signed a milder measure.[12]

Also in 1882, Arthur discovered he had Bright's disease, a kidney condition that is fatal if untreated. In Arthur's day, there was no treatment. Observers of Arthur's actions often thought of him as lazy, but likely the disease already was taking a severe toll and slowing him.

By embracing reform, the machine politician, Chester A. Arthur, had alienated his former supporters. He was unable to gain the nomination in 1884, and spent his final days in office largely on ceremonial matters. It was he who dedicated the Washington Monument, and as his last act in office, signed legislation restoring Ulysses S. Grant's commission as general of the army. Surprisingly, in view of the Stalwart's attitude toward his reforms, they offered him election to the U. S. Senate as he left the presidency, but he turned it down.[13]

Chester A. Arthur was "one of the nation's great political surprises, for few expected a man of his limitations to do a commendable job, and he was successful to a degree that has not been acknowledged by his fellow politicians, the press, the great mass of his countrymen — and, most of all, historians."[14] He had faults, but he had virtues as well. He initiated little legislation, but in many ways he was surprisingly progressive. His ideology prevented him from dealing successfully with the economy, but that trait he shared with all other presidents in the latter part of the nineteenth century.

It is obvious that those who rank presidents either pay him little attention, or find it difficult to know where to place him. Thus, the rankings tell us little in his case. And that is another trait he shares in common with his fellow presidents.

22

GROVER CLEVELAND
March 4, 1885–March 4, 1889

When Grover Cleveland took office in March 1885, he became the first Democratic president since the Civil War. In fact, along with Woodrow Wilson, he became one of only two Democratic presidents in the entire period from the end of Buchanan's term in March 1861 until the beginning of the term of the New Deal President, Franklin D. Roosevelt, in March 1933. Democrats held the presidency for only four terms in that long span of more than seventy years.

Historians have tended to be quite varied in their treatment of Cleveland. Some have placed him in the "near great" category. In the 1962 Schlesinger poll, for example, he ranked eleventh of thirty-one.[1] Clinton Rossiter thought even more highly of him. After listing eight "greats," Rossiter placed Cleveland first among the six who followed. Cleveland's "persistent display of integrity and independence," he said, "brought him very close to greatness in the Presidency."[2] He did well, but less well — thirteenth ("high average") — in Schlesinger, Jr.'s, 1996 study of thirty-nine.[3] Genovese, on the other hand, was considerably less impressed. Cleveland to him was average — albeit ranking at the top of that category — and came in seventeenth of thirty-nine.[4] The Fabers went further; while putting Cleveland twenty-third among their thirty-nine, they indulged in a bit of mild aspersion-casting. Cleveland, they said, in their opinion was among those presidents ordinarily "ranking significantly higher than they deserve."[5]

Perhaps the reason for the variation was the very nature of Cleveland's record. Although he was unquestionably a man of integrity, he was extraordinarily conservative and thus in most instances did not even attempt to lead vigorously. In this connection Vincent De Santis quoted Thomas Bailey as saying that "not all effective leadership is of a positive nature." He also quoted a complementary comment by William Leuchtenburg, who said that even negative achievements were "something of a virtue when too many politicians were saying 'yes' to the wrong things." Therefore, thought De Santis, Cleveland was "remembered less for his accomplishments (or his personal brilliance) than for his character — specifically, for his courage, firmness, uprightness, and sense of duty."[6]

All these, to be sure, are excellent qualities, and all are worthy of praise. Whether they are sufficient by themselves is the question. We must ask whether judgment and understanding — even wisdom — also may be required to arrive at a favorable assessment of overall performance as president.

After all, presidential actions affect people's lives. The effect that actions have depends upon more than the extent to which courage and a sense of duty motivate them. Actions can be beneficial or destructive, regardless of whether they are firm, and regardless of how "upright" is the person who has taken the action. An examination of Cleveland's actions — positive and negative — is essential in evaluating his performance as president. If they had generally a positive effect, it does him no justice to praise him grudgingly based on his character alone; if their effect was negative, his character should not shield him from criticism. This is not to diminish the value, of course, of the qualities for which Cleveland continues to receive praise. In an era known since the Civil War for corruption at all levels of public life, they assumed an even greater importance than normal.

Cleveland brought an extensive background to the presidency, all acquired in his native New York. He had been sheriff of Erie County and later mayor of Buffalo, and had practiced law. When he received the presidential nomination, he was governor of New York — the most important state in the Union. Although he was a firm Democrat, he had never been associated with the predominant, pro–Southern, faction of the party, and he had supported Lincoln's policies during the Civil War.

He also brought with him a scandal: a charge that he had fathered an illegitimate child. Republicans gleefully chanted: "Ma Ma, where's my pa? Gone to the White House, Ha Ha Ha!" Just before he received the nomination, the *Buffalo Evening Telegraph* splashed a lurid headline across its page one: "A TERRIBLE TALE, A Dark Chapter in a Public Man's History, The Pitiful Story of Maria Halpin and Governor Cleveland's Son." There appears to be no doubt about the affair, but Cleveland seems to be been one of several possible fathers. Nevertheless, said the historian Henry Graff, although he "never acknowledged the child to be his, … he had contributed to the boy's support." Graff speculated that Cleveland may have been protecting the memory of his late friend, Oscar Folsom. "The Gesture honored the memory of his friend," Graff said, "and spared his widow and daughter from shame." Graff noted that Halpin had named her son, Oscar Folsom Cleveland.[7] Whatever the merit of Graff's speculation, protecting Folsom's widow and his daughter may indeed have been uppermost in Cleveland's mind.

After he became president, the forty-nine-year-old bachelor married his friend's daughter, Frances ("Frank") Folsom, then a twenty-one-year-old student at Wells College. Despite the disparity in their ages, she quickly became enormously popular, and was an extraordinary asset to her husband. The happy couple had five children. The first-born, Ruth, came in 1891 and attracted the attention of an admiring public. As "Baby Ruth," to that public, a popular candy bar emerged as her namesake. It was a terrible blow to the Clevelands when she died of diphtheria in 1904.

Despite the scandal, Cleveland's record and image of integrity — political integrity, that is — certainly overshadowed that of his Republican rival, James G. Blaine. In addition to suspicions regarding Blaine's possible corruption, his candidacy received considerable damage when he addressed a group of Protestant clergymen in New York City. The Reverend Samuel Burchard of the Murray Hill Presbyterian Church introduced Blaine and charged that the Democrats were the party of "Rum, Romanism, and Rebellion." Blaine did not disavow the remark, nor, apparently, did he sense that it would cause Catholics to disavow his candidacy. There was, however, no landslide.

After a narrow victory, Cleveland and his running mate, former Indiana governor Thomas A. Hendricks, became president and vice president.[8] Hendricks had been the Democratic vice presidential nominee in 1876 when he and Tilden lost the disputed election to Hayes and Wheeler. He had tried unsuccessfully to obtain the presidential nomination in 1880. He tried again in 1884 but ultimately accepted once more the second spot on ticket. His persistence paid off at last, but only briefly. He did not live until the end of the term, and in fact died before completing his first year in office.[9]

In 1885 when Vice President Hendricks died in office, the existing succession act specified that the president pro-tempore of the Senate was next in line to succeed to the presidency after the vice president. At the time of his death the Senate had not yet chosen its president pro-tempore, so for several days there was no chosen successor if Cleveland were also to die. The following year, Cleveland signed into law a succession act superseding the 1792 law. The new legislation placed cabinet secretaries next in line of succession after the vice president, beginning with the secretary of state. The revised law remained in place until Congress changed it again under President Harry Truman.

Cleveland's inaugural address was brief and undistinguished. He selected a cabinet that for the most part was businesslike and effective. Postmaster General William Vilas, for example, worked diligently to bring railroad officials to justice who had overcharged for transporting mail. He even proposed that the government own and operate the mail cars. He failed, but did direct public attention to the wrongdoing. Although Cleveland was no imperialist, for a variety of reasons including coastal defense, he supported plans for naval expansion.[10] He also signed into law the Interstate Commerce Act of 1887 creating the Interstate Commerce Commission to assist in correcting abuses by the railroads, although the Commission had no real powers at the time. The same year he signed the Dawes Act intended to integrate Native Americans into the predominant culture and to provide citizenship to those who acculturated, and he signed the Hatch Act establishing agricultural experiment stations in the states. Some of his actions "laid the groundwork for changes that would afterward be associated with the rise of Progressivism."[11]

Nevertheless, Cleveland was quite conservative. His orientation was clearly toward business, and despite his discomfort with great disparities in wealth he had no sense that government had a role to play in assisting those in need. In vetoing a bill to provide aid to Texas farmers suffering severely from drought, for example, he wrote, "I do not believe that the power and duty of the general government ought to be extended to the relief of individual suffering which is in no manner properly related to the public service or benefit." He followed with words that later would have seemed outrageous: "though the people support the government," he said, "the government should not support the people."[12] It is ironic that as a century passed, such sentiments again made their way into the public discourse.

Cleveland's record on strengthening the presidency was mixed, but on balance he did strengthen the institution. On the one hand, he considered it improper to pressure Congress to approve legislation. Consequently, although he favored lowering the tariff, he made no real effort to achieve tariff reform. Along the same lines, he disdained the press and therefore failed to connect adequately with the public. He was both the only president who refused to attend the press association's annual Gridiron Dinner (after it had begun in 1885), and the last one who refused to provide reporters with working space.[13] On the other hand, he strongly protected the institutional independence of the executive, and in that regard was a strong president. It was Cleveland who, in his first term, brought about the repeal of the notorious Tenure of Office Act.

There had been tension between the Cleveland and the Senate regarding appointments. Under the provisions of the Act, the president could suspend, but not remove, most appointees. As is often the case, the controversy reached a peak with regard to one specific case. Cleveland nominated John D. Burnett to replace George M. Duskin as U.S. attorney for Alabama. The Senate demanded all papers regarding the suspension and appointment.

Cleveland provided all documents with regard to Burnett's appointment, but refused to furnish any material pertaining to Duskin's suspension. The Senate passed a resolution criticizing Cleveland for refusing to cooperate, and Cleveland in turn issued a public message to the Senate accusing it of infringing upon his constitutional authority as chief executive. The impasse ended when someone noticed that Duskin's term had expired during the controversy, and the Senate then confirmed Burnett. The public had overwhelmingly sided with the president, and subsequently Congress voted to repeal the Tenure of Office Act, with both Republicans and Democrats supporting repeal.[14]

Cleveland also used his veto to good advantage. Rossiter wrote that the 414 vetoes of his first term symbolized Cleveland's "integrity and independence."[15] De Santis, too, pointed to the influence on the presidency of Cleveland's vetoes, saying that "he was the first president to use the veto freely," although he noted correctly that many of the 414 vetoes of his first term were to turn back private pension bills affecting only one person.[16] Genovese drew the same conclusions, saying also that "Cleveland was the first president to use the veto power freely," and remarking that he vetoed more bills than all his predecessors combined.[17] So, one should note, did President Ulysses S. Grant, whose use of the veto has attracted little attention. These observers, and others, make a good case — for Cleveland, if not for Grant. Cleveland's use of the veto assisted in restoring executive power and independence.

In the very close election of 1888, Cleveland ran against the Republican nominee, Benjamin Harrison. Cleveland, like Al Gore more than a century later, won the popular vote. Also like Al Gore, he lost in the electoral college.[18] Unlike Al Gore's loss, however, Cleveland's loss was clear. No Supreme Court decision was required to stop vote counting within a state, or to award the election to Harrison. Despite the popular vote loss, Harrison was the undoubted winner.

One bizarre episode in the race resulted from an early "dirty trick," which led to an astonishingly incompetent action on the part of the British minister to Washington, Sir Lionel Edward Sackville-West. Charles Osgoodby, a Republican orange grower in Southern California, posing as a British citizen and using the false name of Charles Murchison, wrote to the minister asking which candidate would be most favorable to British interests. Sackville-West, in an unbelievable display of poor judgment — especially for a diplomat — responded that Cleveland would be preferable. The press published the minister's letter just before the election, and generated charges among the numerous Anglophobic groups that Cleveland was under British influence. "The time remaining before the election was less than two weeks, too short a period to get a recall from the Foreign Office in London, so Cleveland sent him packing on 30 October."[19] There is no way to know the extent to which the letter affected the election, but any influence would have been detrimental to Cleveland. In such a close election, even a small effect is likely to make a major difference.

In Cleveland's final annual message to Congress, he expressed concern for the greatly-widening gap between rich and poor. He noted that "trusts, combinations, and monopolies" were trampling citizens "to death beneath an iron heel." He decried communism, but asserted that wealth and capital fueling "cupidity and selfishness" undermined the "justice and integrity of free institutions" no less than communism did. His written message, though, attracted no public attention, and "disappeared into the oblivion of the *Congressional Record.*" One circumstance, regardless of any other, would absolutely have kept him from greatness. That circumstance was the tragedy of the Cleveland presidency. Although Grover Cleveland had come to recognize the danger, "he was imbued indelibly with the antistatist Jeffersonianism he shared with fellow Bourbons; it prevented him from making legislative proposals to confront what he recognized."[20]

Cleveland and Harrison rode together to Harrison's inauguration. While Harrison gave his address in a pouring rain, Cleveland graciously held an umbrella over the new president. As they had left the executive mansion, Frances Cleveland had said to a servant, "I want you to take good care of all the furniture and ornaments in the house, for I want to find everything just as it is now when we come back again." And, she said, they would be back. "We are coming back, just four years from today."[21] She was exactly right for four years later, in 1892, Cleveland was again the Democratic nominee, again running against Benjamin Harrison. This time, the victory in both popular and electoral vote went to Cleveland.[22]

The new vice president was Adlai Stevenson, grandfather of the unsuccessful Democratic presidential candidate against Eisenhower in both 1952 and 1956. Cleveland chose a new cabinet with all different members from his first. Also different in the second Cleveland presidency, unfortunately, was a severe economic panic that struck in 1893 just before he took office, and dominated his administration. One positive development was the admission of Utah as a state in 1896.

His solutions were limited by his restricted view of government. He signed legislation repealing the Sherman Silver Purchase Act, restoring the country to a complete gold standard. To secure scarce funds, he persuaded a consortium put together by the financier J. P. Morgan to purchase $60 million in U.S. bonds on favorable terms and pay for them with 3.5 million ounces of gold.[23] Regardless of the need, many members of the public perceived the deal as selling out to bankers.

Cleveland's own health increased his troubles. He developed a painful lesion in his mouth, related in all likelihood to tobacco. Physicians determined that it was malignant, and required immediate surgery. Keeping his condition secret from the public, and hiding the purpose of his trip, he set out for a voyage up New York's East River on the yacht of a friend. Surgeons performed the operation onboard. Working inside his mouth, they removed a portion of his upper jaw, and fitted a rubber prosthesis that did not change his appearance, and permitted him to eat and speak normally. The public knew nothing of the entire episode until 1917, long after Cleveland's presidency, and nearly a decade after his death.[24]

Although Cleveland long had sought tariff reduction, he was unhappy with the Wilson-Gorman Act of 1894. The bill lowered tariff rates overall, but added so many special duties that Cleveland thought it useless. It also added provision for a graduated federal income tax. Cleveland permitted the act to become law without his signature. The next year, a conservative Supreme Court declared the income tax unconstitutional.

As troubles increased in the economy, they increased throughout society. Farmers and urban workers became increasingly restive. Strikes and demonstrations upset the more comfortable elements of society, violated their notions of decorum, and created a fearful atmosphere. Most inflammatory of all was the Pullman Strike.

George Pullman had created a huge company that supplied sleeping cars to the railroads. He had built a company town, and required that all his workers live there. They paid much higher amounts for rent and utilities than were available outside, and "he forced his tenants to buy their food and other necessities from company stores, where prices far exceeded those of regular outlets." Although the village was pleasant to the eye, in fact it was "an instrument of corporate despotism, reproved even by other leaders of big business." In 1894, Pullman cut workers' wages some 25 percent, without reducing his charges. When they protested, he fired them and closed the plant.[25]

In response, the American Railway Union went on strike, and refused to operate trains with Pullman cars. The Pullman officials then attached their cars to trains carrying mail, "confident that any interference with the mail was a federal crime." When the strike continued, Attorney General Richard Olney, a former railroad lawyer, persuaded Cleveland to send in troops. Cleveland did so, despite protests from Illinois Governor John P. Altgeld.[26] That action alone lost the Democrats the support of much of the labor movement.

It did, however, strengthen the powers of the presidency. He used federal power without a request of the state involved — and in fact over its protests. He relied on constitutional authority, rather than statute. Moreover, he had used the military in peacetime.[27]

In foreign policy, too, Cleveland was firm, and at times innovative. He quickly squelched efforts by expatriate American sugar growers in Hawaii to induce the United States to annex the islands. They had hoped to secure the benefits available to American sugar growers. Using harsh language, he succeeded in persuading the British to accept arbitration in a boundary dispute between Venezuela and British Guiana.

Cleveland's policies had contributed to a split in the Democratic Party. When the convention met in 1896, it nominated the populist William Jennings Bryan from Nebraska. Cleveland saw his party's nomination of a radical as a slap in the face. The gold Democrats who could not accept Bryan held a rump convention. After determining that Cleveland would not accept, they nominated John Palmer of Illinois. Cleveland and most of his cabinet supported Palmer, and Cleveland saw conservative Republican William McKinley's success as a victory for his own policies.[28]

One would be hard-pressed to make a case for Cleveland as a great president, although some have come close to trying. No one, on the other hand, could with justice claim him to be a failure. In truth he was honest, hard-working, well-meaning, and greatly restricted by his conservative views regarding the appropriate use of government. To his credit, he retained Theodore Roosevelt, a Republican and a holdover from the Harrison administration, on the Civil Service Commission. The two had developed mutual respect earlier, when he was governor of New York and Roosevelt was a young reform-minded member of the Assembly. Cleveland did succeed to some extent in strengthening the executive, although he was neither unique nor especially noteworthy in that regard.

As we have seen, there have been criticisms of rankings because they place Cleveland too low. There also have been opposite criticisms, saying that rankings put him too high. Let us concede that both criticisms are correct in that no ranking has placed him properly — nor could one.

23

BENJAMIN HARRISON
March 4, 1889–March 4, 1893

Benjamin Harrison, the grandson of former President William Henry Harrison, lost the popular vote in 1888 to Grover Cleveland, but nevertheless ousted him from the presidency by winning a clear victory in the electoral college. He became the twenty-third president without the aid of a congressional commission or of a Supreme Court intervention to decide the issue. His victory was no landslide, but it was decisive, and he carried Republican majorities in both houses of Congress.

"The day after Harrison's victory, the *New York Tribune* congratulated the 'Grand Old Party" on its victory, and the name stuck."[1] The Republican Party had become, permanently, it seems, the "GOP." Harrison's new vice president was Levi P. Morton of New York, a prominent banker from the conservative Stalwart wing of the party.

Harrison was reportedly devoid of humor; one observer, though, said "he possessed a fine sense of humor but kept it a carefully guarded secret."[2] Harrison was a small, seemingly colorless man whose abrupt manner and speech were likely to give offense. He was not good in dealing person-to-person or with small groups, and he had no patience with small talk. For example, he once held a watch in his hand as he greeted the governor of Ohio. He pointed to a pile of papers on his desk and said, "I've got all these papers to look after, and I'm going fishing at two o'clock." He then opened his watch, and waited for the governor to comment and be on his way.[3] The countless enemies he created with his brusque manner no doubt contributed to his political difficulties, and subsequently to his defeat for re-election. On the other hand, accounts indicate that he was a very skilled public speaker, and was at his best in addressing large crowds. A colleague once said that

Harrison "can make a speech to ten thousand men and every man will go away his friend [but] let him meet the same ten thousand men in private and every one will go away his enemy."[4]

He also maintained good relations with the press. Despite his apparent lack of humor, he submitted himself to good-natured jokes at his expense by reporters at the first annual dinner of the Gridiron Club of the press association. Every president since then, except for Cleveland, would follow his example.[5]

At five feet six inches, he was the shortest president except for James Madison. He was a lawyer who until his election to the presidency had held only one elective office: he had served one term as United States senator from Indiana. He had, however, served with distinction in Sherman's Union forces during the Civil War, and had risen to the rank of brigadier general — the last of the Civil War generals to serve as president. By all accounts he had absolutely no qualms about his rather minimal political experience, and had no doubts about his abilities.

As one of the often-forgotten late nineteenth-century presidents, Harrison long tended to be remembered, if at all, merely as the president who occupied the interlude between Grover Cleveland's two terms. In recent years, though, evaluations of his presidency have taken a more positive note. Louis Koenig wrote, in fact, that "history has been kind to Benjamin Harrison. Emphasizing his ability in extracting legislation from Congress — with its centerpiece, the Sherman Anti-trust Act — and his leadership in laying the groundwork for an expanded United States presence in international affairs, some historians hail the Harrison presidency as the most achieving in the half-century between Lincoln and the progressive era of Theodore Roosevelt and Woodrow Wilson."[6]

Surveys of the presidency still are likely, however, to pass over his extraordinary abilities, and to stress instead his acceptance of a whiggish view of the executive. Claims that he was a mere pawn of Congress still are commonplace. It is correct that his whiggish views limited his effectiveness as a legislative leader, but Harrison was far from a passive executive. In fact, he could claim substantial accomplishments for his administration.

The Schlesinger, Jr., poll of 1996 reflected what seemed to be a more nuanced understanding than many, and placed Harrison nineteenth of the thirty-nine rated.[7] Harrison fared considerably worse in Schlesinger, Sr.'s, second poll in 1962 where he ranked twentieth among thirty-one.[8] Genovese dismissed Harrison as having a "very limited view of the president's authority," that "led him neither to propose nor dispose."[9] Harrison, he said, was "content to let Congress rule," and as a result he "exerted little direction or leadership."[10] Accordingly, he placed Harrison in the middle of his "Below Average" category, ranking him twenty-ninth of thirty-nine.[11] The Fabers placed Harrison almost in the same position, tied with the first George Bush for twenty-eighth of thirty-nine.[12] Oddly, though, their narrative reflects a generally positive view, and notes Harrison's solid accomplishments.[13] Perhaps this apparent inconsistency simply reflects the impossibility of a valid ranking.

Harrison delivered his full inaugural address, despite heavy rainfall. Outgoing President Cleveland stood by his side, and sheltered him with an umbrella. The new president spoke of the prospect of additional states, of the dangers of trusts, and of the need to increase veterans' pensions. He called for a larger and modernized navy, and defended the protective tariff. He also sent a warning to the South, saying that the administration of federal laws should be uniform throughout the country.

Harrison had decided upon most of his cabinet members before coming to Washington. Every member shared the same Presbyterian faith as the president. His choices consistently "mirrored his own background."[14] The new secretary of state, James G. Blaine, had held the position under Garfield and Arthur. Harrison delayed announcing Blaine's selection. The delay helped counter speculation that Blaine — a long-time power in the Republican Party and its presidential candidate in 1884 — would be the dominant force in the administration. Harrison's delay in making the appointment and his refusal to appoint Blaine's son, Walker, to the top assistant secretary position in the State Department created a relentless enemy in the form of Blaine's wife — who in any case reportedly was bitter that it was Benjamin Harrison and not James G. Blaine who was president.[15] Friction between Harrison and Blaine grew to such an extent that Blaine resigned just before the Republican National Convention, with timing that was especially awkward for the president — no doubt calculated to be so.[16] In any case, Blaine's health had become precarious before he entered Harrison's cabinet. As it turned out, illness severely restricted his effectiveness, and encouraged Harrison to take a personal role in foreign policy.

The result was substantial. Harrison took firm positions on various matters in negotiations with Germany, Great Britain, Italy, and Chile. It was "the beginning of a new, more determined foreign policy for the United States." Socolofsky and Spetter wrote that "in the Western Hemisphere — from the Bering Sea to the Pacific coast of South America — and on the continent of Europe itself, Harrison would establish an American presence that seemed entirely appropriate by the end of the nineteenth century."[17] He had submitted to the Senate a treaty annexing Hawaii, but President Cleveland withdrew it when he succeeded Harrison in office. Harrison had a delayed victory, though, when the U. S. annexed Hawaii during the McKinley administration.

Harrison's foreign policy achievements included appointing the noted orator and former slave, Frederick Douglass, as minister to Haiti. It was the first diplomatic appointment of an American of African descent. The appointment was consistent with Harrison's commitment to enforcement of the Fifteenth Amendment and to the protection of black rights in the South. He considered equality to be a moral issue. The South resisted all efforts. When Senator Henry Cabot Lodge introduced a bill authorizing federal courts to oversee elections — elections to the U. S. House of Representatives only — Southern members of Congress condemned it as a "Force Bill."

Harrison's unsuccessful attempts to protect black citizens brought an end to such efforts for decades. When real progress did come, it came ironically from Democrats, and it was a century after the Civil War before true protections were in place. Harrison, however, brought the resources of the presidency, as he understood them, to bear on the issue.

Among his appointments, one stands out in retrospect as perhaps his most significant. He appointed the young Theodore Roosevelt to the Civil Service Commission, thus providing the future president with a national platform. Although Roosevelt thought that Harrison had not supported his reform efforts, the president tolerated them. Roosevelt became so popular that President Cleveland, after he succeeded Harrison, kept him on the commission — even though Cleveland was a Democrat.

President Cleveland had signed legislation admitting Oklahoma as a territory, but had not specified a date for settlement. Harrison issued a proclamation on the 23rd of March, 1889 establishing 22 April as the date. The Oklahoma land rush began on noon of that day — although, as became well-known, some settlers entered sooner.

When Harrison assumed office, no state had entered the Union since Colorado's admission in 1876, during the Grant administration. Under Harrison, six new states became members of the Union, a record for any administration. These included North and South Dakota, Montana, and Washington in 1889, and Idaho and Wyoming in 1890.

Harrison had favored increased pensions for veterans, and in 1890 signed into law an act extending coverage to dependents and veterans with non-service-connected disabilities. The same year he signed the Sherman Silver Purchase Act and the highly protectionist McKinley Tariff.

Probably the most important pieces of legislation passed during the Harrison administration were the Sherman Anti-trust Act, also of 1890, and the act creating the U. S. Courts of Appeals. There is no evidence that he attempted any serious enforcement of the Sherman Act. Nevertheless, it had considerable long-term effect.[18] In 1889, Harrison's annual message called for the creation of an intermediate level of federal courts. In 1891 Congress responded to the need, and passed legislation creating nine judicial circuits. The nine Courts of Appeal began hearing cases appealed from the U. S. District Courts, and appeals to the Supreme Court dropped from more than six hundred per year to fewer than three hundred. The Court could only handle some four hundred fifty cases per year, and in 1890 had a backlog of around eighteen hundred cases.[19]

An action by Harrison indirectly, but greatly, strengthened the authority of the U. S. government. Supreme Court Associate Justice Stephen Field previously had served on the California Supreme Court with David S. Terry. Terry had resigned from the court in order to fight a duel with U. S. Senator David Broderick, and had killed Broderick. Terry had married "one Sarah Hill, who was in the midst of a long legal battle to obtain her share of the estate of former United States Senator William Sharon of Nevada. She claimed they had been married secretly; Sharon had vigorously denied the claim until his death in 1885."[20] Field had been performing circuit duty in California, and ruled against Mrs. Terry. He held both Terrys in contempt when they erupted with shouted threats. Mrs. Terry, who had a knife, received thirty days in jail; Terry, who had a pistol, received six months.

When Field returned later on business to California, Attorney General W. H. H. Miller assigned a deputy marshal, David Neagle, to Field for protection. Sure enough, Terry accosted Field, and Neagle killed him. Because there were no federal laws protecting a marshal in the course of duty, both Field and Neagle were charged with murder. The U. S. courts dismissed the charges, but California claimed jurisdiction, and appealed to the U. S. Supreme Court. The Court held that Neagle was acting as "the principal conservator of 'the peace of the United States'" and turned down California's appeal. The *Neagle* decision became one of the greatest assertions of the implied powers under the Constitution of the Government of the United States.[21]

Although Harrison accepted the supremacy of the legislature, he vigorously protected executive authority. He did take action to influence legislation, despite his whiggish orientation. He met with members of Congress, often over dinner for small groups, and informed them what features bills must have to receive his signature. He sometimes sent cabinet members with messages to members of Congress. He remarked that his primary influence on legislation had come from his veto power."[22] In his one term, he cast forty-four vetoes, and was upheld on all but one.

Benjamin Harrison was not a great president. He did not serve in heroic times. However, despite many assertions to the contrary, he was not a passive president. Under the circumstances, he accomplished a great deal, especially in view of his attitude toward executive-legislative relations.

Where, then, should he be ranked? The better question, is "should he be?"

24

GROVER CLEVELAND
March 4, 1893–March 4, 1897

In 1892, Grove Cleveland was again the Democratic nominee for president. Benjamin Harrison, now the incumbent, once again was his opponent. This time Cleveland won (both the popular and electoral vote). The twenty-second president had been elected as the twenty-fourth, making Cleveland the only American president to serve two nonsecutive terms — a feat that has never been repeated.

Cleveland's second term is covered with his first, in Chapter 23.

25

WILLIAM MCKINLEY
March 4, 1897–September 14, 1901

In 1896, the American people had a clear choice between a solid, conservative Republican and a "radical" Populist running also on the Democratic ticket who favored the free coinage of silver, an inflationary policy. The "Gold Democrats" bolted and chose their own, reliably conventional, candidate. The split Democratic Party lost across the board. Republican William McKinley became the twenty-fifth President of the United States. The new vice president was Garret A. Hobart. McKinley had won a majority of the popular vote, 51 percent. It was the first time since Grant's 1872 victory that a presidential candidate had won a clear majority. The Republicans also won control of both houses of Congress.[1] The election dealt a blow to the Democrats, but it was a death blow to the Populists and to the free coinage of silver. Nevertheless, some "Populist arrows later hit their mark." During the Progressive period, amendments to the Constitution incorporated Populist principles and provided for the direct election of senators and for a progressive income tax.[2]

During the new administration, tariffs rose sharply (the Dingley Tariff of 1897), the gold standard became secure (the Gold Standard Act of 1900), and in 1898 the United States annexed Hawaii — as Harrison had sought, but Cleveland had blocked. The McKinley administration worked to ensure the "Open Door" policy in China by which foreign powers had equal access to Chinese markets. It also participated in suppressing the Boxer Rebellion there. The "Boxers" were armies of martial artists, or Chinese boxers, some of whom believed that their training developed their *ch'i* so completely that they could withstand bullets (they discovered that despite their masters' assertions, they could not). The boxers had massacred some foreigners and

177

captured others. The occupying powers, including the United States, moved to crush the Boxers and rescue the hostages. They forced the Chinese to pay reparations. To its credit, the United States used its share to provide scholarships to students from China.

McKinley used patronage skillfully as a political tool. His initial cabinet appointments, however, included two poor choices which brought him difficulty. The ill and elderly Senator John Sherman became secretary of state, and Michigan businessman and politician Russell Alger took over the War Department. Neither was competent for his position. When war came, Alger was "over his head."[3] His inefficiencies led to his forced resignation and to an investigation, but no evidence emerged that would have brought criminal charges. Sherman also resigned, and two new members, John Hay as secretary of State and Elihu Root as secretary of war brought great strength and badly needed competence.

One very important appointment at the sub-cabinet level was Theodore Roosevelt as assistant secretary of the navy (then the number-two position in the Department). The vigorous and innovative Roosevelt did not hesitate to exercise full authority when Secretary of the Navy John Long was on several of his extended vacations. When war began, Roosevelt resigned his position to raise and lead a unit, affectionately known as the "Rough Riders." It performed superbly, and Roosevelt received promotion to colonel on the battlefield. He became a legitimate war hero, and even more popular as a national figure.

Deaths of political figures have often dramatically changed American history. The deaths in office of William Henry Harrison and Zachary Taylor brought a sudden shift of policy to favor Southern demands; Abraham Lincoln's tragic assassination brought an equally tragic Andrew Johnson presidency that sabotaged any effective chance for reconstruction and a two-party South that had any semblance of racial equality; James A. Garfield's assassination brought to office the careful Chester Arthur, who surprised the public — and also his former political cronies — by using the sentiment that Garfield's death generated to support the creation of a merit-based civil service. Vice President Garret Hobart died suddenly on 21 November 1899. He had been a close confidant of President McKinley's, and had served the administration well as President of the Senate. His wife, Jennie, was a great asset as well, frequently stepping in to perform social functions for the ailing First Lady, Ida McKinley, whose serious health troubles included epilepsy. Hobart's death removed a loyal supporter from the administration.

More important, it created a vacancy in the position of vice president. When McKinley ran his successful campaign for re-election in 1900, his new running mate was the most dynamic figure in American politics (if not in American history), the young Governor of New York, Theodore Roosevelt.

Six months after the beginning of McKinley's second term as president and Roosevelt's term as vice president, President McKinley himself died at the hand of an assassin. Theodore Roosevelt, at the age of forty-two, became the youngest man ever to be President of the United States.

Time has dimmed McKinley's image. Whether it was the overwhelming personality and presidency of his successor, or merely Americans' tendency to have a weak grasp of their own history, they tend to remember McKinley faintly, if at all. To some historians, it is another matter. Although his reputation has risen and fallen somewhat through the years, Lewis Gould was not alone when he remarked — numerous times, in fact — that McKinley was the first modern president.[4] He said that historians tend to rate McKinley "in the middle range and lower" among presidents, and that McKinley himself probably would not have been surprised. Greatness, Gould said, attaches to a small group to which McKinley does not belong. Nevertheless, "if standards of judgment include strength as president and impact on the history of the office, then McKinley's tenure gains in importance." He went on to say that on these grounds, "McKinley easily merits a higher place than Hayes or Cleveland."[5]

Such an evaluation would not have grated on the ears of many of McKinley's contemporaries, some of whom in fact would have rated him even higher than Gould did. Nearly two decades after McKinley's 1901 assassination, his reputation still was extraordinary. Shortly after former president Theodore Roosevelt died in January 1919, for example, Progressive leader Joseph M. Dixon — former senator from and former governor of Montana — eulogized the old Rough Rider. In a speech in Missoula, Montana, Dixon said that the Roosevelt would rank among the great presidents. Among whom, he said, were such presidents as Washington, Lincoln, "and perhaps McKinley."[6]

McKinley had been immensely popular. He "turned an accessible and affable face" to the public, and went openly around Washington "as Grant used to do." He also "resumed the regular public receptions that Cleveland had discontinued."[7] James Ford Rhodes, writing in 1922, mentioned his "vast influence with Congress," and quoted Theodore Roosevelt's first annual message in which the new president said that at the time of McKinley's death, he had been "the most widely loved man in the United States."[8] A glowing tribute, *Life of William McKinley: Our Martyred President*, almost immediately after his death, included a chapter describing sympathetic ceremonies held in some two dozen countries around the world.[9]

Today, however, few people other than historians are likely to know much of McKinley, and the historians seem to be generally respectful, but not overly enthusiastic. In Schlesinger's 1962 poll, he fell into the "average" category, and ranked fifteenth of the thirty-one rated.[10] He had risen somewhat in the collective judgment of those who participated in Schlesinger, Jr.'s, 1996 poll, which placed him among the "high average," sixteenth of the thirty-nine.[11] Genovese placed him in exactly the same position.[12] The Fabers, on the other hand, viewed him much less favorably. In their opinion, he was an "intelligent and popular man," but they thought "his failure to prevent the Spanish-American War was disgraceful."[13]

That war unquestionably dominated his presidency. Rhodes, early in the twentieth century, was convinced that McKinley could have avoided that war had he resisted pressures from within his own party.[14] More recent assessment, however, has taken note of the complexities of the situation. Gould, for example, has written that there are two dominant explanations for McKinley's Spanish-Cuban diplomacy. One, the Rhodes position, is that he was weak and yielded to war hysteria. Gould noted that such a view assumes that the Spanish ultimately would have agreed to a peaceful settlement. The second view sees McKinley as a "wily expansionist," who deliberately sought war. Gould noted that the diplomatic record gives no support to either position. Spain held its "grip on Cuba to the end," and atrocities continued there. To have avoided war, Gould said, would have "taken a revolution in attitudes, outside the existing political consensus, to have produced any other result than intense absorption in the fate of Cuba." In fact, he wrote, in view of the Spanish tenacity, "what is remarkable is how long the president was able to obtain time for the conducting of peaceful diplomacy."[15]

The battleship *Maine* exploded in Havana Harbor and sank on 15 February 1898. It seemed apparent to many observers at the time that Cuban sabotage had caused the explosion. Careful studies by modern military historians have not been definitive regarding the precise cause of the tragedy, but the evidence suggests that it may well have been an accident. Regardless, the effect on the public was electrifying. McKinley's critics have argued that he should have rallied public opinion against war after the loss of the *Maine*, but as Gould asks, "what could he have said?"[16] Spain and the United States each was convinced that it was in the right. The Americans sent troops to Cuba to end an excessively brutal civil war, "against a foe that had resisted all attempts at peaceful compromise." Gould asserted that the war reflected a "better side of American life than posterity has recognized. If the war that ensued was not splendid," he wrote, "it had come in a way that dishonored neither the two countries involved nor the presidency of William McKinley."[17]

The McKinley administration had moved quickly — with the strong assertion of power by Acting Secretary of the Navy Theodore Roosevelt — to assure naval victory against the Spanish fleet in the Philippines. That victory was complete, and resulted in utter destruction of the Spanish naval presence there with almost no American casualties. America clearly had become a world power, and "men who were close to the White House agreed that William McKinley ran the war on the American side." By so doing, he considerably expanded the presidency.[18]

McKinley, then, was a strong president. Gould certainly had a point when he argued that McKinley should rank ahead of Cleveland or Hayes. The basic question, though, is why cannot his presidency simply be permitted to stand on its own merits? Does not comparison of such disparate figures in such different times under such varying circumstances obscure the true issues and make it more difficult to arrive at a sound evaluation of any one of them?

26

THEODORE ROOSEVELT
September 14, 1901–March 4, 1909

Theodore Roosevelt was the first vice president to go on to win the presidency in his own right after having succeeded to a vacancy in the office. To date there have been three others, Coolidge, Truman, and Lyndon Johnson. When Roosevelt won election in his own right, his percentage of the popular vote was the highest that any presidential candidate had received until that time. He had enchanted the popular imagination.

The new president brought with him a reputation as a rancher and sometime lawman in the Wild West who could handle the worst the frontier could hurl at him. That included assorted ruffians and outlaws, punishing and ceaseless labor, and fierce weather. The public knew of the determination and courage that had enabled him to build a powerful body after a frail and sickly childhood — as a writer, he made certain that they knew. They knew him as a champion of political reform, and as a legitimate war hero in the Spanish-American War. Political bosses knew these things, too. Republican boss and Ohio Senator Mark Hanna feared for the future. "Now look," he said, "that damned cowboy is President of the United States."

Roosevelt's background included much more than acts of physical valor. He had a powerful and broad intellect, and was a prolific author on a wide range of subjects. Among other things, these included American history, biography, military history, and wildlife. He was renowned for scientific studies on big game animals and songbirds. Harbaugh pointed out that Roosevelt was a statesman "whose interests were more catholic than all but a handful of his country's men of letters and probably most of its college professors." His breadth, said Harbaugh, "was incredible. He knew, often in the original, Villon, Ronsard, Mistral, Körner, Topelius, Goethe, Dante, Dumas, and hundreds of others. He was versed in the minor Scandinavian sagas, the Arabian tales, the core of Rumanian literature. And he even earned," Harbaugh noted, "honorary presidency of the Gaelic Literature Association." Moreover, he had "read the bulk of his own country's literature and knew personally perhaps a majority of the nation's best writers." This was, Harbaugh observed, "a rare quality in any man of action," but was "a unique quality in a President."[1] He remarked that there were other intellectual presidents, such as Jefferson, the Adamses, and Wilson — Clinton, who served after Harbaugh wrote these words, is the only other one (despite Kennedy's well-crafted image) who even comes close — but his comment that none other had generated Roosevelt's "virile intellectualism" remains accurate.

Always with a reform agenda, TR had been a member of the New York State Assembly, the U.S. Civil Service Commission, and the Police Commission of New York City. He had been assistant secretary of the navy — which at that time was the number-two position in a cabinet-level department. He had been governor of New York, and vice president of the United States. At the age of forty-two, he was president of the United States. John F. Kennedy would be forty-three at the time of his election. Theodore Roosevelt was the youngest person ever to hold the office.

Without doubt, he also was the most dynamic. Roosevelt was the overwhelming force in American politics in the early part of the twentieth century, and soon became a major world influence as well. He would easily have been the first three-term president, except for a rash promise that he made when he won his landslide victory in 1904. That promise — that he would not run again — which had been impulsive and not well-considered, caused his wife Edith to "wince in surprise."[2] It came back to haunt him in 1908. He said he would give his right arm not to have made the pledge.

It is doubtful that anyone ever loved being president to the extent that he did. But he considered his pledge to be binding. Despite pressures to run again, he honored it.

His reputation when he left office was extraordinary. It declined for a time, but since has risen sharply.[3] Much of the reason that it declined at all is attributable to an extensive biography by Henry Pringle in 1931.[4] Pringle's study was well-written and interesting — so much so that it received a Pulitzer Prize — but it was a brutal treatment. However much he may have attempted to be fair, Pringle left no doubt that he disliked his subject and took him no more seriously than he would have an adolescent — a word that he used frequently to refer to Roosevelt. Unfortunately, Pringle influenced a generation in a way that Arthur Schlesinger, Jr. — a friend of Pringle's — correctly described as "mischievous."[5]

John Morton Blum wrote an excellent, and much more balanced, work in 1954.[6] Numerous others followed. Of the later general works that dealt with his presidency, the best are the splendid one-volume study by William H. Harbaugh[7]; Edmund Morris's *Theodore Rex*, the second volume of a projected three-volume work[8]; Nathan Miller's one-volume biography[9]; and most recently, Kathleen Dalton's *Theodore Roosevelt: A Strenuous Life*, which holds its own with any of the others, and is the best at presenting TR's own life.[10]

TR's rankings placed him in the "near great" category in both Schlesinger polls, seventh of thirty-one in 1962,[11] and an improved sixth of thirty-nine in 1996.[12] Genovese similarly placed him seventh overall (of thirty-nine), and categorized him as "near great."[13] The Fabers, too, put him in seventh place; a number of other polls have ranked him as high as fourth.[14] In 1994, the Siena College poll even placed him third, behind FDR and Lincoln, in that order, and ahead of Washington. This reflected the tendency for his ratings to improve; the same poll in both 1982 and 1990 had rated him only number five.[15] Thus, he consistently ranks near the top. This verifies — assuming that the judgments are accurate — that his was a highly significant presidency, and that Roosevelt was important in the history of the executive. That much should be obvious to any student of history, however, even without a ranking. The polls reveal little, if anything else.

Without begrudging McKinley his due, Theodore Roosevelt has the best claim to being the first modern president. In many ways most even of his successors have failed to reach the standards that he set by his examples. Presidential scholar Wilfred Binkley once wrote that outstanding leadership as a rule can come forth only in time of crisis.[16] The Political historian Clinton Rossiter went even further. He wrote that no president could possibly be judged great "unless he holds office in great times."[17]

Ordinarily this is true, which makes TR's performance as chief executive all the more impressive. Only he, among all the presidents who can lay a true claim to greatness, held office at a time of no overt national crisis so severe as to threaten the country's continuation. Arthur Schlesinger, Jr., wrote of Jackson and TR as in a class by themselves. "Of the immortals," he said — no doubt indicating that he would class Jackson also as one with a claim to greatness — only two "made their mark without benefit of first-order crisis. Jackson and Theodore Roosevelt forced the nation through sheer power of personality to recognize incipient problems — Jackson in vindicating the national authority against the state of South Carolina and against the Second Bank of the United States; the first Roosevelt in vindicating the national authority against the great corporations and against raids on the people's natural resources." He quoted the historian and TR scholar Elting E. Morison as describing this "quality of noncrisis leadership" admirably. Morison said, "Theodore Roosevelt could get the attention of his fellow citizens and make them think. He knew how to put the hard questions a little before they became obvious to others; how to make the search for sensible answers exciting; how to startle the country into informing debate; and how to move people into their thinking beyond short-run self-interest toward some longer view of the general welfare."[18] He also, in Eric Goldman's words, "brought the country out of the divisiveness of the 1890s."[19] In that respect — if only in that respect — he resembled a far different president, Eisenhower in the 1950s.

TR was not faced with the task of actually implementing America's Constitution and establishing its governmental institutions as Washington was; he was not called upon to hold the country together and re-establish its unity when it had been torn apart as Lincoln was; and it was not necessary for him to deal with twin crises of America's greatest economic depression followed by the world's greatest war as it later was for his distant cousin Franklin D. Roosevelt. Theodore Roosevelt presided over a time of peace, and in common with few other presidents lost no American lives to warfare.

Rather, he achieved greatness by committing himself to the public interest — the interest of the whole public, not a particular class — and by building upon two keen insights. First, uniquely among presidents until his time, he recognized the need for strength in government to counter the real and growing threats to a free society from corporate industrialism. Second, and at least as important, he not only recognized the potential of the presidency to marshal and apply that strength, but he began to establish ways within America's complex system of government to do so — all without surrendering its institutions to demagoguery. To this end he articulated his "stewardship theory" of the presidency, that "the executive power was limited only by specific restrictions and prohibitions appearing in the Constitution or imposed by the Congress under its Constitutional powers." He set forth his executive philosophy clearly:

> My view was that every executive officer, and above all every executive officer in high position, was a steward of the people bound actively and affirmatively to do all he could for the people.... I declined to adopt the view that what was imperatively necessary for the Nation could not be done by the President unless he could find some specific authorization to do it. My belief was that it was not only his right but his duty to do anything that the needs of the Nation demanded unless such action was forbidden by the Constitution or by the laws.

As a result of his approach, in his words: "I did and caused to be done many things not previously done by the President and the heads of the departments. I did not usurp power," he said, "but I did greatly broaden the use of executive power."[20]

Upon assuming office, Roosevelt announced that he would continue the policies of President McKinley. He quickly left McKinley's policies behind him, however, and proceeded in the direction of Progressivism. He moved rapidly.

Hardly had he become president when he invited the noted black leader Booker T. Washington to the White House — the name he bestowed officially upon the executive mansion — for dinner to discuss ways to strengthen the Republican Party in the South. There was no public announcement of the dinner, but a reporter discovered it, and revealed in print that Washington had dined with the president. Cries of dismay swept the South.

"Southern newspapers loudly denounced the President for letting his wife and daughters sup with a black man." Mississippi bigot James K. Vardaman said Roosevelt encouraged "the violation of white women by black men." South Carolina's notorious racist Senator "Pitchfork Ben" Tillman squealed that "the action of President Roosevelt in entertaining that nigger will necessitate our killing a thousand niggers in the South before they will learn their place again." TR barred Tillman from the White House, and of course was angry and despondent at the reaction, and at "the depth of race hatred the incident uncovered."[21]

Nevertheless, he remarked later that, although his dinner with Washington no doubt had been a political mistake, he was glad that he had asked him. "The clamor aroused by the act," he said, made him feel that it had been necessary. He added that he did not intend to offend anyone's prejudices, but said, "neither do I allow their prejudices to make me false to my principles."[22] The extent of those prejudices is startling. James Ford Rhodes, in an early history of the McKinley and Roosevelt administrations, quoted one young white Southerner as saying at the time that he loved TR and would follow him anywhere, but that he could not "get over ... the Booker Washington incident." He said that he knew Washington's work and appreciated it. Washington had even been in his "mother's parlor and invited to sit down there." He might even have had no feeling about the president and Washington having lunch or dinner by themselves, "But to invite him to the table with ladies," he said, "that is what no Southerner can brook."[23] It is even more startling to recognize that this person's opinion was moderate for the time among whites in the South.

Although TR's record on race was at least as good as that of any president between Grant and Franklin Roosevelt — or perhaps even between Grant and Truman — it was not a strong point of his presidency. He did not repeat the Washington invitation, nor did he move vigorously on racial matters. His record is even marred by one outrageous incident in 1906 in which he discharged three companies of black soldiers. There had been a disturbance including a shooting in Brownsville, Texas and some of the townspeople charged that black troops had been involved. Roosevelt was angry that none of the troops would identify anyone who participated. He always denied that race had been a factor in his decision, but although he did not back down, he clearly was uncomfortable with his action, and did not refer to it in his 1913 *Autobiography.*

The episode certainly is not to Roosevelt's credit. It is tempting — and easy — to conclude that he acted out of racial prejudice. Writers of course generally have leaped to that conclusion. Even the judicious Kathleen Dalton assumed that TR's action reflected "racial condescension," although she did point out thoughtfully that the discharge decision "had the markings of a bad judgment call made in a hasty, tired moment."[24] Certainly TR may have acted out of prejudice. It may even be the most likely conclusion. It is impossible to know with certainty, but there is another possible explanation.

Roosevelt had a strict sense of military discipline. His definition of integrity would include an assumption that a soldier had a duty to identify another who committed wrongdoing. As a matter of fact, the service academies today at Annapolis, Colorado Springs, and West Point operate with just such an honor code. As I have written elsewhere, "regardless of whether race was involved, injustice certainly was. The existence of the racial element points up the injustice, which might have gone unnoticed had it been absent, but it is possible that TR may have been criticized for the wrong reasons.[25]

Nothing slowed the new president down. In February of 1902, when he had been in office for fewer than six months, TR directed Attorney General Philander C. Knox (whom he inherited from McKinley) to file suit to break up the Northern Securities Corporation. As he described that new corporation in his *Autobiography*, it resulted from the action of a "small group of financiers desiring to profit" from governmental "impotence." The tycoons J. P. Morgan, James J. Hill, and E. H. Harriman had combined a number of railroads, including the huge Northern Pacific and the Great Northern, and "had arranged to take control of practically the entire railway system in the Northwest."[26] The explosive news of the suit came as a shock to the business community. Morgan came to see the president and told him, "if we have done anything wrong, send your man to my man and they can fix it up." TR refused, saying later that Morgan had illustrated Wall Street's point of view, which was that the President of the United States was simply a "big rival operator" with whom he could work out a deal.[27] If that indeed had been the nature of the presidency before, Theodore Roosevelt had changed it dramatically.

The Supreme Court, to the surprise of conservatives (and others as well), ruled in favor of the government. It upheld the Sherman Anti-Trust Act and found the Northern Securities Corporation to be in violation of its provisions. The Court ordered dissolution. Its vote was by the narrowest of margins, five to four, and Roosevelt was outraged that his own appointee, Oliver Wendell Holmes, Jr., voted in the minority against him. Still, he had won. He went on to order suits against the American Tobacco and the Standard Oil Companies. "Both," he said, "were adjudged criminal conspiracies, and their dissolution ordered."[28]

As a pragmatist, TR would compromise as necessary. On conservation of natural resources, however, he fought any attempt to dilute his program — the strongest in history. All in all, his administration added five new national parks, beginning in 1902 with Crater Lake National Park in Oregon. The others, in 1903 and 1904 respectively were Wind Cave National Park in South Dakota and Sullys Hill National Park in North Dakota. Platt National Park in Oklahoma and Mesa Verde National Park in Colorado followed in 1906. In addition to these were 150 national forests; 51 federal bird reservations, including Pelican Island, Florida; 4 national game preserves; 18 national monuments; and 24 reclamation projects. In 1902 he signed into law the Newlands Reclamation Act, which was one of twenty new federal irrigation projects, including the Theodore Roosevelt Dam in Arizona. The extensive web site of the Theodore Roosevelt Association lists each of these measures.[29]

Roosevelt had an emotional commitment to the "bond between man and wilderness," as Dalton put it.[30] He succeeded in persuading Congress to transfer supervision of forests from the Department of the Interior — which had been noted for corruption in numerous previous administrations — to the Department of Agriculture, and he placed his friend and professional forester, Gifford Pinchot, as head of the new Forest Service. His concern, however, was broader than merely the "preservation of animals, forests, and water resources. As a historian he understood how damaging deforestation had been to topsoil in other countries." He cited China and North Africa as examples, and wrote that erosion seriously damaged the environment, greatly disrupting agriculture and other economic activities. Congress failed to heed many of his warnings, and the dust bowls of the 1930s were the consequence. He may have developed special sensitivities to the dangers of air pollution because of his own asthma. He ordered industries in the District of Columbia to cease pouring out smoke, and took steps to prevent federal agencies from polluting the air.[31]

Air pollution was extreme in American cities at the time, because coal was the dominant source of heat for homes and buildings. In 1902, miners in eastern Pennsylvania struck in protest of their working conditions, which involved long hours, low pay, and danger on the job. The resulting coal shortage with winter looming threatened disaster. Roosevelt called United Mine Workers President John Mitchell along with the mine owners to his office to negotiate. The owners were haughty, and refused negotiation, saying they resented being summoned to meet with a criminal. They called for troops to crush the strike.

Mitchell, on the other hand, was courteous and completely cooperative. He surprised and impressed Roosevelt, who let the owners know that if troops came, it would be to operate the mines, not to defeat the workers. Faced with the president's determination, the owners agreed to arbitration. They refused to accept a union representative on the arbitration commission, but agreed to a mining engineer, a military officer, a businessman, a federal judge, and an "eminent sociologist." In a brilliant move, TR appointed E. E. Clark, who was president of the Brotherhood of Railway Conductors, as the "eminent sociologist."

TR wrote in his *Autobiography* that he would never forget the mixture of relief and amusement when he grasped the fact that the owners would "submit to anarchy rather than have Tweedledum," yet if he called it "Tweedledee they would accept it with rapture." He said sardonically that it gave him "an illuminating glimpse into one corner of the mighty brains of these 'captains of industry'."[32] The owners, having saved face, agreed and the strike came to an end on 15 October 1902.[33] The situation had been so dire, that, as TR put it, "even so naturally conservative a man as Grover Cleveland wrote to me, expressing his sympathy with the course I was following." Roosevelt thus became the first president to intervene in a labor dispute as a neutral party — let alone with sympathy for the workers — rather than to do the bidding of the owners.

TR was elated after settling the coal strike, and said he felt like throwing up his hands "and going to the circus." Other matters, however, intruded into his euphoria. In early 1903 he discovered that many Post Office administrators were involved in corruption that dated from the McKinley administration and involved profiting from government contracts. Although it involved Republicans, he resisted the wrath from his own party, "faced the scandal squarely and with impressive tact," and moved vigorously to clean up the department.[34] That year he also signed into law the Elkins Anti-Rebate Railroad Act which prevented large shippers from receiving from the railroads — and sometimes extorting from them — rebates that gave them even greater advantage against smaller shippers. In addition, he signed legislation creating a new Department of Commerce and Labor, and appointed George Cortelyou as its secretary.

Some of the most dramatic aspects of Roosevelt's presidency are reflected in his highly successful foreign policy. During his first year in office, "he deftly and secretly warned the Germans, by an implicit threat of war, to stay out of Venezuela." He understood "the propensities of weak Latin American regimes for running up and then defaulting on debts to foreign bankers."[35] Italy, the United Kingdom, and Germany had taken military action because of Venezuelan debts, but it was the Kaiser whom TR suspected of harboring territorial designs in violation of the Monroe Doctrine. He persuaded the parties to submit their differences to International Court at The Hague, and thus gave strong support to the principle of arbitration for international disputes.

In the years leading up to the Second World War, some writers hostile to Roosevelt alleged that in his 1913 autobiography and later, he at best exaggerated the situation and his role in it.[36] Sometimes they asserted that TR was simply producing anti–German propaganda to boost the Allied cause. Pringle's unfriendly, but careful, biography, for example, accused "the former President" of being "quite willing" in his historical writings "to let patriotism's warmth obscure cold fact."[37] It spoke of the "obvious impossibilities of TR's narrative."[38] Pringle did concede, though, that TR's letters at the time — long before the First World War — did provide support for Roosevelt's position. He even admitted that "in all probability Roosevelt hastened the acceptance of arbitration by Germany," but could not resist adding that there is "no possible doubt that he dramatized and heightened the part that he played," and that "arbitration would have come in any event"[39]—a dubious assertion at best.

Postwar studies have documented as clearly as can be done when secret negotiations are involved, that TR described his role accurately. The secrecy had been essential to avoid challenging Germany in public and making a peaceful solution impossible. Dalton's excellent description of the episode is brief, but fully documented.[40] Morris's is lively, and much more extensive.[41] He recounted an incident in which Admiral Dewey said that he had been part of an operation that had been "an object lesson to the Kaiser." [42] TR called the admiral to the White House to admonish him. Although he could not bring himself to subject the "old warrior in medals" to a presidential dressing-down, he did write him to suggest gently that in the future he watch his words. TR's words themselves carry wisdom even into the twenty-first century. He said that it would be well to avoid causing trouble with any foreign power, and also to avoid giving substance to the charge from some other countries that "as a nation we are walking about with a chip on our shoulder. We are too big a people," he wrote, "to be able to be careless in what we have to say."

The year 1903 also brought other substantial accomplishments in foreign policy. That year Roosevelt brought settlement to the Alaskan boundary dispute, which secured the Alaskan gold fields to the United States, and he secured ratification of the Cuban Reciprocity Treaty. In November, he afforded protection to Panamanian rebels who seceded from Columbia, and recognized the new Republic of Panama. He then proceeded to negotiate and sign the Panama Canal Treaty. The following year, he outlined the

"Roosevelt Corollary" to the Monroe Doctrine, which asserted that the United States would enforce the Monroe Doctrine by intervening in situations of "chronic wrongdoing" in the hemisphere that would otherwise invite European intervention.

He justified his conduct in Panama — which he considered the "most important action [he] took in foreign affairs," by equating it with Jefferson's Louisiana Purchase. To the charge that he usurped authority, he replied merely that what he did was to exercise efficient authority "when nobody else could or would" do so.[43] There would have been no Canal at all without his actions. He said that one could argue that it would have been better to have no Canal than to have built it under such circumstances, but that it is "hypocrisy, alike odious and contemptible," to argue that America should have built the Canal, but not the way he did it.[44]

Regardless, this would have been an extraordinary list of accomplishments for any administration. These, however, came in TR's first term — which, one should remember, at three and one-half years was not even a full term. On 8 November 1904, he won his landslide re-election. Alton B. Parker, a lackluster opponent, was the Democratic candidate.

Roosevelt was delighted to be, at last, President of the United States in his own right. He was less delighted with his new vice president; the Republican National Convention had chosen the conservative Indiana Senator Charles W. Fairbanks. Fairbanks, Alaska, was to bear his name, and chances are that TR would have been delighted if the new vice president had chosen to spend his time there. Although long before he became president, he had advocated a key role in government for the vice president, TR would not — and did not — permit a vice president in whom he had little confidence to figure prominently in his administration.

Shortly after his inauguration on 4 March 1905, the Republican president happily attended the wedding of his niece, Eleanor, the daughter of his late brother Elliott. The groom was their young and distant cousin, a Democrat, Franklin D. Roosevelt. The new couple almost three decades later would become First Lady and President of the United States.

In September of that year because of Roosevelt's initiative and his skillful negotiation the Russians and the Japanese signed a treaty ending the Russo-Japanese War. The Japanese had attacked and destroyed the Russian fleet. They clearly were in the ascendancy, but the war dragged on, and Russia had almost unlimited manpower. "He failed to consult his cabinet, the State Department, or Congress about his mediation" of that war — and this was consistent with his having been the first president to use executive agreements to circumvent the treaty process.[45] TR arranged for the negotiations to be conducted in Portsmouth, New Hampshire, and personally supervised the proceedings, deftly handing and bringing together the two very difficult parties. At times, he despaired of success, but succeed he did.[46] He had "demonstrated exceptional diplomatic skill and openness to new cultures and peoples in the negotiations." In no way was he a "bigot with a closed mind. It also helped that he had studied Japanese history and culture."[47] As a result of his mediation, on 10 December 1906, he became the first American to win a Nobel Prize — the Nobel Prize for Peace.

To date, only Woodrow Wilson (TR's nemesis) and Jimmy Carter among presidents have joined Roosevelt as Nobel laureates. TR donated his substantial prize money to a foundation to establish a permanent "Industrial Peace Commission." He explained to his children that he and Edith had discussed it, and although he would rather save the money for them, he felt it improper to do so because it had come to him as a result of his official duties.[48]

For several reasons, Japan weighed heavily on Roosevelt's mind. He had great respect for Japanese culture and capabilities, and saw the Empire of the Rising Sun as a direct threat to American interests in the Pacific. He also was far ahead of his time in his concern for a possible German-Japanese alliance against the United States. The State of California, where prejudice against Japanese was strong, made American-Japanese relations all the more difficult. The proud Japanese public and its officials were outraged — as was the president — against discriminatory and humiliating measures that Californians had adopted against Japanese residents there.

As president, Roosevelt had no authority over California policy, but he attempted to negotiate with local authorities. At first he had little success, and South Carolina's Senator "Pitchfork Ben" Tillman ranted about efforts to force "Mongolization" in California, and the potential for race-mixing in the South. The San Francisco School Board had adopted a policy of segregation, which Morris described as treating Japanese children as black children were treated in Alabama. "Roosevelt decided on a moderation of his attitude," Morris said, "not just to soothe redneck neuroses, but because of the much more dangerous mood of the Japanese government."[49] TR persuaded San Francisco's mayor to readmit Japanese children to the public schools contingent upon an informal agreement with Japan to limit Japanese emigration to the United States. The resulting "Gentleman's Agreement" defused the tension, although Japan hardly forgot the insult.

TR continued to project the United States into world politics. At first he refrained from taking a stand in the dispute between France and Germany over Morocco, although he did send a delegation to the resulting Algeciras Conference. When it deadlocked in January 1906, he secretly sent a message, intervening as a disinterested mediator, and ultimately brought about a settlement that for the time being preserved Moroccan independence and kept the status quo in Europe.[50]

For the Roosevelt presidency 1906 was a banner year. That year he won passage of landmark legislation that pointed the way to the future. The Hepburn Act protected consumers by strengthening the powers of the Interstate Commerce Commission over railroad rates and practices. Protecting the public in another, and more direct, manner he signed into law the Meat Inspection Act, and the even more important Pure Food and Drug Act. At the same time, he captured the public's attention in quite a different fashion. He and Edith in a grand spectacle supervised the wedding in the White House of his daughter Alice to an Ohio member of the U.S. House of Representatives, Nicholas Longworth. He intrigued the public yet again when he and Edith journeyed to Panama to inspect the construction of the new Panama Canal. It was the first time that a President of the United States had left the country while in office.

The next year brought a severe economic panic, but also the voyage of the "Great White Fleet" around the world. TR considered the trip to be his most important contribution to peace.[51] No large convoy had ever completed such a voyage, and many naval experts considered it to be impossible with the equipment available; ships would break down, the rough seas around the Horn were too formidable, and the like. Without consulting his cabinet or Congress, TR directed the fleet — a convoy extending for more than three miles and including sixteen battleships — to depart from Virginia. At first, the destination seemed to be California, but the fleet then proceeded across the Pacific.

There was considerable opposition to the cruise. "The head of the Senate Committee on naval Affairs announced that the fleet should not and could not go because Congress would refuse to appropriate the money." The president announced in response that it was going; that he had enough money already appropriated to take the fleet to the Pacific, "and that if Congress did not choose to appropriate enough money to get the fleet back, why, it would stay in the Pacific. There was," TR wrote in his biography, "no further difficult about the money."[52] Presidential historian Clinton Rossiter asked of TR, "who can say he did not act grandly when he started the fleet off around the world and left it up to Congress to buy enough coal to bring it back?"[53] The fleet did return, on the 22nd of February 1909, more than a year after it had set out. A few days later, and the Bull Moose presidency would be at an end.

The voyage was a huge success. It demonstrated, and corrected, weaknesses in gunnery and seamanship, it impressed the American people and instilled pride in American accomplishment, and it sent a message to other countries — including Japan, although Roosevelt was quite careful not to make it a show of belligerence — that the United States had become a first-class naval power.

As great as any of Roosevelt's successes was his program of conservation of natural resources. In the face of condemnations from western members of Congress, he had managed to accomplish "more than any other president to save trees and wilderness areas — he quadrupled federal forestland until 172 million acres were protected by law."[54] The most dramatic of his actions on behalf of the environment equaled in "grandness" his feat in sending the fleet around the world.

On 22 February 1907, a member of his own party tried to scuttle Roosevelt's conservation efforts. Republican Senator Charles Fulton of Oregon added a rider to a bill that TR needed for his forest program, the Agricultural Appropriations bill. The rider stipulated that within the States of Oregon, Washington, Idaho, Montana, Colorado, or Wyoming only Congress — not the president — could create or add to a forest reserve. The president could not veto the bill without eliminating the money the Forest Service needed to operate; if he signed it, he no longer had the authority to create forest reserves in the six northwestern — and heavily forested — states.

Both Theodore Roosevelt and his chief forester, Gifford Pinchot, had killer instincts — unlike some politicians then and especially later, however, they "fought cleanly."[55] Roosevelt had the bill that he needed to sign, but that stripped him of his authority. If he did nothing, it would become law in ten days without his signature. TR set the bill aside, and, with Pinchot and his staff, began a clean but deadly fight on behalf of conservation.

Working together they managed to save "all the public lands Senator Fulton thought he had saved from being saved." Clerks worked day and night to complete "all the paperwork necessary for the President to proclaim twenty-one new forest reserves, and eleven enlarged ones, in the six states specified"[56] before the ten days elapsed. The president then officially proclaimed the additional reserves, which constituted some sixteen million additional acres to be protected. Only then did he sign the bill stripping him of the authority to do so. Had he acquiesced, those acres would no longer be a source of controversy. They would have been ruined decades ago, and no longer would there be anything to save.

So, what can one say of the presidency of Theodore Roosevelt? Oklahoma became a state during his administration (in 1907). TR was a powerful national symbol, unifying the country east and west at a time when the wounds from the north-south conflict still were raw and bleeding. He saw as his greatest presidential achievements "the settlement of the coal strike, the construction of the Panama Canal, the ending of the Russo-Japanese War, the voyage of the Great White Fleet, 'the irrigation business in the West,' and finally," as he put it, "the toning up of the Government service generally."[57] Elting Morrison noted that TR had proposed "all the basic reforms that became law during the Taft and Wilson administrations — and some that awaited the coming of the New Deal."[58] Some critics sniff that Taft brought more anti-trust actions in his four years than Roosevelt did in his almost two terms, and conclude from that TR was more bluster than action. They fail to understand that a paved road is easy to follow; TR not only paved that road, but had blazed the trail before there was any path at all. It was he who made the later actions feasible.

There was vastly more to this first twentieth-century president than his critics recognized. John Milton Cooper, Jr., summarized the breadth of TR's influence with admiration.[59] He had thrown the weight of his office behind both the arts and scientific discovery, including providing support for the Smithsonian Institution and urging the creation of a National Gallery of Art. He had boasted that he had given the country "the most beautiful coinage since the decay of Hellenistic Greece." His hobbies and enthusiasms "reflected an aspect of his leadership that was serious, important, and virtually unique among American presidents. Lewis Einstein later commented that Roosevelt seemed to him to reincarnate the Italian Renaissance ideal of rounded and encompassing thought and action." Cooper said that TR pursued during his presidency what historian Jacob Burckhardt had called "the state as a work of art."[60] No better praise is possible for an American president.

Theodore Roosevelt had his faults, to be sure. Many of his ideas were quaint by today's standards. Some were misguided, and some clearly were wrong. He was, however, a powerful leader and one devoted to responsible, constitutional government. He preached and operated by his "Great Rule of Righteousness," that demanded that every man — or woman — be treated as an individual on his or her merits. He created a presidency that had not existed previously — one fully consistent with the Constitution, if not with custom. That presidency enabled the United States to compete in the new, interconnected, technologically sophisticated, complex, and highly dangerous world that loomed as he left office.

He was great, and knew it. He needed no ranking to tell him where he — or any other president — placed. Nor should we.

27

WILLIAM HOWARD TAFT
March 4, 1909–March 4, 1913

William Howard Taft had been Theodore Roosevelt's secretary of war, and was also his handpicked successor to be President of the United States. The Taft presidency had its accomplishments and has always had its defenders. Without doubt there have been many that were worse. It would be unwarranted and unfair to classify it as a failure.

On the other hand, no one — likely not Taft himself and certainly not TR, the man who engineered his selection as president — would list Taft among the greatest presidents. The only possible exception to this broad statement might be Helen ("Nellie") Herron Taft, his wife. It was she who pushed a somewhat-reluctant Taft toward the presidency in the first place. He would always have preferred to be on the United States Supreme Court.

Taft was an able man, and man of principle and integrity. He also was a good administrator. In view of his position, however, what he was not was as important as what he was. He was not a skilled politician — in fact, not only did he dislike politics, he had never run for office before running for president. He also did not have what a later president dismissed as "the vision thing." Moreover, although he did desire to protect the independence of the executive, he had a restricted view of its place within the American political system, and he lacked a sense of its potential to contribute to the public good.

These lacks are puzzling when one considers his previous association with the vibrant and innovative Theodore Roosevelt, and his key position within the Roosevelt administration. Taft was committed largely to laissez-faire, but despite that commitment he had pledged to support Roosevelt's policies. Some explanations for this contradiction are his "personal friendship with Roosevelt, his party loyalty, his unfortunate habit of permitting those closest to him to make his decisions for him, and his lack of contact with, indeed dislike of, reformers and progressives even before he became president."[1]

Genovese rated Taft number twenty-three, the top of his "below average" category.[2] He provided a brief, but quite good, summary of the Taft presidency and of Taft's views. Genovese described Taft's view of presidential authority — a view well known to be vastly more restricted than TR's. "He opposed Roosevelt's theory that the president has a large unspecific 'residuum of powers'." In 1916, Taft wrote that TR's view "ascribing an undefined residuum of power to the President is an unsafe doctrine" that might lead to "injustice to private right." Genovese pointed out that, in contrast to TR, Taft "argued for a strict construction of Article II. The executive should exercise only power that is expressly or implicitly granted by the Constitution." As Taft, himself, put it, "such specific grant must be either in the Constitution or in an act of Congress passed in pursuance thereof. There is no undefined residuum of power which he can exercise because it seems to be in the public interest."[3] A greater contrast to TR's dynamic views could hardly be possible.

The 1962 Schlesinger poll treated him more kindly. In it, Taft rated sixteenth overall (of thirty-one), which placed him among those in the "average" category.[4] In the Schlesinger, Jr., poll of 1996, Taft's placement was similar, twenty-second of thirty-nine, still "average."[5] The Fabers, too, reacted much the same. They placed Taft twenty-first among their thirty-nine.[6] They captured much of the twenty-seventh president's essence when they wrote that Taft was dull, but "in the sense of being boring, not in the sense of being dimwitted."[7]

Thus, in contrast to the records of many presidents, Taft's seems to have generated little or no controversy among most observers. In his defense, he shared with very few presidents a liability completely beyond his control. Like John Adams, Andrew Johnson, and Harry Truman he had, so to speak, a very difficult act to follow. His supporters — and especially TR's detractors — have pointed out that Taft did remain quite aggressive against the trusts, and that he even filed more anti-trust suits in his one term than TR had in two.

This is correct, but misleading. TR was the pioneer "trust buster," who pointed the way. It is to Taft's credit, though, that he continued the Roosevelt policy — at least his anti-trust policy. The Taft administration's largest anti-trust victories were against the Standard Oil Company and the American Tobacco Company. In terms of its political effect, though, one might argue that the largest of the Taft administration's anti-trust suits was against the United States Steel Corporation.

In 1907, an economic panic had been threatening the American economy. J. P. Morgan had asked President Roosevelt if his U.S. Steel Corporation could acquire the Tennessee Coal and Iron Company in order to halt
the increasing panic. TR agreed that "he would not invoke the Sherman Act
to block the purchase." The sale went through immediately, "the market rallied, and the panic was over."[8] On 27 October 1911, however — ironically, it
was TR's fifty-third birthday — the Taft administration did file a lawsuit
accusing US Steel of having violating the Sherman Anti-Trust Act when it
acquired Tennessee Coal and Iron. The "indolent Taft had not read the documents before they were filed — a blunder in itself," said TR's biographer
Nathan Miller, but regardless, TR "angrily called the allegations an attack
upon his honor." The thrust of the lawsuit was that the company had duped
the Bull Moose. When the Supreme Court finally settled the case nearly a
decade later in 1920, it upheld Roosevelt's position.[9] The suit was a major
addition to TR's litany of complaints against Taft, and contributed to the
break in their friendship.

It also is to Taft's credit that he came to support an income tax, although
he at least initially would have preferred a corporation tax — the Supreme
Court had declared an income tax unconstitutional, and Taft was sensitive
to any criticism of the Court.[10] Nevertheless, he did support the proposal
and ratification of the Sixteenth Amendment to the Constitution to make
such a tax possible. The Amendment became part of the Constitution on 3
February 1913, almost exactly a month before Taft left office. His administration could add to its list of accomplishments the addition of two more
states to the Union. New Mexico and Arizona, in 1912, became the final
states of the contiguous forty-eight.

Taft's tin ear with regard to politics, however, led to his siding with his
secretary of the interior, Richard A. Ballinger against the head of the Forest
Service, Gifford Pinchot. His dismissal of Pinchot was one of several acts
that led Theodore Roosevelt to believe that Taft was betraying his programs,
and helped widen the split between the Republican old guard and the Progressive "Insurgents." Pinchot had charged Ballinger with improperly sell-
ing federal lands in Alaska to private interests. Although a congressional
investigation of the questionable action cleared Ballinger of any illegalities,
his action was a clear signal to the Progressives that he had no commitment
to their programs of conservation. Taft lost again when Ballinger resigned
in 1911.

Taft did sign into law the Mann-Elkins Act, in 1910. The new law
strengthened the Hepburn Act and gave added authority to the Interstate
Commerce Commission to set railroad rates and ban greater charges for short
than for long hauls. Taft had opposed the Progressive Insurgents who had
strengthened the bill.[11] Presidential scholars Milkis and Nelson noted the

irony that it was Taft's "most dramatic assertion of presidential leadership [that] proved to be his political undoing." They wrote that in the 1910 congressional primaries Taft worked to defeat such Republican progressives. Although Taft had criticized TR for "meddling in the legislative process," his own meddling in the nominating process was "an unprecedented effort by a president to influence congressional support for his legislative program." Taft's efforts in the primaries, they said, were "aggressive, albeit surreptitious." More to the point, they were "manifestly unsuccessful."[12]

Taft's political skills were no better in dealing directly with Congress. He had favored lower tariffs, but — consistent with his view of executive-legislative relations — gave Congress little guidance when it dealt with tariff revision. The resulting Payne-Aldrich Tariff of 1909 did lower some duties, but sharply raised others. Altogether, it clearly was a confused mix of actions that reflected the influence of special interests, and as such it generated great controversy. Taft nevertheless praised the new bill as "the best tariff bill that the Republican Party has ever passed, and therefore the best tariff bill that has been passed at all."[13] In view of the controversy surrounding the bill, Taft could hardly have done more to reduce his support among his own party.

In foreign affairs, Taft and his secretary of state, Philander C. Knox, developed the doctrine that came to be called "Dollar Diplomacy." They openly used the Department of State to protect American business abroad, and encouraged American investors to buy up foreign debt in Latin America so that there would be no incentive for European countries to meddle in the Western Hemisphere.

Although Helen Taft had a burning ambition to see her husband become president, and although Theodore Roosevelt successfully worked for Taft's nomination and election, until Taft actually sat in the White House, she had always thought TR would not follow through. President and Mrs. Taft were at dinner on 25 February 1912 when they heard of TR's comment that he would accept the Republican nomination that year if offered. The statement was in response to a letter from seven Republican governors urging TR to run again.

As Taft passed the notice around the table for the guests to read, Helen said bitterly, "I told you so four years ago, and you would not believe me." Taft replied, "I know you did, my dear, and I think you are perfectly happy now. You would have preferred the Colonel to come out against me than to have been wrong yourself."[14]

Despite TR's victories in most of the primaries, the Taft forces controlled the convention and re-nominated the president. With no effort to mollify the Progressives, the convention also re-nominated the arch-conservative Vice President James S. Sherman of New York to run again. The Taft campaign was lackluster, and both TR and the Democratic candidate, New Jersey Governor Woodrow Wilson, dismissed him and directed their campaigns at each other.

Vice President Sherman died a few days before the election, and Taft continued without a running mate. It did not matter. Taft came in a poor third, carrying only Utah and Vermont, and garnering only their eight electoral votes. For the first and only time, a minority candidate came in ahead of a major-party candidate. Former President Theodore Roosevelt, the Bull Moose Progressive candidate, carried six states, and received eighty-eight electoral votes. Taft lost out even in the popular vote. He received just over 23 percent, and TR received more than 27 percent. The victor, however, was Democrat Woodrow Wilson. Although he received not quite 42 percent of the popular vote, he swept up 435 electoral votes.[15]

It was a massive loss, but Taft's defeat "restored his zest for life and sense of humor." He no longer felt the heavy burden, and knew that he was not indispensable.[16] His biographer Paolo Coletta said that Taft had not been a bad president but, in fact, "a rather good one."[17] He had both failures and successes, but when "challenged by [Roosevelt's] New Nationalism on one side and [Wilson's] New Freedom on the other, he had retreated to a defense of conservative constitutionalism.[18] He was clumsy politically, and could never connect with the people. As *The Nation* put it, "he brought his fate upon himself.... Placed in the White House by grace of Theodore Roosevelt, he is now expelled from it as revenge of Theodore Roosevelt."[19] The conservative Taft thought of himself as a Progressive, and in fact was no reactionary. His alliance with the Old Guard, however, at the expense of the Progressive movement that had put him in office, split the Republican Party and ended it as a progressive force.

William Howard Taft was a decent man who conducted a decent presidency. He was able, but his talents were not those he needed to be President of the United States. He was insensitive not only to his friend, Theodore Roosevelt, who placed him in the presidency, but also to his party and to the mood of—and needs of—his country. A study of his presidency reveals his strengths — and he had strengths — and his weaknesses. Comparing him with other presidents tells us nothing.

WOODROW WILSON

March 4, 1913–March 4, 1921

Woodrow Wilson, formerly Governor of New Jersey, President of Princeton University, university professor, and lawyer, was the first and only President of the United States to have a Ph.D. degree. His degree from Johns Hopkins University was, in fact, one of the first such degrees in the United States. When he took office, he already "had a national reputation both as a scholar and as a popular intellectual leader."[1] He became the second American president, following Theodore Roosevelt, to win the Nobel Prize for Peace, one of only three in the country's history who have done so. Jimmy Carter was the third. Wilson was the first president to address Congress in person since John Adams, returning to a long-dead practice that not even Theodore Roosevelt had seen fit to restore.

Wilson's presidency, like that of his idol, Jefferson, is especially difficult to evaluate. Its accomplishments were enormous. So, too, were its failures. Those who play the game of ranking presidents, though, have tended to share Harry Truman's admiration of Wilson, although slightly less effusively. They generally place him quite high. Truman — who in no way, incidentally, was the greatest admirer of Franklin Roosevelt — said that in many ways Wilson was "the greatest of the greats."[2] The 1962 Schlesinger poll placed Wilson fourth out of thirty-one rated, among the five it designated as "great."[3] Arthur Schlesinger, Jr., reported that President John Kennedy expressed surprise to him that historians rated Wilson so well in his father's poll, below only Lincoln, Washington, and FDR in that order. "Though a fine speaker and writer, Wilson, in Kennedy's view," Schlesinger said, "had failed in a number of cherished objectives. Why did professors admire him so much? Schlesinger suggested a reason: after all, he quipped, Wilson was "the only professor to make the White House."[4]

In Schlesinger, Jr.'s, own 1996 poll, Wilson was seventh of thirty-nine, in the lower half of the "near-great" category (that poll listed only Lincoln, Washington, and FDR as "great").[5] Genovese, too, ranked him "near great," and put him sixth of thirty-nine.[6] Rossiter thought even more highly of Wilson, ranking him along with Jackson just under his two leaders, Lincoln and Washington. Rossiter (apparently forgetting the Adamses and Theodore Roosevelt) said that "Wilson was the best prepared President, intellectually and morally, ever to come to the White House."[7] The Fabers also placed him behind only Lincoln and Washington, third overall, although in their ranking he tied for third with FDR, not with Jackson (who could manage in their study no higher than ninth).[8]

Thus it is clear that rankings tend consistently to place Woodrow Wilson without qualification near the top. That fact alone, in view of the complexity of Wilson's presidency with its dramatic failures alongside successes, should lead a thoughtful observer to question the value of any ranking scheme. As Walter Dean Burnham put it, Wilson's case presented a "dichotomous or schizoid" profile. "On some very important dimensions," he said, in his view Wilson was an outright failure, while on others he should "rank very high indeed."[9] No single ranking or quantitative measure could reflect this.

Wilson won the three-way election of 1912 with less than 42 percent of the popular vote, but with a smashing victory in the electoral college. He received 435 of the 531 electoral votes. The race all along was between him and the Bull Moose Progressive candidate, former President Theodore Roosevelt. The incumbent, President William Howard Taft, was a distant third, carrying only Utah and Vermont, with a total of 8 electoral votes.[10] Much of Wilson's eight years as president saw the continuation of the contest with TR.

Reformers in general had hoped for a Roosevelt victory, and were dismayed at his defeat. They soon discovered, however, that Wilson with his "New Freedom" followed in TR's footsteps as a great reformer. Neither man, of course, would have admitted to the similarity of their domestic programs.

But Wilson's very domestic success brought controversy. He became, in John Milton Cooper, Jr.'s, words, "one of the two or three most controversial presidents in American history." For domestic legislative accomplishment, only FDR's New Deal from 1933 to 1936, and LBJ's Great Society in 1964 and 1965 "rival Wilson's accomplishments with the New Freedom between 1913 and 1916." He also came to share controversial status with Jackson and Jefferson "for much the same reasons." He functioned primarily as a party leader, and like both of these predecessors "he headed a coalition that advanced the interests of particular sections and occupational groups in opposition to the interests of others, with overtones of class conflict."[11] As for his twentieth-century predecessor, both TR and Wilson were partisans, and both championed "the people" versus the "special interests." The advantage, though, was Roosevelt's, whose "ideological position had allowed him to appeal to national unity, pursuit of transcendent ideals, and renunciation of self-interest. As a result, Roosevelt had enjoyed advantages in reputation and in aspects of leadership that eluded Wilson."[12]

The title of Cooper's book on TR and Wilson, *The Warrior and the Priest*, was perfect. Wilson brought a priestly asceticism to the presidency, but also a leadership no less bold than TR's. Rather than reveling in his victory, he called off the inaugural ball that had been a tradition since James Madison's presidency. He did the same for his second term. "His Republican successors — Warren G. Harding, Calvin Coolidge, and Herbert Hoover — also did without them."[13] Wilson was aware that he would need help to implement his bold measures. His austere impatience rendered him unfit for the normal give and take of politics, so, as John Morton Blum put it in his graceful study of Wilson, "he found subordinates who would do what his temperament precluded." The most useful of these — a man who nevertheless had no office or formal title — was Colonel Edward M. House of Texas. House, Wilson said, became his "second personality."[14]

Working with enormous skill and astonishing speed, Wilson managed to secure some of the most momentous legislation in American history. He attempted to function, "as much as the American system permitted," as a prime minister. Ironically, he was less successful in that regard than Lyndon Johnson would be a half-century later.[15] He called Congress into special session and kept it in session continuously for a year and a half. Such a thing had never happened before.[16] Astonishing everyone and horrifying some, on 8 April 1913 he journeyed to the Capitol and addressed the assembled legislators in person. No president since John Adams had done so. Jefferson — who in any case disliked public speaking — had begun the practice of communicating with Congress only in writing. As a part of his calculated effort to display republican simplicity, he had argued that direct addresses were too reminiscent of a monarch speaking to Parliament. Wilson, on the other hand, long before he entered politics had taken issue with Jefferson's decision.[17] Although he was a committed Jeffersonian, Wilson was considerably more aware of the need for effective government than was the Apostle of Liberty. Effective government, he believed, required direct and continuous cooperation between legislators and the executive.

As Cooper put it, "by making legislation his top priority, the new president brought his best skills into play." These led to passage of "his great trio of New Freedom measures," tariff reform, the Federal Reserve System, and "the combination of the Clayton Anti-Trust Act and the Federal Trade Commission Act.... All of these measures went from proposal to enactment within the eighteen months between April 1913 and October 1914."[18] The Underwood tariff lowered rates and revamped the tariff for the first time since before the Civil War. To compensate for loss of revenue, Congress attached to the new tariff law a graduated income tax that the recently ratified Sixteenth Amendment to the Constitution made possible. Wilson signed the Underwood-Simmons tariff bill with its income-tax rider on 3 October 1913.[19] Thus the first income tax actually applied since the Civil War became ultimately the basis for financing the Government of the United States. The long-overdue Federal Reserve System was "no less sweeping in its impact on the American economy than the income tax and tariff changes."[20] It provided for federal-private cooperation in supervising the country's chaotic banking system and for the first time made it possible to regulate money supply and interest rates. Also of great import was ratification of the Seventeenth Amendment providing for direct election of senators. This time, though, the credit should not go to Wilson. Ratification came 8 April 1913, barely a month after he took office.

Wilson should, however, receive some credit for the Nineteenth Amendment, removing sex as a criterion for voting. Although in the 1912 race, neither Taft nor Wilson supported women's suffrage — TR was the only candidate then who did — Wilson ultimately revised his opinion. By 1915 or so, he had begun to support the suffrage amendment. After its proposal by Congress, the requisite three-fourths of the states ratified it on 18 August 1920.

Wilson's domestic legislative record far exceeded that of Theodore Roosevelt — and also those of almost every other president, for that matter — but TR had laid the groundwork that made Wilson's achievements possible. It takes nothing away from his achievement to note that it was "distinguished by its scope rather than its originality," or to recognize that "Wilson's achievement would have been impossible had not others laid a political and intellectual foundation for him."[21] Wilson's ideas drew upon Bryan's populism and TR's activism and progressive reforms. As Cooper noted of TR and Wilson, "too ready a comparison of their partisan and legislative records is misleading because they faced such different tasks in the White House. Roosevelt had followed the delicate, daunting course of awakening and unbending a solidly conservative party. Wilson led an aroused, reasonably united reform-minded party." Strong elements among Wilson's own Democrats actually pushed him to do more. "If Roosevelt had won in 1912 and had carried Progressive congressional majorities in with him, he might have wrought comparable legislative feats."[22] As it was, both the first Roosevelt's and Wilson's presidencies fed into the startling developments in the 1930s of Franklin D. Roosevelt's New Deal.

Woodrow was not the only Wilson who created a foundation for the future. His wife, Ellen Axson Wilson, not only discussed policy with her husband, but also acted on her own initiative. She had heard of the squalid living conditions of most of the District's black population, and after inspecting some of the slums herself bought stock in an organization that provided "model low-cost houses," the Sanitary Housing Company. She became active in many reform efforts around the District, including working for better conditions in public hospitals, and better lighting, ventilation, and sanitary facilities in government buildings — especially for women workers. She blazed "a trail that would be greatly broadened by Eleanor Roosevelt and other First Ladies."[23] With regard to her specific causes, she had little lasting effect. On 6 August 1914, she died — another victim of Bright's Disease, the kidney ailment that had killed Chester A. Arthur, and Alice Lee Roosevelt, TR's first wife.

Wilson badly needed her influence. Intellectually, as committed as he was to humanitarian causes, he tended to think in global terms. Individual injustice often fell beneath his notice. Personally, he was stiff and unbending, but she had given him "strength and love. Her gentleness mellowed even his austerity; her thoughtfulness made him considerate beyond his inclinations. She was," as Blum put it, "a great lady. For any man such a wife would have been important," he said, but "for Wilson she was indispensable." Her death left him "crippled emotionally," and he experienced "a frosty loneliness no human being pierced for many months."[24] His despair finally lifted when he met Edith Bolling Galt, a widow, and in December 1915, married her. She, too, was a devoted wife, but she was no Ellen Axson.

Nor was Wilson a race baiter along the disgraceful lines of Mississippi Senator James K. Vardaman, Georgia's Tom Watson, or South Carolina's "Pitchfork Ben" Tillman, but he accepted the notions of black inferiority that were prevalent, especially in the South. He was a Southerner, and so were many of his Cabinet. He apparently thought racial segregation to be rather unimportant. At least he tolerated it in government departments. Under Wilson, segregation increased, especially in the Treasury and Post Office Departments. When Monroe Trotter along with a group of other black citizens met with Wilson in November 1914 to protest segregation, the president lost his temper and ordered them out of his office. He admitted later that he had acted rashly, and that he regretted his display of anger — but nothing changed administration policy.[25]

And nothing angered former President Theodore Roosevelt more than Wilson's refusal to arm the United States. Even with mounting reports of German atrocities, Wilson refused to be drawn into the European war that had begun in 1914, or to prepare for that eventuality. He seemed to believe that the United States could remain aloof and unaffected by the war, even when Americans began dying on passenger ships that had become targets for

German torpedoes. In May of 1915, the Germans sank the liner *Lusitania*, after the German Embassy in Washington had published warnings to Americans to stay off the ship. An outraged TR called it an act of piracy, and said that if he had been president, the first thing he would have done when the notice appeared in the press would have been to hustle the German ambassador out of the country — on the *Lusitania*![26] A few days after the tragedy, Wilson drove TR almost to a frenzy with a speech declaring that the United States was "Too Proud to Fight." Largely because of TR's campaign, "preparedness" thus became a major issue, and Wilson — who always was inclined to view disagreement (let alone opposition) as disloyalty — became furious at Roosevelt.

In 1916, Wilson won re-election against Republican Charles Evans Hughes on the slogan "He Kept Us Out of War!" Wilson's victory was narrow; he received slightly less than 50 percent of the popular vote, and slightly more than 52 percent from the electoral college (277 to Hughes's 254),[27] but he did win. He became the first president to serve two full, consecutive, terms since Grant left office in March of 1877.

In the meantime, his Mexican policy added to the historical ill will that Mexicans felt for the United States. He intervened in the Mexican Revolution, thinking to foster democracy and human rights. Blum correctly referred to Wilson's "naïve belief that he could formulate and decree a solution to that country's problems," and noted that Wilson "never really learned that *all factions* in Mexico considered his repeated intrusions unwarranted invasions."[28] He ordered several military actions — including seizing and occupying the city of Vera Cruz with such confused motives that he appeared to be seeking "like the jingoes 'ready to blow up the whole place'," and going after the bandit Pancho Villa, who had conducted cross-border raids, and whom he earlier had naïvely supported.[29] At least he did avoid a general war with Mexico.

But try as he would he could not avoid becoming involved in the World War. He had said in a speech in January 1917 that there should be "peace without victory." Then, on 28 February, an intercepted secret memorandum from the German foreign minister, Arthur Zimmerman, became public. The memorandum instructed Germany's representative in Mexico to ensure the Mexican government that it could regain all the previously owned Mexican territory (Texas, New Mexico, Arizona, California, etc.) if the Mexicans would attack the United States in the event that America went to war with Germany. Despite public outcry, not even the Zimmerman Memorandum persuaded Wilson; he delayed yet another month before acting. When German submarines then sank three American vessels, Wilson finally, on 2 April, asked Congress for a declaration of war against the Central Powers. Congress declared war on the 6th.

Wilson retaliated against his enemy, TR, when TR pleaded with him to be permitted to raise a division and lead it against the Germans. TR even offered to relinquish command and take a junior position, but Wilson would have none of it. A plea from French Premier Georges Clemenceau had no effect. Clemenceau sent a public letter to Wilson, saying that nothing would be better for morale than to know that Roosevelt would be coming. "The name of Roosevelt has legendary force in this country," he said.[30] The meeting between TR and Wilson had been cordial — Wilson said later that "there is a sweetness about" Roosevelt that he found "very compelling. You can't resist the man." But resist him he did. Later, in response to TR's continuing criticism of his policies as being too little too late, Wilson even remarked: "The best way to treat Mr. Roosevelt is to take no notice of him. That," he said in one of his less humanitarian moments, "breaks his heart...."[31]

It took some time but Wilson, hampered though he was by his failure to prepare, ultimately put America on an effective war basis. The military draft sent a million troops overseas. Later would likely have been too late. As it was they were just in time, and made the difference.

At home, Wilson's management of the war was a two-edged sword. Traditional American liberties crumbled. The government, through the mechanism of a new Committee on Public Information under the directorship of George Creel, conducted a massive propaganda campaign. It became unpatriotic to teach the German language in high schools. German music, including Beethoven and Wagner, no longer filled concert halls. Sauerkraut became "liberty cabbage" (in more sophisticated times, we have "freedom fries"). Worse were the overt violations of the First Amendment. Wilson signed into law the Espionage Act in 1917 and the Sedition Act in 1918. Although they provided a method of combating sabotage and obstruction of the war effort, their greatest effect was to suppress freedom of speech.

There were few arrests for actual acts, but many for pure speech. People went to federal prison literally for criticizing the war effort or the government. Even the statement "war is contrary to the teaching of Christ," brought jail time. Eugene Debs, persistent Socialist candidate for president, received a sentence of ten years in prison for speaking out against the draft. Wilson would never consider a pardon. Theodore Roosevelt spoke out forcefully against the excesses. *The Nation* magazine in a famous editorial asked why he remained unjailed, and TR dared the authorities to come after him. They did not. *The Nation* credited his opposition — coming as it did from one with such stature — with having saved the right of wartime free speech.[32] That may have been exaggerated, but Roosevelt, hardly a free-speech absolutist, certainly helped to modify the Wilson government's excesses.

Wilson, the Jeffersonian, followed the harsh example of his honored predecessor. Loyal Americans had not seen such a level of oppression since

Jefferson's embargo policies. In this regard, it would have been better had Wilson followed the example of President Madison rather than that of President Jefferson — although Jefferson's was the more successful of the two presidencies.

Wilson outlined his view of the future in his famous "Fourteen Points" speech to Congress on 8 January 1918. The war ended with an armistice on 11 November 1918. Committed to making "the world safe for democracy," Wilson insisted on negotiating personally, and set sail in December to head the American delegation in Paris. He spent February and March in the United States before returning to Paris. While home, he found that more than enough senators to defeat a treaty insisted on certain conditions. The resulting treaty bore his imprint, and ignored the wishes of the senators. It brought him the Nobel Prize for Peace.

The treaty called for a League of Nations and self-determination for nationalities, as well as for harsh measures for the defeated Germany. When the Senate considered it for ratification, Wilson stubbornly refused to consider any alteration. He set off in September on an extensive speaking tour around the country to build support for his position. Wilson's efforts to appeal directly to the people, coupled with other factors including his oral delivery of messages to Congress, have caused a number of scholars to misinterpret the attitudes of the Founders, and to criticize Wilson for laying the groundwork (even more than TR) of what they term rather grandly, "the rhetorical presidency."[33] One may be pardoned for suspecting that those who dislike the idea that presidents resort to rhetoric would much prefer the approach of a Taft, who believed that presidents by and large (no pun intended) should reflect merely the will of Congress.

On the 25th, a sudden stroke caused him to abandon his tour. On 2 October, another stroke left him completely paralyzed. Blum put it bluntly, but accurately: "the stroke did not kill Wilson, but it would have been kinder if it had."[34] He was totally disabled for nearly two months, and thereafter he was too weak to function adequately. For three months or so Edith denied him visitors, and determined what it was he would — and would not — see and hear. She would return papers with the notation, "the President directs," or "the President orders."[35] She vetoed any consideration of resignation, or temporary assumption of power by Vice President Thomas Marshall. The government of the United States was leaderless and adrift. Edith even persuaded Wilson that he would be sufficiently fit to run for a third term, but when the time came the Democratic National Convention quietly turned his bid aside.

Even though he appeared to have recovered to a great extent physically, his mental functioning was severely impaired. He could no longer read, nor could he concentrate for more than a few minutes at a time. His normal tendencies to be self-righteous and to see matters only in stark contrast of good and evil intensified. He refused to permit his followers to vote for ratification of the treaty unless it were completely unchanged. He even suggested that opposition senators resign and immediately run for re-election to see if voters favored their position. The treaty failed. Certainly, Wilson's inability to compromise doomed it.

He had hoped that the Democrats might win in 1920. Republican Warren G. Harding, however, won by the largest popular-vote landslide that any candidate had ever received until that time. He was the first president to receive 60 percent of the popular vote. Wilson took his victory well, and went to the Capitol to attend Harding's inauguration. He was too weak to remain, however, and left early.

Wilson's presidency ended even more sadly than Jefferson's had. He was broken in body, and certainly impaired in mind. He had failed to achieve his dream, but he had made a valiant effort. Nevertheless, his principles continued as motivations, and his spirit remains alive in the Charter of the United Nations.

29

WARREN G. HARDING
March 4, 1921–August 2, 1923

Warren Gamaliel Harding became President of the United States following two of the most dynamic and tumultuous decades in American history. It is common to hear that the country was tired of frenetic activity, and that it was tired of reform. It very likely was. Above all, however, it was tired of Woodrow Wilson. Harding promised a return to what he called "normalcy," and the people elected him by a landslide — an enormous landslide. His vote percentage put him in the same category (at least in that respect, if *only* in that respect) with no more than three other presidents: FDR in 1936, LBJ in 1964, and Nixon in 1972. He was, that is, the first president to receive 60 percent of the popular vote, and he remained popular while in office.

Yet rankings of presidents usually find him rated below every other — or at least very close to the bottom. He is in last place in both the original 1948 Schlesinger poll and in its 1962 follow-up.[1] Maintaining family consistency, Schlesinger, Jr.'s, 1996 study also kept him at the bottom.[2] President Truman's daughter, Margaret, wrote of Harding that "Dad did not hesitate to call him our worst President."[3] She maintained the momentum, extending the attack by declaring Florence Kling Harding to be the worst of the first ladies.[4] The ranking by the Fabers places Harding somewhat higher than most studies do, making him thirty-third. They ranked him above Coolidge, Reagan, Nixon, Arthur, Pierce, and Grant in that order.[5] Harding's "positives" slightly exceeded his "negatives," they concluded.[6]

Thomas A. Bailey, one of the early students of presidential "greatness," thought that Harding's presidency was better than several others, but that does not mean that he thought Harding to be outstanding.[7] Hardly anyone would go that far, except for a handful of anti-government ideologues who favor his tax cuts and relative passivity. One Joshua Hall, for example, who is director of something called the "Buckeye Institute Center for Education Excellence," suggested that Harding's tax cuts were designed not "to reward big business and wealthy friends," but rather reflected a "principled desire" to shrink government (as opposed, perhaps, to "unprincipled desires" such as those to eliminate poverty and poor working conditions). Hall spoke favorably of a study that rated presidents on one measure only: the extent to which they reduced government spending as a percentage of GDP. Harding placed third, Hall said approvingly, and added that "often the best thing government can do to help the American people is to get out of the way."[8] Single-mindedness certainly does not preclude high-mindedness; it is, however, distressingly close to simple-mindedness.

As Eugene Trani and David Wilson have written, the strongest defender of Harding's administration "among respected historians," is Robert Murray. They quote Murray as saying that "in concrete accomplishments, his administration was superior to a sizable portion of those in the nation's history."[9] Harding, Murray concluded, set the tone for Coolidge's administration. Trani and Wilson note that other historians have disputed some of Murray's conclusions, but that his works and others have "partly rehabilitated Harding." Harding was no simpleton. He was a shrewd politician who had some accomplishments to his credit, and who was not implicated in the scandals that rocked the country when they became known after his death. Trani and Wilson conclude, however, that Harding as president cannot receive high marks. He provided no moral leadership, had little "understanding of forces at work in the United States after the World War," he sought at all costs to avoid controversy, and he was unwilling to use the government's power to aid the country in adjusting to post-war conditions.[10] He was a transition president who failed to bring to the office the strength that could have been of enormous benefit to the country.

Harding certainly was not a great president. It would be a stretch even to say that he was a good president. The customary view that he was a failure, though, may be unduly harsh in view of the things that he did actually manage to accomplish. Moreover, since his administration's many flaws certainly did not damage the country to the extent that, say, the policies of Pierce, Buchanan, or Andrew Johnson did — not to mention those of some more recent presidents — it would seem questionable at best to say that Harding was America's worst president. Yet there was enough wrong with the Harding presidency to make the harsh evaluations understandable.

With much more assurance, one can say that calling Florence Harding the worst first lady not only is unfair, it is nonsense. She was a strong, talented woman who was an enormous asset to her husband, and who in many ways was quite admirable. Fortunately, Carl Anthony (among others) has presented a more well-rounded view that should offset Margaret Truman's one-dimensional portrait.[11] Truman's book is valuable. It presents first ladies from the unusual point of view of one who has lived in the White House as a member of a first family. At its best — as in its perceptive and thoughtful treatment of Mary Lincoln — it is excellent. But for more reliable judgments — judgments based on sound and recent scholarship — other works are much better, the best being those by political scientist Robert P. Watson.[12]

Although the Harding Inaugural Address was undistinguished, he did lay out a program, part of which was a coherent agenda. He called for tax reduction and an emergency tariff increase. He displayed thoughtful concern for transportation. Railroads, he argued, were in bad condition. He did not specify a program, but called for Congress to study the issue. He did argue that rates were too high. He also took note of the very poor condition of America's highways. The automobile had advanced far beyond the capacity of American roads to accommodate them. An act of 1916 had arranged for federal support for road building, and Harding called for federal supervision of construction. Continuing his expression of concern for transportation, he called for improvement to the merchant marine, and encouragement for civil and military aviation. The emerging communication systems of radio and cable required regulation, as well, he pointed out. Additionally he called for the creation of two new agencies, a veterans' bureau and a department of public welfare that would coordinate government activities in education, public health, working conditions, sanitation, and the like.[13] He specifically rejected participation in a "super-government," by which he meant the League of Nations, although oddly he did speak of the potential benefits of an "alternative association."[14]

Harding's Taft-like view of executive-legislative relations did not work in his favor, nor in favor of his program. After he gained experience in the presidency, Harding became frustrated and attempted to take a hand in directing legislation — specifically to secure subsidy for American shipbuilders. He was unsuccessful, despite huge Republican majorities in each house. The results of the congressional elections of 1922 reflected Harding's lack of leadership, and his inability to provide cohesion to his party and its numerous factions. Although Republicans retained control of both houses of Congress, their huge majorities became quite narrow.

The 1920s, despite being a time of relatively passive executives, did not become a decade with congressional dominance. Those days were gone. Harding certainly looked more back to the days before Roosevelt or Wilson, but too much had changed for a McKinley-style leadership. Harding addressed Congress directly, as Wilson had done, the most obvious symbol that a new dynamic had been created within the government.

Harding did achieve the tax cuts that he desired as well as an increase in the protective tariff. One major result of his program and his determination to increase economy in government was the establishment in 1921 of the Bureau of the Budget. It was perhaps Harding's major achievement. "Harding was not the first president to advocate a national budget system. Both Taft and Wilson had supported measures to strengthen the president's authority in fiscal affairs. But Harding did what Taft and Wilson were unable to do — he secured budget legislation from Congress."[15] With the very capable Charles G. Dawes as its director, the Bureau was able to assist Harding in reducing expenditures enormously, and in greatly increasing efficiency. The Budget and Accounting Act 1921 that established the Bureau, for the first time gave the president legal authority over the expenditures of executive agencies.

Foreign policy during the Harding administration for the most part did not lead to major advancements, although there were some significant developments. The United States absolutely and finally refused to participate in the League of Nations. Ultimately, the Harding administration secured peace treaties with Germany, Austria, and Hungary thus formally ending the Great War. Harding also hosted the Washington Conference for the Limitation of Armaments from November 1921 to February 1922 at which the great powers agreed on arms reductions. With regard to Mexico, Harding overruled his secretary of state Charles Evans Hughes, and agreed to a conference with the new Mexican government. He accepted the outcome, which led to formal recognition. "Generally, the Harding administration pointed the way to what later became the Good Neighbor policy."[16] His Latin American policy in general was considerably more successful than Wilson's had been.

Harding was known as a kind, genial man. Many historians charge that he was lazy, but he worked long and hard at the presidency. He was, to be sure, intellectually lazy in the sense that he was indecisive and sought to avoid controversy, but despite criticism of the time he spent playing golf, playing cards, and the like he spent no more time in recreation than many other presidents have.

Harding was compassionate. In December of 1921 he released socialist leader Eugene Debs from jail, where he had languished ever since the Wilson administration had convicted him for speaking out against the draft. The starchy Wilson always had refused to consider clemency. Earlier, Harding had received a delegation in his office that had come to plead on Debs's behalf. When he responded that he would attend to the case immediately, one member spoke up and demanded that the president answer "yes" or "no" on the spot. Another member of the group, Kansas editor William Allen White, had been disturbed by the outburst, but was "pleased by Harding's dignified retort: 'My dear woman: you may demand anything you please out of Warren G. Harding. He will not resent it. But the President of the United States has the right to keep his own counsel, and the office I occupy forbids me to reply to you as I should like to do if I were elsewhere'."[17]

Harding signed the Sweet Act establishing the Veterans' Bureau on 9 August 1921, but he opposed the veterans' bonus for which the American Legion was lobbying. Such a bonus would have made it impossible to achieve one of his major goals, budget reduction. Moreover, he "was against subsidizing individuals, no matter what the disguise."[18] Times were hard, and unemployment was high. The rationale for the bonus was that it would help redress the imbalance between low military pay, and what the veterans would have earned in civilian life.

Especially considering the brevity of his term, Harding was able to go a long way toward restructuring the Supreme Court, ensuring its conservative bent. He named four new justices. The most important appointment was that of former president William Howard Taft, whom Harding appointed Chief Justice on 30 June 1921. Taft became the only person to have served both as President of the United States and Chief Justice of the United States Supreme Court; in fact, no other president has ever served on the Court in any capacity.

Harding spoke out against lynching in a message to Congress the month after he took office. On 26 October in Birmingham, Alabama he called for equal opportunity for blacks. Even though he cautioned against seeking social equality because he said it was not possible at the time, his speech aroused fury among some Southern politicians. Despite his apparent personal sentiments, his administration did little for black rights. Its record with regard to advancing the rights of women was better, and Harding signed several pieces of legislation, including some that provided small steps toward better maternal and child health.[19]

One of Harding's major advantages was his appearance. He looked very presidential. Part of that image was the appearance of robust health. It was misleading. Harding's health was precarious. He suffered from high blood pressure and a failing heart. On 2 August 1923, not yet two years into his term, Harding died. He had undertaken a trip to Alaska, and was on the way back when the end came in San Francisco. He was buried in his hometown of Marion, Ohio.

Shortly after his death, the notorious scandals erupted, but they had begun to surface beforehand. Many of Harding's appointments had been outstanding: Dawes at Budget, Hughes at State, Herbert Hoover at Commerce, and Henry Wallace at Agriculture. Andrew Mellon at Treasury was highly capable. Other appointments, however, were disastrous. A few months prior to his death, Harding had discovered that Charles Forbes, who headed the Veterans' Bureau, had defrauded the government by making illegal sales and accepting kickbacks. Harding reportedly shook Forbes, calling him a "yellow rat," and a "double-crossing bastard!" Seeking to avoid a scandal, though, Harding permitted him to flee to Europe before accepting his resignation. The president lamented to William Allen White, "My God, this is a hell of a job. I have no trouble with my enemies, I can take care of my enemies all right. But my damn friends ... my God-damn friends, White, they're the ones that keep me walking the floor nights!"[20] Forbes's associate, Charles F. Cramer, committed suicide. Forbes himself finally paid a fine and received a prison term.

Harding's reputation suffered the most from the Teapot Dome scandal. Secretary of the Interior Albert Falls had persuaded Navy Secretary Edwin Denby to agree to the transfer of naval oil reserves from the Navy Department to the Department of the Interior. There were two such reserves in California, and one at Teapot Dome, Wyoming. Harding agreed to the transfer; along with Denby, he accepted Falls's argument that Interior was better equipped to handle drainage from the reserves onto private property.

Outcry from conservationists who feared that Falls would permit private development led Secretary Denby to resign. Although his intentions had been to protect the navy's oil, not to encourage development, he became the first casualty of what later were major scandals. Falls did lease oil reserves to petroleum companies, and resigned his position shortly thereafter. Following Harding's death, investigations determined that Falls had accepted bribes in return for the leases. He was convicted, and became the first American to be sent to jail because of his conduct as a cabinet officer. Also after Harding's death, his attorney general, Harry Daugherty, was indicted for connection with a different scandal involving illegal payoffs, but he was not convicted.

Harding had not known of the worst of these scandals, and there is no evidence connecting him with illegal acts. As Trani and Wilson noted, however, "he appeared to be far more concerned with political liabilities of a scandal than in securing justice."[21] Certainly this, as they concluded, was among the most troublesome aspects of Harding's presidency. His reputation has suffered accordingly, and revelations of extra-marital affairs added further damage.

Harding trusted friends who betrayed him, and the Great Scandals were the result. It has been these that have led those who rank presidents to render such harsh judgments against him. As important as the scandals were, though, were they really the most important things to consider? Rarely have rankings taken note of the fact that Harding was a conservative who accepted the idea of aid to business, but for whom "helping the individual citizen in need lay outside" his view of what government should do. If others benefited from his policies, he had no objection, but his administration "was unwilling to use its power to alter society in a way to help its less fortunate members. The conservative bias toward wealth was all too apparent."[22] Did not more harm result — certainly more immediate harm to people — from such a philosophy of government and the presidency than from the scandals? Least relevant of all were the improprieties in his private life. Perhaps they were the most interesting parts of the Harding presidency, but clearly they also were the least significant.

Hence, an evaluation of Warren G. Harding as president must conclude that he was flawed in important ways. He was not a great president; he was not a good president; he was not a failed president. He was not corrupt, but he failed to take adequate action against those who were. He trusted the wrong people. His policies failed to alleviate distress for all but the wealthy. Even though he served barely longer than Zachary Taylor, not quite seventeen months in office, he did have some substantial accomplishments. Moreover, any damage that his presidency caused was far less than that from some other administrations. The example that he set of releasing the harmless Eugene Debs from his ten-year sentence demonstrated to the country that kindness and geniality have their place, even when seeking strict justice. The country could have done worse — in fact, it has done so, decidedly.

$\boxed{30}$

CALVIN COOLIDGE
August 3, 1923–March 4, 1929

    Vice President Calvin Coolidge was sworn in as the thirtieth President of the United States when President Warren G. Harding died in office. He became the second vice president to fill a vacant presidency and then go on to win nomination and election in his own right. From the time he assumed office, he worked quietly and effectively to undercut rivals, and to ensure that the nomination would be his.

    Coolidge had arrived at the presidency with a strong background — at least so far as the positions that he had held is concerned — but there was little in his record that was outstanding. He had served in both houses of the Massachusetts legislature, had been mayor of Northampton, had been lieutenant governor and governor of Massachusetts, and had been Vice President of the United States. He presided over the Senate with little understanding of the legislative process, and most of the senators "ignored him, for he seemed to know nothing about national politics."[1] In all these positions, his wife, Grace, had been an enormous asset "as he climbed the political ladder," and her warm and outgoing personality "made up for her husband's social inadequacies."[2] In none of them had he made much of an impression.

    There was, however, one exception. He did achieve national prominence when he was governor from a well-publicized comment that he made during the Boston police strike of 1919. "There is no right to strike against the public safety by anybody, anywhere, any time," he had said. His comment was most welcome to much of the comfortable element of the country. In the words of Coolidge's admiring biographer, Robert Sobel, it was a time when they were fearful that strikes were a "harbinger of the coming sovieti-

217

zation of the United States."[3] Perhaps even more memorable was his statement in January of 1924 to the Society of American Newspaper Editors that "the chief business of the American people is business." To be fair, however, the comment is at least somewhat less one-sided if not lifted from context. Coolidge also said in the same speech that wealth was a means, not an end. As his thoughtful biographer Robert Ferrell remarked, Coolidge was "too intelligent to rest his ideas on William Graham Sumner."[4] Sumner was a Yale sociologist, the most prominent American exponent of Social Darwinism and the doctrine of "survival of the fittest."

"Silent Cal" was the source of much humor because of his alleged reluctance to speak. Actually, although he was shy, he did have a sense of humor. He also carefully cultivated his image. Despite his dour demeanor, he had a keen understanding of public relations and was popular while in office. He needed all the public relations skills at his possession. His physical appearance suffered greatly when contrasted with that of his predecessor. Harding looked presidential; he was tall, dignified, and experienced. He was an "accomplished orator," who could convince each person in a huge audience that he was communicating to him or her personally. "Coolidge, in contrast, had never been an engaging speaker." When he was lieutenant governor, the ongoing joke was that the governor could fill any hall, and Coolidge could empty it.[5] It is to his credit that he overcame his limitations in this regard, and caused the public to warm up to him.

Kansas editor and Republican contemporary William Allen White remarked that "no other president in our day and time has had such close, such continuous and such successful relations with the electorate as Calvin Coolidge had."[6] His inaugural address and other statements convinced the public that his commitment to business represented "idealism in its most practical form."[7] He courted reporters, treating them well and holding frequent press conferences. He missed no chance to be photographed, and was always available to present even his private life to the public. Above all, he compensated for his lack of stage presence by making use of a new medium, the radio, taking care to sell himself more than a political program. "I am very fortunate that I came in with the radio," he once remarked. "I can't make an engaging, rousing, or oratorical speech to a crowd, ... but I have a good radio voice."[8]

This is all the more noteworthy when one considers Coolidge's tendency to be not only curt and insensitive but also overtly rude. He could be harsh both to his family and to outsiders. Some observers have wondered how Grace could have stayed with him. For example, he did not even tell her of his decision not to run in 1928, and she heard it elsewhere. Also, he grew angry if she ever gave any indication that she was interested in politics.[9] Nevertheless, there was warmth in the marriage regardless of the appearance that it may at times have presented. Perhaps surprisingly, the Coolidges were free with their hospitality, and did entertain constantly.

Perhaps some of Coolidge's eccentricities, if one may so label them, resulted from personal tragedy. Many contemporaries who knew of his habit of sleeping eleven hours a day — nine hours at night and a two-hour nap in the afternoon — thought of him as lethargic. He may have been, but he may also have been suffering from deep depression. During the campaign of 1924, the Coolidges' sixteen-year-old son Calvin, Jr., developed a blister on a toe while playing tennis at the White House wearing tennis shoes without socks. It rapidly became infected, and in those pre-antibiotic days it burgeoned into a massive and generalized infection, and he quickly died. Both Grace and Calvin Coolidge were devastated.

The mixture of skill and awkwardness, of ability and passivity, of triumph and tragedy, of withdrawal and a commitment to public service that Calvin Coolidge presented might seem to complicate any objective evaluation of the Coolidge presidency. Those who come up with presidential rankings, though, do not hesitate to place him at a precise point on their lists. He ranks far down toward the bottom. His below-average placement put him twenty-seventh of thirty-one in Schlesinger's 1962 poll,[10] and thirtieth of thirty-nine in Schlesinger, Jr.'s, 1996 study.[11] The Fabers, too, put him in the bottom ranks, thirty-fourth of thirty-nine,[12] as does nearly every other ranking. There is a remarkable consistency.

No doubt this consistency results from the fact that Coolidge, in terms of exercising the powers of his office, was one of the most passive presidents in history. He "raised inactivity to an art. When it came to exerting his will on matters of public policy, Coolidge felt even less responsibility to act than had Harding."[13] If newspaper accounts were correct, one later president disagreed with criticisms of Coolidge. Presidential inactivity seemed to be a positive factor to a president who announced that "government is not the solution; government is the problem." Ronald Reagan allegedly looked to Coolidge as his favorite president.

President Coolidge signed into law the most stringent restrictions on immigration in American history. They were calculated not only to reduce immigration overall, but also to restrict and even ban certain racial and ethnic groups. During House debate on the 1924 measure, one representative presented the issue baldly. "On the one side," he said, "is beer, bolshevism, unassimilating settlements and perhaps many flags — on the other side is constitutional government; one flag, stars and stripes; a government of, by and for the people; America our country."[14] The provision excluding Japanese immigration was popular in California, although Secretary of Commerce Herbert Hoover, whose home was in California, argued against it. Coolidge himself opposed the provision. Sobel wrote that it was not Coolidge's "style" to veto the measure, and that it "was another step on the road to war."[15] No one can say with certainty what effect it had on later Japanese aggression, but it certainly contributed to Japanese resentment against the United States.

The Coolidge administration sharply reduced taxes. In 1926 legislation cut top rates in half, and in 1928 reduced rates yet again.[16] Throughout his time in office, he reduced the debt and kept the budget steady.

Coolidge did make use of his veto. The veterans' bonus bill was a notable example. His message was typical Coolidge: "No more important duty falls on the government of the United States than the adequate care of its veterans," he said, "But I do not favor the granting of a bonus."[17] Congress passed it over his veto. It provided veterans with paid-up government insurance policies, and allowed them to borrow up to 25 percent of the policies' value. Similarly, despite the crisis in American agriculture that was driving farmers off their land, Coolidge vetoed measures to provide aid. He opposed price supports or other measures. "No complicated scheme of relief, no plan for government fixing of prices, no resort to the public treasury will be of any value. Simple and direct methods put into operation by the farmer himself are the only real sources for restoration" of farm income, he said.[18]

In short, as Coolidge's biographer Robert Sobel put it, "the progressives continued to view him as a tool of business, the farm bloc as the enemy of rural America, and the intellectuals as the personification of Babbitry."[19] Sobel argued that these perceptions were inaccurate, but they nevertheless form a rather good summary of the Coolidge administration. Even Sobel conceded that "Coolidge's critics also might have charged him with being ineffectual and timid and with ignoring important issues," pointing out, for example, that although Coolidge spoke in the abstract of the injustice of racial prejudice "he refused to go beyond that." Coolidge would praise "tolerance and liberalism," but he would not "take the next step — confronting the bigots by discussing specifics, not philosophy."[20] Moreover, Sobel noted, Coolidge's "timidity — his unwillingness to take political risks — can be seen time and again throughout his life." Such a record, one would think, would commend itself to very few observers.

At least one time, President Coolidge did take a bold step. On 2 August 1927, the fourth anniversary of President Harding's death, Coolidge announced simply, "I do not choose to run for president in nineteen twenty-eight." This was "the great political bombshell of 1927, the effects of which lasted until Coolidge left the presidency in March 1929."[21] On that day, the Coolidges attended the inauguration of the new President of the United States, Herbert Hoover, and embarked by train to their home in Northampton, Massachusetts.

There was an interesting situation that resulted during the Coolidge administration with his vice president, Charles G. Dawes. Dawes, whom

Harding had appointed the first director of the new Bureau of the Budget, was one of the most distinguished persons ever to hold the vice presidency. He had practiced law, held an engineering degree, was an accomplished musician and composer, had risen to brigadier general in World War I, had held several government posts and declined several offers of cabinet positions, and was blunt and outspoken — a quality that the vice presidency does not encourage. As he embarked upon the vice presidency he received the Nobel Peace Prize for his work on the Dawes Plan, a program that reduced reparations payments from Germany and helped strengthen its economy.

As vice president, he opposed Coolidge's passivity and his refusal to use the government to relieve social troubles — supporting the farm bill that Coolidge vetoed, for example. This was unusual, certainly in modern times, but he immediately had become controversial, and ineffectual — even for a vice president. Three things stand out. On inauguration day, he candidly chastised the Senate for its hidebound rules, and criticized the practice of filibuster. Senators to not take kindly to criticism — merited or not — especially from vice presidents. He sent a letter to Coolidge informing (and annoying) the president, saying simply that he did not wish to attend cabinet meetings. Indirectly, and inadvertently, Dawes was responsible for the defeat of Charles B. Warren, Coolidge's nominee to replace Attorney General Harry Daugherty who left the cabinet after being dismissed in 1924. Senate leaders of both parties had assured Dawes that the nomination would not come up for a vote that afternoon, so Dawes left the Senate and went to his hotel for a nap. He received an emergency summons that the vote was indeed taking place, and that it was tied. Had he been presiding, he could have cast his tie-breaking vote in favor. As it was, by the time he had rushed back to the Senate, one senator changed his vote, and there no longer was a tie to break. Warren's nomination went down to defeat. Coolidge then nominated John G. Sargent. The Senate confirmed Sargent, and Vice President Dawes had become a laughingstock.[22]

An early attempt to "rank Coolidge among the other presidents,"[23] is interesting both because it treated him somewhat more kindly than the later more formal studies have, and because it predated Arthur Schlesinger's initial presidential ranking by approximately two decades. Before the public had thought of turning to rankings of presidential greatness, a journalist and politician from Massachusetts, Sherwin Lawrence Cook, said that Coolidge "is not among the great American presidents. Neither is he among the presidential failures." He said that the "serviceable Coolidge" stood amidst the "great bulk of our presidents," but did not lead them. Cook prudently, by the way, omitted "the first Harrison, Taylor, and Garfield, who died too soon for estimates." The presidents in this middle group, he said, were "able, honorable, generally useful" men. He thought Coolidge to have "neither the great qualities of Hayes, the deep intellect of [Benjamin] Harrison, nor the tact of Van Buren. On the other hand, both in purpose and ability," Cook concluded, Coolidge transcended "a Polk or a Fillmore."[24]

Whatever Coolidge's merits, he adamantly refused to approve use of government resources to provide assistance when needed, and within government itself his ideology prevented him from using the power of the presidency to influence legislation. As Ferrell noted, there was only one "positive program of a social nature advocated by the Coolidge administration," and that was road construction. Even it had roots in a previous Democratic administration's Federal Aid Road Act of 1916. All other "involvements of the administration in issues of American society" were negative. The federal government by and large did nothing for civil liberties, leaving them to conservative — if not reactionary — courts. Regarding immigration, it went along with the peoples' desires to reduce it, and exclude Japanese immigrants. Finally, it "looked with a jaundiced eye toward the decade's proposed great social experiment of using the wartime facilities at Muscle Shoals in Alabama to lift the entire Tennessee Valley out of that region's decades-old poverty."[25] Ultimately, under Franklin D. Roosevelt, Muscle Shoals became the New Deal's famed Tennessee Valley Authority. It was an enormously successful venture, but those of the Coolidge persuasion in future years — who, for reasons of pure ideology completely disregarded its demonstrated benefits as irrelevant — prevented it even from being considered seriously as a model for other, similar, projects.

To be sure, as Sobel went to pains to point out, one should not blame Coolidge for failure to foretell the future; the historians who have faulted him all have the benefit of hindsight.[26] Nevertheless, although times appeared to be prosperous, there were ominous signs in the economy. Caseloads in settlement houses and charity agencies were rising, for example. There was huge speculation and there were other troubles in the booming stock market that even Sobel noted. These were signs about which Coolidge did nothing, and of which he took no note.

One should not say that Coolidge caused the Great Depression that was soon to come, but it is clear that he did nothing to avert it. Perhaps he had no part even in planting the seeds of the disaster, but at the very least he permitted them to be watered. Calvin Coolidge thus was not a great president — his enormous popularity notwithstanding — or even a good one. He added nothing positive to the presidency, or to the country. He was, however, a reflection of what the powerful interests in the country wanted at the time. The failure, if such it was, was not solely his administration's but also was the country's. Can such a record truly result in a precise placement on a rating scale?

31

HERBERT C. HOOVER
March 4, 1929–March 4, 1933

Herbert Hoover brought a sterling background to the presidency. Some authorities believe that he was the most capable administrator ever to be president. He left office four years later, however, with his presidency in shambles. Unemployment was at record highs, the economy was a disaster, and countless homeless people lived in tarpaper or packing crate shacks, groups of which came — unkindly, but under the circumstances understandably — to be called "Hoovervilles."

Shortly after Hoover assumed the presidency, the stock market crashed. Prices had begun to slip in October, fell sharply on "Black Thursday," 24 October, and plummeted disastrously on "Black Tuesday," the 29th. The Great Depression was to follow. In no way was Hoover responsible for the Crash or the Depression, and he took many actions attempting to alleviate the distress. Unfortunately, they were too little, too late, and unsuccessful. Although he had a background as a progressive and was a notable humanitarian, Hoover adhered paradoxically to a rigid doctrine of individualism, a restricted presidency, and strictly limited government. He was far from a passive president, but his absolute unwillingness to consider direct financial aid to persons in need gave a false impression of heartlessness, and his absolute conviction that expanded government could bring only evil rendered him impotent. His conviction that character and individualism could solve the crisis was his undoing.

Hoover's poor political skills contributed substantially as well. Moreover, he was not publicity minded as Coolidge had been, and did not present himself well to the public. He also was notably thin-skinned, and carried a grudge. In addition to his many fine qualities, he clearly had a dark side.

Times were hard. Criticism — even condemnation — came from people in need, from writers, and from throughout the country. Understandably, much of it came from the Democrats, some from conviction, and some for purposes of plain partisan politics. Few presidents since have been the target of such partisan vilification until Bill Clinton became the object of ferocious Republican venom in the 1990s.

Hoover would certainly not have fared well in presidential rankings when he left office or for the next decade or so. Since then — although assuredly his name will never be found high on any rating with the slightest pretense to objectivity — there has been a certain rehabilitation in his reputation. President Truman had appointed Hoover to a commission to suggest government reorganization (the first "Hoover Commission") and thus had helped restore his public image by the time Schlesinger first began the ranking effort in 1948. Both in that poll and in Schlesinger's 1962 follow up Hoover placed in the "average" category.[1] A number of other ratings have put him in a similar position. Schlesinger, Jr.'s, 1996 poll, however, rated Hoover a "failure," above only Nixon, Andrew Johnson, Buchanan, and Harding, in that order.[2] Genovese ranked him "below average," twenty-eighth of thirty-nine,[3] while the Fabers' ranking put him in a similar position, thirtieth of thirty-nine.[4]

Still, Hoover has always had his defenders. Generally, though, they have been fierce partisans whose basic purpose was to condemn Hoover's successor, Franklin D. Roosevelt, and FDR's New Deal policies. One example of this was a Hoover biography by a senior editor of *The Reader's Digest*, Eugene Lyons, in 1964. In both prose and praise it was typical of the *Digest*, as was the revulsion it expressed for FDR.[5] To Lyons, criticism of Hoover was essentially communist inspired.[6] Hoover had the depression defeated, only to have it recur with his defeat.[7] Hoover himself ever after shared this opinion. To be sure, there are historians and analysts who defend the Hoover administration, who note its many innovations and attempts to right the economy, and who praise Hoover's political insights (if not his political skills).[8] Most defenses, though, come from political partisans who condemn Roosevelt's moves toward "big government," yet who praise Hoover and are inclined to argue that it was he who laid the groundwork for the New Deal, but fails to receive credit! Such attempts to have it both ways — eat one's intellectual cake and have it, too — are distressingly common.

Only three months into his presidency, on 15 June, and before the Crash, Hoover signed into law the Agricultural Marketing Act of 1929. This resulted from a special session of Congress that he called at the request of Senator William Borah of Idaho and other western senators to deal with the plight of agriculture. The Act's purpose was to control surpluses, and to lend money to support the formation of agricultural cooperatives. It established a Federal Farm Board that would coordinate federal activities but would not attempt to control farmers.

The western farmers were the object of the act, but they were "far less enthusiastic than was the president" about it. Not only was it "vaguely drawn," but they had wanted a considerably more forceful role for the government.[9] The *New York Times* asked why the president faced a "formidable party revolt" in the Senate after only two months in office. As the Hoover scholar Martin Fausold pointed out, "much of the answer involved Hoover's belief in the executive branch's hands-off approach to the Congress." It is a reflection of his personality, and his lack of political skill, that Hoover considered that "Congress represented the politicians," while he represented the people.[10] To some extent, he had in this regard adopted a neo–Jacksonian position while having none of Jackson's political sensitivities. Hoover was unwilling to engage in the rough-and-tumble activity of politics, and — perhaps arrogantly — considered political bargains to be beneath him. He soon paid the price for his aloofness. That aloofness did not mean that he was unconcerned about public attitudes, though. He was a pioneer among presidents in attempting to assess public opinion in a relatively systematic manner.[11]

As the country moved toward the Great Depression following the crash of the stock market, Hoover somewhat reluctantly on 17 June 1930 signed into law the Smoot-Hawley Tariff, hoping that it would provide some relief for farmers. In keeping with his view of congressional independence, he had provided hardly any guidance as the measure proceeded through the legislative process.[12] The new tariff sharply raised many rates. Many authorities in retrospect blamed the highly protectionist measure for worsening conditions by setting off an international tariff war. Whatever Hoover's intention, the tariff failed to help him in the November congressional elections. They replaced large Republican majorities in each chamber with an evenly divided Senate and bare Republican control of the House.

In December Hoover requested that Congress fund additional public works projects to help provide jobs for the unemployed. His efforts to combat the depression "made little news during the first half of 1930, attracting far less attention than the ratification of the London Naval Conference Treaty," the tariff, or his nominations to the Supreme Court.[13] Those nominations included Judge John J. Parker of the U.S. Court of Appeals, who faced exaggerated charges that he was anti-union and anti-black. In rejecting Parker, the Senate for the first time in the twentieth century turned down a Supreme Court nomination.[14] Hoover succeeded in appointing Charles Evans Hughes — former associate justice and the 1916 Republican presidential candidate — as chief justice, and two associate justices, Owen J. Roberts and Benjamin Cardozo.

In January 1931, the Wickersham Commission issued its report on prohibition. Hoover had appointed the commission under the direction of former attorney general, George Wickersham, to investigate enforcement of the dry laws. Throughout the 1920s, enforcement had been lax, but Hoover had tightened it considerably. The Wickersham Report concluded that enforcement had nonetheless been unsuccessful, but did not recommend repeal of the Eighteenth Amendment. "The prohibition amendment manifested for Hoover such a strong mixture of societal ordering and individual behavior that it was one of the most compelling of his commitments as president. Thus he staunchly stood by prohibition until late in his presidency, and then would forsake it only out of dire political necessity.[15] This was one of the most dramatic examples of the rigidity of his principles — although Hoover was not a teetotaler — and of his poor political judgment.

Another example of Hoover's poor judgment was his reaction to federal development of the area at Muscle Shoals, Alabama, on the Tennessee River. The government had constructed a dam there to supply electricity to two nitrate plants during the First World War. After the war, although Henry Ford had considered developing the area — using the nitrates for fertilizer rather than explosives — no buyer could be found for these facilities; they sat unused.[16] Private power companies purchased the electricity. Senator George Norris of Nebraska long had argued that the nation should make use of the power for the benefit of the region and its residents. In recognition of the country's great need for development, Congress finally passed Norris's bill to do just that. Hoover earlier had signed legislation to build a dam on the Colorado River to produce public power, and construction for the Hoover Dam began in 1930. That project, however, was a mixture of municipal and private effort, and provided for repayment of the cost to the federal government. Hoover argued that the Muscle Shoals project would compete with private industry, and on 3 March 1932, he vetoed it.[17] Hoover's belief in development of the country's river basins, and his recognition of the economic crisis, could not overcome his rigid ideology — especially in the face of a huge outcry from private power companies that had profited considerably from their purchase of the cheap power.

The most dramatic example of his inept actions, however, came in 1932 when he and Secretary of War Patrick J. Hurley sent General Douglas MacArthur — who used a flamboyant show of force — to disperse veterans who had come to Washington to pressure Congress into early payment of the bonus authorized by law in 1924. Hoover's record with regard to veterans' affairs had generally been good, although he had vetoed a 1931 bill to permit them to borrow up to 50 percent of their bonus. Congress overrode the veto. His reaction to the march wiped out any good that he had accomplished previously. Hurley and MacArthur clearly exceeded Hoover's orders — in fact, they did so defiantly — but Hoover had sent him, and the buck stopped with him. When they refused to apologize publicly, Hoover assumed full blame himself. Moreover, at the end of the campaign the president had the poor judgment to remark in irritation to a Minnesota audience, "Thank God, you have a government in Washington that knows how to deal with a mob."[18] The veterans had come to Washington in May, and troops drove them away on 28 July. Any possibility that Hoover might have been re-elected three months later in November vanished in that fiasco.

Matters became even worse in the last few weeks of the Hoover administration. All across the country, banks began to fail. Hoover urged the Federal Reserve to insure bank deposits, but the conservative board of governors refused. Hoover sought Roosevelt's assistance, but the president-elect — wishing not to compromise his own plans — argued that power still resided with the incumbent and the Federal Reserve.

The Hoover foreign policy was hardly more successful than his domestic efforts.[19] He did move for a moratorium on reparations from Germany and on payment of war debts to the United States to help counter the depression worldwide. Nor was he an isolationist. In contrast to many in his party, he favored participation in the World Court and the League of Nations, and he moved in the direction of the "Good Neighbor" policy toward Latin America of the Roosevelt administration. Those authorities who argue that he anticipated the New Deal policy, however, seem to be exaggerating. Substantial differences from the Hoover approach emerged when the Good Neighbor policy matured. Not only was there a difference in tone — with FDR's warmth contrasting sharply with Hoover's frosty official policies — but FDR committed United States policy, whereas Hoover merely assured the friendship of an administration.[20] When Japan invaded Manchuria in 1931, however, he did nothing, and Japanese aggression continued to include occupation of Shanghai and bombing of its civilian population. The Hoover response, the so-called Stimson Doctrine (Secretary of State Stimson actually had favored a more forceful policy, but Hoover rejected it), was to refuse to recognize as Japanese any territory that Japan had seized by aggression in violation of the Kellogg-Briand Pact outlawing war. As events of the next decade indicated, the Hoover policy failed to in any way to restrain the Japanese.

Hoover's most significant piece of legislation was the Reconstruction Finance Corporation of 1932. It provided federal loans to banks, railroads, and agricultural organizations to stimulate business activity and provide jobs. In an obvious way, however, it undercut his commitment to his own principles. Fewer people than ever supported him when it became clear that he would authorize money to corporations, while still maintaining that any direct payment to citizens would "destroy their character."

Hoover adhered completely to his strict view of constitutional principles, and "grimly resisted" all such demands. He strove mightily to marshal the resources of the federal government, but as a rule refused to use those resources to do more than to exhort private organizations to act — are people hungry? Then urge the Red Cross to feed them (food from the Red Cross, apparently, did not destroy "character" as food from the government assuredly would).

Hoover would always believe that direct federal assistance, however great the need, was unconstitutional. As Milkis and Nelson remarked, he put nineteenth-century principles to their most severe test. By committing himself so fully to them "even in the face of national calamity," he discredited them.[21] The more he worked to retain the solution of problems within the restricted framework of his individualist ideology, the more he paved the way for the thing he most feared: an activist federal government.

Hoover's tragedy was that he had a humanitarian commitment demanding some rather drastic changes in society. He also had a commitment to preserving minimal government, which made those changes impossible.[22] His two commitments were sincere and firmly held; they also were incompatible. One canceled out the other.

After the Roosevelt vote buried Hoover in 1932, the relationship between the two men was especially bitter. Both attempted some sort of cooperation at various times, both had their own political goals in mind when they did so, and both were met with lack of communication, or even by refusals. "The struggle between the two men was the more painful because they had enjoyed a pleasant social relationship when both served under Wilson."[23] Hoover felt especially betrayed because when he and Roosevelt had met at Hoover's invitation to discuss European war debts, the forthcoming Geneva conference on disarmament, and a proposed international economic conference, nothing positive came from the meetings. Hoover thought that he had been gracious, and had offered to help Roosevelt. "What Hoover overlooked was that he was willing to aid only if Roosevelt totally conformed to his views; he would not accept even minor differences."[24] For his part, Roosevelt refused to act jointly with Hoover, contending that so long as Hoover was in office, he and only he had the power. The tense relationship reflected both Hoover's rigidity, and FDR's refusal to be lured into committing to Hoover's policies.

On inauguration day, Hoover and Roosevelt rode together to the capitol. They both attended the swearing-in of Vice President Garner, and then proceeded to the Capitol's rotunda. After FDR's inaugural address, the two presidents shook hands, and the Hoovers made their way to Union Station to take the train for New York and the company of friends. Hoover was ready to offer advice and help to Roosevelt's administration, but no request came.[25] (Ironically, Hoover had never sought advice from former President Coolidge.) After a time in New York, they boarded another train for their transcontinental journey home to Palo Alto.

When Coolidge left office, he had recognized that the times had passed him by; not so Hoover. "For the rest of his long life would relive the period from 1914 to 1933, arguing and rearguing the past."[26]

Hoover believed, and continued to believe, that the country's welfare depended upon him, and that the Roosevelt presidency would be disastrous. Despite his Quaker heritage, he continued to hold a bitter grudge against Roosevelt and the New Deal; the animosity burned for the rest of his life. That post-presidential life was longer than that of any other former president.

For more than three decades, Hoover remained active. On the one hand, he published book after book, and continued to be defensive and ideological. He told his gushing biographer, Eugene Lyons in 1947 (assuming that Lyons quoted him accurately — and the words certainly ring with authentic Hoover flavor) that "we definitely had the depression licked, but the election of the new Deal reversed the trend and perpetuated the depression."[27] He said that the slogan of a "welfare state" had "emerged as a disguise for the totalitarian state by the route of spending." As Arthur Schlesinger, Jr., noted, this is pure "historical nonsense." There are threats to liberty, but they do not come from welfare spending. "There is no example on record of progressive social legislation leading to totalitarianism."[28] On the other hand, when Hoover accepted congressional appointment to head the first "Hoover Commission" on the reorganization of government in 1947 and President Truman accepted his report, the Hoover reputation's rehabilitation began, at least to some extent. He continued to devote his enormous time and energy to public service and efficient government in various ways until well into his eighties.

Hoover died on 20 October 1964. His wife, Lou Henry Hoover, a fellow Stanford graduate in geology and a career woman in her own right, preceded him in death, dying in 1944. The Hoovers are buried in West Branch, Iowa.

Whatever Herbert Hoover's talents and desires, they failed him in the presidency. He struggled valiantly to use them to solve one of the greatest crises that the republic had faced, but for ideological reasons he refused to use the appropriate tools. Despite allegations to the contrary from partisans, his efforts were no more successful than a carpenter's would be if he or she tried to drive a screw with a hammer. No matter how able the carpenter, how hard he or she tries, or how good the hammer, it will not work. Hoover's skills and his ideology were unsuited to the task for which he attempted to use them.

Certainly one should evaluate Hoover favorably if the criterion is good intention or native ability. If one factors in judgment, however, or looks for success, the result must be damning. Only ideologues will argue that Hoover succeeded when he dealt with the Great Depression. Few others would even contend that he approached it with all the measures at his disposal. Just as some recent presidents blame their failures upon their predecessors, Hoover — for the rest of his life — attempted to blame his upon his successor.

32

FRANKLIN D. ROOSEVELT
March 4, 1933–April 12, 1945

Franklin D. Roosevelt, the Democratic Roosevelt, distant cousin to former Republican president Theodore Roosevelt and husband of TR's niece Eleanor, was the only president in the history of the United States to serve more than two terms. Because of the Twenty-Second Amendment to the Constitution of the United States — a posthumous slap at this political giant by his outclassed Republican opponents who were unsuccessful in their attacks on him while he was alive — he was the last who could be elected more than twice. Ironically, however, the Amendment secured his unique status. Also ironically, for a half-century, the only presidents whom the Twenty-Second Amendment prevented from running for a third term were popular Republicans, Eisenhower and Reagan. It was not until the election of 2000 that the Amendment restricted a Democrat, Clinton, protecting the Republicans from what otherwise would assuredly have been a third Clinton term, thus causing them at last to be grateful for their spiteful action, and to breathe a collective sigh of relief.

Ranking after ranking identifies FDR as the greatest president since the nineteenth century. Most place him above all presidents except for Lincoln, or possibly Washington. Regardless of the inherent shortcomings of rankings, when they place these three presidents at the head of the list, they are getting at least something right.

FDR took office during the most severe economic crisis in America's history. His inaugural address, however, was one of optimism and reassurance. He pledged a "New Deal" for the American people, and said reassuringly, "The only thing we have to fear is fear itself." From a strictly realistic point of view that was far from the truth. In a symbolic sense, though, it was right — and it worked. After four gloomy years of Hoover, it inspired the country. It also began the construction of FDR's image as one of the greatest presidents in history. He broke with tradition immediately when he appointed his cabinet. Frances Perkins, the new secretary of labor, was the first woman to hold a cabinet position.

Roosevelt moved quickly and vigorously. His first order of business — literally the day he took office — was to deal with the banking crisis. With nervous depositors withdrawing their money, banks were failing throughout the land. To prevent further runs on their assets and avert collapse of the country's financial system, FDR ordered the banks closed.

The "bank holiday" also permitted the government to submit them to audit. Additionally, he called Congress into special session to begin on 9 March. Literally within hours it passed his Emergency Banking Act. The new legislation directed the issuance of Federal Reserve notes to prevent failures, and provided for banks to issue preferred stock that they could use as security for loans from the Reconstruction Finance Corporation.[1] With their new security, the banks that were sound began reopening only a few days after shutting their doors. By executive order, in April FDR took the United States off the gold standard. When he had told a banker and his budget director of his intentions, "one or the other of them lamented the decision as marking the end of western civilization."[2]

The beginning of FDR's administration has become the stuff of legend as "The First One Hundred Days." So dramatic were the accomplishments that the hundredth day of any new president's term has come to provide a convenient — and nonsensical — marker for journalists to pontificate regarding the course of the new administration. It is highly unrealistic, of course, to evaluate any president against the standard that such an outstanding leader set during a crisis so enormous.

During the New Deal's first hundred days the president sent request after request to Congress, and bill after bill followed. He asked on 15 March for farm legislation; for unemployment relief on 21 March — this "came to include a Civilian Conservation Corps, Federal Emergency Relief Administration, and Public Works Administration." On 29 March came his proposal for regulation of securities; on 3 April a measure to avert foreclosures on farm mortgages; on 10 April the Tennessee Valley Authority. "And so it continued, climaxing on May 17 when Roosevelt requested Congress to enact a national industrial recovery bill."[3] To explain his programs and marshal public support, he resorted to a new and powerful medium of which he was a master: radio.

His "Fireside Chats" endeared Roosevelt to a nation starved for reassurance. Freidel noted that FDR had perfected the "low-key and informal" radio conversations when he was Governor of New York. "Roosevelt used to imagine," Freidel wrote, "that he was engaged in explaining a policy to his tenant farmer at Hyde Park." The Fireside Chats were "notably effective, in part because Roosevelt shrewdly made rare use of them," Freidel said.[4] They also were effective because, as never before, they enabled Americans to sense a direct connection with their president.

Among the new programs, the Civilian Conservation Corps, or CCC, was especially popular. It provided jobs with shelter and food at minimal pay for thousands of unemployed youth, housing them in camps in rural areas under quasi-military conditions. The CCC was "a long-time cherished project of Roosevelt before he took office, so his wife assures us."[5] Under the direction of military officers who administered the camps, CCC workers engaged in conservation projects, built roads in rural and forest areas, otherwise made substantial contributions, and in general got their lives in order.

An indication of the popularity of the CCC may be seen in the reactions of residents in Wheatland, a strongly Republican and then extremely isolated Missouri village. In a study of the community in 1939, the author discovered great hostility toward the New Deal. It was "ruining the country." It "meddled" with business and with the way "farmers know how to do things." It ruined character. On the other hand, the residents accepted the CCC because it "built boys up" and "learnt 'em things."[6]

Congress passed the Tennessee Valley Authority Act on 18 May. Senator George Norris of Nebraska had long sought such legislation, but it languished during the Coolidge years. When Congress had finally passed Norris's program in1932, it fell victim to a veto from President Hoover who did favor development of the river basins, but who considered the potential competition with private generators of power to be "socialism."

The Tennessee Valley Authority, or TVA, grew out of the federal government's buildup during the First World War. It had constructed the Wilson Dam at Muscle Shoals, Alabama, on the Tennessee River to supply electricity for two plants that it had built to provide nitrates for explosives. After the war, efforts to sell the facilities to private companies found none interested in paying what they were worth — although Henry Ford briefly considered developing the area — and private power companies purchased the dam's electricity at give-away rates to re-sell at great profit.

FDR recognized that they were "valuable installations capable of producing electric power and fertilizer on a large scale" that were not being utilized.[7] He saw no reason why they should not be, and every reason why they should. This illustrates the stark contrast between the practical Roosevelt and Hoover the ideologue. FDR journeyed along with Senator Norris and other dignitaries to inspect the installation. "As Roosevelt stood by the roaring spillways, almost within sight of farmhouses still lit with kerosene lamps, he avowed he would put the wasted power to work as a part of a program to develop the entire Tennessee Valley." Later he spoke at the Alabama State Capitol in Montgomery, and said that TVA should serve as an example to future generations. It would tie industry, agriculture, and flood prevention into a "unified whole over a distance of a thousand miles so that we can afford better opportunities and better places for millions of yet unborn to live in the days to come."[8] Where FDR looked, he saw possibilities for government to help provide a brighter future. Small wonder that the people found him a welcome contrast to Hoover. Under the Hoover administration, they had experienced a president who, even in the midst of a crisis, could see no potential for expanded government other than regimentation and "socialism."

Among TVA and other milestones in the First One Hundred Days was the Agricultural Adjustment Act. For the first time there was national coordination to crop production. To deal with the great oversupply that suppressed farm prices, the government would pay farmers to control their output. In addition, there was the elimination of national prohibition. Although he had not been persuaded that federal insurance of bank deposits was wise, "in June, 1933, it was forced upon him, and came to be listed as one of his notable achievements."[9] After FDR's election, Congress had proposed the Twenty-First Amendment repealing the Eighteenth. Although repeal did not come until December, Congress at the president's request authorized immediate production and sale of beer and wine, thus revising the Volstead Act that Congress had passed over President Wilson's veto. The Eighteenth Amendment did not mandate prohibition; it merely authorized Congress to establish it. The National Industrial Recovery Act (NIRA) was probably the most ambitious, and least successful, of the new programs in the One Hundred Days. The new National Recovery Administration worked under its terms, cooperating with industry to develop codes of fair employment and competition.

The flurry of activity continued during the remainder of Roosevelt's first administration. In 1934 he signed into law the National Housing Act, and legislation creating the Securities and Exchange Commission. He appointed Joseph P. Kennedy, the father of future President John F. Kennedy, to chair the SEC. In 1935, he signed the Wagner Labor Relations Act that for the first time recognized labor's legal right to bargain collectively.

Also in 1935 came the Rural Electrification Administration (REA) and the Works Progress Administration (WPA). The REA brought electricity to vast sections of rural America that private power companies for economic reasons had refused to service, and the WPA made the federal government the employer of last resort, providing jobs to millions of unemployed workers. The WPA, under the direction of Harry Hopkins, constructed huge numbers of court houses, city halls, other public buildings, airports, and runways; it built tens of thousands of bridges and hundreds of thousands of miles of roads in a country still lacking adequate highways; it built countless miles of hiking trails, constructed parks and sidewalks, and completed conservation projects throughout the country. Some of the things that the WPA built for the country remain in use after nearly three-quarters of a century.

Additionally, the WPA included a Writers' and Artists' Project that put unemployed artists to work on various projects such as painting murals in public buildings; the Writers' Project brought forth a remarkable series of guidebooks on every state and region — some of the finest such materials ever published. Those who have enjoyed John Steinbeck's *Travels with Charley* may remember that he said he wished he could have taken the entire set of the guidebooks with him on his journey, because they were well written, and gave the best account of the United States ever produced. There was a similar WPA project for musicians, which among other things provided free concerts across the land. Playwrights and actors provided live theater where it had never before existed.

Critics charged that the WPA was "made work." It was inefficient; a boondoggle. Writer Eugene Lyons of the *Reader's Digest* praised Hoover precisely because he had not "set millions to raking leaves, flailing water, daubing walls, writing guidebooks and gibberish to gloss the facts of joblessness." On the contrary, Lyons wrote, Hoover's "system left the unpleasant truth starkly exposed."[10] Well, yes it did — exposed and unchanged. Lyons lauded Hoover because he had *not* made jobs for the unemployed. The WPA's writers and artists came under the strongest attack because some of their works contained political themes, even radical themes. There is no denying one simple fact, however. Millions of workers needed jobs, and the WPA gave them jobs.

By far the most important achievement of the New Deal, however, was the Social Security Act. Roosevelt worked diligently to achieve the milestone legislation, which he signed in August of 1935. Since its inception, Social Security arguably has been the most popular government program ever adopted, and clearly it is the best and most efficient large-scale income-maintenance program in the world. The Social Security Act provided unemployment insurance as well as the familiar Old-Age Benefits, or the Survivors' Benefits that were added in the 1939 amendments. It has grown through the years to cover virtually the entire population, and its value to the country is almost impossible to overstate. Because of Social Security, the elderly by-and-large have been lifted from poverty. Despite questionable allegations of fiscal troubles ahead, the system was well planned, and it remains sound. It will continue to be sound unless those who wish to turn the clock back to the days of Coolidge and Hoover convince the public that radical revisions are necessary to "save" the system.[11]

Despite the successes of the New Deal, it ran into a major roadblock: the United States Supreme Court. In early May 1935, the Court struck down the Railroad Retirement Act, "casting doubt on the social security legislation"[12] that was to come the following August. Then, on 27 May, the day that New Dealers came to call "Black Monday," the Court handed down three decisions striking at Roosevelt's administration.[13] Two especially angered FDR. *Humphrey's Executor v. The United States* reduced the president's authority to remove appointees, an authority that Chief Justice Taft had upheld in the *Myers* case in 1926. The Court in *Humphrey* declared that the president could not remove members of independent regulatory commissions. *Schechter Poultry Corp. v. The United States* struck down the NIRA as unconstitutional. Ominously, the Court in the Black Monday cases was unanimous. Some observers have concluded that this was the end of what they term the "first New Deal." A second was to follow.

FDR spoke out against the decisions, but he bided his time. In the 1936 Democratic National Convention his forces were so strong that they succeeded in eliminating the party's restrictive rule that required two-thirds of the delegates to choose its presidential and vice presidential nominees. The two-thirds rule had been in place since Andrew Jackson had engineered it over a century earlier. It had given the South a veto over Democratic nominees ever since.

In the election in November, FDR won an unprecedented landslide. Only LBJ's 1964 victory even today has surpassed it. Because of the new Twentieth Amendment, he began his second term on 20 January 1937, rather than the traditional date of 4 March. On 5 February, he submitted a message to Congress proposing his infamous "court-packing" plan. He called for legislation permitting him to nominate an additional justice for every one on the Court who had reached the age of seventy, up to a maximum Court size of fifteen. This would have permitted him to appoint a new justice — intended to be liberal — to offset the votes of the elderly conservatives. Congress, the press, and the public reacted vigorously, often in fury. Despite cries of "dictatorship" and "subversion of the Constitution," there is no doubt that Congress has the authority to set the size of the Court.

The justices clearly were frightened that the Court was in danger. For whatever reason, they began to uphold New Deal programs — some that were little different from those they had originally stricken. Then, Justice Willis Van Devanter, one of the conservatives on the Court, retired, and FDR was able to appoint his first Supreme Court justice (Hugo Black, in 1937). Before the end of the 1930s, he had appointed a total of four (the others were Stanley Reed, 1938; Felix Frankfurter, 1939; and William O. Douglas, also in 1939). In addition, Senator Joseph Robinson, who had sponsored the Court-packing plan in the Senate, died. The plan evaporated. It never came to a vote.

In a sense, FDR had won as he himself thought. The Supreme Court no longer was an impediment to the New Deal, and never again struck down a New Deal measure. Most writers, though, argue that he paid too heavy a price. He caused great friction in the Democratic Party, they say, and he no longer had the firm support of Congress. Although no one can prove the point either way, FDR may have lost less than it seems on the surface.

Regardless of the reason, the Court did change its course. FDR did have more opposition in Congress than in his first term, but presidents always have more congressional opposition in their second terms. It certainly is not definite that the proposal for the Court caused this. In addition, FDR did run for a third, and even a fourth, term — and he was successful. It seems somewhat questionable, therefore, to assert with any certainty that the struggle over the Court was the reason why he was no longer so dominant in his relations with Congress.

In 1938, angry at congressional resistance, FDR sought to influence primary races and defeat some of the most prominent conservatives. The result of the "Party Purge" was unspectacular, at best. He was embarrassed at the outcome because of strong press coverage.

Students of the presidency rightly consider reorganization of the executive to have been one of the most significant developments of the Roosevelt administration. FDR appointed three prominent political scientists — Louis Brownlow, Luther Gulick, and Charles E. Merriam — to a President's Committee on Administrative Management. The resulting "Brownlow Committee" recommended a number of reforms, some of which Congress after lengthy deliberation incorporated in the Executive Reorganization Act of 1939.[14] The legislation gave the president limited authority for two years to reorganize executive agencies. The result was an executive order that, among other things, created a new Executive Office of the President (EOP). The EOP included a White House Office and an expanded Bureau of the Budget (BOB); BOB previously had been within the Treasury Department.

There were other considerations, however, that soon superseded those of organization or of the New Deal. Germany was on the march in Europe, and Japan was threatening in the Pacific. The Second World War was on the horizon, and the mood in America, including the Congress, was predominantly isolationist. In 1935 Congress passed a Neutrality Act placing an embargo on munitions to countries at war. In 1936 it added a prohibition against loans to belligerents. The height of isolationist sentiment came in 1938 with the introduction of the Ludlow Amendment to the Constitution, which would have required a national referendum before the United States, could enter a war. Although the amendment failed, some polls showed as many as 75 percent of the people favored its principle.[15] As war became ever more likely, FDR had to find ways to assist Great Britain, which ultimately was standing alone after the Germans had conquered nearly all of Europe.

Recognizing the need for unity, "he invited two eminent Republicans to join his cabinet."[16] Henry L. Stimson who had been Hoover's secretary of state became secretary of war, and Frank Knox, an old Bull Moose Progressive who had been Landon's vice-presidential running mate in 1936 became secretary of the navy. In 1940, Congress passed a conscription law, the first ever in peacetime.[17] FDR managed to transfer fifty aged destroyers to Britain in return for the use of some naval and air bases. "Two of the bases would be a gift in exchange for the destroyers, and the remaining five would be a gift. The naval and air bases were to be in Newfoundland, Bermuda, the Bahamas, Jamaica, St. Lucia, Antigua, Trinidad, and British Guiana." He merely informed Congress of the arrangement.[18] This took place while he was in the midst of his precedent-shattering race for a third term.

Vice President Garner had broken with FDR over the third term, and had begun to oppose parts of the New Deal. He briefly challenged Roosevelt for the presidential nomination, but quickly failed and wound up back in his home town of Uvalde, Texas, his political career at an end. FDR insisted that his new running mate be Secretary of Agriculture Henry A. Wallace of Iowa. The convention was reluctant, but an appearance by First Lady Eleanor Roosevelt, and her powerful speech arguing that the president needed those with whom he was comfortable and upon whom he could rely, carried swung the convention to Wallace.

After his third election, Roosevelt carefully began to edge the public away from isolation. In a press conference on 17 December, he argued that assistance to Great Britain and the Allies was similar to lending a garden hose to a neighbor whose home is on fire. He does not insist on payment for the hose, FDR said, merely on its return following the fire.

In his annual message to Congress on 6 January 1941, Roosevelt made his famous "Four Freedoms" declaration. He looked forward, he said, to a world founded on "four essential human freedoms," freedom of speech, freedom of religion, freedom from want, and freedom from fear.[19] The public responded enthusiastically. FDR deftly had connected two traditional American freedoms, freedom of speech and religion, with two additions that were freedoms *from*, freedom from want and freedom from fear. In March after his inauguration, Congress passed the Lend Lease Act of 1941, supplying the Allies with military equipment. After the surprise attack by the Japanese on Pearl Harbor in Hawaii on 7 December 1941, there was no more need to work against isolationism. German and Italy followed the Japanese attack with declarations of war against the United States. On 8 December 1941, Franklin D. Roosevelt presented his simple and eloquent message to Congress. "Yesterday, December 7, 1941— a date which will live in infamy — the

United States of America was suddenly and deliberately attacked by the naval and air forces of Japan."[20] Congress eagerly granted FDR's request to declare war.

The only dissenting vote came from Representative Jeanette Rankin of Montana. Rep. Rankin was in her second, and final, term in the House. She had served a previous term some two decades before at the beginning of the First World War. At that time she also had cast the only vote against going to war. She thus became distinctive for at least two reasons: she cast a vote against both world wars, she was alone in each case, and she was the first woman to serve in Congress.

A few conspiracy theorists along with a handful of intensely partisan opponents have accused FDR of knowing that the Japanese would attack Pearl Harbor and of doing nothing in order to jolt the country into acceptance of war. This is nonsense; it was the Japanese, not Roosevelt, who attacked. It is absurd to think that he would have permitted such great damage to the Pacific Fleet in order to "shock" the public. The public would have been just as shocked by an attack on Pearl Harbor with the fleet moved out to sea away from harm, or with an alert to the military that there was an impending attack so that it could have responded.

There were, it is true, some indications that the Japanese would be moving to attack somewhere, but there was no indication that the move would be so audacious. There had even been Japanese speculations about an attack on Hawaii, including a Japanese comic book that Naval Intelligence sent to FDR. To be sure, the book did begin with an attack upon Pearl Harbor. Roosevelt received the comic book, however, in 1934 — over seven years before the strike.[21] In 1941, an attack in Asia or nearby seemed much more likely. Interestingly, American comic books after George W. Bush became president but before the actual events of 9/11 had included stories based on attacks by airliners on the World Trade Center.

When anything serious happens, there frequently are items of intelligence that, in retrospect, "should" have been warnings — but often only in retrospect. If, for example, there are thousands of warnings of various terrorist attacks and one takes place, it is tempting to accuse officials of not acting on that warning. Of course, in that circumstance there are also thousands of warnings that were *not* valid. Only after the fact can any isolated bit of information seem thoroughly persuasive — and in this instance, even after the fact there was nothing definite in 1941 that related specifically to Pearl Harbor.

The war — as wars do — brought even more power to the president. Roosevelt centralized much control in his own hands, rather than delegating it to various agencies. He violated many tenets of good administrative practice. It was no secret that he set agencies at odds with one another, and that the "right hand did not know what the left hand was doing." He often would let one authority go off on its own, reining it in when necessary to keep it in line. Although he sacrificed efficiency, he was thus able to retain New Deal values during wartime, and he "blocked the tendency of his industrial administrators to centralize production in a way that would turn the process of post-war conversion into a bonanza for the country's largest industries."[22] Because of his enormous skill, FDR's personal administration worked well. In a manner reminiscent of Jefferson's administration that could work well only under a Thomas Jefferson — of whom there was only one — FDR's administrative style could work well only under a Franklin D. Roosevelt — of whom there also was only one. Toward the end of his life, as his energy began to lag, some fraying around the edges had become apparent.

The nature of war always brings threats to civil liberties. The record was vastly better in the Second World War under FDR than in the First World War under Wilson. There was a major exception, however — one of huge proportions. The military commander of the West Coast, General John De Witt, reflecting racist fears and a prevailing West Coast hostility toward residents of Japanese descent, made one of the most absurd official statements ever on record. His hysterical illogic led to tragedy.

There had been rumors of sabotage, of furtive signals from shore to mystery ships off the coast, of Japanese crops planted in such a manner as to point the way to military bases, and the like. De Witt admitted that none of this was true. He said, however, that "the very fact that no sabotage has taken place is a disturbing and confirming indication that such action *will* be taken."[23] The racist motivation is clear when one notes that persons of German and Italian descent were of little or no concern, nor were those of Japanese descent in Hawaii, where they were considerably more numerous but where there was less racism.

Nevertheless, the entire political establishment in California and in the military, and all the cabinet except for the new attorney general, Francis Biddle, agreed with De Witt and recommended internment. Roosevelt therefore ordered all persons of Japanese descent removed immediately from the military zone. He directed that it be done "as humanely as possible." The order included not only Japanese aliens but also native-born American citizens who had been so unwise as to have selected a Japanese ancestor. More than one hundred thousand people were rounded up, and ordered to bring only what they could carry. The order affected the "entire state of California, the western half of Washington and Oregon, and the southern part of Arizona."[24] Ultimately, those removed to the "relocation centers" lost their property in addition to their loss of years of freedom. Ultimately, also, the U.S. Supreme Court in two cases, *Hirabayashi v. United States* (1943), and *Korematsu v. United States* (1944), upheld the government's actions.

Eventually, in 1998 — more than a half-century later — the U.S. Congress, at the urging of President Clinton, voted a small reparation ($20,000) to those still alive who had been relocated. Even then, there were objections that "the Japs got what they deserved." In wartime, people — officials and others — frequently are caught up in emotions that lead them to take actions that most of them later regret. The Roosevelt administration was not alone in its actions; the Canadian government treated its Japanese residents in a similar manner. Eventually Canada, too, paid reparations to the survivors of its relocation policies.

Another questionable part of the record of the Roosevelt administration pertained to its reaction to the genocidal policies of the Nazis. The United States did admit Jewish refugees but not nearly so many as needed admission. The Allies never did bomb Nazi concentration camps, probably as the result of a decision by FDR himself.[25] FDR's view was that the best way to aid the Jews was by devoting maximum military force to ending the war.

Many people, especially in retrospect, believe that bombing the concentration camps would have been a great symbolic strike at Nazi bestiality. Regardless of the merits of such arguments, FDR's actions regarding the Jews were not the bright spot of his administration. The historian Michael Beschloss has summed up the controversy quite well. He quoted Arthur Schlesinger, Jr., as arguing "rightly," that FDR "more than any other person, deserves the credit for mobilizing the forces that destroyed Nazi barbarism." Nevertheless, Beschloss said, "a half-century later, one of the most controversial aspects of Roosevelt's World War II leadership is the American failure to bomb Auschwitz."[26] This is true enough, but as Beschloss also wrote, FDR's flaws "are overshadowed by greatness." In 1939 and 1940, his leadership on Germany was superb. "Against the advice of hard-boiled advisers who warned that most Americans were isolationist, the President risked his career by campaigning for military preparedness and aid to Britain." The key point is, as Beschloss put it so well, that "had Roosevelt been more meek or shortsighted, Hitler might have won World War II."[27] As this implies, it is important to evaluate a president on the full record not merely on one part of it.

That record was extraordinary. Franklin D. Roosevelt established much of what Theodore Roosevelt had begun. He implemented a new public philosophy that energized government to protect the public — at least to some extent — from want and from repression by concentrations of private economic power. He insisted on "unconditional surrender," which, although controversial at the time, succeeded in removing Japan and Germany from the list of countries that were continuing threats to world peace. This is the major theme of the recent extraordinary book by Michael Beschloss: after more than half a century, Roosevelt's policies — and those of his successor, Harry Truman — have stood the test of time.[28] Because of these two leaders, there had been a true reformation of two aggressive countries, one of which twice in two generations had shattered Europe.

No discussion of the Roosevelt administration would be sufficient without consideration of the extraordinary role that Eleanor Roosevelt played as First Lady.[29] She was a tireless voice for the oppressed and for social justice. She was indispensable in her assistance to FDR, and in helping him develop enlightened views. She was a force unto herself, both politically and socially. She was the first major voice in government during the twentieth century supporting the extension of civil rights; her activities for women's rights also helped pave the way for future advances.

Among many innovative roles that she assumed, one that remains unique among First Ladies was her acceptance of a formal governmental appointment. Roosevelt had created an Office of Civil Defense (OCD), and had appointed New York Mayor Fiorello LaGuardia as its director. Its purpose was to encourage broad participation among the public as volunteers. At LaGuardia's request, Eleanor Roosevelt accepted appointment as OCD's assistant director. Although she provided extraordinary service and found great satisfaction from the position, Roosevelt's enemies in Congress were quick to attack her on any pretext. She resigned in order to prevent damage to the agency, but it was clear that "her dream of the OCD as a people's movement had come to a humiliating end."[30] Enemies of the New Deal always found the president's wife to be a more satisfying, and less dangerous, target than the elusive president himself. Although other First Ladies since then have been targeted — notable ones being Betty Ford, Rosalynn Carter, and Nancy Reagan — not until Hillary Clinton was another so vilified as was Eleanor Roosevelt.

As the war was entering its final stages, and after several notable conferences with Allied leaders, Franklin D. Roosevelt died suddenly. He was at his retreat in Warm Springs, Georgia. The cause was a cerebral hemorrhage. The date was 12 April 1945. He was buried on his home estate, at Hyde Park in New York.

The new President of the United States, Harry S Truman, appointed Eleanor Roosevelt in 1946 to the United States delegation to the United Nations. President John F. Kennedy also appointed her to the UN. She devoted the rest of her life to writing and public service. Eleanor Roosevelt died on 7 November 1962, and was buried at Hyde Park with the late president.

33

HARRY S TRUMAN

April 12, 1945–January 20, 1953

Harry S Truman, the Man from Missouri, as president shared a disadvantage with several of his predecessors. John Adams followed George Washington; Andrew Johnson followed Abraham Lincoln; and William Howard Taft followed Theodore Roosevelt. One might add Martin Van Buren — who followed Andrew Jackson — to the list. Along with these earlier presidents, Truman stepped into the office to replace a giant.

The presidencies of Adams, Van Buren, Andrew Johnson, and Taft suffered accordingly, but their own shortcomings added to their woes. Truman's presidency, too, suffered from unfavorable comparisons with that of his immediate predecessor, the charismatic Franklin D. Roosevelt. Truman's unassuming manner and appearance, his clipped uncultured Missouri accent, and his apparent lack of sophistication contrasted markedly with the demeanor of the suave, patrician but magnetic and exciting FDR.

Yet Truman's presidency is quite distinct from others who have had to follow America's strongest leaders. Alone in this group he left a record that, although mixed, included many extraordinary accomplishments — and he left the presidential office as strong as he had found it. Alone in this group the criticisms, even condemnation, that he faced in office — "To err is Truman," his Republican adversaries gleefully chortled — have not only faded, but reversed, with time. They have appeared progressively minor as the years have passed, and as admiration for the honest, straight-talking, and decisive Missourian has come almost universally to supersede them. Truman has worn well.

The current admiration for Truman is widespread, although inevitably not universal. Now and then revisionist historians take delight in attempting to demolish what they perceive as the Truman myth — that of the small-town boy who brought integrity, plain-speaking, decisiveness, and common sense to the White House — especially since the enthusiastic public reception of David McCullough's highly favorable biography in 1992.[1] Nothing stimulates the ire of many academicians so much as a popular work in their specialties. This is especially the case if the work, however well-researched and well-written, becomes a best seller.

The most recent attack on Truman seems quaintly out of date. Revisionist Arnold Offner echoes the Old Left cry that the Cold War was the result of Truman's policies, not Stalin's.[2] Amusingly, critics on the far right accuse him of the opposite; right-wing extremist literature is filled with bleats about "perfidy" on the parts of FDR and Truman who, its fevered authors imagine, sold out U.S. interests to those of the Soviets.

Among revisionist historians — serious scholars as opposed to the extremist right — critics of presidents agree in diminishing their subjects. They do so, however, usually from one of two opposing and inconsistent perspectives. Some, such as Offner, cast blame upon their subjects, charging that they were responsible for much that turned wrong. Another school, on the other hand, takes away credit without levying much in the way of blame, denying that great figures have much influence in the long run in any case.

Certainly historical forces are important, and "great figures" are not responsible for the whole of historical development. Nevertheless, it is tempting to conclude that anyone who can say with a straight face that things would have been much the same without, say, a Washington or Lincoln (or a Jesus, Napoleon, Gandhi, Einstein, Mao, or Hitler), or that the presidency would have developed much as it has without the Roosevelts, Wilson — and yes, even Truman — are likely reacting with bitterness to their own (unfair, of course) lack of influence on long-term events. To provide current perspective, could any serious and informed person, Republican or Democrat, liberal or conservative, American or French (or Iraqi) argue that America in 2004 would be the same with a President Albert Gore as with a President George W. Bush?

The initial Schlesinger poll of 1948 of course did not rank Truman; he was still president. The follow-up 1962 poll, however, placed him ninth of thirty-one, "near-great."[3] He ranked ninth also in Genovese's ranking,[4] eighth in Schlesinger, Jr.'s, 1995 study,[5] and the Fabers rated him fifth overall.[6] As early as 1956, the presidential historian and political scientist Clinton Rossiter placed Truman eighth, among his eight "great" presidents. He praised Truman's abilities as a "technician," who "had few equals in the long history of the Presidency. Most experienced students of public administration," he said, "agreed that he organized his time, which meant a seventy-hour week, and distributed his energies, which were legendary, with the sure touch of a professional." Yet, Rossiter noted, Truman after all was not a professional. It meant that "he learned his job on the job with astounding success."[7] As Rossiter said, he handed an office to Eisenhower that was no less grand than the one he inherited from Roosevelt. "Looked at in the light of what took place during the term of every other man who succeeded a great President — John Adams, Madison, Van Buren, [A.] Johnson, Taft, and Harding — this may well appear as Truman's most remarkable accomplishment," he wrote.[8]

Truman lived to see much of the process of rehabilitation, and surely it came as no surprise to the former president. This is not to suggest that it was a question of ego. Rather, Truman had a superb ability to analyze a political situation, and as a keen student of history, he simply knew full well that his accomplishments were outstanding.

The new president was sensitive to the damage that Wilson had caused by his inability to keep the United States from withdrawing into isolationism at the close of the First World War. He therefore took advantage of the international spirit that Roosevelt had encouraged. As his first official act, he announced that the United Nations conference would meet as scheduled in San Francisco on 25 April 1945.[9] He quickly met with the cabinet and assured the members that he intended to continue Roosevelt's policies, but that final decisions would be his.

Truman's immediate responsibility as president was to deal with the war and its aftermath. Hitler committed suicide at the end of April, less than a month after Truman took office. The most recent — and the most thoughtful — study of the effects of the Roosevelt-Truman policies toward Germany is that of Michael Beschloss, who has argued that the wartime leadership of these two presidents was largely responsible for the emergence of a reformed Germany; a Germany that would no longer be a threat to the world.[10] To accomplish this, it had been necessary to impress upon the Germans that they truly had been defeated. It was important that there be no repetition of a "stab-in-the-back" legend such as the one that followed the First World War. That legend had convinced many Germans that they lost only because of internal disloyalty. It also was essential to develop democratic attitudes among the German public. To accomplish this required the avoidance of harsh measures that would generate resentment. Only after they had stood the test of time for a half century was Beschloss confident in concluding that the FDR–Truman policies had been a success. At the century's end, German aggressiveness had vanished, German democracy was secure, and a strong but non-threatening Germany had served successfully as a bulwark to Soviet expansionism. Roosevelt had laid the foundation, but Truman followed through and built the superstructure.

As for Japan, it was the war in the Pacific and Asia that brought about what surely was Truman's most controversial action: the use of the atomic bomb. It should give any thoughtful American pause to recognize that his or her country is the only one that actually has used nuclear weapons. Truman himself had no doubt, and consistently expressed confidence that his decision had been appropriate. Even he, though, worried about "killing all those kids," and about the future of nuclear warfare.[11] General Eisenhower when he heard of the bombing quite naturally wondered if it had been really necessary to "hit them with that awful thing."[12] It is easy in retrospect to condemn the decision, but things were not so simple at the time.

The standard argument is that the bomb saved lives by making an invasion unnecessary, an invasion that would have taken countless lives on all sides. The rejoinder has been that a demonstration — on an uninhabited island, for example — might have been sufficient. Truman and his advisers considered and dismissed the idea as unrealistic. They concluded that it would have been unlikely to convince the Japanese leaders who were so stubborn as at least to border on the fanatic. A blockade was another possibility, but it would have been not only costly, but lengthy. Such a war of attrition would have created the likelihood that the Japanese leaders would have attempted "to negotiate a peace that was less than humbling," and that the American people would tire of the war, and withdraw their support from the effort needed to bring it to a successful conclusion.[13] Truman concluded that what has come to be the standard argument was correct.

Richard Frank, author of the most recent study of the issue, after examining vast amounts of material not available to Truman and his advisers, has concluded that they were right. As brutal as the bomb was, its use "saved not only American and Japanese lives but also Chinese and other nationalities, as well as prisoners of war."[14] As historian and Truman biographer, Robert Ferrell, put it, the Japanese regime had to be shocked out of its complacency; but "a terrible shock it proved to be," he said, "involving tens of thousands of people who had nothing to do with the self-serving schemes of Tokyo officialdom."[15] Right or wrong, it was a judgment call, and Truman was characteristically decisive.

One often-overlooked factor, also, was American public opinion. The blast over Hiroshima took place on 6 August 1945. A poll on 8 August showed approval from 85 percent of Americans.[16] Americans were in a vengeful mood. Their country had been attacked directly. The numbers of their war dead were huge. Anti-Japanese war propaganda had been effective. Apart from propaganda, though, there could be absolutely no doubt that Japanese troops had behaved with unspeakable brutality — and that the brutality was deliberate: it had resulted from official policy. If Truman had decided not to use the bomb, he could well have been treated as a war criminal himself when the people — incited by grieving parents and families as well as by politicians — discovered that it had been available, but unused. The American system of government would surely have been weakened, and it is entirely within the realm of possibility that it might even have crumbled.

As it was, the people elected substantial Republican majorities to Congress in the off-year election of 1946. Republicans in the new Eightieth Congress and their conservative Southern Democratic allies moved speedily to show their animosity toward the late President Roosevelt, and proposed the Twenty-Second Amendment to the Constitution. The Amendment prevents any president from being elected more than twice.

As the presidential scholars Milkis and Nelson put it, the debate on the Amendment "painted a thin gloss of constitutional philosophy over a highly partisan issue." Sometimes it was so thin as to be nonexistent. Representative Karl Mundt of South Dakota said openly that the move grew "directly out of the unfortunate experience we had in this country in 1940 and again in 1944." There was no consideration of the Founders' deliberate decision to "place no restrictions on presidential reeligibility." Ratification came from states with Republican governments and from those in the South. Even then, it took nearly four years, an unusually long time.[17] With one exception, no amendment to the Constitution has taken so long to ratify.[18]

President Truman had no way to stop the Amendment. Amendments do not require presidential signatures; they bypass presidents and go directly to the states for ratification. In any case, they already have support from two-thirds of each House of Congress. The late Clinton Rossiter, a political scientist and presidential historian and a conservative himself, condemned the limitation, and pointed clearly to its dangers. It reflected, he wrote, "a shocking lack of faith in the common sense and good judgment of the people." It added an element of rigidity to the Constitution, and, he said, "sooner or later we will find ourselves trapped in a severe national emergency and be anxious to keep the incumbent President in office." The Amendment, he added, "disfigured the Constitution with words that still express the sharp anger of a moment of reaction rather than the studied wisdom of a generation." He said that it was, indeed, "an undisguised slap at the memory of Franklin D. Roosevelt."[19] Ironically, since the Amendment exempted any president in office while it was ratified, for a half-century the only two presidents who came within its strictures were the popular Republicans, Dwight Eisenhower and Ronald Reagan — either of whom could probably (and in Eisenhower's case, certainly) have been re-elected.

Although it did not affect him, Truman shared the disdain for the Twenty-Second Amendment. He saw it clearly for what it was: an "endeavor to handicap the presidency." He was characteristically forthright in describing it as a "monstrosity," and one of the worst Amendments "ever added to the Constitution. "It is as bad as that short-lived Prohibition amendment," he said. He, like Rossiter, recognized that it could be tragic "in the event the nation is confronted by a grave emergency."[20] Truman was equally blunt in assessing blame. The amendment, he wrote, "was sponsored by that famous Eightieth Congress as a reflection upon a great President, Franklin D. Roosevelt."[21]

From the beginning of the Republic until the Twenty-Fifth Amendment, ratified over two decades after Truman became president, a vacancy in the vice presidency remained unfilled until the next election. The succession act in effect when Truman took office dated back to 1886 during Cleveland's first administration. It placed the secretary of state next in line to become president if vacancies occurred simultaneously in the offices of president and vice president.

As a new president with no vice president, Truman was sensitive to the power that he had to appoint a secretary of state who was an unelected official in line to succeed him. Truman was a politician committed to the electoral system, and believed it inappropriate for a president to be in a position to appoint his successor. A young, and still unseasoned, Senator J. William Fulbright of Arkansas, in fact, when the Republican Eightieth Congress took office reflected the discontent with the president by suggesting that he appoint Michigan Republican Arthur Vandenberg secretary of state, and then resign so that Vandenberg could become chief executive.[22]

To remedy a situation that he considered defective if not outright dangerous, Truman requested a revision in the line of succession. Congress responded with the Succession Act of 1947, which remains in effect. In the event of a double vacancy in the two top offices, the speaker of the House becomes president. If there is no speaker, the post falls to the president pro-tempore of the Senate. In the highly unlikely case that both congressional offices are vacant, the succession would revert to the cabinet, beginning with the secretary of state.

Truman's reasoning was certainly understandable, as was his preference for an elected rather than an appointed official. It probably was a mistake to change the succession, however. A secretary of state would be likely to carry on the policies of the administration, and avoid an abrupt change that the voters had not chosen. A House speaker, on the other hand, might even belong to a different party, and in any case could well introduce a radical change in direction. Consider, for example, the policy reversal that would have resulted if Tip O'Neill had replaced President Reagan, let alone the disruption that would have taken place if Newt Gingrich had replaced President Clinton.

In another change, sound administrator that he was, President Truman signed into law the National Security Act of 1947. Seeking to unify the armed forces, the Act created a new cabinet agency, the Department of Defense. At the sub-cabinet level, it separated the Air Corps from the army to become a new Department of the Air Force. The Department of War became the Department of the Army; it and the Department of the Navy lost cabinet status and became units of the Department of Defense. Under the Act's provisions, the Secretaries of the Air Force, Army, and Navy are not cabinet officers; they report to the Secretary of Defense who is the member of the cabinet.

That year the president also announced the "Truman Doctrine," pledging aid to countries threatened by "direct or indirect aggression."[23] Communist threats to Turkey and Greece brought about the policy shift, and it was a direct response to Soviet expansionism and to Soviet support for insurgent communist revolutionaries. Truman succeeded in securing aid from Congress to the two beleaguered countries, each of which remained outside the area of Soviet domination.

In 1948 Truman recognized the new state of Israel. With bipartisan support, he also signed into law an amazingly farsighted measure, the Marshall Plan. It was the most massive program of foreign aid in history. Secretary of State Marshall had proposed the plan to rebuild the ravaged states of Europe, and Truman wisely seized upon it. Although the Soviets could have participated, they refused. The plan clearly aimed at blocking Soviet influence, and at creating markets for American goods, but only the most cynical observers can deny that it contained a healthy component of altruism. And regardless of motivations, it filled a desperate need for an entire continent, if not in truth for the world.

When the Soviets closed the roads to Berlin, shutting off access and supplies to the Allied sector of the city deep within the Soviet zone of East Germany, Truman acted forcefully. The United States along with the French and the British conducted a massive airlift of food and other necessities. The Berlin Airlift was classic Truman, and it was his policy. "We were going to stay, period," he said. Since no feasible suggestions came from American agencies or from abroad, "it was left to the president to decide, which he did on June 28," 1948.[24] There was no war, and the Soviets eventually removed their blockade, but to force it, the airlift continued for approximately a year.

In domestic policy, however, Truman's relations with the Republican Eightieth Congress were bitter. Moving to restrict organized labor, for a major example, Congress over labor's strenuous objections in 1947 passed the Taft-Hartley Act. Truman, along with labor, objected to several provisions that reduced labor's rights as set forth in the New Deal's Wagner Act of 1935. He cast his veto, but Congress overrode it. Truman termed his program the "Fair Deal," to complement and complete FDR's New Deal. Although he had some success — on such matters as the minimum wage and housing — the bulk of his measures, most notably calls for comprehensive national health insurance, went down to defeat. A striking success was his order to desegregate the armed services, but this resulted from Executive Order 8981, rather than from congressional action.[25] Congress at the time was totally unreceptive to civil rights. Truman, himself, had come a long way from his earlier racist views. "Students of the Truman administration, almost without exception, have been certain about the president's conversion, and with much new evidence available the change of mind seems irrefutable."[26] That change of mind apparently resulted from reports of atrocities in the South, and from meetings with sober and thoughtful black leaders. It led to legislative proposals, which went nowhere, but also to court briefs, which did; they ultimately contributed to the basis for the Supreme Court's landmark desegregation decision in 1954.

Hardly anyone other than Truman himself thought that he could win re-election in 1948. In fact, so pervasive is the view that the Democrats then had faced overwhelming disadvantages, that accounts frequently assert that Truman offered Eisenhower the Democratic nomination — and more — in 1948. Until recently, there was only one source for this, and that source under the circumstances is hardly the most reliable: Eisenhower himself.

As Eisenhower biographer Stephen Ambrose carefully put it, "Late in 1947, Harry Truman called Eisenhower to his office, where — according to Eisenhower — he made a most remarkable offer. If Eisenhower would accept the Democratic nomination, Truman said he would be willing to run as the vice-presidential candidate on the same ticket."[27] Truman denied any such offer.

There had, indeed, been "dump Truman" and "draft Eisenhower" movements. "The president's own party did not want him." FDR's son, James, supported Eisenhower, said Truman biographer Robert Ferrell. As carefully as Ambrose, he wrote that "Truman naturally was incensed over this opposition. In preceding years he may have thought a little about Eisenhower's candidacy."[28] Truman himself, however, said flatly that it was untrue that he had suggested that Ike run in 1948. "Oh no," he said, "I didn't do that. I didn't encourage him to seek the Presidency on the Democratic ticket, because I was going to run myself in 1948."[29] Ferrell even cited evidence that Ike ambitiously sought nomination by *both* parties.[30] The most recent evidence presents new information that suggests a truth somewhere between the Eisenhower and Truman versions.

In July 2003 the Truman Library reported that an archivist had discovered a previously unknown Truman diary. It contained an entry in Truman's handwriting describing a discussion he had with General Eisenhower about MacArthur's "superiority complex." In the entry for 25 July 1947, Truman wrote: "Ike & I think MacArthur expects to make a Roman Triumphal return to the U.S. a short time before the Republican Convention meets in Philadelphia. I told Ike that that he (Ike) should announce for the nomination for President on the Democratic ticket and that I'd be glad to be in second place, or Vice President." Truman added that "Ike won't quot [*sic*] me & I won't quote him."[31] So, rather than offering Ike the nomination, Truman outlined a hypothetical situation in which he might do so. Ike may have exaggerated Truman's position, but the truth seems closer to his recollection than to Truman's flat denial.

In protest against efforts by Northern Democrats to ensure black civil rights, the Governor of South Carolina, J. Strom Thurmond, led a faction that split from the Democratic Party (the States' Rights Party, or "Dixiecrats") and entered the race attacking Truman from the right. Former Vice President Henry A. Wallace, angered over Truman's strong anti–Soviet policies, split another faction from the Democrats (the Progressive Party), and entered the race attacking Truman from the left. Truman, for his part, ran hard against the "Good For Nothing, Do Nothing, Republican 80th Congress." His famous "whistle stop campaign" took him all over the country. He won decisively. No doubt one the high points of his life took place when he posed grinning while holding aloft the famous *Chicago Tribune* front-page blunder, a huge headline saying "Dewey Defeats Truman."

Second terms frequently bring more trouble to presidents than their first terms, and Truman's was no exception. Minor scandals arose that permitted opponents to decry "the mess in Washington," which became a major campaign issue in the 1952 election. In China, Mao won in 1949 and drove the Nationalists to the Island of Taiwan (Formosa). Truman and the Democrats were the target of allegations that they had "lost China," as though it had been America's to begin with. The Cold War proceeded. Truman earlier had authorized research on thermonuclear weapons, the hydrogen bomb, and in 1952 the United States tested the first such device, which dwarfed even the fearsome atom bomb. Soon, with Soviet developments, there were two thermonuclear powers — two antagonistic thermonuclear powers — and the danger to the world, and America's anxiety, increased.

Additionally, in 1950, an obscure senator from Wisconsin, Joseph McCarthy, after having searched frantically for a campaign issue that he could use to secure his re-election, discovered that he could cause hysteria nationwide by alleging that he had discovered "communists in government." In West Virginia in his first speech on the subject, McCarthy charged that he had evidence of 205 communists in the State Department. The next day in Utah, the number was fifty-seven. Thereafter, the number varied with each reference. He consistently refused to reveal any names — and in fact never did reveal any evidence to substantiate his wild charges — but he caused national turmoil, and in 1952 campaigned against the Democrats by saying that they were guilty of "twenty years of treason."

This is not to say that the United States had no communist movement, or that communists had no effect. There undoubtedly were spies who transmitted classified information — especially information regarding nuclear weapons — to the Soviets. The "Red Scare" that developed, however, was out of proportion to anything that actually existed. McCarthy and others, including many members of the House Committee on Un-American Activities (HUAC), used the notion of widespread communist influence to advance their own political careers.

One young politician whose career during the Truman administration benefited from the Red Scare and from his position on HUAC (as it came to be called) was a young member of the House from California, Richard M. Nixon. Nixon was a central figure in the case of Alger Hiss, who had been accused of having passed information to the Soviets when he was a young official in the State Department. Hiss denied the charges and ultimately received a prison term for perjury. Nixon used his newly won prominence to secure election to the Senate in 1950, and to the vice presidency on the ticket with Eisenhower in 1952.

Having been elected to office first in 1946, Nixon's rise in politics was meteoric. He received considerable criticism for his role in the Red Scare, but his actions were reasonably moderate for the time. To be sure, among his many strengths ethics did not appear to be prominent. Undoubtedly, he was a vicious — even an unscrupulous — campaigner. He was not, however, an irresponsible demagogue on the order of McCarthy. Nixon's enemies, of course, even if they were to agree, would consider this to be an instance of damning with faint praise.

A true crisis energized the Truman administration in 1950, in divided Korea. When troops from the Marxist-Leninist north invaded the south, Truman on 28 June sent U.S. troops in response. The United Nations endorsed his action, and the Korean War was underway. During the war, Truman's efforts to deal with the threat of a steel strike, which under the circumstances he considered a danger to national security, brought him in 1952 one of his most serious setbacks. He refused to use the Taft-Hartley Law. When the strike threat continued, he seized the steel mills, and sent troops to operate them. The Supreme Court in a surprise decision, *Youngstown Sheet and Tube Company v. Sawyer*, rebuked the president and ruled that he had acted unconstitutionally.[32] The decision clearly was a blow to the administration, which could cite precedents for Truman's action.

As Milkis and Nelson have pointed out, Theodore Roosevelt had threatened to seize coal mines and operate them by army troops if a strike continued; Franklin Roosevelt actually did seize "the North American Aviation Plant at Inglewood, California, on June 9 1941, six months before Pearl Harbor, arguing that his power to act derived from the 'aggregate' of the Constitution and the laws"; and the Supreme Court had not "ruled against a president in the exercise of prerogative power" since 1866.[33] Nevertheless, although the decision was important, and although some authorities have concluded otherwise, it did not shatter executive power — nor was it even a major blow against the president's authority as commander-in-chief. A major difference in circumstance between his action and others was that by the time Truman acted, Congress already had legislated on the subject. The majority of the justices in *Youngstown* either voted to uphold the president, or to apply the decision only to the specific case. Therefore, it was not a rejection of TR's stewardship theory of the presidency, that the president can take actions necessary for the public good provided that neither the Constitution nor the laws prohibit them.

The war was a continuing disaster for the Truman administration. After initial victories under General of the Army Douglas MacArthur, who advanced far into North Korea, Chinese troops entered the war and forced the Americans to retreat. Thereafter, the war dragged on, taking an enormous toll on all sides. Fearing the start of a Third World War, Truman would not permit MacArthur to cross into China, or to bomb Chinese territory. MacArthur, characteristically convinced of his own infallibility, blasted the Truman policy in public, and even sent critical letters to Republican leaders in Congress. On 11 April 1951, Truman removed the General from all of his commands (he also headed the American government in occupied Japan, where he had done an outstanding job).

MacArthur returned to an enthusiastic public. He even presented a maudlin speech to a joint session of Congress, quoting what he said was an old song, "Old Soldiers Never Die; They Just Fade Away." There were calls for Truman's impeachment and worse.[34] The controversy, however, faded more quickly than the old soldier when top military officials supported the president. It became clear that MacArthur had directly violated orders, and had been openly insubordinate.

On the more positive side, Truman outlined the program for his second term in his 1949 inaugural address. His fourth point became the famed "Point IV" programs of technical assistance to foster development in Third World countries.[35] Although the State Department was initially reserved and Congress was slow to act, it ultimately passed legislation that Truman signed into law on 5 June 1950. When members of Congress subsequently attempted to slash funding drastically — charging that the program was "idealistic" (a damning indictment), and it made use of "the taxpayer's money" (another)— Truman actively lobbied key members and succeeded in securing funds to implement what clearly was an excellent idea.

Point IV did more than merely provide American aid. It also called for assistance from other governments. Although it faced frequent impediments from Congress and from other governments, and although it never lived up to its full potential, Point IV did have numerous positive effects and became the basis for enlightened programs in subsequent administrations.

In 1949 Truman also succeeded in securing ratification of the North Atlantic Treaty that formed the basis for NATO, the North Atlantic Treaty Organization, that provided a foundation for resistance to Soviet expansion.[36] He was also remarkably successful in "proposals relating to the management of the federal government." Congress followed his recommendations, and in June 1949 enacted a Reorganization Act, which permitted the president within a certain time period to submit reorganization plans that would become official unless either the House or the Senate disapproved. Later that year Congress voted to improve the pay of upper-level officials and to reform "the salary structure for much of the civil service."[37] These were outgrowths of the recommendations of the Hoover Commission, and they brought considerable improvement in government efficiency. During his second term, Truman also presided over a massive reconstruction of the White House. It had deteriorated so substantially that it actually had become dangerous. For an extended period, the Trumans moved into Blair House while the White House was undergoing renovation.

Truman decided that he would not be a candidate for re-election in 1952. His popularity was so low that chances of victory would have been dim in any case. They would have become even dimmer when the Republicans nominated the beloved wartime leader Dwight Eisenhower as their candidate. His running mate was the young and outspoken California senator Richard Nixon. The Democrats nominated Illinois Governor Adlai Stevenson, the grandson of Vice President Adlai Stevenson who served with Cleveland in his second term. His running mate was Alabama Senator John Sparkman.

The campaign was especially brutal. Senator McCarthy's charges of "twenty years of treason" set the tone, and more responsible Republicans condemned corruption and "the mess in Washington." President Truman graciously invited General Eisenhower to the White House for a briefing. The bitterness of the campaign increased when Eisenhower refused to come. He won strongly.

Despite his anger, Truman invited President-Elect Eisenhower to meet and work with him to smooth the transition to the new administration. Eisenhower did so. Truman's initiative established "a precedent for the cooperation of old and new administrations in the period between election and inauguration days." As McCoy described it, this demonstrated that Truman "had one more innovation in him before he left office."[38] The outgoing president on 6 January added nearly fifty thousand acres to Olympic National Park. A short time before, he had approved a settlement of an impending coal strike to avoid bequeathing a major problem to Eisenhower, and had submitted an *amicus curiae* brief to the Supreme Court in the case of *Brown v. Board of Education*. His last official act was on 19 January 1953, when he signed a letter recognizing the seventy-fifth anniversary of the Civil Service System, and blasting those who would weaken it.[39]

"On inaugural day Eisenhower refused to do the traditional thing and come into the White House to greet the outgoing president; he simply drove up on his car and sent word he was ready to go to the capitol."[40] After the inauguration, the Trumans returned by train to Independence, Missouri. Along the way, crowds greeted them at many stops, especially in Missouri, to wish them well.[41] At the time there was no Secret Service protection for former presidents, nor was there a pension. The Trumans lived simply, and the former president busied himself with numerous activities, including writing. As long as he was able, he remained highly accessible to the public.

Harry S Truman, thirty-third President of the United States, lived almost two decades in retirement. He died on 26 December 1972 at the age of eighty-eight. His widow, Bess, survived him, living until 18 October 1982. She lived until the age of ninety-seven. The Trumans are buried on the grounds of the Harry S Truman Library and Museum in Independence, Missouri.

There has never been a perfect president, and certainly Harry Truman had his faults. He could be petty, he was irascible and outspoken, his sense of loyalty to his friends sometimes outweighed his normally sound judgment. His loyalty program — albeit intended to preempt truly draconian measures as well as to ensure the absence of subversives in government posts[42] — was misguided and pernicious. It actually played into the hands of the enemies of civil liberties.

Harry Truman was nevertheless a man of extraordinary ability, and one of unquestioned integrity. He was decisive and thoughtful, and he accepted any blame for the consequences of his actions. In a time of unusual turmoil, he shepherded the country into a new era. Not all of the precedents he set were positive, but he left the presidency, and the country, as strong as he had found them. In fact, because of his excellent administrative skills and his success in reorganizing the executive branch to make it more efficient, in a very real sense he left the presidency stronger than he had found it. Under the circumstances, it would be asking the superhuman to have expected more. How he compares to any other president — each of whom served under completely different conditions — or whether it is even possible to achieve any accuracy at all in drawing such a comparison not only is irrelevant but is meaningless.

34

DWIGHT D. EISENHOWER
January 20, 1953–January 20, 1961

General of the Army Dwight David Eisenhower, perhaps the most popular leading military figure of the Second World War, became President of the United States on 20 January 1953. His popularity brought Republican control of both houses of Congress. He was the first Republican president in twenty years.

In many ways he was a president especially appropriate for the time. The country was weary; weary of depression and its aftermath, weary of the Second World War and also of its aftermath, and weary of twenty years of reform. Moreover, the Korean War was underway. There is little doubt that Americans needed reassurance, and perhaps a period of rest. However devoid it was of content — reminiscent of the Whigs' "Tippecanoe and Tyler too" more than a century earlier — the slogan of the victorious Republicans' 1952 campaign, "I Like Ike," seems to have captured the country's mood in a way more than anyone at the time recognized.

One thing Americans especially liked about Ike was that in 1953 he did, indeed, go to Korea. As he had said he would, he brought an end to the Korean War. It was no victory, and was in fact inconclusive, but the armistice preserved South Korea's independence.

Eisenhower's critics during his eight years as president saw him as passive; saw his two terms as a time of stagnation. He had none of the suave charm of FDR, garbled his syntax in press conferences, peppered his comments with no such salty phrases as those of Truman, and he seemed hardly to be in control. Subsequent scholarship, however, has demonstrated how wrong such a view was. Eisenhower was a strong leader. He not only knew what was going on, but controlled his administration tightly and effectively.

His was, in the words of one later scholar of his presidency, a "hidden-hand presidency."[1] He kept his control from public view, but when he chose to do so, directed developments from behind the scenes and was often effective. There were times, however, when for one reason or another he chose to keep hands off. The question regarding Eisenhower no longer is whether he was in control — he was.

Nor is the question whether he, as the first Republican in twenty years, attempted to reject the Roosevelt-Truman modern presidency (one might say the TR-Wilson-FDR-Truman modern presidency) and attempt to return to the days of Coolidge and Hoover. He clearly did not. Ike was a domestic conservative, but he had no intention of dismantling the New Deal. For example, Social Security was Franklin Roosevelt's landmark domestic achievement. Ike tried in 1953 to expand the system and failed. He repeated his request the next year. "With an election coming in November, Republicans were more amendable to improving rather than destroying the system, and Eisenhower got a bill that increased benefits and put ten million people not previously covered into Social Security."[2] In 1956 Eisenhower signed into law the addition of disability benefits to the Social Security program, which was an enormous expansion of the key New Deal measure.

Milkis and Nelson provided what probably is the best capsule description of Eisenhower's approach and his major achievement. "Like the Hoover Commission, and in contrast to the Twenty-second Amendment," they wrote, "the presidency of Dwight Eisenhower fostered bipartisan acceptance of the modern presidency." Nevertheless, they said, "Eisenhower's contribution was reluctant."[3]

Eisenhower, "did badly in the Schlesinger 1962 poll." He "accused the scholars of equating 'an individual's strength of dedication with oratorical bombast; determination, with public repetition of a catchy phrase; achievement, with the exaggerated use of the vertical pronoun'." He, as Schlesinger, Jr., described it, wondered who historians thought they were to "arrogate to themselves the judging of presidential performance?"[4] Obviously, there is some substance to the question. Both Coolidge and Kennedy agreed that "only presidents can really understand the presidency."

At one level, of course, this contention is not open to argument. As for evaluating presidential performance, however, that notion cannot — especially in a democracy — be tolerated. The alternative to judgment by historians, as Schlesinger pointed out, would be to argue that "only presidents would have the qualifications to rate presidents."[5] Certainly that would be nonsense — voters are called upon to do so every four years. And, assuredly, there would be even some presidents whose judgments at best would be open to question.

Truman was, according to Schlesinger, the only president to wade into the rating waters. He named his eight best, chronologically, as Washington, Jefferson, Jackson, Polk, Lincoln, Cleveland, Wilson, and FDR. Characteristically, Lincoln was the only Republican to make the list. Most contemporary listings would include two Republicans: not only Lincoln, but Theodore Roosevelt as well. Truman's list of the eight worst — except for the clearly terrible Pierce and Buchanan — were all (again it is hardly a surprise in view of President Truman's partisanship) Republicans or Whigs. These (again chronologically) were Taylor, Pierce, Buchanan, Grant, Benjamin Harrison, Harding, Coolidge — and Eisenhower.[6] Considering that it was Truman doing the rating, the inclusion of Ike might have been a foregone conclusion.

As for the formal surveys, Schlesinger, Sr.'s, 1962 poll placed Ike twenty-second among thirty-one, eleventh of the twelve he rated "average."[7] By the time of Schlesinger, Jr.'s, 1996 poll, Eisenhower had risen to tenth among thirty-nine, which placed him "high average."[8] Genovese rated him twelfth of thirty-nine, "above average,"[9] while the Fabers placed him much lower, twenty-fourth.[10] Reuters reported a poll on 21 February 2000 that included not only historians but also politicians "pundits," and others who were "knowledgeable." It rated Eisenhower ninth, ahead even of Lyndon Johnson and Jackson.[11] Thus, one who wishes to take polls seriously could find evidence to justify placing Ike almost anywhere on the scale. That alone should be enough to demonstrate that the polls are hardly a precise — let alone a scientific — measurement of the performance of a president.

In view of the characteristics of the Republican congressional leaders of the time, it is little wonder that, as an internationalist, "in his first months in office, Eisenhower had far greater difficulty with his own party than with the Democrats." He thought that Republican senators, especially the Old Guard, were unable to understand that their team had come to include, not oppose, the White House."[12] Milkis and Nelson quote the distinguished historian Oscar Handlin to the effect that "Eisenhower made palatable to most Republicans the social welfare legislation of the preceding two decades. In the 1950s, the New Deal ceased to be an active political issue.... No other figure could have achieved that transformation."[13] It would be difficult to overestimate the importance of that achievement.

Throughout his presidency, Eisenhower adhered to the traditional conservative goal of a balanced budget. He was ruthless in holding down expenditures, including military expenditures. In fact, he reduced Truman's military budget by 20 percent,[14] but he was insistent on preserving sufficient revenues to pay for needed programs. In words that hardly any Republican would recognize a half century later — in fact words would send a chill to the very marrow of the bones of twenty-first-century Republican legislators — Ike, the beloved Republican icon said in a press conference that he would never agree to the elimination of any tax that would cause a reduction of revenue.[15]

In his first State of the Union message, Ike called for a "new, positive, foreign policy." He wanted a powerful military, but as a fiscal conservative he wanted one "that did not burden the economy." That meant tight military budgets. Under the circumstances, it also meant a heavy reliance on nuclear weapons. Inevitably, the press, and hence the public, began to refer to the Eisenhower policy as "The New Look."[16] This took its name from popular culture — from women's fashion, to be precise. In 1948, as the wartime shortages of fabric and other resources had eased, fashion designers retreated from the short skirts and relatively sparse use of material seen in the war years to huge, sweepingly full, nearly ankle-length skirts that set the tone for the opulent 1950s. The designers and fashion writers were markedly successful in popularizing their term, "the New Look," which then spilled over into politics.

In contrast to some of his successors decades later, Eisenhower believed that, as he put it in a national security directive, a "sound dollar lies at the very basis of a sound capability for defense."[17] His insistence on economy plus force, which meant heavy dependence upon nuclear power, ultimately meant that American policy had to be based upon the definite possibility of nuclear strikes. It also meant reliance upon covert action.

Truman had used the CIA as it had originally been intended: to gather intelligence and evaluate it. Ike, on the other hand, decided to use it in a vastly more activist role. He thought it could be used much more effectively than Truman had used it, and that it "indeed could become one of America's chief weapons in the Cold War."[18] Shortly after the July 1953 armistice in Korea, for example, Eisenhower ordered a CIA-backed coup in Iran to topple Prime Minister Mohammed Mossadegh. "Do it, he told the CIA, and don't bother me with any details."[19] This, the "CIA's first big-time coup," restored the monarchy and brought the Shah to power. That same year saw the United States enter into the Southeast Asia Treaty Organization (SEATO), pledging support to countries in the region facing communist threats.

The following year, Eisenhower first articulated the "domino theory," stressing the need to protect Southeast Asian countries from communism, asserting that the fall of one would lead to the fall of others as with a row of dominoes. This may have been only words, but they were words that were to have a profound effect in years to come. Although he refused to send troops when the French ultimately were forced from their colony in Indochina, Eisenhower provided support for the government of Ngo Dinh Diem in the newly formed South Vietnam, created by the partition of Indochina.

Regarding the nuclear buildup and the reliance on nuclear weapons, when the Chinese in their controversy with the Nationalists on Taiwan bombarded the islands of Quemoy and Matsu, beginning in 1954 — islands that are so insignificant that they now are virtually forgotten — Eisenhower demonstrated that although he worked diligently to avoid it, he was quite prepared "to wage nuclear war."[20] Vice President Nixon had announced in a speech that tactical nuclear weapons had become "conventional," and would be used against aggressors. Eisenhower endorsed this, saying that he saw no reason why they "shouldn't be used just exactly as you would use a bullet."[21] Ultimately, for a number of reasons the threatened crisis receded. Although Chiang Kai-shek on Taiwan rejected Eisenhower's initiatives, the administration treated the cessation of overt hostilities as a victory.

Some historians later agreed, calling it a triumph. Ambrose was among them, saying that the "beauty" of the policy was that not even Eisenhower knew whether he would resort to nuclear weapons. Pach and Richardson, however, pointed out that this gives Eisenhower "too much credit for keeping his options open and controlling the course of events." On the contrary, they argued, it is "by no means clear that Eisenhower forced the PRC [Peoples' Republic of China] to back down." Moreover, Ike limited his own flexibility by "secretly promising to defend Quemoy and Matsu and, over the long term, by agreeing to a mutual defense treaty with Nationalist China. Despite Ambrose's claim," they wrote, "Eisenhower knew that he would use nuclear weapons in the event of war" with China.[22] The difficulty with the policy was twofold: it created a potentially disastrous condition under which the use of nuclear weapons was a strong possibility — and over a minor issue, at that — and it surrendered American options, as Eisenhower himself recognized, by basing them upon the unpredictable actions of the erratic Chiang.

In 1956, the Hungarian uprising took place. The Hungarians reinstalled as premier, Imre Nagy, whom the Soviets had deposed in 1955. The Soviets sent in tanks, and crushed the rebellion. Despite breast-beating cries of "roll back communism," and encouragement from the Eisenhower administration to "captive nations" to throw off communist oppressors — encouragements that blanketed the Eastern European airwaves from Radio Free Europe, a CIA-backed American propaganda organ, and implied that American support would be forthcoming — Eisenhower was too realistic and too prudent to intervene in a situation so close to the Soviet Union and so important to their policies. Subsequently, there was a marked decline in calls from the United States for citizens in Eastern Europe to stand up to the Soviets, and throw off the oppressor's yoke.

Also that year, the Israelis, the British, and the French invaded Egypt. The action was a response to a previous nationalization of the Suez Canal.

The Eisenhower administration introduced a resolution in the UN for a cease-fire and withdrawal. A UN force moved in, and the invaders accepted a cease-fire.[23] An outcome of the turmoil in the Middle East was the Eisenhower Doctrine, which promised not only to come to the aid of countries in the region faced with communist threats, but to strengthen them with military and economic assistance.[24]

To be sure, Eisenhower was, as Milkis and Nelson said, a reluctant adherent of the modern presidency. He thought that that the Democratic era had upset the constitutional balance between the executive and Congress. Thus, in his first year he submitted no legislative program, but as he grew in experience he came to recognize the importance of executive leadership with regard to legislation. There continued to be issues, however, upon which he elected not to exercise firm leadership when it seemed to be needed. One of those issues pertained to "McCarthyism."

The 1952 election had been especially bitter. The new Vice President Richard M. Nixon had faced a storm of opposition, and weathered it. At their extreme edges, the Republicans had crossed over the boundaries of propriety when they had charged the Democrats with "Twenty Years of Treason." The phrase was a favorite of Senator Joseph R. McCarthy, Republican of Wisconsin, who was tearing the country apart with reckless charges of communism. Although McCarthy had campaigned for Eisenhower, he came to demonstrate to Republicans why it is unwise to cultivate a rattlesnake. After President Eisenhower had been in office a year, the rampaging senator had begun to speak of "twenty-*one* years of treason."

Eisenhower did speak out against McCarthy's tactics but did not refer to the senator by name. In fact, during the election, in deference to a request from McCarthy, Eisenhower had deleted a segment praising General Marshall — his wartime mentor and Truman's secretary of state — from a speech that he gave in Milwaukee, in McCarthy's home state. McCarthy had insisted that Eisenhower not defend Marshall — whom McCarthy had viciously attacked — in Wisconsin, but rather "in another state." Ambrose wrote of Eisenhower and the incident, "that he was ashamed of himself, there can be little doubt."[25] Truman considered Ike's deference to McCarthy at the expense of a dedicated public servant to be nothing less than dishonorable, which contributed the campaign's bitterness.

As McCarthy continued his demagoguery — it had been effective in 1952; Wisconsin's voters had returned him to the Senate for a second term — Eisenhower continued to hold himself aloof from the fray. He told friends, including his brother, Milton, that he would not "get into a pissing contest with that skunk," which is precisely what Milton and others were urging him to do.[26] Some friendly analysts have concluded that Eisenhower worked behind the scenes and brought McCarthy down.

Milkis and Nelson, for example, while quoting contrary opinions —
Alonzo Hamby, they said, argued that Ike let McCarthy run amok — concluded that the president used "the media and his congressional allies to
undermine McCarthy's political effectiveness."[27] Eisenhower biographer
Stephen Ambrose, however, wrote that Eisenhower's assault against
McCarthy was "so indirect as to be scarcely discernible," and he said it was
"one which contributed only indirectly — at best — to McCarthy's downfall."[28] Undoubtedly, Eisenhower's own acceptance of the Republican rhetoric
charging that the Truman administration had been "riddled with communists"— leading even Ike himself to sound somewhat like McCarthy and to
flirt with the word "treason," as he did in the Milwaukee speech[29]— hampered him in dealing with the out-of-control anti-communist crusader.

Eisenhower simply thought that the best way to handle the senatorial
loose cannon was to ignore him. Ultimately, McCarthy did self-destruct. He
challenged the U.S. Army and was discredited by his performance — for the
first time televised to the entire country — in the ensuing Army-McCarthy
hearings in 1954. The Senate censured him, and he faded from prominence,
dying of acute alcoholism in 1957. He caused incalculable damage, however,
and it seems likely that Eisenhower could have prevented much of it simply
by having acted.

Another major issue that Eisenhower handled badly by deciding for too
long to ignore it was civil rights. "No one is more anxious than I am to see
Negroes receive first-class citizenship in this country," he said to a group of
black leaders in May of 1958, but told them that they had to "be patient."[30]
It was an issue that he preferred not to confront, and his own sentiments, at
best, were in conflict. He was reluctant to offend people, but those whom
he was reluctant to offend almost always were Southern segregationists.[31]
Although he strongly favored the right of all citizens to vote, and insisted
with equal vigor upon the authority of the federal courts, he did not speak
out in favor of *Brown v. Board of Education*, and, when asked, he equivo-
cated.

Ultimately, the governor of Arkansas, Orval Faubus, assigned the
Arkansas National Guard to Little Rock High School to prevent black students from entering. Eisenhower federalized the Arkansas Guard, and sent
U.S. troops to protect the black children and enforce their rights. He could
hardly have acted otherwise as President of the United States, when a governor openly defied the orders of a federal court. He had, however, submitted a mild civil rights bill to Congress. Although it was weakened even
further, the arm-twisting tactics of Senate Majority Leader Lyndon Johnson, brought eventual passage of the bill. It was the first civil rights legislation that had made it through Congress since Reconstruction. Jackie
Robinson, the famous player who had broken the color line in major league

baseball, urged Ike to veto the bill, as did the great black leader A. Phillip Randolph, the head of the Brotherhood of Sleeping Car Porters.[32] Dr. Martin Luther King, Jr., however, urged the president to sign the bill, as did Roy Wilkins of the National Association for the Advancement of Colored People (NAACP). "If you are digging a ditch with a teaspoon," Wilkins argued, there is something wrong with your head if a man comes along and offers you a spade but you "don't take it because he didn't offer you a bulldozer." His argument recognized that a small victory is better than none. Eisenhower signed the bill.

In his fight with the Old Guard, Eisenhower had to work diligently to head off the Bricker Amendment. The amendment was an absurd attack on the presidency itself— and even on the central government — but it had considerable popular support. The Old Guard unanimously endorsed it, as did most other Republicans and some Democrats. White supremacists backed it "to defend against international threats to racial segregation," in order to prevent "socialized medicine: from being "foisted upon the American people" medical societies supported it, and "the United States Chamber of Commerce endorsed it to forestall destruction of 'vital parts of our free enterprise system'."[33] Its sponsor was Senator John Bricker from Ohio, the Republican Vice Presidential Candidate on the ticket with Thomas E. Dewey in 1948. Bricker's amendment to the Constitution would have forbidden executive agreements, and would have banned any treaty that affected "matters essentially within the domestic jurisdiction of the United States." A reasonable interpretation of the amendment would even have ruled out a treaty that conflicted with a state law.[34] Eisenhower worked skillfully to undercut the proposal, attempting to do so without alienating Senator Bricker — who, by the way, lost his Senate seat in the Democratic sweep in the offyear congressional elections in 1958. Bricker, however, was under no illusion about the source of his defeat. He said that it was "Eisenhower — nobody else" who preserved the executive's authority in international affairs.[35]

The Eisenhower administration had a number of substantial accomplishments. Among them were the admission of the final two states, Alaska and Hawaii, and the development of the Interstate Highway System. Ike had a personal interest in highways. As a young army captain in 1919, he had accompanied an army convoy literally across the country, from Washington, DC, to San Francisco. The roads were atrocious, and the convoy took more than two months to make the journey. Along the way, the heavy military vehicles crashed through more than one hundred bridges (which the army then repaired). As president, Eisenhower remembered this experience, and was aware of the difficulty in moving goods and personnel across the country. He considered it a threat to national security, and the Interstate Highway system was the result — and is Eisenhower's enduring monument.

The Interstates have been a mixed blessing. They certainly have had destructive effects in many ways, but on balance, this most extensive public works program in human history has been beneficial to the country. Ike was justified in the pride he took in his accomplishment. Also important to the country's transportation was the St. Lawrence Seaway that made the Great Lakes accessible to ocean traffic. He signed legislation authorizing in 1954 that authorized cooperation with Canada in its construction, and in 1959, while he was still in office, the Seaway opened.

Although Eisenhower was aware of the dangers of nuclear testing, the Atomic Energy Commission, the military, and others (including some scientists led by the fanatically pro-nuclear physicist, Edward Teller, the "father of the hydrogen bomb")— consistently minimized the risks and reassured Americans that the tests presented no undue health hazard. Eisenhower sought to meet with The Soviet leaders to achieve an agreement to halt testing. He and Khrushchev had arranged a summit meeting, but shortly before it was to take place, Eisenhower — unwisely as it turned out — authorized a flight over the USSR to take spy photographs. The flights, by the U-2, an extremely high altitude airplane, had been going on for years. Although somewhat apprehensive, Eisenhower was confident that no Soviet missile could reach the U-2 at its extraordinary altitude, and he gave his approval. He was mistaken. The Soviets shot down the plane, and after presidential denials that it was a spy plane — Eisenhower himself destroyed his credibility by alleging that it was a weather plane that had "strayed off course" from Turkey — produced not only the wreckage, but the CIA pilot, Francis Gary Powers, "alive and kicking." Soviet leader Khrushchev destroyed the summit meeting with an angry rant just as it was beginning.[36] Any further such talks were doomed for the remainder of the Eisenhower administration.

Both Harry Truman and Dwight Eisenhower were excellent administrators. Each added to the institutionalization of the office of the presidency. Ike studied the reports of both the Brownlow and the Hoover Commissions, and he acted accordingly. The line of authority that he established ran from the president to his chief of staff, Sherman Adams, "to the rest of the president's team, and back again." He also "created the first White House office of legislative liaison."[37] It worked well.

Eisenhower also, in 1953, had presided over the creation of a new cabinet department, the Department of Health, Education, and Welfare. Its first secretary was a Texas newspaper publisher, Oveta Culp Hobby. He thus had appointed the second woman to serve in the cabinet. Moreover, he contributed to the growth in importance of the vice presidency.

The office had always been an anomaly. Vice President Jefferson had refused a request from President Adams to join a diplomatic mission to

France; his motives were political, but his excuse was that he was a legislative officer and not part of the executive.[38] In the 1890s, Theodore Roosevelt had suggested a key role for the vice president. As president, however, he was burdened with a vice president for whom he had little respect and therefore did nothing to enhance Vice President Fairbanks's role. The independently-minded Charles G. Dawes, vice president under President Coolidge, simply refused to attend cabinet meetings.

FDR, on the other hand, in his first term used Vice President Garner (previously speaker of the House) as his legislative liaison. By the time Ike took office, the Twenty-Second Amendment was in effect. By denying a president a third term, the Amendment suggested an increased political importance for the position of vice president, at least in a president's second term. Eisenhower invited Vice President Nixon to meet with the cabinet, assigned him various duties within the party and sent him on good-will missions abroad. Nixon had little influence over policy — and the Nixons had no social relationship with the Eisenhowers at all — but the president had made him more active than previous vice presidents.[39]

Vice President Nixon had received the Republican nomination, but in one of the closest elections in history, he and his running mate U. N. Ambassador Henry Cabot Lodge, lost to the young Senator John F. Kennedy, running with Senate Majority Leader Lyndon B. Johnson. Although Nixon had never been a favorite of Ike's, his defeat embittered the old soldier who saw it as a rejection of his administration and its policies. The president was resentful also of the restricting effect of the Twenty-Second Amendment. According to John Eisenhower, his son who also served as his deputy chief of staff, regardless of age and poor health President Eisenhower would have run for a third term if he could have done so.[40] The first victim of the vindictive Republican attack upon the memory of FDR thus was its own war-hero president. Given the closeness of the 1960 election, there is little doubt that the popular Ike again could have carried his party to victory.

On 17 January 1961, Eisenhower gave his stirring Farewell Address. "In the councils of government," he warned, "we must guard against the acquisition of unwarranted influence, whether sought or unsought, by the military-industrial complex." That combination, he said, must never be permitted "to endanger our liberties or democratic processes. We should take nothing for granted." As Ambrose pointed out, these were the words of a soldier-prophet.[41] Eisenhower's departure was eloquent, and his words are as vital today as when he uttered them.

After attending Kennedy's inauguration, the Eisenhowers "sneaked away through a side exit." They drove to a club in downtown Washington, where they were guests of Adm. Lewis Strauss, who hosted a luncheon. They dined with members of his cabinet and a few close friends. "Then it was off for Gettysburg, along the route they knew so well, and home to the farm."[42]

Ike died on 28 March 1969, shortly after his vice president, Richard Nixon, at last became president. Mamie lived another decade, dying on 11 November 1979. The Eisenhowers are buried in Abilene, Kansas.

Eisenhower's was an enormously important presidency. He accomplished great things, and had great failures as well. He had roots in the nineteenth century, and yet also looked ahead. His greatest success was in doing what in all probability no other president then could have done: he brought the Republican Party into the twentieth century — and that century was half over before he even took office. The party, the presidency, and the country were stronger when Eisenhower left office than when he assumed it.

He was the first Republican president since Theodore Roosevelt even to recognize that it was desirable — let alone that it was necessary — for the party to modernize. It was his tragedy, and that of the party and the country as well, that the innovation was not permanent. As the century drew to an end, the party of Eisenhower, that had begun to look forward, reverted to its old ways. It began again to take its cue from its pre–New Deal presidents. Once again the Party of Lincoln turned its collective back on the future, and turned its collective face to look backward.

35

JOHN F. KENNEDY

January 20, 1961–November 22, 1963

John Fitzgerald Kennedy was forty-three when he was elected President of the United States, and when he assumed the presidency. He was the youngest person ever to be elected president, and was the second youngest ever to hold the office. Theodore Roosevelt, who was forty-two when he replaced the slain William McKinley, was the youngest. Kennedy was the first president, and thus far the only one, who was a Roman Catholic.

Kennedy was also probably the least healthy of all the presidents. He had been the least healthy member of the United States Senate even while he was its youngest, and he was equally unhealthy in the presidency. He was in constant pain. "In a lifetime of medical torment, Kennedy was more promiscuous with physicians and drugs than he was with women."[1] That, one must concede, was considerable.

He also consistently hid the severity of his condition. During the campaign he had denied that he had Addison's disease (an adrenal insufficiency) and had said that his health was excellent. "The campaign statement was not true. Kennedy had received the last rites of the Catholic Church at least four times as an adult. He was something of a medical marvel, kept alive by complicated daily combinations of pills and injections."[2] In spite of this, he radiated an aura of health — and vigor. Regardless of the merits of his deceptive statements, no one can challenge John Kennedy's courage, physical and otherwise, and his determined ability to function in spite of his pain.

The election could hardly have been closer in the popular vote. Fewer than twenty thousand votes separated the losing Vice President Nixon from the victorious Senator John F. Kennedy. Kennedy's margin in the electoral college, on the other hand, was comfortable.[3] The myth persists that Mayor

267

Richard Daley's Chicago Democratic machine "stole" the election by adding spurious numbers to the count in Cook County, Illinois, but that Nixon's "statesmanship" led him to refuse to contest the result. He was willing to sacrifice victory, so the story goes, to avoid the turmoil that a contested election would involve.

A look at the facts suggests something far different. First, there likely was pro–Democratic corruption in Chicago — certainly there have been a number of reports indicating that there was. On the other hand, there may also have been pro–Republican corruption outstate. A discovery of urban corruption might well have been offset by revelations of corruption in rural and small-town areas. Shrewd politician that he was, it is likely that Nixon would have considered the entire situation too dangerous to touch — a "can of worms."

Regardless of that, Kennedy could have *given* Illinois to Nixon, and he still almost assuredly would have won the presidency. Even with fifteen Southern electors going to the States' Rights Harry Byrd, Kennedy had 303 electoral votes to Nixon's 219; Illinois's total was twenty-seven, far too few to have changed the result. The allegations persist, however.

Seymour Hersh, in his lurid treatment *The Dark Side of Camelot,* labeled it "the stolen election." He dismissed the electoral-vote argument above by saying that Illinois's loss would have enabled unpledged electors from the South to throw the election into the House. Perhaps, but it would have taken more than the fifteen electors who did vote for Harry Byrd to do so. Even Hersh, though, quoted Nixon as saying that he might not win a recount, and he could not risk being called a sore loser. Hersh concluded that Nixon had no chance, because the Chicago machine would have managed any recount.[4] He ignored the fact that the federal government could investigate fraud, and that a Republican administration was still in office.

What Hersh did not know when he wrote, what the public did not know, and what apparently not even election specialists knew until the disputed election of 2000 brought it to light, was how imprecise vote counts are in this country. It is quite possible, given the poor systems of recording and of counting votes, that Nixon really was the winner. On the other hand, it is at least equally possible that an accurate assessment would have given Kennedy a more substantial majority than the razor-thin result that he did get.

It is true that all else being equal if Nixon had carried both Illinois and Texas he would have won. Kennedy, however, had shrewdly selected Senate Majority Leader Lyndon B. Johnson of Texas as his vice presidential running mate. There are many contradictory stories as to how this occurred. What really happened will never be known. What is known is that Johnson's presence on his ticket helped Kennedy narrowly carry the Lone Star

State — which at that time had only twenty-four electoral votes, fewer than Illinois.

Regardless of the extremely close election, there was excitement in Washington at the inauguration. Despite a heavy snowfall — which brought huge, characteristically Washingtonian traffic snarls — even many Republicans felt elation at Kennedy's promise to "get the country moving again," and to lead with "vigor." "Vigor" had become the watchword of his new administration. "Getting the country moving again" could well be interpreted to have meant a more aggressive foreign policy than Eisenhower's.

At the same time, his charming young wife, Jacqueline, proved to be a strong asset who was a favorite with diplomats and leaders from other countries. She was a favorite as well with the public, which followed with interest her redecoration of the White House. She hid her snobbery, and also her extravagance, well. In order to avoid having to deal with "fat little ladies," she developed to an art what she called the "PBO" (polite brush off), and most often foisted off "semi-official" White-House visitors on the vice president's gracious wife, Lady Bird Johnson. Margaret Truman wrote of Jacqueline that "a lot of her PBOs were rooted in a visceral repugnance for average Americans."[5]

Serving as more or less an informal minister of culture, Jacqueline Kennedy brought a dazzling array of artists, writers, and musicians to the White House. It was her dedication to culture that to a great extent gave John Kennedy — who had little use for the arts — his reputation as an intellectual.[6] She was so successful that people who should have known better were convinced. A popular history, for example, could say of Kennedy that "not since Jefferson had any President been so interested in art, letters, and learning, or himself so involved in them." It went on to say that Washington, "perhaps for the first time, became a cultural as well as a political and social capital."[7] Even if this view of Kennedy were correct, the passages reflect total ignorance of the White House during Theodore Roosevelt's presidency.

To be sure, Jacqueline Bouvier Kennedy had a less than pleasant side. Nevertheless, she was an outstanding first lady who was an enormous asset to the country. She was a courageous and talented woman who contributed much during her brief stay in the White House.

Kennedy and the Democrats built their campaign on the existence of a "missile gap," alleging that the Soviet Union was far ahead in nuclear missiles. It was not. The charge was irresponsible and untrue. After Kennedy took office, it became clear that the missile gap had never existed. Ike, the old soldier, had known what he was talking about. The missile gap vanished when Kennedy took office, just as surely as the "weapons of mass destruction" vanished when U.S. troops set foot in Iraq in 2003.

Eisenhower had been right all along when he said that the Russians were not ahead in nuclear technology or in the number of missiles. In any case, he had argued, why build more missiles than could be used regardless of how many the Russians had? But the Republicans were on the defensive. When Kennedy at his inaugural spoke of the torch being passed to a new generation, born in this century, he subtly portrayed himself as the "anti–Eisenhower."

Clearly, however, he shared several principles with Eisenhower and with Truman before him. Among them were "containing communism and preventing world war."[8] Additionally, they shared a civic responsibility that later had largely vanished from American politics. When Kennedy said, "ask not what your country can do for you, ask what you can do for your country," he sounded an idealistic note that was in stark contrast to bombast from later politicians who appealed for votes by openly courting naked self-interest and encouraging hostility to any sense of community obligation.

Later politicians tended to abandon calls for sacrifice or common purpose. They often campaigned primarily upon a platform of cutting taxes. They said to the voters, "you can spend your hard-earned money more wisely than the government can."

Kennedy avoided such simple-minded approaches. Taking his cue from historian Frederick Jackson Turner — who had argued that the frontier and the spirit it created had made American character what it was — Kennedy asserted that he would lead the country to a "New Frontier." He was responding to misgivings Turner expressed in 1893 about the closing of the frontier. The census of 1890 had announced that it was gone. What, Turner had wondered, would this mean for America's development when such a vital factor no longer existed? Kennedy adopted Turner's long-ago concern as his administration's metaphor, and asserted that the "New Frontier" his administration would supply would be a "frontier" of space, the arts, the intellect — in fact, the height of human experience — that would enhance the American character.

The image that Kennedy and his administration projected was one of youth, energy, and excitement replacing age, fatigue, and boredom; brilliance banishing dullness. It was time for the beautiful people. Kennedy's administration indeed was filled with people who were young, bright — and also highly privileged. In addition, they were people who worshipped power. Garry Wills has observed that presidents such as Washington and Eisenhower had a commitment to duty rather than to power. They used power but were aware of its dangers. They therefore were wary, and used it carefully. Wills believed that John Kennedy, by contrast, was tempted by the belief that there was nothing *but* power.[9] One might add also, that he and those around him — Jacqueline most of all — believed in style. Both concerns, power and style, suggest why it was that JFK was attracted to James

Bond novels — and in fact how it came to be that he popularized them with the public.

So powerful was the projected image of the Kennedys, that those who rank presidencies tend to rate JFK rather well, fifteenth place or higher, despite the brevity of his time in office. The Fabers even rank him in the top ten; in their rating he is in eighth place.[10] The Reuters poll of 2000 also put JFK in eighth place.[11] This latter poll reported the opinions of "politicians, pundits, and other knowledgeable individuals," as well as historians. The more a poll includes a popular audience instead of historians and political scientists, the higher Kennedy is inclined to rate simply became of the glamour of "Camelot," the Kennedy White House. "Kennedy" is the one presidential name from history — apart from Washington and Lincoln — that any citizen is likely to know; even citizens who may be unaware that there were two Presidents Roosevelt, one from each party, are likely to thrill to the Kennedy image.

Hardly had the young president taken office when he was involved in an enormous fiasco. On Monday, 17 April 1961, a CIA-backed force of Cuban exiles landed in Cuba at the Bay of Pigs. Long before the week had ended Cuban forces had routed the small force which had vainly expected air cover and other support. Romantic notions of the planners that the invaders could disperse into the mountains and serve to rally an uprising among the Cuban people were exposed for what they were: delusions. Later, President Kennedy explained to former President Eisenhower that he had denied support from American forces because he wanted to keep America's role hidden. Ike pointed out politely that everyone already knew that the United States was behind the invasion. There was nowhere else, he told Kennedy, that the force could have obtained its weapons or the ships to get to Cuba.[12] Kennedy spoke to the public and accepted full blame for the debacle.

Many writers, though, have fostered the myth that the invasion was an Eisenhower plan that Kennedy had "inherited." Although there had been planning during the Eisenhower administration — and even steps toward such an attempt — the operation undertaken was purely a product of Kennedy and the CIA. In any case, the buck stopped with Kennedy.

Garry Wills has provided one of the harshest criticisms of the disastrous effort. "The distinctive note of the Bay of Pigs invasion was that it was a military operation run *without* the military's control," he wrote, "an invasion force created specially by the CIA itself." It involved guerrilla uprising, assassination, amphibious landing, propaganda and the like. "Later," Wills said, "the plan would look so crazy that people could not credit its acceptance in the first place. But it made sense to a James Bond fan."[13] It is hardly less crazy to think that President Eisenhower, America's premier general and the organizer of the Normandy invasion, would for a minute have entertained a military invasion — including a very difficult amphibious landing — without control from, or even the participation of, the military. Kennedy's candid acceptance of blame, however, impressed the public. He did not parse words or blame the CIA, and his popularity remained high.

In June, Kennedy journeyed to Vienna to meet with Khrushchev at the Vienna summit. Soon thereafter he told James Reston of the *New York Times* that the Russian leader had "savaged" him. It was, JFK said, "the worst thing in my life." He said that because of the Bay of Pigs Khrushchev thought of him as inexperienced. He "probably thinks I'm stupid," Kennedy lamented. "Maybe most important, he thinks that I had no guts."[14] In August, the East Germans built the infamous Berlin Wall, sealing off West Berlin. It was a trying year.

Disasters were not the only things that characterized Kennedy's first year as president, however. Although Kennedy could take little credit for it, the states in April ratified the Twenty-Third Amendment granting presidential electors to the District of Columbia. In May, Kennedy issued an executive order creating the Peace Corps. The idea was not original with Kennedy or his administration. In fact, he initially had reservations, but he ultimately recognized its value and supported legislation to continue the program.[15] Volunteers by the thousands went around the world to provide services to communities in developing countries, to serve as good-will ambassadors for America, and to learn from other cultures.

The program was far from perfect, but it was on the whole a rousing success. Living in India in 1978–1979, fifteen years after the end of the Kennedy administration, I found servants who spoke no English but who had children named "John Kennedy." It was fairly common to see Kennedy's picture displayed in positions of reverence, alongside those of Gandhi. More than anything else, the Peace Corps had been responsible for creating that good will.

Also in May 1961, Kennedy signed legislation designed to cement relations with Latin America and create an "Alliance for Progress." That same month, Alan Shepard returned successfully from a sub-orbital journey into space. Kennedy announced that the United States would "put a man on the moon" by the end of the decade. Although he was no longer alive to see it, the event took place in 1969, well within the time frame he had set as the goal. The Alliance for Progress was less successful than the space program. The assistance provided was inadequate and there was little progress in encouraging democratic reform.[16] There were even some counterproductive aspects. It did, however, put the administration on record as seeking cordial relations with countries in Latin America, and did bring about some modest economic improvements.

In 1962 Kennedy faced one of the most serious challenges of any president in history. The administration discovered that the Soviets had stationed nuclear missiles in Cuba. After consideration of a military strike to destroy them, Kennedy accepted the recommendation — from his brother Attorney General Robert Kennedy, among others — to "quarantine" Cuba; that is to impose a naval blockade. Kennedy announced the situation to the public in a television broadcast on 22 October. "On 24 October.... Soviet ships approached the quarantine line.... On 27 October, Secretary of Defense Robert McNamara wondered whether he would live to see another Saturday. But on 28 October, the president and Soviet Chairman Khrushchev struck a deal. The Soviets would remove the missiles, and, in turn, the United States would pledge not to invade Cuba. The United States also confidentially promised to dismantle Jupiter missile sites in Turkey."[17] The young president had stood firm, and achieved a great diplomatic and public relations triumph.

On the other hand, although it was successful, Kennedy had chosen a very dangerous course of action: confrontation instead of diplomacy. One needs to be cautious in criticizing a policy that worked, and it did work, but it is important to consider why it happened. Kennedy's reckless policies — including "Operation Mongoose"[18] to undermine the Cuban economy and attempt some truly bizarre efforts to kill Cuban leader Fidel Castro — almost assuredly helped bring about the crisis in the first place. Never, before or since, has the world been so close to destruction.

This tense situation in all probability helped bring about the 1963 treaty banning nuclear testing in the atmosphere. Since the nuclear age had begun, nuclear testing had been systematically poisoning the atmosphere, the people, and the land — even those of the countries doing the testing. Few people remember that "it was Khrushchev who had first proposed negotiations on a test ban, in February 1955. This was after the discovery that the fallout from an American test in March 1954 ... had killed or maimed Japanese fishermen and islanders hundreds of miles from the test site on Bikini Atoll."[19] Adlai Stevenson in his 1956 campaign had proposed banning tests, and President Eisenhower was furious. Eisenhower's policies led directly to an enormous amount of highly dangerous fallout all over the world, but nevertheless he pursued a ban in his second term. Not until Kennedy, though, did a ban materialize.

As with the Peace Corps, the idea of banning nuclear testing may not have been original with John F. Kennedy, but this should take from him none of the credit. "The Limited Test Ban Treaty was officially signed in Moscow on August 5, 1963, with Secretary of State [Dean] Rusk leading the U.S. delegation, which included senators from both parties and U.N. Ambassador Adlai Stevenson," who had, as indicated, advocated such a treaty in 1956.[20] Later, President Clinton negotiated a comprehensive test ban treaty that would have eliminated all nuclear testing, not merely those in the atmosphere. In one of the most irresponsible acts in its history, the United States Senate refused ratification.

No examination of the Kennedy presidency, however brief, should ignore what Reeves called "John F. Kennedy's role in precipitating the U.S. disaster in Vietnam."[21] Kennedy did not cause the war. The Johnson and Nixon administrations must bear the true blame. Nevertheless, "most historians believe that the decisions Kennedy and his advisors made between 1961 and 1963 made it more likely that Johnson would seek military solutions in Vietnam."[22] Johnson had a choice; so, later did Nixon, but so had Kennedy. He inherited a Vietnam problem from Eisenhower, and he left to Johnson a larger problem than he had inherited.[23]

Regarding civil rights, Kennedy's enthusiasts give him credit for the great progress made during the 1960s and 1970s. Civil rights were not uppermost on his agenda, and he came late to support of the movement that got well underway during his presidency. In his eloquent inaugural address, he had to be persuaded to include the topic at all, and what he included could hardly have been more vague. He spoke of "human rights to which this nation has always been committed and to which we are committed today *at home* and around the world." Harris Wofford, staff director of the U.S. Civil Rights Commission, had encouraged Kennedy to include civil rights, and the result was the addition of "at home."[24] As the pressure for civil rights increased, so did Kennedy's interest, and his strong rhetorical support for reforms.

Among the many dramatic civil rights developments during the Kennedy years — James Meridith's move to break the color line at the University of Mississippi, sit-ins, freedom rides, and the like — two especially stand out. On 11 June 1963, George C. Wallace, Governor of Alabama, made his symbolic protest, making good on his vow to "stand in the schoolhouse door" to prevent black students from registering at the University of Alabama. The other was the great March on Washington on 28 August 1963.

By previous arrangement with the Kennedy administration, Governor Wallace acquiesced when Kennedy called the Alabama National Guard into federal service and U.S. marshals escorted the two black students, Vivian Malone and James Hood, to their dormitories. That evening, Kennedy went on national television to give an eloquent address on civil rights, stressing the moral issue involved. As he promised, he sent a civil rights bill to Congress, and gave it administration support. The historian James Giglio has argued that Kennedy's bill would have resulted in a civil rights law if he had lived.[25] This is dubious, at best. It was his successor, Lyndon Johnson, who knew how to get legislation passed — and who was personally and thoroughly committed to the cause. Kennedy had not been markedly effective as a legislative leader, and no subject elicited more congressional obstruction than civil rights. LBJ managed to secure the Civil Rights Act of 1964, and should receive full credit. Quite likely he was the only one who could have done so.

Wallace lost in his effort to prevent integration, but in a sense, he won. His actions catapulted him onto the national scene and launched his subsequent third-party bids for the presidency. His national campaigning changed the rhetoric of American politics, and in to a large extent made possible the subsequent victories of the Republicans nationally, based on a "Southern strategy."

The March on Washington was one of the most extraordinary events in American history. It was the occasion of Dr. Martin Luther King, Jr.'s, great "I have a dream" address. Some three hundred thousand or so descended upon the capital city from all over the country. There have been huge gatherings since, but this one was unique. The weather was bright and beautiful, and despite concerns that such a huge crowd could be tumultuous, the spirit along the streets was cheerful — and unprecedented. People, white and black, would smile and speak to strangers. Only one who was there to experience the day can understand how it was that in the entire city of Washington, DC, a full twenty-four-hour period elapsed without a single reported crime. Four decades later, it remains unforgettable.

One program behind which Kennedy threw his weight enthusiastically was Medicare. Health care for the aged had been an issue since the Truman administration. Kennedy put the prestige of his office behind the program, and to his credit was willing to challenge the American Medical Association (AMA), then arguably America's most formidable lobbying power, to achieve government support for hospitalization coverage. His efforts were powerful, but so were the resources of the AMA, which brought forth a secret phonograph recording to play for groups of physicians' wives to stimulate anti–Medicare letters to representatives and senators.[26] The record, "Ronald Reagan Speaks Out Against Socialized Medicine" (part of the AMA's clandestine "Operation Coffeecup") helped defeat the proposal until the Johnson administration.

Kennedy served fewer than three years. He died in Dallas, Texas, on 22 November 1963, from an assassin's bullet. His brief, glamorous, glittering presidency had come to an abrupt and sadly premature end. Vice President Lyndon B. Johnson, a towering political figure in his own right, replaced the slain pioneer of the New Frontier, and "Camelot" was no more.

Along with Kennedy, presidents who served less than a full term (not including Tyler, whose time in office was only one month shy of four years, and Chester Arthur who lacked only six months) were William Henry Harrison, Zachary Taylor, Millard Fillmore, James A. Garfield, Warren G. Harding, and Gerald Ford. It would seem especially questionable to rank any of these, but only the most conscientious ratings exclude even Garfield and Harrison. Thus, those who produce presidential rankings rush to include the brief Kennedy presidency.

By some measures, he had been far from a success. He began with fiasco at the Bay of Pigs, and ended with failure to find a "stable non–Communist formula for South Vietnam." In fact, shortly before his death, "a military coup in Saigon was accompanied by the murder of South Vietnamese President, Ngo Dinh Diem." He likely recognized, said the historian Eric Goldman, "that Vietnam was his great failure in foreign policy," while he also had failed to achieve his "big four legislative proposals — civil rights, tax reduction, Medicare and federal aid to education."[27] On the other hand, Goldman noted, "there were other ways of remembering the murdered President."[28] People remembered his courage, his good will, and his inspiring presence.

His was an important presidency. Kennedy succeeded in establishing respect for the United States around the world, and he stimulated enthusiasm for government and public service at home. His record is decidedly mixed. His accomplishments were few, but important. Establishment of the Peace Corps and, especially, gaining ratification of the Limited Nuclear Test Ban Treaty were splendid. So was his image. The detrimental side of his legacy is more subtle, but also very important. How could it be possible to "rank" such a brief, and varied, presidency, and what does such an attempt gain in understanding?

36

LYNDON B. JOHNSON
November 22, 1963–January 20, 1969

There have been good presidents in the past half-century, even charismatic presidents (at least in today's popularized meaning of the term), the perceptive presidential scholars Marc Landy and Sidney Milkis have said, but they lamented that since Franklin D. Roosevelt, presidential greatness has disappeared. A great president, as they defined it, is one who seizes the opportunity and who has the capacity "to engage the nation in a struggle for its constitutional soul." They believed that for greatness to emerge there must be a "conservative revolution;" it has to be conservative in order to avoid alienating too may Americans who would otherwise refuse to follow. Only one president since FDR, they thought, had even tried. That was Lyndon B. Johnson.[1] They said LBJ came the closest to greatness of any president since FDR, and they noted "an undeniable element of greatness in him."[2] Wilson Carey McWilliams went further. LBJ was, he wrote in an essay of the same name, "The Last of the Great Presidents."[3] Greatness of course is in the eye of the beholder — and in the word processor of the evaluator — but LBJ clearly stands out.

No less than the hero of a Greek tragedy, LBJ was larger than life. His virtues were monumental; his flaws also. In his long-range contributions to the United States and to American society, his virtues are likely to loom even larger as time passes, and his flaws to seem progressively less significant.

Johnson tends to rate rather high in the polls. Arthur Schlesinger, Jr.'s, 1996 study rated him lower than most, and still he came in at fourteenth, the upper third.[4] A number of other polls rank him no lower than twelfth, and some as high as ninth.[5] Nevertheless, as with Wilson, Nixon, and even Jefferson, LBJ presents special challenges to any ranking attempt. Schlesinger

277

quoted Walter Dean Burnham as referring to LBJ's "dichotomous or schizoid" profile, ranking on some measures as an outright failure while on others "very high indeed."[6] Even more so than for most presidents, therefore, a single rating for Johnson cannot help but distort the nature of his presidential performance.

LBJ assumed office under tragic circumstances, but he moved quickly to make the most of his presidency. He urgently sought national unity, and vowed eloquently to continue the policies of the stricken Kennedy. "Cynics at the time and since credited Johnson with a good but largely contrived performance," said the presidential historian Robert Dallek — the author of a thoughtful study of the Johnson presidency. "By their lights," he continued, "LBJ was a 'wheeler dealer' who launched his 1964 election campaign the day after becoming President. His appeals for continuity and unity were good politics aimed more at serving himself than the national interest." Dallek correctly disputed this. Johnson certainly could be manipulative and even devious, Dallek said, but "this was not the case with the transition from JFK to himself and to much of what he did in domestic affairs." He conceded that Johnson obviously thought about the coming election, which was but eleven months away. He asked, though, "what career politician, who had spent much of his life running for office, could have, or even should have, done otherwise?"[7] In any case, LBJ intended to carry on the Kennedy legacy — which unfortunately contained the looming conflict in Vietnam — but, more than that, he was determined also to go far beyond Kennedy's proposals; he sought to achieve a record that overshadowed even the New Deal accomplishments of his own mentor, Franklin D. Roosevelt.

Throughout his administration, as she had been throughout his entire career, Lady Bird Johnson was a tremendous asset. She was shrewd and thoughtful, and was a keen political adviser to her husband. In the later years of his presidency when the strains began to tell on him, "she was the civilizing force that checked Lyndon's erratic, intemperate behavior and helped him channel so much of his raw energy into making the government work as well as it did." All indications are that the marriage was strong, despite LBJ's transgressions; both partners appear to have found it highly rewarding.[8]

LBJ acted to centralize power over the party and, through "his budget and his White House staff, to concentrate information, publicity, and decisions in the Oval Office."[9] Following along the administrative path that Truman and Eisenhower had blazed, his administration succeeded in securing congressional approval for two new cabinet departments: the Department of Housing and Urban Development (1966), and the Department of Transportation (1967). The first HUD secretary was Robert C. Weaver. FDR had appointed Frances Perkins as secretary of Labor, the first woman to serve in the cabinet, and LBJ, in Weaver, had appointed the first African American. On 13 June 1967, he also appointed the great civil rights lawyer, Thurgood Marshall, to the Supreme Court as its first black justice.

Johnson supported two new amendments that became part of the Constitution during his presidency, although of course he had little to do with the first other than to support it. On 23 January 1964, the Twenty-Fourth Amendment achieved ratification from the states. It declared that the right to vote could not be denied for failure to pay a poll tax — or any other tax. Although it applied only to national elections (president, vice president, senators, and representatives), those states that had used poll taxes to limit voting quickly repealed their restrictive laws. On 11 February 1967, came the Twenty-Fifth Amendment, including some of the most important provisions relating to the presidency in the Constitution.

Johnson and Truman both had been concerned during the first parts of their presidencies when there was no vice president. LBJ's personal experience had led him to think deeply about the vice presidency and about the need to fill some gaps in the Constitution relating to the office. Those experiences included having served as a vice president himself, and having succeeded to a presidential vacancy. Moreover, he had been Senate majority leader during the Eisenhower administration when the president had had three severe illnesses.

He therefore knew very well of the vagueness that existed regarding power arrangements between a president and vice president under such conditions. Johnson had had a heart attack when he was in the Senate, and was acutely aware of the need for some formal arrangement specifying the circumstances that would govern a transfer of power from one to the other. He and Vice President Humphrey reportedly had a written understanding between them — Kennedy and he, and Eisenhower and Nixon, had similar arrangements[10]— but LBJ was sensitive to the need for something clearly spelled out in the Constitution. He therefore strongly supported the efforts of Senator Birch Bayh, a Democrat from Indiana, to develop such an amendment. Congress proposed the Twenty-Fifth Amendment in April, 1965; as indicated, it received ratification in 1967.

The Twenty-Fifth Amendment created a procedure that for the first time made it possible to fill a vice presidential vacancy without having to wait until the next election. Under its terms, the president nominates a candidate who takes office upon confirmation by the *both* houses of Congress — for all other appointments, only the Senate confirms. The Twenty-Fifth Amendment also settled any lingering question — if any still existed — regarding the status of a vice president who succeeded to a presidential vacancy. Section 1 reads as follows: "In case of the removal of the President from office or his death or resignation, *the Vice President shall become President* [emphasis added]. Additionally, the Amendment sets forth procedures by which a vice president can become acting president temporarily, in the event a president cannot carry out the duties of the office.

As a creature of Congress, LBJ took special pains to work with members of both the House and the Senate. Calling into question the overblown notion of the "rhetorical presidency,"[11] LBJ much preferred to work quietly with Congress than to appeal directly to the general public. As Goldman noted "for a strong President, he resorted to the practice relatively little."[12] And, for a time, success followed success.

In his State of the Union Address on 9 January 1964, LBJ declared a War on Poverty. Johnson had always had a burning resentment against deprivation and discrimination. Even so relentless a critic as Robert Caro, in his engaging, consistently hostile, and inexcusably one-sided biography of LBJ's early years, could not disguise Johnson's genuine feel for children and others who had been ground down by bigotry and poverty.[13] Beginning speedily and continuing for some time came a number of programs with varying degrees of success: Head Start, the college Work-Study Program, affirmative action, fair housing measures, Community Action Programs, consumer protection, and more. In addition, there were great strides forward in environmental protection.

On 22 May 1964 in a speech at the University of Michigan, Johnson announced the metaphor for his entire presidency: it would work toward achieving the "Great Society," with justice, liberty, and abundance. On 2 July, he signed into law the most important and far-reaching piece of legislation on civil rights since the Reconstruction period, the Civil Rights Act of 1964. On 20 August, he signed into law the Economic Opportunity Act to coordinate the various programs of the War on Poverty.

Unfortunately, shortly after the 1964 Civil Rights Act there was a riot in Harlem. The "long hot summer" repeated itself in 1965 and 1966 with greater riots in other cities. Instead of meeting force with force, LBJ spoke out for full integration.[14] It was a time of general unrest apart from civil rights demonstrations. Not only were there urban riots, but the New Left had become organized to incorporate among other things a "Free Speech Movement," and ultimately, anti-war protests. The new feminist movement also was in full swing and was gaining power.

The election of 1964 was a landmark in numerous ways. The right wing of the Republican Party seized control from the moderate and liberal Republicans (yes, in those days there were liberal Republicans) who had supported Eisenhower. In a raucous convention, they gleefully nominated Senator Barry Goldwater for president. People today may remember Goldwater from his later years. He had mellowed considerably by then. During his campaign he spoke rashly for the far right, and suggested — rather, he declared overtly — that a Goldwater presidency would be as reckless as his campaign rhetoric.

As LBJ later wrote, early in the campaign Goldwater made a series of statements "implying that he would more than willingly threaten to use, or even use, nuclear weapons to gain American ends. Statements such as 'I want to lob one into the men's room of the Kremlin and make sure I hit it' created the image of an impulsive man who shoots from the hip, who talks and acts first and thinks afterward."[15] Goldwater also suggested using tactical nuclear weapons in Vietnam, and — as though he had a political death wish — he steadfastly — although one must concede honestly — refused to soften the rhetoric of the Republican right, regardless of his audience. He insisted, for example, on criticizing anti-poverty programs when in Appalachia; he condemned Social Security and any thought of Medicare when he was speaking to aged populations in Florida; and he blasted public power when he spoke in Tennessee, where the TVA had permitted a deprived area to develop by providing inexpensive electricity. He also had voted against the Civil Rights Act.

Johnson had selected Senator Hubert H. Humphrey as his running mate; Goldwater selected Representative William Miller as his. Goldwater declared in his acceptance speech that "Extremism in defense of liberty is no vice; moderation in support of justice is no virtue." The campaign revolved around his slogan, "In your heart you know he's right." Rejoinders flew rapidly from the Democrats. "In your head you know he's wrong," they said, or "In your heart you know he's Far Right." Some said, "In your guts you know he's nuts." In early October, a rather common bumper sticker in Washington, DC, read, "Goldwater for Halloween." The Republican bumper sticker "AuH20" (chemical symbols for gold and water) were clever, but hardly a match.

Johnson and Humphrey won an enormous landslide.[16] Goldwater carried only his home state of Arizona and — a portent of things to come for the Democrats — five states of the Deep South: Louisiana, Mississippi, Alabama, Georgia, and South Carolina. Only three other presidents have polled 60 percent in the popular vote: Harding in 1920, FDR in 1936, and Nixon in 1972. Johnson remains the only presidential candidate ever to gain 61 percent — the greatest popular vote percentage in American history.

The Democratic landslide carried large majorities (but not uniquely so) of Democrats, many of them liberal, into Congress, especially in the House. It created an unusual opportunity. Congress, whether controlled by Republicans or Democrats — despite assertions from the right to the contrary — is almost always very conservative. Even when the Democrats are a liberal party, their ranks always include a substantial number of conservatives (in recent times called "Boll Weevils") who frequently join with Republicans to create a conservative majority.

LBJ's Eighty-Ninth Congress, from 1965 to 1967, was one of the very rare (almost nonexistent) times in history when it has been possible to put together fairly consistently a liberal majority. He made the most of it, although even then it required great and skillful effort. There has been a tendency among academics — after all, he lacked Kennedy's style, and they abhorred his accent, both important measures of quality, to be sure — to attribute Johnson's victories to the landslide election and to underestimate "not only the originality of the Great Society but also Johnson's contributions to getting the programs enacted." In fact, FDR "had enjoyed an even bigger advantage in 1937 and had not achieved nearly so much that year," said historian William E. Leuchtenburg, who remarked that the country did not properly appreciate LBJ. No less astute an observer than Senate Majority Leader Mike Mansfield told Leuchtenburg that "Johnson has outstripped Roosevelt, no doubt about that. He has done more than FDR ever did or ever thought of doing."[17]

On 11 April, LBJ signed into law the Elementary and Secondary Education Act, providing federal assistance to local school districts. On 30 July, in a ceremony at the Truman Library in Independence, Missouri, with former President Harry Truman in attendance he signed the Medicare Act — the culmination of more than two decades of struggle to provide assistance to the elderly in paying for the costs of health care. Harry and Bess Truman the next year received the first two Medicare cards, numbers one and two. On 6 August, he signed the Voting Rights Act of 1965, providing federal registrars in states that had repressed black voting; he intended to ensure African-American citizens their right to vote. Johnson had been able to prevail on civil rights by persuading the Senate Republican leader, Everett Dirksen of Illinois, to line up Republicans in support. The existence at the time of a liberal wing of the Republican Party helped greatly.

Ever since the Civil War, the Democratic Party had relied upon a guaranteed bloc of Democratic votes in the "Solid South" as the bedrock of its strength. In supporting civil rights, Johnson knew full well that he would damage, possibly even kill, the Democratic Party. Yet he persisted.

He knew, as civil rights leader Andrew Young said, that action on civil rights was the way really to "save the nation," but he also knew that it "was not politically expedient."[18] It is true that LBJ knew the bill would secure his place in history, and that as a Southerner he had to make it stronger than Kennedy's proposals to demonstrate his sincerity to his party's liberals. Only six Southerners in the House voted for the bill. Johnson telephoned one of them, Rep. Jake Pickle from Texas, to tell him how proud he was of Pickle's courage. He confessed that as a member of the House, "he had lacked Pickle's courage to vote for a civil rights bill."[19]

Nevertheless, when the bill passed, LBJ "seemed deflated." His aide, Bill

Moyers asked "why he was so glum. 'Because, Bill,' he replied, 'I think we just delivered the South to the Republican party for a long time to come.'"[20] Numerous other Johnson aides have commented through the years that LBJ knew that by working for the best interests of his country, he was working against the interests of his party. For a professional politician to take action that damages his party because it is the right thing to do, reflects a true act of conscience. Those who condemn Johnson merely as a cynical manipulator who had no principles, one who sought nothing but power and political advantage, should consider the record carefully. Regardless of its dark side, Lyndon B. Johnson's record reflects him as a true humanitarian.

LBJ astonished nearly all observers. Those who had assumed that he, as a Texan, would be a captive of the oil industry were amazed to find him a staunch advocate for environmental quality, highway beautification, and the arts. No president since Theodore Roosevelt, certainly not John Kennedy, did as much for the arts and humanities. He succeeded in securing legislation creating the National Endowment for the Humanities, and the National Endowment for the Arts. He hoped for even more. "Though Johnson won passage of his air and water quality and highway beautification bills, they were less than what he wanted." He recognized that more would be needed, especially with regard to the "Highway Beautification Act, which Mrs. Johnson had made, along with Head Start, major First Lady projects."[21]

Vietnam, of course, came to overshadow everything. Few people today remember just how strong was the consensus that the United States had to intervene to stop communism. Liberals and conservatives, right and left, Democrats and Republicans — nearly all agreed. The Republicans, in fact, including former President Eisenhower who had first spoken of the domino theory — that the fall of one Southeast Asian country to Marxism-Leninism would inevitably lead to the fall of others.

The increasing escalation, increasing protests, and decreasing prospects for victory all are familiar. Some observers have argued that recently-published White House tapes suggest that LBJ refused to withdraw because he feared that he would be impeached.[22] They conclude, understandably, that he was sacrificing American troops to preserve his own position.

More plausible, however, is that he feared what would happen to the country and the world if he were impeached and removed from office. The Republicans already had rejected the Eisenhower internationalists. They already had fielded a candidate in 1964 who threatened nuclear war. What might they do if liberal forces fell apart?

The reaction to the "loss" of China under Truman had been venomous enough, and LBJ could have feared an even more brutal reaction if he were to "cut and run." He would have been charged with being "the first American president to lose a war." The forces aligned to take over could well have caused those who stood in the wings in 1949 to appear tame by comparison.

Regardless, Vietnam did more than tarnish a presidency, it shattered the country, and came close to destroying Johnson himself. Certainly Johnson must share the blame. Kennedy inherited the Vietnam situation from Eisenhower, and bequeathed a more troublesome situation to Johnson. Johnson in turn inherited a troublesome situation from Kennedy, and bequeathed a much worse situation to Nixon. Johnson, though, should not have to bear the blame alone for what he bequeathed to Nixon. There was much to go around.

Johnson's last year as president was painful in many ways. It was the year of assassinations; both Martin Luther King, Jr., and Robert Kennedy fell to assassins' bullets. On 31 March 1968, LBJ announced in a televised address that he would not be a candidate for re-election, and that he would not accept a nomination. He did this, he said, to encourage national unity. Doris Kearns called it an act of courage.[23] Robert Dallek said that Democrats and Republicans alike "described his decision as an act of selfless statesmanship."[24] Clearly, he felt a great relief. Then, in June, Chief Justice Earl Warren retired from the Supreme Court.

LBJ nominated Associate Justice Abe Fortas to succeed Warren, but the Senate refused to act. Fortas asked that his name be withdrawn.[25] The combination of Republicans and conservative Southern Democrats held the chief justiceship open for more than a half year. They made no secret of the fact that they would confirm no appointee until after a new president took over the presidency in January of 1969. They were counting on a Republican who would appoint a conservative. In the early twenty-first century, of course, conservatives complain bitterly if their own judicial nominations do not all receive speedy confirmation, but the delaying action began in 1968. It was the start of their long and largely successful effort to politicize the judiciary.

The 1968 Democratic convention in Chicago was the scene of great riots, and it felt to Johnson as though his presidency were unraveling. Vice President Hubert H. Humphrey won the Democratic nomination. In November, he narrowly lost the race to former Vice President Richard M. Nixon. The race was almost as close in the popular vote as the narrow Kennedy victory over Nixon had been in 1960.

Nevertheless, right up to inauguration day, 20 January, LBJ was as active as usual. After Nixon's inauguration, the Johnsons and their daughters drove to the Bethesda home of Marny and Clark Clifford for a farewell luncheon. Lady Bird later remarked that it was one of the most "significant and dear parties" that they ever attended.[26] Afterward, they drove to Andrews Air Force Base from which they flew on to their home in Texas. Doris Kearns summed it up poignantly. After "thirty-two years in public life as Congressman, Senator, Vice President, and President," she wrote, LBJ "returned to the hill country, where, as his father had told him, 'the people know when you're sick and care when you die'."[27] LBJ's death came on 22 January 1973. Four years after he left office, he succumbed to a heart attack. He is buried on the LBJ ranch in the Texas hill country, where his widow, Lady Bird, as of this writing, at the age of ninety, still lives.

As painful as the last days were, LBJ's legacy remains. True, the Nixon administration began dismantling some of his programs. Others, though, survived, and some Nixon even expanded. Despite some assertions to the contrary, the presidency remained strong and vigorous when the Johnson administration left office. Because of Lyndon Johnson, the country achieved at last a firm civil rights law, equality in voting, Medicare, and so much more. Much of what we take for granted today as part of the American way of life — even at the same time that reactionary politicians and their henchmen in the field of economics point with scorn to the "failed Great Society Programs" — came directly from those programs, and from LBJ. Lyndon Johnson's Great Society was a huge success in that it made the United States a better country. Those who argue to the contrary should openly admit that they would prefer a nation without the Civil Rights Act, the Voting Rights Act, Headstart, Medicare, assistance to the arts, environmental protections, and on and on.

Assessing greatness is subjective, as are rankings. Dallek saw LBJ as a "flawed giant." About that there can be little dispute. If monumental flaws preclude greatness, then LBJ cannot be great. On the other hand, is there a great political figure without flaw?

In any case, Lyndon Baines Johnson, thirty-sixth President of the United States, was a giant. As his flaws — treated with that most powerful medication, tincture of time — shrink and recede into the past, his monumental virtues and the enormity of his accomplishments will be all the more visible. Eventual recognition of his greatness is likely — even if now it remains in dispute.

37

RICHARD M. NIXON
January 20, 1969–August 9, 1974

Richard Milhous Nixon, thirty-seventh President of the United States, has a number of distinctions. No other sitting vice president has run for president, been defeated, and then returned to run again successfully. No other president has been implicated personally in what clearly fell under the Constitution's reference to "high crimes and misdemeanors." No other president has resigned from the office. Two vice presidents have done so, John C. Calhoun under President Andrew Jackson, and Spiro T. Agnew, who served under Nixon himself. Not only was Nixon the sole president in more than two centuries under the United States Constitution to resign, but both he and his elected vice president did so.

There were some intense partisans who defended Nixon as he left office. One business school dean, for example, missed no opportunity to declare confrontationally, "I'd vote for him again in a minute!" Some of the diehards vowed to lie in wait until it was possible to bring down a Democrat as payback.

Except for such zealots, however, there were few defenders of Nixon when he departed in disgrace. Of course, the passage of time tends generally to bring less passion and more perspective. It now is possible to recognize that there was more to his presidency than The Dark Side, however prominent that was.

Within two decades after Nixon's exit in shame, the prominent and thoughtful historian Forrest McDonald could write that he believed Nixon one day would be classed as a great, or near-great, president.[1] That, under the circumstances, seems highly doubtful. One need not go to such lengths to make the case that the Nixon administration did make some positive contributions, as even many of those who remain highly critical of Nixon now recognize. Former Democratic Speaker of the House Thomas "Tip" O'Neill, for example, more than a decade after Nixon's resignation noted that it was ironic that Nixon's pre–Watergate record was better than most liberals had recognized. O'Neill mentioned the opening to China and the ultimate end to the war in Vietnam, and said that even in domestic policy Nixon was more moderate "than his image would suggest."[2]

Still, as one might anticipate, most rankings place him quite low, often classing Nixon as a failure.[3] Schlesinger's 1996 study placed him thirty-sixth of thirty-nine rated,[4] as did the Fabers.[5] Genovese[6] put him one step lower, at thirty-seventh, and Ridings and McIver[7] squeezed him up to thirty-two. Nevertheless, Nixon presents special challenges — even if it were valid to rank presidents. As Schlesinger quoted James MacGregor Burns of Nixon, "how can one evaluate such an idiosyncratic president, so brilliant and so morally lacking?"[8] Burns said he guessed he would even it out and call him average. If there is one thing that Richard M. Nixon or his presidency was not, it was "average"— this one fact alone should be sufficient to demonstrate the flawed nature of rankings.

Both Nixon and Lyndon Johnson came to the presidency from relatively deprived backgrounds; certainly, neither was to the manor born, nor did either benefit from a privileged upbringing. Each struggled to make something of himself, and each did so by virtue of enormous effort and talent. Each bore the scars of insecurity as a result, but the results were vastly different.

Johnson's background brought him a burning hatred of poverty and discrimination, and he marshaled his prodigious energy in an attempt to eliminate them. It made him a reformer, even a revolutionary, who upon occasion could act upon pure conscience. In other words, despite his great faults, he had a great heart.

Nixon, too, had dreams of improving the world, but his insecurity brought him merely burning hatred. He directed much of this toward those who assumed an air of superiority — such as the Kennedys, whom he considered "glamour boys"; he despised those with style and inherited privilege. His background also led to an "inner contempt and hatred he felt for those who disagreed with him."[9] He compiled a huge "enemies list." His background produced not a reformer, but a hater who seethed with resentments; resentments that could suppress his conscience as he gleefully attempted to "screw his enemies," real and merely perceived. Rare, indeed, would there be a Nixon supporter who could praise him because of his great heart.

For eight years, Vice President Nixon was a loyal supporter of President Eisenhower, and he carried out his duties well. His eight years as vice president also were years of humiliation, bringing him no praise and little recognition from the president he served so faithfully, and requiring him to fight for his political life to avoid being "dumped" from the ticket in 1956. In 1960 he barely lost a heartbreaking election — and it was to a Kennedy.

In 1962 Nixon ran for, and lost, the governorship of California. In a bitter rant, he condemned the press, saying he felt sorry for the reporters, because he was withdrawing from politics and that meant they would not have "Nixon to kick around any more." Six years later, in another narrow race, he was elected President of the United States.

That race, 1968, involved three candidates. Vice President Hubert Humphrey was the Democratic nominee. Humphrey was an old liberal warhorse and civil-rights activist, but many liberals considered him tainted by his support of LBJ's Vietnam policies. Alabama Governor George C. Wallace ran a strong nationwide third-party campaign on his "American Party" ticket. He emphasized "states' rights" as a well-understood code for racial segregation. Nixon ran as a "law and order" candidate — another code word that Wallace also encouraged — and hinted at a plan to bring a speedy end to the war in Vietnam.

"Those who have had a chance for four years to bring peace and have failed, do not deserve another chance," Nixon thundered on 9 October 1968 — a saying made famous four years later while the war continued to rage by a Democratic campaign button saying only "Remember Oct. 9th." Nixon "had made the liberal trend of the Warren Court one of his most promising issues." He had pledged to reconstruct the judiciary by nominating only strict-construction conservatives to serve as judges.[10] This, too, as with "states' rights" was a direct appeal to Southern segregationists — a part of Nixon's successful "Southern strategy." Additionally, he had chosen as his running mate Governor Spiro T. Agnew of Maryland, a border state that in addition to a strong segregationist heritage also had a Deep South culture on its Eastern Shore.

In addition to the Southern strategy, there is the possibility of a much more sinister tactic that the Nixon campaign employed in the 1968 victory. Presidential historian Robert Dallek, in his research on Lyndon Johnson, came across material suggesting that LBJ was aware of highly damaging material from the National Security Administration files. According to that material, Nixon's agents had convinced North Vietnamese officials to stay away from peace talks until after Nixon assumed the presidency — thus prolonging the war and causing untold death and devastation.[11] Another great crime at least as serious as those associated with Watergate would have to be charged against Nixon's record if these charges are true.

When charges that he had accepted an improper gratuity caused Associate Justice Abe Fortas to resign, Nixon nominated a Southerner to the Supreme Court, Clement F. Haynesworth, a conservative from South Carolina. Nixon worked to stimulate letters of support for Haynesworth from such groups as Farm Bureaus, bar associations in the South, and the National Rifle Association. He went so far as to persuade Representative Gerald Ford to launch an impeachment drive — unfortunate and ultimately futile — against sitting Justice William O. Douglas. The effort backfired, and alienated even some Nixon supporters who would otherwise have supported Haynesworth.[12] On 21 November 1969, the Senate rejected Haynesworth's nomination. Liberal groups and many unions objected to Haynesworth as not having an adequate "judicial temperament," although there is little doubt as to his qualifications.

Nixon responded with a vastly worse nomination, G. Harrold Carswell of Florida, a sitting judge on the U.S. Court of Appeals. Nixon vindictively had sought a nominee even further to the right than Haynesworth, and he found him. Unfortunately for the nomination, although Carswell was much more conservative, he was much less competent and was a racist as well. As his record became known, even many Republicans shied away from him as not worthy of a spot on the Court. Senator Roman Hruska, a Republican from Nebraska, attempted to defend Carswell against charges of mediocrity, but his argument — although it became a classic — did Carswell no good. Hruska said something to the effect that even if Carswell were mediocre, there were millions of mediocre people in the United States and they deserved representation on the Supreme Court, too!

For his part, Nixon asserted a strange constitutional doctrine that antagonized the Senate yet further. He said that the issue was the "constitutional responsibility of the President to appoint members of the Court," and whether "this responsibility can be frustrated by those who wish to substitute their own philosophy ... for that of the one person entrusted by the Constitution with the power of appointment."[13] As senators from both sides of the aisle were quick to point out, that not only was arrogant, it was nonsense. "Appointment" includes senatorial confirmation as well as presidential nomination. Moreover, Nixon was arguing that it was improper for the Senate to consider a nominee's judicial philosophy — he made no such charge when the Senate because of philosophy and partisanship had refused to consider LBJ's nomination of Abe Fortas as chief justice. At the same time, he had made it crystal clear that he would select his nominees based on nothing but their philosophy.

Nixon had not dreamed that the Senate would turn back two nominations in a row but, in April 1970, it did. Nixon recorded later in his memoirs that the two rejections constituted "an unprecedented partisan display."[14] He then proceeded again to play to the South by announcing bitterly that he had concluded that he could not successfully nominate any Southerner who believed, as he did, in the strict construction of the Constitution.[15]

Nixon's stock with the South soared. Many segregationists nodded in agreement when the Senate unanimously confirmed Nixon's next nomination, Harry Blackmun — from Minnesota.

Carswell, by the way, had assured Nixon that he would stay on the federal bench as Nixon had requested. Yet within a few weeks, he saw what he thought was an opportunity to convert his new notoriety into a political career. Disregarding his pledge to Nixon, he resigned his judgeship in order to run for a seat in the United States Senate from Florida. He did not even survive the Republican primary. The last news item regarding Carswell before his death in 1992 appears to have been a report of his arrest on 24 June 1976 in a public men's room in Tallahassee for soliciting sex.

Nixon defended the Carswell nomination in his memoirs, and condemned those senators who "used the issue of competence as camouflage for their real reason, which was their disapproval of his constitutional philosophy." Reading between the lines of Nixon's self-serving work, however, one can detect a vague and deeply camouflaged admission of error. "Looking back," Nixon wrote, "I have no quarrel with some of those senators who voted against Carswell because of their belief that he lacked the superior intellectual and judicial qualities to be a Supreme Court Justice."[16] Nixon himself had to concede, however grudgingly, that Carswell might not have been the best person to assume a seat on the United States Supreme Court.

Nixon ultimately succeeded in placing four justices. Warren Burger, a strong conservative replacing the liberal Earl Warren, had already easily become chief justice. After the Haynesworth/Carswell debacle, as indicated Nixon successfully nominated Harry Blackmun of Minnesota. Later he placed Lewis F. Powell of Virginia on the Court. The last Nixon appointment was an extreme conservative, William H. Rehnquist, from Arizona. Rehnquist had a controversial background regarding voting by minorities, but he had a brilliant record, and no one could question his competence.

It was characteristic of Nixon to try to have things both ways. He did enforce court-ordered integration, all the while assiduously courting Southern segregationists by — among other things — letting it be known that he had no choice. Court orders, he said, would be carried out so that they treated "this part of the country with the respect that it deserves." Tom Wicker has said that there was more school desegregation under Nixon than under any other president. Wicker conceded that Nixon had worked openly against busing and had refused to use the symbolic power of the presidency to disavow racism.

Nonetheless, he said, Nixon "got the job done," which was the destruction of the dual school system, when no one else had been able to do so.[17] One should remember, though, both that it could not have been done before — LBJ had paved the way making it possible for Nixon to achieve school desegregation — and that Nixon was indeed acting under compulsion from the courts. The Court had declared in *Alexander v. Holmes County* (1969) that segregation had to end immediately, and Nixon responded that he would carry out the order, even if he disagreed with it. He was careful to make clear that he "did not feel obliged to do any more than the minimum that the law required."[18] In fact the Nixon Department of Justice — fortunately without success — opposed extension of LBJ's 1965 Voting Rights Act.

Some three decades later, George Shultz wrote an op-ed piece for the *New York Times* crediting Nixon with school desegregation.[19] Shultz, secretary of state under Ronald Reagan, had been Nixon's secretary of labor. He said, correctly, that Nixon had declared *Brown v. Board of Education* to have been "right in both constitutional and human terms" (this was in a "white paper" on 24 March 1970), and that he intended to enforce the law. Shultz said that Nixon asked him and Vice President Agnew to head a cabinet committee to work toward school desegregation. Shultz "became de facto chairman," he said, with help from counselor to the president Daniel P. Moynihan, when "the vice president said he wanted no part of this effort." Shultz and his team then formed bi-racial committees in the seven states at issue, all in the Deep South, to proceed. He quoted Wicker's conclusion that school desegregation under Nixon was his administration's "outstanding domestic achievement," and, said Shultz, "I believe he was absolutely right."

Two days later, however, the *Times* printed a rebuttal letter from Joseph A. Califano, Jr., who had been an aide to LBJ and who later became secretary of health, education, and welfare under President Jimmy Carter.[20] Califano said that Shultz's piece re-wrote history. "Throughout his presidency, Richard M. Nixon pursued a Southern strategy intended to play on white resentment and fear of Lyndon B. Johnson's civil rights agenda." Califano said that when he became secretary in 1977, "more than 80 percent of the staff of H.E.W.'s Office of Civil Rights, which was responsible for school desegregation, was under the control of federal courts," and that judges had found the Nixon administration repeatedly guilty of failure to enforce civil rights laws. It took him as secretary many months, he said, to get the office in order because of Nixon's undermining of those laws.

Despite Wicker's praise of Nixon for desegregating schools, his view of Nixon was decidedly mixed. He quoted civil-rights lawyer Roger Wilkins as saying later that Nixon had sent "cultural signals" to the public indicating that racism was permissible, signals such as opposition to busing and comments sympathetic to segregationists. Wilkins said that this was the worst thing the Nixon administration did, that it made "possible the later presidency of Ronald Reagan, with his 'grotesque' civil rights policies."[21]

As the later release of the presidential tapes during the Watergate scandal made clear, expressions of bigotry in the president's office were frequent, and were directed at many groups in addition to blacks. When the White House diaries of key Nixon aide H. R. Haldeman came out in 1994, for example, they quoted conversations between Nixon and the evangelist Billy Graham speaking of "satanic Jews," and condemning Jews for being pornographers and controlling the media, injecting left-wing bias. Graham strongly denied Haldeman's account. In 2002, however, the National Archives released the relevant tapes. They verified the conversations between Nixon and Graham, and in fact made it clear that they were worse than Haldeman had presented them. Graham had told Nixon that he had many Jewish friends who did not know how he felt about them. If Nixon were re-elected, the revered evangelist told the president, perhaps "then we might be able to do something."[22]

Wicker nevertheless stood firm in his belief that, with regard to segregation, Nixon was the right president for the time. In this regard, Wilkins was surely the more perceptive. Nixon built upon the Wallace constituency to incorporate previously Democratic blue-collar groups into an anti-government phalanx within the Republican Party that responded not only to Wallace's bigoted appeals, but later also accepted many of the Reagan efforts to turn back the New Deal's legacy.

In Nixon's first term, he became known for "Nixonomics," rather startling departures from traditional conservative approaches to the economy. He held discussions with employers ("jawboning" was the popular term) in an effort to counter both unemployment and price increases. Ultimately, in a presidential action that remains unique in peacetime, he imposed temporary wage and price controls.

Nixon implicitly accepted the direction laid down by the New Deal, although he did away with the Office of Economic Opportunity from LBJ's Great Society, and undercut the Community Action Program. Still, he expanded Social Security and other measures of income maintenance, and extended the government's regulatory reach by accepting such measures as affirmative-action programs, the Environmental Protection Agency, and the Occupational Safety and Health Administration. He signed the Environmental Quality Policy Act of 1969, the Water Quality Improvement Act of 1970, and the National Air Quality Standards Act pf 1970.

Complaining of its cost, he vetoed a water pollution control act in 1972, but Congress passed it over his veto (when it did so, Nixon attempted to prevent enforcement by "impoundment," that is, by impounding and refusing to spend funds Congress appropriated. His practice of impoundment precipitated one of his major confrontations with Congress). In 1972 he signed the Consumer Product Safety Act. He even went so far as to propose a radical "Family Assistance Plan" (FAP), an enlightened measure that would have included a "negative income tax" and a guaranteed annual income, but he did not support it aggressively. For a variety of reasons Congress failed to pass it. Conservatives, for example, thought it did too much and opposed it. Liberals thought it did too little and therefore foolishly opposed it, thereby demonstrating the truth of the saying that the best is often the greatest enemy of the good. Elements of the New Left — as unperceptive and as politically unrealistic as the liberals — called the FAP the "Fuck America's Poor" plan. Perhaps they thought the poor were better off with nothing than with a plan that would bring some credit to the hated Nixon.

The Nixon penchant for having it both ways was evident in social legislation as much as it had been in civil rights. In 1972, he signed into law an act raising Social Security benefits by 20 percent. He had previously opposed the increase, indicating that it was too great. When Congress forced it upon him by attaching it to a measure he needed, he signed it into law, timed the checks to go out just prior to the 1972 elections, and included a slip with each of the millions of Social Security checks telling beneficiaries that their benefits were permanently increased because of legislation that he had just signed.

Nixon's greatest interest was in foreign policy, and it was foreign policy in which he achieved most greatly. By far his most stunning triumph was his opening of relations with China, and his dramatic surprise trip there in February of 1972. It is commonplace to note that no Democrat could have done this without being blasted by charges at best of being "soft on communism," or at worst of committing treason.

Republicans had condemned Truman and Dean Acheson, his staunchly anti-communist secretary of state, as having "lost" China. Joe McCarthy had an audience-pleasing line in his speeches condemning "Dean Acheson's Cowardly College of Communist Containment." Nixon, as a well-known anti-communist who had begun his political ascent by investigating allegations of communism when he was a young member of the House Committee on Unamerican Activities, had considerable armor against such charges. Among the most paranoid fringes of the far right, there were accusations that Nixon himself was a communist agent, but these were so ludicrous that they made no impression. Against a Democrat, however, such irresponsible charges likely would have been widespread and would have become campaign issues. As it was, Nixon was able in 1971 to negotiate and secure approval of a treaty banning the use of chemical weapons, and in 1972 to negotiate and secure approval of SALT I, a strategic arms limitation agreement.

The most severe trouble that confronted Nixon from abroad was the same that LBJ had faced: Vietnam. Demonstrations continued on college and university campuses and elsewhere across the country. Nixon grew to loathe the demonstrators as though they had been Kennedys. He sought to find "peace with honor," to end the war without withdrawing. His solution was "Vietnamization," in which Vietnamese troops were supposed gradually to assume all of the fighting. In the meantime, he expanded the war into neutral Cambodia.

The Cambodian invasion — that the administration hoped to minimize by calling simply an "incursion"— caused an outburst of campus demonstrations. On 4 May 1970, National Guard troops fired into a crowd of students at Kent State University in Ohio. The crowd included some peace demonstrators, and others who simply were changing classes.[23] Four students, two men and two women, died. Nixon made a public statement against violence, with no word of sympathy for the murdered, "or their families, or the eight wounded students."[24]

The war's continuation did not damage the president's re-election in 1972. Secretary of State Henry Kissinger — to Nixon's great annoyance — announced in October that he and the North Vietnamese representatives had worked out a peace agreement.[25] The North Vietnamese said that the terms were no different from those that they had agreed to accept back in 1969, but the administration disagreed.

The election this time was no cliff-hanger as in 1960 or 1968. In November Nixon carried every state except Massachusetts and the District of Columbia.[26] He became one of only four presidents (along with Harding, FDR, and LBJ) to achieve 60 percent of the popular vote. In Paris the following January the Americans and the Vietnamese finally agreed formally to the American withdrawal.

The war had not damaged Nixon's re-election, nor did another potential disaster: Watergate. On 17 June 1972, Washington, D.C. police arrested five burglars at the Democratic National Headquarters at the upscale Watergate apartment complex. Quickly it came to light that the five were employees of the Committee to Re-Elect the President (CRP — widely known for various reasons as "CREEP") working directly under authority of White House officials. They were attempting to plant eavesdropping equipment, electronic "bugs."

The media did report the break-in. Nevertheless, although the election was only six months away, they did not give it high visibility. "For all of Nixon's anger at the newspaper and television reporters in July of 1972, they were actually doing him the greatest possible service by concentrating on McGovern, Vietnam, and the financing of his home improvements while all but ignoring the Watergate story."[27] There were many unfolding developments before the election; they actually were reported, but only briefly, without emphasis, and usually as parts of other stories or on inside pages.

The Democratic national chairman, Larry O'Brien, for example, requested a special investigation, and the Democratic Party filed a lawsuit. Presidential press secretary Ron Ziegler's statement that the FBI was conducting an investigation received more media attention than the Democrats' legal actions. Astonishingly, a short item buried deep on page 21 in the New York Times and rarely even mentioned elsewhere, reported that CREEP had requested that there be no hearings in court on the matter until after the election, so as not to damage the Nixon campaign. Even more astonishingly, the court granted the request.[28] Thus, although there was considerable information available about the Watergate break-in before the election, the public heard little of it, and the president went on to his landslide re-election.

After the election, the story was quite different. People who previously found it easy to pay no attention suddenly discovered that they no longer could overlook what came to be called, simply, "Watergate." In depth investigative reporting by the Washington *Post's* reporting team of Bob Woodward and Carl Bernstein along with the no-nonsense rulings of U. S. District Judge John Sirica (who, incidentally, was a conservative Republican) brought more and more information to light. Each new revelation made the situation look worse. No longer was it possible for officials — or, for that matter, for the public — to take seriously dismissive comments from the White House that the whole situation was merely a "third-rate [whatever that is] burglary."

Presidential scholar Michael Genovese called it, quite correctly, "the most serious scandal in the history of U. S. presidential politics." He noted that it was the first time that a president himself had been personally involved in "the crimes of his administration. Watergate was a different kind of scandal," he said, "Richard Nixon was a different kind of president."[29]

The Watergate conspiracy began with the establishment of the "Plumbers," a group charged with stopping "leaks" from the administration. From the Plumbers flowed wiretappings and efforts to destroy Nixon's political enemies, or those whom he thought to be his enemies. This included the burglary of the office of a Los Angeles physician, Dr. Lewis J. Fielding, who was a psychiatrist treating Dr. Daniel Ellsberg. Ellsberg had openly released the Pentagon Papers to the *New York Times* (they dealt with Vietnam policy before Nixon took office, but their release infuriated him nonetheless). The burglary team included among others Howard Hunt and G. Gordon Liddy. They were seeking information with which to discredit Ellsberg, but found nothing of use.[30] True police-state tactics had come to the United States.

In addition to activities of the Plumbers, Nixon and his inner circle sought to ensure a landslide re-election. They raised huge amounts of money, legally and illegally, and conducted a campaign of "dirty tricks" to destroy Democratic front-runners. Their goal was to ensure nomination of a weak candidate. Nixon and his administration had launched a direct attack upon

the electoral system and upon the American system of constitutional gover-
nance. Then came the cover-up, an effort to deny that there had been any
wrongdoing.[31] With the revelation that Nixon had secretly taped all conversations in his office, and the successful effort to secure the tapes, the truth
came out. Nixon had been indirectly involved in some of the activities, and
directly involved in most if not all the efforts at covering them up.

Nothing like it had ever before been seen in American politics. Top presidential aides received jail terms, the president himself became an "unindicted
co-conspirator," and impeachment efforts began. Despite the pleas from
Nixon apologists that "all presidents do it," they do not. No other president
had done anything remotely approaching in seriousness the Nixon transgressions. The most nonsensical excuse of all is to say that "other presidents
have been worse, they just haven't been caught." This is ridiculous on its
face. If they have not been caught, how could anyone know?

The few efforts at presidential impeachment in American history have
been highly partisan — with the exception of this one. To be sure, some of
the participants may have had partisan motives, but in no way was the move
to impeach Richard Nixon a Democratic effort directed at a Republican
president. Prominent Republicans joined with Democrats in recognition that
the president had demonstrated his unfitness for the office. A bipartisan
majority of the House Judiciary Committee recommended impeachment to
the House of Representatives. Facing almost certain impeachment and conviction, President Richard M. Nixon submitted his resignation, and on 9
August 1974 became the only president ever to relinquish the office prior to
the ending of his term.

Less than a year before President Nixon's resignation, Vice President
Spiro T. Agnew had resigned. In many ways, Agnew had become an embarrassment to Nixon. Although Nixon used him to make political attacks as
Eisenhower had used Nixon, himself (leading some to call Agnew "Nixon's
Nixon"), Agnew frequently blundered, and was inclined to veer off into the
outrageous. From a political point of view, however, he did have one major —
and largely unheralded — accomplishment. His incessant attacks on media
reports that were not markedly pro–Nixon gave rise to the myth of the "liberal media." Although never accurate and increasingly less so as the years
went by, the notion that the media are "liberal" persisted. That it remains
an article of faith to many observers decades later is a tribute to the power
of repetition: anything, plausible or not, can become accepted if only the
public hears it repeated often enough. Much of the repetition has come from
numerous politicians who find it greatly to their advantage.

After the landslide re-election of the Nixon-Agnew ticket, charges surfaced that there had been corruption in Agnew's dealings when he had been
county executive of Baltimore County, and also when he had been Gover-

nor of Maryland. He resigned on 10 October 1973 in an agreement to ensure that he would serve no time in jail. Nixon thus became the first president to have an opportunity to invoke the new Twenty-fifth Amendment.

With the ratification of that amendment during the Johnson administration, it became possible for the first time to fill a vice-presidential vacancy before the end of the term. President Nixon did invoke the Amendment, and nominated Gerald Ford, the minority leader of the House of Representatives, to fill the spot that Agnew had vacated. Both houses speedily confirmed the new vice president who took office in December of 1973. Thus, when Nixon resigned the presidency on 9 August 1974, Vice President Ford became the new president. The next month, on 8 September, President Ford in an effort to bring the matter to an end issued a full pardon to former President Richard M. Nixon.

There were many good things, both foreign and domestic, that came out of the Nixon administration. It was not all bad, even though nearly all else falls under the shadow of Watergate. So thoroughly has the term entered the language, that lazy or weak-minded reporters and politicians now routinely add "gate" as a suffix to any political scandal. Since the Nixon administration, we have heard of Koreagate, filegate, troopergate, travelgate, Monicagate and on and on. Such nonsensical shorthand trivializes the truly serious Watergate, and tends to "water" everything down to the same level in importance.

There were also notable things that came during the Nixon years that were not directly his doing. On 20 July 1969, Neil Armstrong became the first being from earth to set foot on the moon, thus fulfilling John Kennedy's pledge to put a man on the moon before the end of the decade. On 5 July 1971 the Twenty-sixth Amendment became part of the Constitution. It provided that no state could set a voting age higher than 18. In 1973, the Supreme Court handed down its landmark ruling *Roe* v. *Wade*, denying states the power to forbid abortions in the first trimester. Ironically, Nixon's appointee Justice Harry Blackmun, wrote the majority opinion.

Richard M. Nixon lived for two decades after his departure from the presidency — a long time for a former president. He died on 22 April 1994. His wife, Pat, had died the year before, on 22 June 1993. They are buried in Yorba Linda, California at the Richard Nixon Library.

Undoubtedly, Richard Nixon left his mark. His was a most important presidency. He began reshaping the federal judiciary by appointing to the bench those who already had been judges with solid conservative records, so they would be more likely to remain reliably conservative during their lifetime tenures (clearly, though, Justice Blackmun surprised him). His excesses — such as in impounding, or refusing to spend, funds that Congress appropriated if he did not favor the programs involved — led Congress to reassert its power. American government is marked generally by tension between Congress and the president. Nixon's presidency caused Congress for a time to be more assertive regarding its share of the power of government.

The Nixon presidency in many ways actually was a great success. It opened relations with China. It expanded the Johnson administration's efforts to restore the environment. It oversaw, however reluctantly, the destruction of the South's dual system of public schools. Nixon himself rebuilt the Republican Party and attracted some traditionally Democratic groups into its embrace, all the while moving it toward the right. He accomplished this while accepting numerous progressive measures, and without engendering the anti-government attitudes that were to come later. For better or worse, he also succeeded in his deliberate effort to begin a massive shift of the federal judicial branch to the right.

At the same time, Richard Nixon was a great failure. He brought disrespect to the presidency, and brought criminal activities into the very heart of the executive branch. He did nothing to condemn racism. He misused the power of his office in a fashion extraordinarily dangerous to the Constitution and to American citizens. He was forced from office, which weakened the presidency.

Nixon may well have been the worst man ever to be president — assuredly, many presidential scholars would agree that he was. The Nixon presidency, though, may not have been the worst. At least with regard to policy and threats to the rights of Americans, his presidency looks almost good when compared with some since. How then could it be possible to "rank" such a confusing figure?

38

GERALD R. FORD
August 9, 1974–January 20, 1977

There were many unique things about the presidency of Gerald Ford. The brevity of his term (895 days) was not among them; it was unusual, but not unique. Presidents William Henry Harrison, James A. Garfield, Zachary Taylor, and Warren G. Harding were in office a shorter time (Harding only by a matter of days). Kennedy also served a truncated term, but he was president somewhat longer than Ford was.

As others have done, Ford came to the office by becoming vice president and then by filling a presidential vacancy. Every other vice president who filled a presidential vacancy, though, had been an elected vice president. Ford was the only one who had been appointed. Moreover, he was the only vice president ever to replace a president who had resigned, rather than one who had died in office. Finally, he was the only vice president to fill a presidential vacancy and then go on to appoint his own vice president — in his case Nelson Rockefeller. It had been impossible previously — before the Twenty-Fifth Amendment — for others succeeding to the presidency to do so, and the occasion has not arisen since Ford's administration. Of course, Ford also was unique in having become president without ever having been elected either to that office or to the vice presidency.

Unique or not, Gerald Ford was a welcome replacement for the great creator of turmoil, Richard Nixon. With Ford in office, the Washington atmosphere shifted abruptly. Nixon had been an imperious president; it was symbolic that he had (however briefly) dressed the White House guards in costumes that would have fit in the most pretentious king's court of earlier times — drawn perhaps from an operetta — until ridicule had forced a return to relative simplicity. Ford, on the contrary, was a down-to-earth fellow who cooked his own breakfast and who gave the impression that he could identify with "the average Joe." The news media reported that he and his wife, Betty, even slept in the same bed. News of this sort gratified the public, and perhaps even slightly titillated some of its members.

This did not mean that Ford had an easy time as president. The war in Vietnam appeared to be over, at least for Americans, but many issues had festered. Ford had come to the office without substantial administrative experience, and had little time to learn on the job. What he did bring to the tasks that he faced, as even his detractors had to concede, was good will. No longer was there even a hint of the malevolence so plainly on display in the Nixon administration. It was a most healthy change, but in time many people would come to ask whether it was enough. Some things Ford did well, some not so well, and some likely were beyond the capabilities of anyone to handle, especially give the shortness of his administration.

One of Ford's initial acts was to nominate former New York Governor Nelson Rockefeller, a representative of the liberal wing of the Republican Party, to be his new vice president. The congressional hearings on his nomination were intense. An embittered Ford complained that it had taken Congress four months to confirm Rockefeller's nomination. He did not become the new vice president until December.[1] Ford blamed Democratic partisanship for the delay. Democrats had wanted, Ford believed, to postpone confirmation until after the congressional elections in November. Undoubtedly, though, hostility to Rockefeller from the Republican right played a role as well.

Those who rank presidents tend to rate Ford more or less as average.[2] The Fabers place him rather lower, putting him no better than thirty-second in their listing of thirty-nine.[3] Perhaps the polls would rank Ford more favorably had it not been for two things. First, after a brief honeymoon with the press and the public, he issued a "full, free, and absolute pardon" to the disgraced former President Richard Nixon. "Ironically, by pardoning Richard M. Nixon, President Ford had adopted the kind of decisive, 'take charge' action of which many of his critics believed he was not capable. Yet more than anything else that Ford did as president, this one decision influenced the press and public perceptions of his leadership."[4] Second, largely because of an incident that took place in June 1975 upon his arrival in Salzburg, Austria, the unfortunate myth developed that Ford was a bumbler with questionable intelligence. He had fallen while descending a staircase from his airplane, and the resulting photograph appeared time and again.[5] This image, coupled with his somewhat slow and deliberate speaking style, gave comedians and political opponents a chance to portray the graceful and athletic Ford in a highly misleading manner — and they seized the opportunity gleefully.

As for the Nixon pardon, it came as a surprise. Ford announced it on 8 September, a month after taking office. He feared a divisive effect on the country if he did not attempt to set the Nixon controversy to rest.[6] The Historian Stephen Ambrose wrote of Nixon's statement that he accepted the pardon with the "hope" that it would remove "the burden of Watergate." Nixon had conceded that there were those who believed his actions had been illegal, and "said he understood how his 'own mistakes and misjudgments ... seemed to support' that belief." Ambrose noted the widespread outrage at the pardon and also at "Nixon's self-serving statement."[7] Ford's Gallup approval rating within a month took an unprecedented dive to 49 percent from 71 percent, his friend and press secretary Jerald terHorst resigned his position in protest, and Ambrose said that at the time he himself had been among "those millions of Americans who were furious with Ford." With reflection, though, his attitude changed. "Seventeen years later," Ambrose wrote, "I find the case for a pardon to be irrefutable. All the arguments that made Ford decide to pardon as soon as possible were accurate: the last thing the country needed was to continue to be torn apart by Richard Nixon." If Nixon had been tried and convicted, Ambrose said, he would have had to be pardoned anyway. Ambrose's ultimate conclusion was that "Ford was both wise and courageous to pardon Richard Nixon."[8] As the years have passed, Ambrose's judgment appears to have been increasingly sound — and Gerald Ford's judgment appears also to have been increasingly sound. In any case, no other president has been faced with a decision whether to pardon a predecessor. Can Ford, then, be compared meaningfully to other presidents who faced no such issue?

To help offset the criticism on the pardon, Ford agreed to appear before the House Committee on the Judiciary to answer questions, despite the absolute power that the president has over pardons. Congress has no role whatsoever in the process, although various members may indulge in political posturing. Ford appeared before the committee in October. It was, as he wrote in his memoirs, "the only way to eliminate, once and for all, the lingering suspicion that there had been a deal."[9] Ford's testimony may not have laid such suspicion to rest, but the controversy did dwindle. It helped that Leon Jaworski, the Watergate special prosecutor, had announced that in his opinion, the pardon was justified.

Undoubtedly, terHorst's resignation was damaging. He had an easy way with the White House press Corps, and he brought a refreshing informality to press briefings.[10] He certainly contributed to the favorable public impression of Ford during his first month as president.

It was not only Ford's press room that was strikingly different from its counterpart during Nixon's time in the White House; the atmosphere of the entire Ford presidency shifted dramatically away from Nixon's. For example, when Nixon's aides discussed leniency for those who had refused military service in Vietnam, "next to statistics showing that Harry Truman had established an Amnesty Board and had pardoned 1,523 persons who had evaded service during World War II, Nixon scrawled an angry 'never'."[11] By contrast, Ford — in the same month that he issued Nixon's pardon — announced a clemency program for those who evaded military service during the Vietnam War.

Ford actually had suggested clemency in August, somewhat boldly raising the issue at a meeting of the Veterans of Foreign Wars. Rather than issuing a blanket amnesty, Ford created a Presidential Clemency Board that would deal with cases on an individual basis and permit "draft evaders" an "earned reentry" into society. The PCB completed its duties in a year, ending officially on 1 September 1975.[12]

In 1974, Ford signed into law the Campaign Reform Act establishing the first limits on campaign contributions. At least as important were its provisions for public funding of presidential campaigns through a voluntary "check off" on individual income tax returns. The amount at the time was $1.00 per taxpayer. Also in that year he signed legislation abolishing the old Atomic Energy Commission (AEC). The Commission's reputation had become poor for a number of reasons, many resulting from its inherent conflict of interest: it had the obligation to regulate nuclear safety, but also to encourage the production and development of nuclear energy. Under the Ford administration an Energy Research and Development Administration and a separate Nuclear Regulatory Commission replaced the AEC.

Concerned with inflation, President Ford attempted to apply countermeasures. He submitted legislative proposals, including a request for a tax increase — shortly before the congressional elections. He designated inflation public enemy number one, and called also for voluntary anti-inflationary actions. One part of his campaign involved distributing "WIN" buttons, for "Whip Inflation Now." As one would expect, the campaign was barely successful, if at all.

Ford's concern with inflation as opposed to unemployment — they had come together in an unusual circumstance that officials and the press came to term "stagflation" — reflected the views of his most conservative advisers, Secretary of the Treasury William Simon and Chairman of the Council of Economic Advisers, Alan Greenspan, each of whom he had inherited from the Nixon administration. Following their lead, Ford at first refused to admit that the economy was in recession. He finally had to admit that it was, and that he had been wrong to concentrate his efforts on combating inflation instead of unemployment. He had suggested a small tax surcharge, as conservative orthodoxy had mandated, and reversed himself to favor a tax cut to stimulate the economy. The far right, "led by Simon from within the administration and Reagan from without, contended that Ford had abandoned conservative orthodoxy and the tax surcharge before it had been given a chance to bring inflation under control," yet predictably they also criticized Ford's "windfall profits tax" as "penalizing success."[13] Reagan had not yet departed from his conservative fiscal principles as he did when he became president.

The press criticized Ford's "flip flops" on the economy. He ultimately signed a tax cut measure that was much larger than he wanted, but warned that he would offset the revenue loss by resisting calls for additional spending. He then did use the veto liberally to cut additional spending measures from the Democratically controlled Congress, which sought to provide jobs by providing new programs. In all, he vetoed sixty-six bills — a large number considering that he served only some two and one-half years. Congress overrode twelve of those vetoes.

In 1975, South Vietnam finally fell. New York City faced bankruptcy, and Ford initially refused to provide financial assistance. The New York *Daily News* ran a banner headline: "Ford to City: Drop Dead." In Ford's defense, he had never promised the city anything, and he insisted that there was nothing personal in his decision. He thought the city had been fiscally imprudent, and feared setting a precedent that would result in other cities seeking federal assistance which would put greater pressure on the federal budget.[14] In November, in fact, satisfied that the city had raised taxes and reduced its budget, he signed legislation providing loans to help it weather its crisis. In addition, Ford signed several laws to provide consumer protections. The year 1975 also brought personnel revisions in the cabinet.[15] Some of these would have important implications for the future.

For several reasons, Ford had little confidence in Secretary of Defense James Schlesinger. Among those reasons was friction between Schlesinger and the forceful Secretary of State, Henry Kissinger. Ford fired Schlesinger, and replaced him with a young White House aide, Donald Rumsfeld. This smoothed the way for the Helsinki Accords that Kissinger had favored, a pact among dozens of countries, including the USSR, designed to lessen tension between East and West. For Rumsfeld's new deputy, Ford selected a young Richard Cheney. Similarly — with no way of knowing that he was laying the basis for a new political dynasty — he asked for the resignation of Richard Colby as director of the CIA, and replaced him with George H. W. Bush. Finally, because of a threat from his party's right wing — specifically from former California Governor Ronald Reagan — Ford thought his chances for the 1976 nomination would improve if he asked Vice President Nelson Rockefeller not to run again. Rockefeller agreed.

Also in 1975 Ford signed faced his most serious foreign-policy incident. On 12 May, forces of the communist Khmer Rouge government of

Cambodia had seized an American merchant ship the *Mayaguez*, and held its crew captive. Within days, and after heavy fighting, American Marines brought the crew's release.[16] There was criticism of the action. For one thing, forty-one Americans were killed — a greater number than the thirty-nine crew members rescued — and another fifty were injured. Ford scholar John Robert Greene was critical, but conceded that "all told, it was the biggest political victory of the Ford presidency."[17] Ford's approval ratings improved sharply.

In 1976, a potential public-health disaster loomed. Ford's reaction was thoughtful and decisive, yet it damaged his reputation still further and decreased public confidence in his presidency. In February, an army recruit at Fort Dix, New Jersey, became suddenly ill with influenza. He died within twenty-four hours. Public health experts identified the viral strain as identical with, or highly similar to, the "Spanish flu" that had swept the world in 1918-1919. Despite a generally-cavalier attitude toward "the flu," the potential of a severe flu epidemic dwarfs any other natural public-health concern.

The flu in 1918-1919 was a pandemic, the worst wave of disease in recorded history. More then a half-million died in the United States, and elsewhere it was even worse. Some *twenty million* perished around the world. Young, healthy, adults seemed no less vulnerable than the frail and elderly. Nothing like it has been seen before or since, but the strain found at Fort Dix — named the "swine flu" — suggested to virologists and epidemiologists that such a pandemic was building to strike the following winter.

Obviously, the case was not clear-cut. Scientists deal in probabilities, rarely in certainties. Possibly, neither a pandemic nor an epidemic would develop. If the swine flu were to emerge, it might be less dangerous than feared. If, however, there were a swine flu epidemic and it turned out to be as serious as the Spanish flu had been, the severity of the consequences could hardly be imagined. President Ford decided to embark upon a mass National Influenza Immunization Program (NIIP), one that would inoculate every American against the swine flu virus.

Laboratories quickly developed the vaccine. Huge numbers of people received inoculations in a short time. There were some defective batches of vaccine that caused illness or death. More than a hundred people were affected. The swine flu epidemic failed to develop; the flu had killed only one person. Those who were victims of the inoculations suffered or died needlessly.

The widespread view was that the program had been a failure, and that the president had made a foolish decision. The predictions, however, had been based upon the best scientific information available. The function of a president is to assure that the best possible information is available, and then to decide accordingly and accept the possibility that the decision might be wrong.[18] Gerald Ford did so. Considering the circumstances, one should give him at least the benefit of the doubt — if not, indeed, credit for firm, decisive, and potentially vital action. Certainly the likelihood of a swine flu epidemic was greater than the threat from biological terrorism that has concerned Americans since 9/11.

Did Ford take political considerations into account? No doubt he did, as a president must. Was there contradictory advice urging caution? There was, but the president had to decide one way or the other. Either way could have been wrong. The NIIP was flawed, but it was based upon sound scientific information that was not fabricated or exaggerated. The result did demonstrate the possibility of mass, energetic, and effective public-health protective measures. To condemn it because no epidemic developed is unwarranted; if the swine flu had swept the country as had been a real possibility, the NIIP would have saved countless lives. Ford would then have been hailed as a hero. Had he failed to act in the face of such a truly documented threat, he would have been condemned for failure to do his duty.

Gerald Ford's First Lady, Elizabeth Bloomer (Betty) Ford, was a great asset to the nation, although unfortunately not always to her husband's presidency. It says much about the state of the country at the time that large numbers of people found her to be unacceptable. She was refreshingly forthright at a time when forthrightness was suspect, especially from a woman, and most especially from a president's wife. It made many citizens uncomfortable when Betty Ford spoke of life as it really is — and was — rather than to hide behind polite but misleading conventions.

She and former first daughter Margaret Truman were friends, and Truman has described Ford's bout with breast cancer a month after moving into the White House (the same month as the Nixon pardon). At a time when it was "indelicate" to speak of such things, Betty Ford went public in order to encourage women to seek medical examinations.[19] She also openly supported, and worked for the ratification of, the proposed Equal Rights Amendment (ERA) for women. Her husband had supported it since he had been in the House, and the Republican platform had done so from its proposal in 1972 until the Reagan forces seized the party and rejected the ERA in the 1980 platform.

This support antagonized many conservatives and much of the Bible Belt. Phyllis Schlafly organized her Eagle Forum to oppose the ERA, and joined with various fundamentalist churches and such extremist groups as the John Birch Society to condemn it. The arguments they used were similar to — and in many cases identical with — the arguments from similar forces against the Nineteenth Amendment that in 1920 had ensured the vote for women.

Betty Ford became even more of a lightning rod when she appeared on the CBS program *60 Minutes*, on 21 August 1975, "eleven days after her husband had announced he was going to seek the GOP nomination in 1976."[20] Morley Safer asked her opinion of the Supreme Court's position on abortion, and she replied that it was a "great decision." As for marijuana, it had not been available in her youth, she said, but if it had been, she might have tried it. What would be her reaction if their seventeen-year-old daughter were "having an affair?" She said she wouldn't be surprised, she said, because Susan was a "perfectly normal human being," but she certainly would counsel her. In response to the predictable huffing and puffing, she sent out a letter explaining — and softening — her comments. Her poll numbers then gradually rose to high levels.[21] If the country had not been ready for such frankness, she helped it mature. Unfortunately, those who resented her resented her with great fervor.

Gerald Ford had initially announced that he would not run for re-election but changed his mind. He and former Georgia Governor Jimmy Carter debated, as Kennedy and Nixon had done in 1960. There were to be three debates. In the first, on 26 September in Philadelphia, Ford did very well. In the second debate, on 6 October in San Francisco, he made the strange statement that there was "no Soviet domination of Eastern Europe, and there never will be under a Ford administration." The questioner, Max Frankel of the *New York Times*, gave him a chance to recover, and Ford made it worse. He named a number of Eastern European states and said that they did not "consider themselves dominated by the Soviet Union." Greene suggests that Ford may have meant that these countries were not part of the Soviet Union.[22] He also wrote that it was the "error of a tired politician, behind in the polls, who had reacted carelessly. It did little to help combat the image of Ford as not up to the job, and it stoked the fires of those critics who questioned his intelligence."[23] The third debate, on 21 October in Williamsburg, Virginia, added little. Ford has said in his memoirs that what he meant was not to deny that the Soviets had troops throughout Eastern Europe, but that he was confident that the Soviets did not dominate the "heart, soul, and spirit" of the people.[24]

Certainly, the second debate was damaging. Nor did it help when Ford had to fire Secretary of Agriculture Earl Butz, in the midst of he campaign. Butz had been guilty of numerous transgressions. The end came when he told a racist joke — demonstrating that he was a bigot — where the press could hear him — demonstrating that he was not an especially smart bigot. The joke was vicious, crude, and was completely unfunny. Butz's blunder revealed him to lack values, prudence — and also a good sense of humor. Ford went on to lose the 1976 election to Jimmy Carter.

He had underestimated the threat from the forces of the far right that inspired a challenge to his nomination by Ronald Reagan, and it had split his party. He had let the right wing dictate his choice of Robert Dole as his running mate. Dole brought little strength to the ticket, and perhaps was a detriment. By and large, Ford had campaigned quite well, but the gaffe on Poland and Eastern Europe haunted him. Nevertheless, the election was very close. Ford took 48 percent of the popular vote to Carter's 50 percent, and carried twenty-seven states. Carter carried twenty-three plus the District of Columbia, but he won 297 electoral votes to Ford's 240. Ford could easily have won if things had been slightly different.

Gerald R. Ford is a decent man who was a decent president. A popular history treats him as a "caretaker president," and said that "the Mayaguez incident notwithstanding, the Ford years were colorless."[25] This is nonsense, as I hope this chapter demonstrates. Despite his reputation, Ford was no Whig, and generally was firm and decisive. He did not achieve — and perhaps did not even aspire to — greatness. As he put it in his inaugural address, he was a "Ford, not a Lincoln." If his administration to some extent lacked cohesion, or vacillated now and then, one must remember how sudden was his emergence as president, and how briefly he held the office. Ford was a cautious fiscal conservative, but he accepted the necessity for an activist government. Moreover, he accepted the obligation of that government to contribute to the quality of the environment, and to the lives of America's citizens.

Perhaps Ford's greatest accomplishment was that he contributed much to the healing of the country following Watergate. James Cannon, who had been an aide to Vice President Rockefeller, has written that Ford's greatest accomplishment "was that he restored the integrity of the Presidency by the example of his own honesty and trustworthiness."[26] Cannon also quoted presidential biographer Edmund Morris as saying that "Gerald Ford was our most underrated modern President."[27] Perhaps so — one can make a good case that he was — but he did have one great failure: his inability to be re-elected.

This was the greatest tragedy of the Ford administration. For other presidencies, this may not be a tragic circumstance. Ford's defeat, however, permitted the forces of the far right to take over the Republican Party — quasi-anarchist forces that threw aside traditional conservative principles as well as modern liberalism, mounting an attack government itself — and positioned them to take advantage of later developments and become dominant.

39

JAMES EARL (JIMMY) CARTER

January 20, 1977–January 20, 1981

It is difficult today to remember what a very popular President Carter initially was. He was "Jimmy," not James Earl. He walked to the White House from the Capitol following his inauguration, rather than being enclosed in the luxury of a limousine. He was an outsider, untainted by the ways of Washington. Above all, he had been unconnected to Richard Nixon. The public accepted him as they had accepted President Ford as a man of integrity; in Carter's case, they accepted him also as a man of brilliance.

However intense and glorious Carter's presidential honeymoon was, it was brief. Some of the unraveling of his presidency clearly reflected his own personality and his stubborn self-righteousness. He was determined to do the right thing — regardless of any consequences, political or otherwise — and he had no doubt that he knew, always, what was the right thing. Less directly, his campaigning as an outsider and his championship of deregulation set the scene for the full-fledged attack upon government itself that came after he left office.

At first, Carter sought to use the cabinet for his major source of advice. Moreover, he did not appoint a chief of staff, and all senior staff reported directly to him directly. Textbook writers are fond of referring to the "spokes of a wheel" model, and of drawing illustrations of a wheel representing the president in the center, and staff members at the far ends of the wheel's spokes.

The typical treatment of the Carter presidency notes that he tried to do too much himself. Such commentaries almost universally use as the perfect example that Carter personally kept control of all White House detail right down, as they say, to scheduling the tennis court. Undoubtedly this is the prevailing view of Carter's administration, but one should note that it is not universal. Presidential scholar Erwin C. Hargrove has studied the Carter administration intensively, for example, and concluded that there is "little evidence that Carter got bogged down in details and failed to see the forest for the trees, a criticism outsiders sometimes leveled."[1]

Regardless of the truth in this instance, it illustrates that scholars as well as journalists and the public can be led astray by accepting as fact things that they hear repeated frequently. Regardless of whether "everyone knows" something, it is dangerous to accept it without verification. Representative Cynthia McKinney of Georgia, for example, lost her race for re-election in 2002 after a flood of reports that she had made outrageous comments regarding the responsibility for the events of 9/11— but there is only hearsay, no record of any such comments. Vice President Dan Quayle was ridiculed over and over for saying that Latin Americans spoke Latin — but it had been a joke about him, and he actually said no such thing; Vice President Al Gore received incessant jeers as a presidential candidate for having claimed to be the inventor of the Internet — a claim that he never made. Thus, whatever Carter's faults as an administrator, and he had his faults, it is not clear that the conventional wisdom regarding his obsessive concern for trivial detail presents anything like a valid picture, let alone an explanation for his difficulties.

Halfway through his term, Carter recognized that he did need a chief of staff, and appointed his aide, Hamilton Jordan, to the post. The White House Office did appear to function better as a result, but the change came too late.[2] Even when he did appoint a chief of staff, his first appointee came with considerable baggage. Undoubtedly the worst of Jordan's encumbrances was tense relations with many members of Congress. Jack Watson later replaced Jordan, who assumed duties relating to Carter's re-election campaign.

One innovation of Carter's worked extremely well, however. His use of Vice President Walter Mondale as a major adviser was unprecedented and highly successful. Mondale, a former senator, was a Washington insider who could bring a wealth of knowledge and insight to an inexperienced administration. Moreover, his liberalism helped balance Carter's conservatism, especially on economic issues. Carter kept Mondale fully informed on domestic matters, "and was one of only four people — along with the president, secretary of state, and national security adviser — to have a daily intelligence briefing."[3] Carter did more than any predecessor to help develop the unrealized potential of the vice presidency. He also made First Lady Rosalynn Carter a complete partner in government in a much more formal sense than previous presidents had done. He invited her to sit in on cabinet meetings, and used her openly as a key adviser.

This brought the predictable bleats of protest from those who saw woman's place as in the home. They ignored Mrs. Carter's outstanding abilities, and sniffed that the people had elected Jimmy, not Rosalynn, Carter. Such critics overlooked the obvious fact that the people had not elected cabinet secretaries either.

Rosalynn Carter filled her role as first lady with great distinction. As Kaufman put it, "she blazed new trails in assuming a major role in the administration. She frequently substituted for Carter at ceremonial affairs, advised him on important policy matters, and helped plan political strategy. In June 1977, she visited seven Latin American countries as an official envoy of the United States and conducted high-level negotiations with foreign leaders."[4] At home she worked diligently for ratification of the ERA.

Carter, to be sure, must bear the blame for some of his difficulties, but certainly not for all. Much of his trouble came purely from circumstance. Jimmy Carter was a singularly unlucky president. The ironic fact that he was the only president in the twentieth century to have no opportunity to place a member on the Supreme Court was also symbolic of the misfortunes beyond his control that plagued his presidency. Even Harding, Kennedy, and Ford — none of whom served a full term — appointed a justice (in Harding's case, even a chief justice). Carter, who did serve a full term, completed that term without a Court vacancy.

Political cartoons showed a steady decline of Carter's presidency and the country's view of Carter himself. Initially, the typical cartoon showed a grinning president with an enormous smile and large teeth as his most prominent characteristic. As his prestige dwindled, so did Carter's image. Cartoonists changed their drawings so that Carter became progressively smaller. Ultimately his most prominent characteristic no longer was the grin, now forgotten, but rather tiny stature, knee-high to other figures in the cartoons.

A huge instance of Carter's bad luck came with the growing inflation that was the aftermath of the OPEC oil embargo during the Nixon administration. Interest rates were heading up to record levels for the United States. The most enormous instance of bad luck for the administration, though, came in Iran on 4 November of 1979. Radical students, violating all traditions of conduct governing international affairs, seized the American embassy in Teheran. Their action was a result of the Iranian revolution that brought to power a religious totalitarianism headed by the Ayatollah Ruhollah Khomeini — who, by obviously managing the occupation of the embassy, violated all traditions of international decorum. In the Second World War, for example, neither the Allies nor the Axis powers held hostage any diplomatic personnel from countries that were their enemies.

In Iran, on the contrary, the radical students were so outraged by Carter's decision to permit deposed Iranian ruler, Shah Reza Pahlavi, for humanitarian reasons to enter the country to receive treatment for terminal cancer, that they stormed the American embassy and held its personnel hostage. They demanded as a condition of their release that America extradite the Shah to Iran for execution. On Khomeini's orders, the Iranians did release women and black captives. Others, fifty-two in all, they held as prisoners for the duration of Carter's administration: 444 days in all.

Every night on the news, Americans saw apparently frenzied mobs shouting "death to America," and calling the United States "the Great Satan." Every night, Carter's presidency looked increasingly impotent. In reality, however, Carter worked diligently and skillfully to free the captives. In addition to diplomatic initiatives, he froze Iranian assets in the United States and ceased oil imports from that country. On 24 April 1980, he dispatched a military rescue mission — and once more his bad luck came into play. A fierce sandstorm arose, disabled helicopters, and made it necessary to abort the effort. In the withdrawal, a collision in the air resulted in the deaths of several military personnel.

Finally, Khomeini agreed to release the hostages and the Carter administration agreed to release Iranian assets in the United States. Even then, however, in a gesture unquestionably designed to humiliate President Carter, Khomeini held the prisoners until the moment of President-Elect Ronald Reagan's inauguration. He did not release them until the moment Jimmy Carter stepped from office. Humiliation notwithstanding, Carter had successfully ended the embassy crisis; after their 444 days of captivity, he had achieved the captives' release. No prisoner had been killed, and none had even been harmed. The news media, though, had made it all appear to be a huge failure of Carter's administration.

Throughout the 1980 election campaign, the Reagan team derided Carter's handling of the hostage crisis. They warned that Carter might pull an "October surprise," arranging for release just prior to the election. They were implying that Carter would handle the issue in such a manner as to improve his election chances. Later, allegations surfaced that it was the other side that had worked to time the hostage release — not for Carter's, but for Reagan's advantage — just as there had been allegations that the Nixon campaign had secretly worked to prolong the war in Vietnam to prevent an agreement before the 1968 election that might have helped Humphrey's bid for the presidency.

In 1991 Gary Sick, a former member of Carter's National Security Council, made the charge. Sick "had been intimately involved in the hostage episode," and "made a startling assertion in the *New York Times*." He amplified his charge in a subsequent book, *October Surprise*. Sick conceded that he had no "smoking gun," but wrote that his computer analysis of a database suggested that "the Iranians were promised large quantities of arms once the new Reagan administration took office," if they held the captives until after the election. Sick accused Reagan's vice presidential running mate, George Bush, of having participated in at least one meeting between Reagan campaign managers and Iranian officials to discuss arms for hostages.

Bush indignantly denied the charge. Moreover, "the director of the Ronald Reagan Library, Ralph Bledsoe, has said that he can find no evidence in Reagan's 1980 campaign files to support Sick's theories," and no member of Carter's campaign at the time suspected such a deal. Perhaps lending some credence to the charge is the known fact that the Reagan administration later actually did provide arms to Iranian militants in the hope that they would release hostages. Moreover, former President Carter himself, who is not one to make reckless charges, "has since stated his belief that there might be substance to Sick's charges." The Senate in October 1991 "voted to conduct an inquiry, but the next month, Senate Republicans were able to block funding for it."[5] Thus there was never an official investigation of Sick's serious charges.

Most of those who play the ranking game barely squeeze Carter into the "average" category. The 1981 Porter Poll put him twelfth of fifteen "average" presidents, or twenty-third of thirty-six overall; the Chicago *Tribune* poll the following year put him twenty-seventh overall of the thirty-six; the Murray-Blessing Poll, also in 1982, put him eighth of nine "averages," or twenty-fifth in the full list of thirty-six; and the Reuters 2000 poll ranked him twenty-second of forty-one.[6] Ridings and McIver placed Carter in nineteenth place among forty-one ranked.[7] Those who might still be inclined to take rankings seriously should be warned that both the Reuters poll and that of Ridings and McIver include not only Garfield, who served only six months, but also William Henry Harrison, who served only one. Their evaluations of these two unfortunate presidents are remarkably similar: Reuters put Garfield in twenty-ninth place and Harrison in thirty-seventh, while Ridings and McIver rate them thirtieth and thirty-fifth respectively. The Fabers, who had the good sense to leave these two short-lived presidents out of their study, put Carter in a rather favorable place, sixteenth among the thirty-nine that they ranked.[8]

Because of his great service after leaving the presidency, Carter once more is highly popular. Popular esteem today, though, could not help him when in office. Recognizing the country's unrest in 1979 — skyrocketing inflation, gasoline shortages that caused seemingly interminable waits at filling stations in many cities — Carter withdrew to the presidential retreat at Camp David, and met in soul-searching seminars with members of the clergy, scholars, psychiatrists, literary figures, and political experts. After eight days, he emerged to address the country on the evening of 15 July. He set forth a comprehensive and innovative energy plan, and admitted that a crisis of confidence had beset the nation.

Reaction was favorable, until a few days later when he abruptly dismissed many of his cabinet members. The press immediately savaged him, charging that it was a frantic action by a president who had no control of his administration. Suddenly, although he had not used the word, his address had become the "malaise" speech. "Much of Carter's problem was that his outsider's approach to the presidency required effective popular leadership to appeal to the people over the heads of interest groups and legislators. Yet rousing the American people," despite having run an effective campaign, "was not Carter's strong suit."[9] It has become a truism to say that Jimmy Carter was a poor president, but he is perhaps the best *former* president the United States has ever had.

Carter did, however, have substantial successes as president. Recent evaluations of his administration itself— not only those of his post-presidential career — often are more favorable than those that came immediately after he left office. Most writers assessing the Carter presidency soon after it ended "regarded it as a failure." Some observers went further. The journalist Haynes Johnson, for example, in 1980 wrote *In the Absence of Power* that Carter's presidency had been "a tragedy."[10] Later, however, evaluations from such scholars as political scientists Charles O. Jones and Erwin Hargrove were more favorable. They pointed out that Carter often received criticism because he determined to do the right thing regardless of the political consequences, suggesting that this might not have been such a bad thing. Others have argued that daunting situations would have faced any president at the time such as the aftermaths of Vietnam and Watergate, the emergence of PACs (political action committees), the breakdown of the congressional seniority system, and the weakening of parties. They say correctly that such things as the Panama Canal Treaties, energy reform measures, protections for Alaskan wilderness areas, and the Camp David accords were substantial accomplishments. As Aaron Wildavsky wrote, Carter may not have been a brilliant president, but "he did a lot better than he was credited with doing."[11] Moreover, there are ways of assessing presidencies beyond a mere cataloguing of legislative accomplishments.

Burton Kaufman, who has written one of the best studies of the Carter presidency, noted that Carter "furthered the earlier efforts of President Gerald Ford to heal some of the wounds caused by the Vietnam War and the Watergate affair," and concluded that he deserves "considerable credit for the quiet manner" in which he did so. Carter, he said, was "neither mean-spirited nor conspiratorial." Still, Kaufman observed, he had to side with the earlier critics of the Carter administration. The country was not "ungovernable," as Carter apologists contended, nor have the apologists been wise in so easily passing over "the elemental fact that, for better or worse, there is a political process in any system of representative government which no leader can simply ignore on the basis of being above the fray."[12] Kaufman rejected as dangerous the assumption that any leader — however wise and benign — can be a "public trustee" with wisdom superior to the other elected parts of the political system and thus ignore them.

One of Carter's first actions as president — in fact, an action that he took on the day after his inauguration — was to issue a pardon to those who had evaded the draft during the Vietnam War. This was a bold move, far more sweeping than Ford's case-by-case clemency program. He did not pardon those who deserted the military, but, predictably, veterans' organizations were quick to condemn the president anyway.

Carter succeeded in securing two additional cabinet departments. The Department of Health, Education, and Welfare was enormous and unwieldy. A reorganization converted it into the Department of Health and Human Services and a new Department of Education. In recognition of the importance of energy in the modern world, Carter signed legislation granting it cabinet status, and creating the Department of Energy.

In 1978 Congress passed Carter's proposals for civil service reform. It abolished the Civil Service Commission and created an Office of Personnel Management. The administration designed the revisions to make it easier to discharge incompetent employees, and to transfer senior executives among departments and agencies for more efficient management. That year he also achieved his two major triumphs in foreign policy. He persuaded the Senate to ratify the Panama Canal Treaties relinquishing ownership of the Canal to Panama, but ensuring priority access for American shipping. Presidents Johnson, Nixon, and Ford had strongly endorsed such a measure, but Carter ran into opposition from former California Governor Ronald Reagan who used the issue as a way to build political support to challenge Carter in 1980. Carter succeeded despite the powerful opposition that Reagan had created. The Camp David Accords were Carter's other outstanding triumph. They ended the decades-long state of war between Egypt and Israel, and provided at least a rudimentary step toward what may someday be peace in the Middle East.

President Nixon had dramatically opened the door to relations with China. In 1979, President Carter completed Nixon's initiative. He established formal diplomatic relations with the People's Republic. American trade would continue with the Republic of China on Taiwan, but no longer would the United States recognize the Taiwanese government as China's true government.

In 1980, Senator Edward Kennedy mounted a strong challenge to Carter's nomination. After a bruising fight, the Democratic National Convention re-nominated the president. It appeared as though the election would be close, and ultimately Carter and Reagan agreed to debate. Although Carter clearly was the superior in terms of mastery of the facts, Reagan's genial demeanor helped offset fears that he was a dangerous right-wing extremist. Carter, for example, correctly accused Reagan of having campaigned against the Medicare proposal during the Kennedy administration. Reagan defused the issue by smiling and saying, "there you go again" — not so subtly implying that he was the superior of the President of the United States whom he could admonish as though he were a child.

After laughter from the audience died away, Reagan said he had not opposed the principle of assisting the elderly, merely that he had favored a different program that Congress had been considering at the time. Carter was precisely correct, and Reagan's answer was false, but there was no follow-up and the issue died.[13] There apparently was an unquestioned belief throughout the public that Reagan had "won" the debate. He went on to win a narrow majority of the popular vote, and a huge landslide in the electoral college.

Following his defeat, Carter remained active. He signed two major pieces of legislation to protect the environment. One created a "superfund" to clean up the country's worst toxic waste dumps. The other was the Alaskan Lands Bill, the strongest piece of environmental legislation protecting the Alaskan wilderness ever passed.

The Carters attended the Reagan inauguration, and then returned home to Plains, Georgia. At President Reagan's gracious invitation, Carter flew to Wiesbaden, in West Germany, to welcome the newly freed hostages.[14] At home in Plains, the Carters faced a period of readjustment, coming to grips with the trauma of defeat. They also had to turn their attention to finances, because their business had gone into debt while Carter was in the White House. Both Carters became prolific authors, and their book contracts and royalties settled their financial difficulties.

It is impossible to sum up the Carter presidency in a single ranking. He had substantial achievements, and although he received great criticism for being naïve or unrealistic in making human rights the cornerstone of his foreign policy, one should be cautious in accepting such a judgment. Certainly the administration applied the policy inconsistently, and certainly there were times when officials failed to apply it, or attempted to apply it but did so in a counterproductive manner. Still, can one truly be comfortable in saying that the United States of America, with its heritage of rights and liberty, should ignore human rights in its dealings with other countries any more than in its own domestic affairs? Such a counsel of despair, if accurate, would suggest that there is no hope for humankind.

On the other hand, Carter unintentionally provided a foundation for the subsequent destructive move against government itself. In campaigning as an outsider, the clear message was that experience at best was unimportant — or at worst, was even dangerous. His moves toward deregulation, however appropriate they may have been in themselves, gave credence to the subsequent simple-minded notion that all regulation is bad. He contributed to the romantic, unrealistic, and in fact fundamentalist commitment to the market place as the answer to all questions.

Finally, by sacrificing political considerations and holding himself aloof from the fray, Carter discredited his own administration in the eyes of the people. This was his greatest failure. It enabled the one segment of American politics that had failed to develop beyond the oversimplified nostrums of the nineteenth century — the political fundamentalists — to seize control. Once in charge, they grew and prospered. Worse, they succeeded in moving American politics sharply to the right — not only away from "liberalism," as current usage defines it, but also away from sound, prudent, conservatism and fiscal integrity. Carter thus has many superb qualities, and there was much to appreciate about his presidency.

There also is much for which he should answer. Carter doubtless would agree. He was especially "stung" to have "lost to a man he thought immoral to the core: an unprincipled but telegenic B-grade Hollywood cowboy who had ridden into the White House on such 'patriotic' themes as abhorrence of government, xenophobia, and massive tax cuts." He remarked in 1995 that "allowing Ronald Reagan to become president" had been by far his "biggest failure in office."[15] A shared concern for their inability to head off the Reagan phenomenon doubtless contributed to the bond that developed between Gerald Ford and Jimmy Carter after their presidencies.

40

RONALD W. REAGAN
January 20, 1981–January 20, 1989

In 1980, as in 1964, the Republicans in their National Convention turned to a candidate from its far right wing. This time the result was different. Reagan was no more moderate than Goldwater, but he was soothing rather than combative, genial rather than abrasive, probably more willing to heed sound advice than Goldwater had been, and undoubtedly more skilled politically.

His victory — actually more a Carter loss than a Reagan victory — was certainly decisive, but in some respects was less overwhelming than it appeared. Although he carried all but six states and the District of Columbia (garnering nearly 91 percent of the electoral vote), Reagan had less than 51 percent of the popular vote, and many states he carried only narrowly.[1] Nevertheless, it was significant that he carried with him a Republican majority into the Senate. It was the first time Republicans had gained a majority in either house of Congress since the Democrats regained control of both houses following the elections of 1954.

Reagan had been wise to in selecting George H. W. Bush as his vice presidential running mate. Bush had been a major contender for the presidency, and had even charged during the primaries that Reagan by promising simultaneous tax cuts, military spending increases and balanced budgets was offering "voodoo economics." Reagan held no grudge, though, and in choosing Bush, a representative of the Eastern establishment, helped unite diverse wings of the party since Reagan represented the party's upstart Western insurgents as Goldwater had done. Bush proved to be not only an able vice president but also a loyal one.

As an interesting footnote to history, before choosing Bush, Reagan considered something truly innovative. His aides approached former President Gerald Ford to determine whether Ford might accept the vice presidential nomination. It failed to come about. Ford sought assurances that would have made him virtually a co-president, and withdrew from consideration when he did not receive them. In Ford's defense, a former president has a special status, and would bring such unique experience to the vice presidency that there would almost have to be some special arrangement; in Reagan's defense, no sitting president could have agreed to such a sharing of power. The idea was certainly creative, and was fascinating. If in some way it had materialized, it might permanently have changed the relationship between presidents and vice presidents.

No doubt a major Carter error was in agreeing to debate Reagan. Although Carter unquestionably had a much greater mastery of the facts, he was no "crowd pleaser." The people were angry and disenchanted with his administration, but they were skeptical of Reagan the extremist, Reagan the warmonger. Reagan did not have to destroy Carter in debate; he had only to convince the public that he was not dangerous.

This he did with great skill. He seemed to be the affable favorite uncle that people wanted to like. When Carter accused him of beginning his political career by opposing Medicare, Reagan uttered the first of the two most memorable lines of the evening, "there you go again." He went on to say that he had not opposed the principle of caring for the elderly; he simply had favored a different program that Congress was considering at the time. It was not true and Reagan knew it; Congress had been considering no other program that he favored, and Reagan had been a bitter foe of both Social Security and Medicare.[2] Carter was precisely correct, but it did not matter.

Apparently shaken by audience laughter in response to Reagan's quip, Carter never regained his momentum. The second most memorable line of the evening — and probably the most effective — came at the end of the debate. It was Reagan's question to viewers whether they were better off after four years of a Carter presidency than they had been previously. Despite Carter's superior knowledge, the public was convinced that Reagan "won" the debate. And so he had.

The debate was one instance in which Nancy Reagan's keen political judgment had been wrong. She had been reluctant to see him participate. In general, though, her instincts were extraordinarily accurate and her understanding of her husband was flawless. Reagan was a superb campaigner but not a perfect one. He had "uncommon skills," but also a "capacity for self-destruction." Until Nancy Reagan ignored advisers Ed Meese and William Casey and "sought help from Stuart Spencer, a onetime favorite strategist who had been blacklisted for leading President Ford's effort to deny Reagan the nomination in 1976," Reagan had been "running loose." He was in trouble because of his "familiar propensity for unverifiable anecdotes and a willingness to say whatever came into his head. What came into his head were happy thoughts about creationism and Taiwan, and confusion about the origins of the Ku Klux Klan."[3] Spencer, and indirectly, Nancy, brought discipline and professionalism to the Reagan campaign.

Ronald and Nancy Reagan were as close as a couple can be. As a result, she was able to become an outstanding First Lady. "One of Reagan's gifts was his ability to attract people who helped him get ahead, and no one since his mother had helped him as much as Nancy Reagan," wrote Lou Cannon, the biographer who had been close to Reagan and wrote more about him than any other has. Cannon noted that Mike Deaver, after he left Reagan's service, wrote that "Ronnie Reagan had sort of glided through life, and Nancy's role was to protect him." She not only accepted "almost total responsibility for their family and home," he said, but "at the same time remained his closest adviser in public life." As a political team, they were unexcelled. "He was a dreamer, preoccupied with ultimate destinations. She was a practical person who worried about what loomed around the next bend in the road. 'She's more tactical; he's more strategic,' said Stuart Spencer, who was both." One of the keys was that "Ronald Reagan was a striver, but his striving was masked by his courteous, amiable manner and enduring fatalism. Hers was out in the open.... With a directness unusual either in Hollywood or Washington Nancy Reagan favored anyone who helped her husband or advanced his career and opposed anyone who stood in his way."[4] One Hollywood observer remarked that if Reagan had married Nancy earlier, he would have won an Oscar. It is no exaggeration to say that without her, he could never have become president.

Ronald Reagan — former actor, former two-term governor of California — was within three weeks of his seventieth birthday as he took the oath of office as the fortieth President of the United States. The oldest person ever to have been president previously was Dwight Eisenhower. Ike had been three months past his seventieth birthday when he left office. Reagan thus was nearly the same age when he became president as Eisenhower had been when he left it after two terms.

Reagan was unique in another way also, at least unique among modern presidents. He came to office saying "government is not the solution to the problem; government is the problem." A public that had come to expect empty words from politicians suddenly had elected a president who meant what he said — however simplistic — and who sought to undo much of what Americans had accomplished through their government over at least a half century.

Reagan had developed his ideas early, and began to express them in public nearly three decades prior to his becoming president. As far back as

1954, for example, he became a spokesman for the General Electric Company — hosting its popular television program *GE Theater* and speaking at hundreds of banquets, conventions, and other GE activities around the country — and presenting what he called simply "The Speech."[5] The contents of The Speech were essentially the same from presentation to presentation and through the years — leading sometimes to the understandable assumption that Reagan had only one speech to give. It was a powerful one, however, and Reagan did vary details and emphases to tailor it to various audiences. The Speech was the basis for the phonograph recording, "Ronald Reagan Speaks Out Against Socialized Medicine," which in 1961 was the heart of "Operation Coffeecup," the American Medical Association's attack upon the proposed Medicare program.[6] When Reagan delivered the stirring address on behalf of Barry Goldwater's doomed presidential candidacy over nationwide television in 1964 — the address that failed to save Goldwater but carried Reagan to the governorship of California and ultimately to the presidency — it was nothing other than The Speech tailored for the occasion.

At the core of The Speech was a warning of danger from big government. More and more as the years progressed, Reagan developed skill in cultivating the far right of the Republican Party — the descendents of what had been the party's Old Guard — while soothing the general public. As Ritter noted, in private or in talks to selected audiences he was quite uninhibited, while in public addresses he stressed his "eagerness to solve the problems of age, health, poverty, and housing 'without compulsion and without fiscal irresponsibility'."[7] Opposition to Social Security also was a key component of The Speech. Reagan decried the compulsory nature of the program, alleged as early as the late 1950s that it was "bankrupt," and recommended all along that it be converted into a private system. In the 1980 presidential race, his hostility to Social Security gave him trouble, as it had in his 1976 challenge to President Ford for the nomination, so he "muted" it: "He promised repeatedly both to protect the long-term integrity of the system and to maintain benefits for those already receiving them. He avoided explicit commitments concerning future beneficiaries, though that could have been inferred."[8]

Shortly after taking office, the Reagan administration mounted an unprecedented attack on Social Security in the form of sharp reductions — and in some instances elimination — of benefits. In the words of Lawrence Barrett, Reagan "took one more whack at the Social Security system in 1981." That effort, though, was "uncharacteristically inept." It "failed utterly. But the fact that he was willing to act out another of his long-held instincts despite the political price was significant."[9] The reaction to Reagan's anti–Social Security policy was so severe that he promised not to attempt it again. By and large, he honored that promise, but his appointees in the Social

Security Administration (SSA) "tried to cut Social Security through administrative action." Rigidly scrutinizing those who were drawing disability benefits, "they engaged in a large-scale effort to purge the rolls of those whom they considered ineligible. Between 1981 and 1984, the SSA informed nearly a half million" beneficiaries that their benefits would cease.[10] Although they restored benefits to those who won in court, Reagan's officials even defied court orders to change their policies. The courts threatened to hold the agency and its officials in contempt. After a two-year battle, Congress overwhelmingly passed the Disability Benefits Reform Act of 1984 requiring the agency to determine that there had been medical improvement before it could terminate disability benefits. "The protracted battle over disability insurance testified dramatically to the Reagan administration's fervent commitment to challenge the social welfare policies of the past, with or without authorization from Congress or the courts."[11]

Regardless of the immediate loss, Reagan had won a victory of sorts. He did succeed in trimming the Social Security — no longer, for example, would there be there a benefit to college students who are qualified dependents of deceased workers, and no longer would there be a guaranteed minimum benefit to those of especially low earnings. More important to the history of the program and to U.S. public policy, he had made it politically feasible to question Social Security. He had paved the way for efforts ultimately to eliminate it by "privatization." So successful was he in providing this foundation that a subsequent Republican President, the second George Bush, has openly advocated just such a change.

"In the area of social regulation, the Reagan administration's attempt to weaken environmental, consumer, and civil rights regulations also came not through legislative change but through administrative action, delay, and repeal."[12] Reagan issued executive orders directing the Office of Management and Budget to review proposed agency regulations, and he also appointed Vice President George Bush to head a "Task Force on Regulatory Relief" to subject existing rules to "cost-benefit analysis." As a part of the administration's "regulatory relief," there was a hasty de-regulation of the savings and loan industry. As a result, many savings and loans executives, reckless or worse, drove their institutions into bankruptcy. The cost to the country of saving the industry was never fully calculated, but all agreed that it was — and will be — in the hundreds of billions of dollars.

Another cost to the country that cannot be measured resulted from the demoralizing effect from Reagan's constant demeaning of federal employees. The civil service suffered greatly, and positions with the federal government became less and less attractive. Few people of quality are likely to seek positions when the highest authority implies that the positions are useless and those who fill them are worthless.

As President, Ronald Reagan inspired many Americans. He clearly inspired also a renewed and cohesive Republican Party; a party that impressed many observers with its new ideas. What such observers failed to recognize was that the ideas, far from being new, were made of recycled content — old wine in new bottles, outdated merchandise with new labels — they had been prevalent in the 1920s, and in fact in the Nineteenth century.

The political scientist Hugh Heclo put it well when he said in a paper that Reagan's words said nothing new but, rather, that "Reagan continued to uphold something old."[13] The fact that the ideas predated the New Deal did not make them wrong, of course. They were wrong for the other reasons — for the same reasons that Hoover's ideas had been wrong: they were wrong because they were rigid and ill-suited for the times.

Cynically, despite his efforts to undo the New Deal and all of FDR's works, Reagan time and again referred to Franklin Roosevelt as though he were the New Deal president's heir. There is one respect, though, in which Reagan indeed was innovative and did mirror FDR: he sought to re-shape a political era, as FDR had done, although it was FDR in reverse. In an approach remarkably similar in broad outline to that of President Jefferson — and one hardly more suited to modern conditions than Jefferson's would be — Reagan sought to make broad national government impossible by depriving it of revenue.

Immediately upon taking office, Reagan began to implement a rigid politico-economic ideology that had surfaced not long previously under the name of "supply-side economics." He presented his programs to a public always hopeful of achieving a free lunch. Cutting taxes, he told them, would *increase* the government's revenues. Thus, he said that he would reduce taxes, increase military spending, and yet achieve a balanced budget. As an actor, he was able to say this with a straight face but, obviously, it could not, and did not, happen. The budget already was in deficit; the last balanced budget had been the final one that LBJ's administration adopted. With Reagan's tax cuts, the deficit predictably soared. Reagan, the balanced-budget advocate, saw the national debt more than triple under his policies. Incongruously, Reagan numerous times called for a constitutional amendment requiring a balanced budget at the same time that the budgets he sent to Congress were the most unbalanced in history.

This development of a huge deficit from the policies of an administration that had preached the danger of deficits was not the sheer incompetence that it appeared to be — at least not completely. Rather, it was deliberate policy. Senator Daniel Moynihan of New York first identified the scheme.[14] He began by noting that the public accepted Reagan's enormous deficits because it assumed that he couldn't have *wanted* to do it, he must have *had* to. Then, he explained how it was that the administration could have failed to see that the tax cut would have produced a great deficit. In fact, he said, the administration knew what the result would be and pursued that result deliberately. He argued that the deficits were purposeful, but that Reagan's administration miscalculated.

Moynihan wrote that the administration intended to create huge deficits in the early years of Reagan's presidency, and then eliminate them by reductions in domestic spending. It had not recognized that the tax cut would be so great that no feasible cut in domestic spending could compensate, but that is what happened. Reagan and his aides had been trapped by their own rhetoric into a ludicrously flawed understanding of government, Moynihan said. Reagan's own Budget Director, former U.S. Representative David Stockman, later in a "tell-all" book admitted the miscalculations and the lack of understanding. The press at the time had been full of reports that Stockman had been the only person in Washington who truly understood the complicated budgetary proposals coming from the Reagan administration. Stockman conceded that neither he nor anyone else had understood, but that they forged on regardless because of the "awesome stubbornness of the nation's fortieth president."[15] Contrary to the administration's assumptions, there was not massive waste and corruption, and therefore they discovered that there was little to be gained by reform and improved efficiency. They had generated a situation of crisis proportions that convinced even Reagan to support a huge tax increase to offset part of his reductions.

The supply-side argument had been that one could reduce taxes, increase military spending, and still balance the budget. No one, not even Reagan, actually believed it, Moynihan said. He supported his point that "there was a hidden agenda" by calling attention to President Reagan's television speech sixteen days after his inauguration. "There were always those who told us that taxes couldn't be cut until spending was reduced," Reagan had said. "Well, you know we can lecture our children about extravagance until we run out of voice and breath. Or we can cut their extravagance by simply reducing their allowance."

Moynihan made his points over and over, but he found that people would not believe that Reagan would deliberately produce deficits in order to force reductions in the budget. The senator said in his constituent newsletter on 4 January 1986 that he had polled New Yorkers, and found virtually *no one* who believed it. Yet, he said, Friedrich von Hayek, a friend of the President and a Nobel Prize–winning Austrian economist, had confirmed that it had been the view of the White House that Congress could not be persuaded to economize unless deficits became so huge that they convinced everyone that no more money could be spent. Columnist Tom Wicker of the *New York Times* verified that Hayek had made the same comments in an interview in an Austrian periodical *Profil 13*, on 25 March 1985.[16]

What had been so shocking that no one would believe it when Reagan was in office ultimately became obvious to any informed and open-minded observer. It became obvious so gradually, however, that there was no outrage and little resistance. So skillfully had Reagan and his aides paved the way, that in another Republican administration more than a decade after Reagan departed, officials openly advocated tax cuts regardless of the economic circumstances as a way of forcing reduction in the size of government.

Why had the Democratic House become so subservient that it failed to block policies of which it disapproved? It seems clear that many Democrats were terrified of what they perceived as the magnitude of Reagan's victory — forty-four states plus a Republican Senate. Several, in fact, saw the handwriting on the wall and became Republicans. Moreover, although it may seem churlish to say so, Reagan benefited considerably from a potential tragedy shortly after becoming president. Few objective observers can doubt that John F. Kennedy's reputation is greater because of his tragic assassination than it would have been otherwise; even fewer objective observers could fail to see that the shocking events of 9/11 caused George W. Bush's quite shaky reputation to soar and become solid.

Similarly, on 30 March 1981, Reagan was seriously wounded in an assassination attempt. His jaunty manner, "honey, I forget to duck," he said to his wife Nancy, grabbed America's heartstrings. He had become not only President of the United States; he was America's President. A month later, he appeared before Congress to make a televised speech, and shortly thereafter achieved his tax cut, his military increases, and his reductions in domestic programs. When he appeared on Capitol Hill, House Republican leader Robert Michel remarked that he had received "the kind of reception that makes a few of the waverers feel, 'Gosh, how can I buck that'?"[17] There can be little doubt that the sympathetic result to his fight for life contributed to Reagan's success as a legislative leader.

And he was a successful legislative leader, especially at first. In contrast to Carter who tried to do so much, Reagan exercised single-minded leadership and fitted all his proposals either toward enhancing the military or shrinking civilian government. Like Carter, he had campaigned as an outsider; unlike Carter, he did not operate that way. Rather he worked closely with Congress and did not hold himself aloof.

Reagan demonstrated that he could be as effective at executive leadership as he was as a legislative leader. In August 1981, the Professional Air Traffic Controllers Organization (PATCO) declared a strike — illegal, because the controllers were federal employees. Rather then negotiate, Reagan ordered the controllers back to work. When they refused, he fired them all. The firm, decisive, move was popular with much of the public. Many private pilots, particularly members of the Aircraft Owners and Pilots' Association (AOPA), also welcomed it. AOPA members frequently resented all but the most minimal regulation, and considered the controllers to be too arbitrary. Ironically, PATCO had been one of the few unions to support Reagan, and Reagan's move against PATCO members set back the union movement in this country considerably. It was fortunate that there were no disasters caused by Reagan's shattering of the air traffic control system, which took years to re-build. Reagan's luck held.

Reagan has the distinction of having appointed the first woman to the United States Supreme Court. On 19 August 1981 he nominated Sandra Day O'Connor from Arizona to replace the retiring Associate Justice Potter Stewart. She joined the Court when the Senate confirmed her unanimously on 21 September. During his eight years as president, Reagan made a substantial mark upon the highest Court. He elevated Associate Justice William Rehnquist to the position of chief justice, and Rehnquist received Senate confirmation on 17 September 1986. He appointed Antonin Scalia in 1986 and Anthony Kennedy in 1988. Reagan's first choice for the Kennedy seat had been a prominent but highly conservative legal scholar Robert Bork. The Republicans had lost their Senate majority following the 1986 midterm elections, and the Democratic Senate rejected Bork's nomination. His confirmation hearings were bitter as he attempted to defend his record — so much so that outraged Republicans often still refer to a rejected nominee as having been "borked." Bork has spent the rest of his career writing bitter books complaining about his rejection — and inadvertently demonstrating how wise the Senate had been to turn back his nomination. After Bork's rejection and before he nominated Kennedy, Reagan again failed with a nominee, a young Bork protégé, Douglas Ginsburg. Ginsburg's rejection ostensibly was on the basis that he admitted to having smoked marijuana both as a student and as a law professor — a rather flimsy basis for a rejection, it would seem.

Reagan made his mark on other federal courts as well. He had numerous opportunities during his eight years in office to appoint federal judges and judges of the U.S. Courts of Appeals. He and his Justice Department carefully vetted the appointments to select those with very conservative political and legal ideologies. He made great progress in turning the federal judiciary sharply to the right, where it is more likely to erode church-state separation, more likely to enhance state authority at the expense of the national government, and less likely to defend individual rights against government action.

Additionally, the Reagan administration moved in ways that are considerably less visible to the public. Under administration pressure, Congress passed strict new sentencing guidelines incorporating rigid mandatory minimum sentences for many offenses, particularly those that are drug-related. These have taken much of the discretion away from trial judges. Although

those advocating more inflexible "law and order" practices praise such provisions as being "tough on crime," all they do is to transfer discretion from
the judge to the prosecutor. Prosecutors still have complete discretion regarding what charges to bring from the serious to the trivial. A major difference
in effect is that judges at least theoretically are a neutral party; prosecutors
are anything but neutral, and make their decisions on a wide range of issues,
including political considerations and those that will advance their careers.
The guidelines have clearly politicized the justice system to a much greater
extent than it had been previously. Few people outside the system recognize
just how damaging this has been to justice in the United States.

Reagan enhanced his standing with the public in October 1983 by sending troops to invade the tiny island country of Grenada in the Caribbean.
A Marxist government had gained control, and some American students in
a medical school there allegedly felt threatened. The new government was
building an airstrip that American officials said would be used by the Cuban
military to land equipment and personnel on the island. The Americans
quickly liberated the students, deposed the government, and withdrew by
Christmas as Reagan had promised.

In October 1983, the president announced that he would pursue a
"Strategic Defense Initiative (SDI)," a defensive shield against missiles. Critics derided the plan as "Star Wars," and called attention to the astronomical expense involved and to the likelihood that it would never work. Reagan's
view of SDI was more visionary even than its critics envisioned.

There are countless documented incidents of Reagan's inability to separate reality from fantasy — such as his frequent confusion of roles he acted
in film with incidents that he had experienced in real life. At least as startling was his mythic expectation of SDI. According to a later book by his
own press secretary, Marlin Fitzwater, Reagan's attitude toward SDI had
been largely fanciful. Fitzwater clearly respected and admired Reagan but
apparently without intending it to be, his portrait of the former president
in this and other respects was devastating. He reported that "Reagan's staff
twice intercepted" comments that the president had put into written
speeches. Reagan had wanted to speak of "the prospect of an alien force
threatening the earth from space." Fitzwater described Reagan's view as
"bringing all the countries of the world together in a Steven Spielberg defense
of mankind."[18]

In dealing with the Soviet Union the fervently anti-communist Reagan
did demonstrate a true commitment to disarmament and an unexpected
flexibility. In November of 1985, he met with Soviet leader Mikhail Gorbachev and the two agreed to work together to bring a thaw in superpower
relations. Gorbachev, for his part, in 1987 began loosening the tight police-
state controls within the USSR. Reagan thrilled the world, but antagonized

Gorbachev, when he visited West Berlin on 12 June of that year and proclaimed before the Brandenburg Gate, "Mr. Gorbachev, open this gate! Mr. Gorbachev, tear down this wall!"[19] Nevertheless, on 8 December, Gorbachev journeyed to Washington to meet with Reagan, and they signed the INF treaty reducing missiles. The treaty affected only about 4 percent of the nuclear forces, but as the "first U.S.–Soviet treaty of any kind to provide for destruction of nuclear weapons and the first to provide for on-site monitoring of this destruction,"[20] it was highly significant.

After Reagan left office, the USSR finally crumbled into non-existence during the first Bush administration. Reagan's supporters say that Soviet efforts to match the vast expenditures for SDI brought its end. It is amusing to see people who argued against domestic programs by saying that "you can't solve problems by throwing money at them," forgetting their principles and saying that Reagan solved the problem of the Soviet Union and ended the Cold War by throwing money at it. Certainly, Reagan's firmness helped bring an end to the Cold War. So, however, did the efforts of Harry Truman, Dwight Eisenhower, John Kennedy, Lyndon Johnson, Richard Nixon, Gerald Ford, and Jimmy Carter all of whom — along with Reagan — helped increase the internal instability of the Soviet Union. There is plenty of credit to go around. Undoubtedly Reagan deserves a good share of that credit because his policies probably hastened the Cold War's ending.

Reagan did have his setbacks, however, some very serious. After 1982, Congress resisted his demands for further domestic program cuts, and also placed a brake on his pet project providing American support for anti-government rebels in Nicaragua, the "Contras." In April of 1983, terrorists bombed the American Embassy in Beirut, Lebanon, killing many people, including more than a dozen Americans. The following October, a terrorist attack killed 241 American Marines in their Beirut headquarters. Note that Jimmy Carter paid the price for the Iranian seizure of hostages in Teheran, although his diplomatic efforts eventually brought their release unharmed. For Reagan, however, setbacks did not always exact a political price, not even a setback that brought great loss of American lives. Rather than losing his bid for re-election, he won overwhelmingly. Consistently, though, he was firm and resolute; he talked tough. He faced no crisis of confidence. Throughout his presidency there were kidnappings, aircraft and cruise ship highjackings, shootings, bombings, and the downing of a Pan Am flight over Lockerbie, Scotland, killing hundreds. In 1986, as noted previously, a major setback came in the off-year elections when they returned control of the Senate to the Democrats.

Two years before those elections though, Reagan had won re-election by a landslide. In spite of faltering badly in one of the debates with his challenger, former Vice President Walter Mondale, Reagan carried every state except the District of Columbia and Mondale's home state of Minnesota; Reagan received 525 of the 538 electoral votes, a record for the absolute number of his electoral votes. He achieved nearly 59 percent of the popular vote.[21] There was no mistaking the breadth of his victory. Another significant achievement of the election was one with which Reagan had nothing to do. Mondale's vice presidential running mate was Geraldine Ferraro, the first woman ever to be a candidate for president or vice president on a major party ticket.

Despite that victory, Reagan had a troubled second term. Although he had declared strongly that he would never deal with terrorists, he not only dealt with them, he sold them arms in order to induce them to free American hostages. Instead of accomplishing Reagan's goal of freeing the five Americans held captive in Lebanon, the arms initiative resulted in more hostages being captured than were freed." When the terrorists did release hostages, they seized others "and replenished their hostage stocks." As a practical matter, "the Iran initiative had provided more of an incentive for kidnapping Americans than for releasing them."[22] Reagan's aides relayed the funds received from arming America's enemies to the Nicaraguan Contras in direct violation of existing law.

In response to public outcry, Reagan appointed a President's Special Review Board — called the Tower Board because of its head, former Senator John Tower — to investigate the situation and issue a report. Also investigating was a congressional joint committee, which televised its hearings. Two of the key figures in the unfolding investigations were Reagan's national security adviser Rear Admiral John Poindexter and a Marine officer attached to the National Security Council, Lt. Col. Oliver North. When North testified before the congressional committee, he appeared in full uniform, and presented himself as a patriot being unjustly vilified by powerful members of Congress.

Many in the public found him to be a sympathetic figure, although he admitted that he had lied to Congress. Poindexter, North, and others were tried and convicted of various charges, but Poindexter and North appealed and achieved reversals of their convictions because Congress had granted them immunity for their testimony. The Tower Board's report was cautious with regard to the president — who testified over and over that he had no memory of various events — but was implicitly critical of his loose management style.

Although at this writing the United States is in its fourth post–Reagan presidential term, it is still too close to the Reagan era even to hope for the passions it kindled to have dwindled. Fervent partisans such as Grover Norquist continue working to see to it that everything possible bears Reagan's name. Thus far he has succeeded in securing legislation attaching the

Reagan name to a government office building and an aircraft carrier — all while Reagan still is alive — and even to have the name "Reagan" attached to the District of Columbia's most convenient airport; no longer does the capital city have "Washington National." Instead, flying in the face of those who through the centuries have honored America's founding president as "first in war, first in peace, and first in the hearts of his countrymen," DCA has become the Ronald Reagan Washington National Airport. True, the name "Washington" still is there, but only to designate the city that DCA serves. The capital city itself — at least at this writing — still bears the name "Washington," as does the state in the Pacific Northwest. Norquist, though, continues his efforts.

Those who rank presidents fail to share Norquist's enthusiasm and have had difficulty placing Reagan. Whatever else his presidency was, it was far from "average." Schlesinger's 1996 poll, though, rated him just that: fourth from the bottom of the "average" category. His overall placement was twenty-fifth of thirty-nine presidents rated.[23] Genovese also put him twenty-fifth of thirty-nine, but in his ranking system that placed Reagan "below average."[24] Ridings and McIver put Reagan in twenty-sixth place,[25] while the Reuters 2000 poll put him up to eleventh.[26] Neither of these two polls puts presidents into categories, but each included Garfield for his term of six months, and even William Henry Harrison for his term of but one. The Fabers were much harsher in their evaluation of the fortieth president than others have tended to be. In their ranking, Reagan held thirty-fourth place of thirty-nine presidents rated.[27]

On 20 January 1989 the Reagan administration came to an end. It lived on, in a sense, in that Vice President George Bush became the new president. For the first time since 1836 when Vice President Martin Van Buren won the election to succeed a retiring President Andrew Jackson a sitting vice president had won the presidency. Bush's victory was a tribute from the people to the Reagan-Bush administration.

Two days before his term ended, Reagan issued a pardon to New York Yankees owner George Steinbrenner, who had been convicted of making illegal contributions to Republicans. Early in his administration, Reagan had pardoned former FBI agents W. Mark Felt and Edward Miller who had been convicted for authorizing illegal FBI break-ins into the offices of political protesters. The total number of pardons Reagan issued was 406, placing him twenty-third among presidents from Washington through Clinton.[28] Beginning with Gerald Ford, presidents have issued fewer pardons than their twentieth-century predecessors. There had been some question regarding some of the Reagan pardons — specifically that they favored the wealthy, the well-connected, and Republican contributors — but the president's pardon authority is absolute.

Reagan left office still popular. He attended President Bush's inauguration on 20 January 1989, happy to accept the Bush victory as a continuation of the Reagan-Bush administration. Then, the same day, he and Nancy returned to their home in Bel-Air, California.

No one can accuse Ronald Reagan of lacking vision. His view was of a great future for America and for its people, one of limited government, freedom, and individual responsibility. The peoples' heritage of Jeffersonian rhetoric — regardless of their Hamiltonian practices — conditioned them to be receptive to Reagan's view. It was a simple one, and lacking in detail, but it helped explain his genius for connecting with the great American public. "To his political opponents, Reagan's rhetoric was the shining gloss on a harshly conservative public philosophy. But Reagan's words and the political vision they expressed stirred many Americans' deeply rooted and widely shared political values. The simplicity of Reagan's message, the dignity of his public demeanor, even his limited faith in government, captivated the popular imagination."[29]

His simple vision, though, however appealing it may have been to the public in general (if not in specifics), did not provide the conditions that would have led to the benign world he envisioned. His proposals frequently were cruel, and adopted with little awareness — or at worst, with lack of concern — for their consequences on those least able to protect themselves. Although Congress and the courts moderated some of the harsher Reagan proposals by protecting programs "to hold together the bottom tier of the safety net," he engineered a fundamental change in policy outlook. At least for the Republican Party and subsequent Republican administrations, he "successfully shifted the nation's social policy agenda from problem solving to budget cutting, and as long as the federal deficit remains a problem, there is little room for the agenda to shift back."[30] To demonstrate just how successful Reagan was in re-ordering the political agenda, consider what happened when subsequent presidents succeeded in restoring some of the taxes that Reagan had cut. A Democratic president then worked to eliminate the deficit, and bequeathed a surplus to his Republican successor. That successor immediately worked diligently to cut taxes again, and restore the deficit. He was successful in returning to the Reagan framework of considering budget cutting rather than problem solving.

Ronald Reagan, then, must be considered a highly successful president in many ways — at least in a technical sense. He set goals; he achieved many of them both by legislation and by administrative action. Unquestionably, he was one of the most significant presidents in the twentieth century — perhaps in American history.

As discussed in the introduction to this work, however, success in achieving goals alone is no measure of greatness. One must consider the quality of the goals themselves and also their effects. Significance can be bad as well as good.

The goals that Reagan adopted, regardless of whether they were well-meant, included some that are an ill fit in a complex modern world. Two examples among many should suffice. First, is a limited case with a broad influence. It was Reagan's Federal Communications Commission that overturned the Fairness Doctrine. Since 1949, that Doctrine had required television and radio stations to provide equal time for "a free exchange of opposing views, with roughly equal time given to all sides, if demanded, on the public airwaves." When Congress passed legislation restoring the fairness doctrine, Reagan vetoed it. Elimination of the Doctrine paved the way for conservative dominance of the media — despite oft-repeated complaints rooted in propaganda from the right that the media are "liberal." The most extreme reflection of this dominance is radio, which has become saturated by the far right.[31] The second example is much broader. It is the obsession with small government; such an obsession can make it impossible to achieve what should be the goal: *good* government. Reagan's goals in many instances — however benign they appeared — were destructive, and in the long run they must bring damage to Reagan's reputation as fully as they damaged the country that he wanted so much to improve.

No ranking of presidents could possibly reflect Reagan's complicated presidency; the presidency of a man who had such simple goals. Nor could it reflect what was great about Reagan. As one worker, a Democrat, said after hearing him, "I don't like Reagan's policies much, but he doesn't really seem like a Republican; he just seems like an American." That was his greatest strength, and the greatest strength of the Reagan presidency.

41

GEORGE HERBERT
WALKER BUSH
January 20, 1989–January 20, 1993

When George Bush became President of the United States — the first incumbent vice president to be elected president since Martin Van Buren in 1836 — he followed one of the most controversial presidents in American history, Ronald Reagan. Reagan had a genial, easy-going manner that helped to blunt the effect of his hard right policy views. Probably no president since Franklin D. Roosevelt had such devoted admirers as Reagan's, or such fervent — and almost equally ineffective — opponents.

Bush lacked Reagan's magnetic personality, and thus could not retain the former president's public appeal. Reagan's more obsessive supporters turned away from Bush when he adopted policies more in keeping with the times than Reagan's had been, but he was unable to attract Reagan's opponents who saw him as simply an extension of Reaganism. The fact that he clearly carved out his own presidency made no difference.

One factor that did help was First Lady Barbara Bush. With her candor and her white-haired grandmotherly appearance — the Silver Fox, the president called her — the new First Lady was a welcome change from the stiff formality of a Nancy Reagan, and in a country still not adapted to assertive, independent, women she perhaps was a welcome change from Rosalyn Carter and Betty Ford as well. Appearances, though, were deceiving. Barbara Bush had keen political insights. In addition, far more than her husband, she had a combative nature that caused her to go straight for the political jugular. The image that she projected, however, was considerably more benign, characterized more by her best-selling *Millie's Book* — one that she ghost-wrote for the White House dog — than by open political involvement. She was enormously popular.

That Bush was his own man should have come as no surprise. Few presidents in history have brought such a strong background to the office. He had served in the U.S. House of Representatives from Texas, and had given up a safe seat to run unsuccessfully for the Senate. President Nixon then appointed him ambassador to the United Nations. Subsequently he served as Republican National Chairman, and then President Ford appointed him chief of the U.S. Liaison to China (the equivalent of an ambassador; the United States and China were not yet exchanging ambassadors at that time). Ford then appointed Bush to be Director of Central Intelligence. Finally, he had been Vice President of the United States for eight years.

For his vice presidential running mate, Bush surprised nearly everyone at the New Orleans convention and around the country by tapping the relatively unknown Senator J. Danforth Quayle. In choosing Dan Quayle, Bush hoped to make a dramatic move that would appeal to the younger generation. Some of the Bush camp endorsed the move, saying that the Indiana senator looked like Robert Redford. Bush scholar Herbert Parmet wrote that there had seemed to be "no downside to Quayle. He had a decent, if not distinguished record in the Senate."[1] Immediately, however, he became the object of concern.

As Parmet put it, "Quayle came out of New Orleans as the easy butt of jokes, an implausible vice president." Bush, for his part, confided to his diary regarding Quayle's selection, "it was my decision, and I blew it, but I'm not about to say that I blew it."[2] Quayle turned out to be a reasonably good campaigner, although he was overwhelmed in the debate with the Democratic vice-presidential candidate, Senator Lloyd Bentsen. Despite the constant murmur about his abilities, Quayle as vice president turned out not to be incompetent. Bush assigned him to head his "Competitiveness Council," a group that worked to lessen the effects of regulation on business. Quayle vigorously pursued a pro-business and anti-regulation agenda. Parmet concluded, fairly or not, that Quayle undoubtedly was a pawn in the hands "of his ideologue chief of staff, William Kristol."[3] Quayle may well have been acting from his own ideological orientation.

In any case, Bush did keep him on the ticket in his 1992 bid for re-election. This may have been less of a vote of confidence than it seemed, though. Parmet noted Bush's irritation at Quayle's public comments that Bush should have had American forces push farther into Iraq. Bush noted that was a "new right-wing theme," and wrote in his diary that "it doesn't help Quayle with me and it doesn't help him at all." Earlier, Quayle had embarrassed the president with comments about Central America "that appeared blatantly targeted to the right wing." Parmet, in fact, concluded that Quayle "remained a chronic embarrassment" to Bush, but quoted a Republican consultant who remarked off the record that Bush could not drop Quayle from the ticket in 1992. To do so, he said, would have been "to admit that he's made a monumental mistake, and he won't do that." If true, it is a damning indictment of Bush. It would have been highly irresponsible for him to keep a person next in line to the presidency if in his view that person were unqualified.

Bush was only an adequate public speaker, not a skillful one, but he demonstrated in the 1988 election that he could be a ferocious campaigner. In accepting the nomination, he spoke — rather obscurely — of "a thousand points of light" (one of speechwriter Peggy Noonan's efforts at inspirational rhetoric), and implied at least in a vague way some criticism of the hard right by speaking of his desire for a "kinder, gentler" country. He also campaigned forcefully against tax increases. He would be implored to raise taxes, he said, but he would say, "read my lips: No New Taxes!" As much as any other single thing it was that mistaken pledge that would undo his presidency when he later recognized — to his credit — that a tax increase was necessary, and succeeded in obtaining one.

Kinder and gentler or not, some of Bush's campaign tactics were so forceful as to be disreputable. He implied that his opponent, Massachusetts Governor Michael Dukakis, for example, was unpatriotic because he had vetoed a legislative act requiring Massachusetts school children to start the school day by reciting the Pledge of Allegiance — hardly a reliable measurement of patriotism, but effective in a world of sound-bites. Worse was the notorious Willie Horton advertisement criticizing Governor Dukakis for a program that furloughed prisoners, a program that actually began before Dukakis had become governor.

Horton was a black prisoner who had been convicted of raping a woman while on weekend furlough. Bush's advertising showed a huge darkened picture of Horton's scowling face, implicitly sending a clearly racist message. Reports later indicated that Horton himself remarked that even he was frightened of his picture in Bush's advertisements. It was this campaign that finally succeeded in demonizing the term "liberal," the term that had been the most honored label in American politics for over a half century or so.

Previously, the public had associated liberalism with Social Security, unemployment insurance, Head Start, environmental and workplace protections, free public education, protection for bank deposits, and the like. After Bush's 1988 campaign, the positive view had largely evaporated. The most likely image of a "liberal" had come to be one the Republicans had created: a liberal was someone who wished for nothing more than to impose high taxes, and direct them to fund black welfare recipients. Governor Dukakis's poor campaign was so ineffective in countering the distorted image, that it contributed indirectly to the actual solidification of that image.

Despite his fierce campaign, his enjoyment of rugged physical activities, his distinguished war record, and his history as an athlete Bush had to contend with the "wimp factor." In 1980 he had battled with Reagan to achieve the presidential nomination; upon winning, Reagan selected him to be his vice-presidential running mate. During the nomination contest, Bush had pointed out, quite accurately, that Reagan's financial ideas made no sense. They amounted, he said, to "voodoo economics." As Reagan's vice president, however, he was overtly loyal, and completely uncritical. That, of course, is what presidents expect of vice presidents, but, along with Bush's gentle and polite manner, it probably was the source of the "wimp" image. Reagan supporter conservative columnist George Will spoke scornfully of Bush as a lap dog to Reagan. Oliphant cartoons were especially piercing, always depicting Bush as a tall, spindly, Ichabod Cranelike character carrying a purse. They were wickedly witty, and quite unfair — but, of course, unfairness is a common attribute of a political cartoon.

Bush won a substantial victory over Dukakis. It was not so substantial as Reagan's 1984 victory over Mondale, certainly, but in some ways it was as strong as Reagan's 1980 victory over Carter. Reagan in the 1980 election had won 489 electoral votes. Although Bush in 1988 won fewer, a still decisive 426, Bush outpolled Reagan in the popular vote. Reagan had won less than 51 percent, while Bush took 53.4 percent.[4]

Bush by and large was a most successful president in foreign policy, but with some exceptions he had little to show on the domestic side. This is understandable. His background, his interests, and his expertise were in foreign affairs. He had no grand agenda for domestic policy — although he did make rhetorical gestures; he promised, for instance, to be the "education president," and the "environmental president" — nor did his sheltered and privileged upbringing prepare him even to be especially sensitive to the need for one. Unfortunately for him, domestic matters in the absence of some great international crisis generally supersede foreign affairs in the minds of the voters, and are more likely to be the deciding factor in choosing a president. Also unfortunately for him, the final years of Bush's presidency were marred by a serious economic recession.

The 1996 Schlesinger poll put Bush twenty-fourth of the thirty-nine rated.[5] The Reuters 2000 poll rated him somewhat higher, twentieth of forty-one.[6] Genovese put him, still in the average category, in between; he was twenty-second of thirty-nine;[7] that is the same position as in the Ridings and McIver poll (that one rated forty-one presidents).[8] The Fabers put him lower, at twenty-eighth among thirty-nine.[9] Thus, those who rate presidents seem to view George Bush as somewhat colorless, as more or less average. What, though, does that mean? He had been a successful wartime president, and a much less successful domestic one. Communism fell in Eastern Europe on his watch (not on Reagan's); it was during his presidency (not during Reagan's) that West and East Germany reunited, and that the Soviet Union ceased to be. Can such a record show through in a rating — especially a rating that portrays such a president as "average?"

When Bush took office, the "depth of the savings and loan scandals, that offspring of careless deregulation and uninhibited greed, had yet to be fully understood and the damage repaired.[10] In 1989, his first year as president, he had to sign into a law a measure rescuing the industry from the effects of the Reagan policies. The costs over the years would be in the hundreds of billions of dollars, and they still are with us.

Bush did approve two significant pieces of domestic legislation, both in 1990. One strengthened the Clean Air Act. The other, the Americans with Disabilities Act, was a far-reaching measure that has come to affect almost every business and place of public accommodation in the United States. Advocates for the disabled have hailed it as the most extensive anti-discrimination measure since the Civil Rights Act of 1964.

He also had a major influence on the composition of the Supreme Court. In 1990, he appointed David Souter of New Hampshire to replace William J. Brennan. Souter received confirmation and took his seat with relatively little fanfare. Bush's second appointment to the Court had anything but an easy time. In the summer of 1991, he nominated Clarence Thomas to replace the retiring Thurgood Marshall. Both were African American.

Viewed technically from a political point of view, it was a brilliant nomination. Thomas was a hard-right conservative, but many liberals would be reluctant to vote against a black nominee. There was, nevertheless, a bitter confirmation battle. Initially, the discussion revolved around Thomas's minimal qualifications.

Bush, in response to criticisms of his nominee's qualifications, made the ludicrous statement that he had nominated Thomas because he was the one person in the country best qualified to be put on the Supreme Court. Inflammatory charges that he had been guilty of sexual harassment rose to plague Thomas, but eventually worked to his advantage. His Republican sponsors skillfully used the charges to shift the discussion away from Thomas's qualifications, implying that if it could not be proven definitively that he had been guilty of sexual harassment (and it could not be) then he must be confirmed. Judicial qualifications no longer entered into the discussion.

He was confirmed, but by a very close vote. He took his seat after having played the race card. He was the victim of a "high-tech lynching," Thomas finally complained. Many people were embarrassed by the entire episode. The American public had been treated to a spectacle unlike any that had happened before. Although Republican zealots later blamed President Clinton for lowering the level of public discourse, during the Thomas hearings conservative Republican Senator Orrin Hatch railed away on national television about "Long Dong Silver," and that was years before Clinton became president. At any rate, so far as can be determined, no person in the shoddy debate pointed out to the public — or to Clarence Thomas — that the results of lynching had never been to put the victim onto the United States Supreme Court.

It was foreign policy in which George Bush truly made his mark. He began making that mark shortly after assuming the presidency. The Reagan administration had virtually ignored the crushing debt that underdeveloped countries around the world were finding increasingly burdensome. It had taken the position that new loans to pay interest on the old loans were the solution. Bush, however, in 1989 encouraged international banks to write off a portion of the loans, thus easing the pressures and reducing the chances that debt would lead to instability abroad.

One of the most vexing foreign situations to the Reagan administration had been the Marxist Sandinista regime in Nicaragua, headed by Daniel Ortega. It was Reagan's obsession with the Sandinistas that dealt the greatest blow to him and to his presidency when it became known that he had personally approved the sale of weapons to America's enemies in the Middle East — enemies who kidnapped Americans to hold as hostages — and that his aides had illegally diverted profits from those sales to the "Contra" rebels opposing the Sandinistas in Nicaragua. In spite of his firm rhetoric, Reagan had appeared impotent and naïve, and the Sandinistas remained in power.

Bush, however, managed to accomplish legally and without bloodshed what Reagan's bluster, force, and illegal activities could not. He brought international pressure upon the Sandinista regime to agree to free elections, and Ortega did so. Former President Jimmy Carter journeyed to Nicaragua to oversee the elections, and on 25 February 1990 some 80 percent of the voters flocked to the polls. They turned the Sandinistas out of office by a wide margin. Ortega accepted the result and ceded power to the victorious Violeta Chamorro. Afterward, Carter met for a luncheon at the State Department with Bush's Secretary of State James Baker and his top aides. Baker said later that he remembered thinking how misunderstood Carter had been among the Republican right, and how "brilliantly" Carter had debriefed him and his aides.[11]

Another thorn in Reagan's side that Bush inherited was in Panama. Panamanian dictator Manuel Noriega had been implicated in the arms traffic, in drug running, and in money laundering. A U.S. grand jury in Miami had indicted him in 1988 on drug trafficking, but Reagan had resisted advice from his advisers, particularly Assistant Secretary of State Elliott Abrams, that he invade Panama. "Reagan was more militant in words but less in deeds than Bush." He wanted to avoid arousing Latin American resentment. Reagan "on the stump ... was a missionary who sought to spread the gospel of freedom. In the Situation Room, he was often a cautious and uncertain leader who was tugged first one way and then another."[12] Bush, however, images notwithstanding, was a much more resolute and determined leader than Reagan. Whereas he had succeeded in Nicaragua using diplomacy where Reagan had failed by using indirect force, Bush succeeded in Panama by discarding diplomacy, and invading the country. Noriega had set aside the results of elections that would have removed him from power, so Bush on 20 December 1989 sent troops to accomplish what an election could not.[13] Capturing Noriega, the troops brought him to the United States where he was convicted. He now is in federal prison.

Regardless of the Reagan myth, it was on Bush's watch that communist control in Eastern Europe dissolved. In June 1989, Polish voters elected the anti-community Solidarity leaders; on 9 November, the Berlin Wall came down, and West and East Germany re-united on 2 and 3 October 1990; Czechoslovakia elected a noncommunist government headed by Vaclav Havel in December 1989; the Yugoslavian Communist Party lost its monopoly status in January 1990; the poisonous Rumanian dictator Nicolae Ceausescu and his equally brutal wife Elena were executed on Christmas Day 1989; Bulgaria held free elections in June 1990; The United States and Albania established diplomatic relations on 15 March 1991, and by 1992 that most hard-line of communist states had chosen a democratic government. In September 1991, one of the two great superpowers, the USSR, began to dissolve. And so it went.

In the Middle East, Bush was uncommonly successful in putting together an extensive coalition to support his campaign against Iraq's leader, Saddam Hussein, after Iraq had invaded neighboring Kuwait on 1 August 1990. In 1991, that effort culminated in the first Gulf War, "Operation Desert Storm" (prior to the actual war, it was "Desert Shield"). "Fighting had hardly begun, it seemed," when by the end of February it was all over. Some of the military personnel were angry that they received orders to halt short of capturing Hussein. The far right was infuriated.[14] There has been much speculation and much after-the-fact posturing, but no less an authority than former President Bill Clinton said in an interview with the journalist James Fallows that Bush's position had been correct. He had never criticized Bush for failing to depose Saddam Hussein, Clinton said, "because I know the facts. And the facts are that George Bush had to promise not to march on Baghdad to get the Arab support."[15]

Bush's presidency slid precipitously from the high point at the end of the Gulf War. His astronomical approval ratings intimidated most of the major potential Democratic candidates, who refused to enter the race against him. By the time William Jefferson Clinton, Governor of Arkansas, became the nominee, Bush's time had passed. Plagued by a third-party candidate, the erratic Texas billionaire Ross Perot, as well as by the brilliant and articulate young Clinton who connected with the people as well as Reagan ever had, Bush went down to a crushing defeat. Clinton took just over 42 percent of the vote but had a very comfortable 370 electoral votes, almost 69 percent of the total of 538. Perot had accumulated nearly 19 percent of the popular vote (no electoral votes), but Bush's popular-vote total was a mere 37.4 percent[16] No sitting president since Taft had received such a small portion of the popular vote. Even Herbert Hoover at the depth of the Great Depression had received 39.7 percent.[17]

During his term as president, George Bush issued seventy-seven pardons.[18] In 1989, he pardoned the industrialist Armand Hammer, who had been convicted of making illegal campaign contributions to President Nixon. Hammer had donated large sums "to the Bush-Quayle inaugural fund and another $110,000 to state Republican parties."[19] Hammer was an especially controversial figure, a millionaire who was such an advocate of Soviet-American friendship that he had been investigated numerous times as a pro–Soviet activist. More obscure, but highly questionable, was the Bush pardon of "an anti-Castro terrorist named Orlando Bosch, who blew up an airliner in 1976 killing 73." Bush freed Bosch from jail in 1990 "under pressure from his son Jeb and Cuban exiles."[20] Jeb, of course, went on to become Governor of Florida.

Probably the best-known of Bush's pardons was that of former Secretary of Defense Caspar Weinberger "and five others connected to the Iran-contra affair. Bush said Weinberger was an American hero, but the pardon also may have spared him from being called to testify at Weinberger's trial."[21] Nancy Reagan had persuaded her husband not to issue pardons for his people in order to protect his reputation. "Jeffrey Toobin, who had worked for Walsh," the independent counsel, "understood why Reagan did not act. 'For all his surface good nature, he was fundamentally ungenerous to those around him.' Bush was not that way." He believed in loyalty to his people.[22] There was some criticism, but it died quickly; the president's power to pardon is absolute.

Any sound evaluation of the Bush presidency must take into consideration Bush's successes and his admirable qualities. On the other hand, it must also consider his willingness to act contrary to what appeared to be his basic principles when he considered it necessary to succeed. The racist Willie Horton campaign along with the demonization of Michael Dukakis and the general misrepresentation of liberalism should be a major case in point. So was the effort in 1992 to uncover damaging information about Bill Clinton's student days in England — efforts aided and abetted by John Major and his Tory government in a noted attempt (that the Bush administration encouraged) to interfere with America's internal politics.[23] To this must be added Bush's willingness to pander to the far right, despite his awareness of its destructive aspects. His nominations of Dan Quayle for vice president and Clarence Thomas for associate justice of the Supreme Court were only the two most prominent instances. The Quayle selection was potentially the most harmful, but fortunately Quayle did not become president. Thomas, though, is likely to remain on the Court for decades. One might mention, also, Bush's invitation to one of the country's leading purveyors of misinformation and bigotry, Rush Limbaugh, to stay in the Lincoln Bedroom in the White House. When the Clintons moved in, there was a note from Limbaugh addressed to the first Clinton guests in that bedroom, their friends Harry and Linda Thomason. "Dear Linda," said the note (she and Limbaugh knew one another and had grown up together in Cape Girardeau, Missouri), "I was here first, and I'll be back," signed "Rush Limbaugh."[24] Undoubtedly, he has been.

The Bushes spent their last weekend at Camp David. The outgoing president and Mrs. Bush received the incoming Clintons graciously at the White House on 20 January 1993.[25] Also graciously, Bush left a note in his desk for the incoming President Clinton. He said that he didn't want to be overly dramatic — that would not have been his style — but that he did want Clinton to know that he "would be rooting for him."[26] They then attended President Clinton's inauguration, after which they and the Quayles flew by presidential helicopter to Andrews Air Force Base. From there, it was home to Houston for Barbara and George H. W. Bush, who had been the forty-first President of the United States.

42

WILLIAM JEFFERSON CLINTON
January 20, 1993–January 20, 2001

Bill Clinton became President of the United States at the age of forty-six. Only John F. Kennedy at forty-three, and Theodore Roosevelt at forty-two, were younger. Clinton was America's first president born after the Second World War. It has become commonplace to note also that he was the first two-term Democratic president since Franklin D. Roosevelt. Although that is correct, it is misleading. It is equally correct to say that Ronald Reagan was the only two-term Republican president since Dwight Eisenhower.

Harry S Truman filled nearly the full fourth term of FDR's and then won a term of his own. Lyndon B. Johnson filled the unexpired portion of Kennedy's, and then served his own after winning a landslide election. In both cases, there were two consecutive eight-year periods in which a Democrat served as president. It was similar for the Republicans when Nixon won re-election, but Ford completed his second term. It is equally accurate and equally meaningless to say that Wilson, FDR, and Clinton were the twentieth century's only Democratic presidents who served two full terms, or that Eisenhower and Reagan were the only two-term presidents of the century who were Republicans.

Clinton's presidency was an unusually tumultuous one. It began as the kind of success story that embodied the American dream. A child whose father died before he was born and who came from a rather poor home in a decidedly poor, small, Southern state rose to the heights. Clinton graduated from Georgetown and Yale, went to Oxford as a Rhodes scholar, became the youngest governor in the United States at the time, and ultimately became President of the United States.

The American success story seemed to end when Clinton's Democratic Party lost control of both houses of Congress in the 1994 elections. Although there were many close contests involved, and the victories might not have been the overwhelming repudiation of the Democrats that they seemed to be, the clear fact was that in 1994 no sitting governor, U.S. representative, or senator who ran for re-election as a Republican lost to a Democrat. In that sense, the elections were an overwhelming repudiation of the Democrats.

The tide turned once again when Clinton decisively won re-election in 1996, and the Republican speaker of the House, Newt Gingrich, resigned from Congress in humiliation. That triumph may once more have seemed hollow when Clinton became the only elected president in history to be impeached, but returned once again when the impeachment effort backfired upon its perpetrators. They not only were unable to persuade the Senate to convict Clinton and remove him from office — which would have required two-thirds of the senators to condemn the president — but they could not even obtain the simple majority that they no doubt would have used to claim at least a symbolic victory.

Truly, the eight colorful years of the Clinton presidency were extraordinary. The republic had never experienced anything like them. At last, however, the Twenty-Second Amendment — the petty and petulant posthumous blow directed against President Franklin Roosevelt's four electoral victories — benefited the party that had unwisely (and contrary to the wishes of the Founders) inserted it into the Constitution.

Previously, the Amendment had affected only two presidents, Eisenhower and Reagan, each of whom was a popular Republican. Certainly Ike could have won had he run again. As indicated earlier (see chapter 34), his son said that Ike would indeed have run for a third term if there had been no Twenty-Second Amendment.[1] Reagan loved being president, and might have run again had the Amendment not constrained him. His chances for success probably would have been less than Eisenhower's would have been. Ike without doubt retained his keen mental faculties, was not a vague and unconcerned administrator, and even though he was elderly, he was much younger than Reagan who was nearing his seventy-eighth birthday. Moreover, Ike did not have the Iran-Contra scandals to contend with — scandals that were so serious as *truly* to have been grounds for impeachment. Still, Reagan seemed to have retained much of his popularity when he left the presidency, so he might have been re-elected for a third term. The tactics that had worked to put George Bush in office might possibly have worked to keep Reagan there.

In 2000, however, the Amendment that had worked so effectively against the Republican Party that had originated it, unambiguously — and after half a century — worked in that party's favor. Bill Clinton became the first Democrat that it had prohibited from running again. There is no doubt that Clinton would have run for a third term if he had been able to do so. There is hardly any more doubt that he would have been re-elected. He was — and is — the best campaigner in American politics, and he could have campaigned upon the unbeatable issues of peace and unprecedented prosperity. Even the Democratic nominee, Vice President Gore — a less attractive candidate who refused to run on Clinton's record and thus sacrificed his major asset and whom the media constantly savaged — won the popular vote. No one can prove the point one way or the other, but it seems clear that the Twenty-Second Amendment saved the Republican Party from a third Clinton term as president.

Despite the recency of the Clinton presidency, it already is represented in numerous rating efforts. Genovese, for example, rated Clinton low in the average category — twenty-first of thirty-nine — just above the first Bush who held that category's last spot.[2] The Reuters 2000 ranking put him in the same place (it included all forty-one presidents up to that time).[3] Ridings and McIver, too, saw fit to rate Clinton (their list also included forty-one presidents), and they put him lower, in twenty-third place.[4] To their credit, they did mention that the respondents to their poll "indicated they feel somewhere between twenty-five and fifty years need to pass before a rational evaluation of a president can be made." They thus implicitly called into question the rationality of their own evaluation. They were perceptive, however, in noting that "one factor future historians are likely to take into account is the ravenous performance of the nation's media. President Clinton," they said, "has been subjected to more scrutiny than any other president in our history." They conceded that such intense probing would damage any president's reputation.[5] The Fabers, too, included Clinton in their scale, placing him eighteenth, in a tie with John Quincy Adams, among the thirty-nine they considered.[6] Note that all of these rating efforts included Clinton while he was still in office.

The Clinton presidency is so recent that it is unnecessary to treat it in detail. Merely hitting the high spots should suffice. There were so many, that even such a truncated effort will cover more than might seem likely at first glance.

On Clinton's first day in office, he removed the Bush administration's gag order on medical clinics that receive any federal funding. Bush's draconian order not only had forbidden physicians to refer women for abortions, it forbade them even to discuss the subject. More headlines were devoted to "gays in the military," an unsuccessful Clinton effort to expand civil rights. The compromise solution, "don't ask — don't tell," satisfied neither side but was an improvement over previous policy.

Clinton signed as his first bill the Family and Medical Leave Act. Bush twice had vetoed similar legislation. Gun control advocates were pleased when the new president signed the Brady Bill requiring a background check and a brief waiting period before purchasing a handgun. Many conservatives and the National Rifle Association predictably were outraged. On the other hand, conservatives generally were pleased and many liberals distressed when he signed the North American Free Trade Agreement (NAFTA). Union members were especially angry, fearing loss of American jobs, but in the long run building up Mexico's economy is a prerequisite to settling the great tensions—especially in border areas—between Mexico and the United States. NAFTA should be a step toward just such an improvement in Mexico's standard of living. One of Clinton's greatest accomplishments that first year in office was securing approval of his budget package. Its spending cuts and tax increases put the country on the road to elimination of the deficit and toward a balanced budget.

It took considerable political courage to advocate a tax increase in view of the anti-tax fervor that the Reagan years had generated. As it was, the measure barely passed the House, and required a tie-breaking vote by Vice President Gore in the Senate. Not a single Republican in either chamber voted for the Clinton budget—this was extraordinarily rare, and may in fact have been the only instance in history when a budget received not a single vote from the opposition party.

Republicans predicted that dire economic consequences would follow. Instead, the United States entered upon the most prosperous period in its history. During Clinton's eight years in office, the economy registered its fastest growth in three decades. His administration balanced the budget for the first time since LBJ's final budget, and began to operate with a large surplus. Unemployment plummeted as the economy generated tens of millions of new jobs. The crime rate dropped, as did the welfare rolls. The poverty rate also dropped dramatically, especially among black and Hispanic groups, and the stock market soared.

On the other hand, the early Clinton administration suffered several major blows. The first act of domestic terrorism by foreign nationals took place on 26 February 1993, when a truck exploded in the basement of the World Trade Center causing extensive damage. The perpetrators were quickly captured, tried, and convicted. On 19 April of that year, the Justice Department moved against the "Branch Davidians," a religious cult that had been stockpiling weapons and allegedly abusing children. During an attack on the Davidians' Waco, Texas, compound, a fire began, which killed numerous members of the group, including children. It was not the senseless attack as some critics alleged, but it clearly was mishandled. Attorney General Janet Reno took responsibility for the disaster.

The second major act of domestic terrorism took place on 19 April 1995. This time it was not Middle Eastern terrorists but a home-grown variety. Apparently angry over the Waco situation, Timothy McVeigh bombed a federal building in Oklahoma City, killing not only federal workers — including Social Security personnel — but also children in a day-care center. McVeigh, too, was captured and convicted, and Clinton quickly secured passage of anti-terrorist legislation. This was not the first terrorist act by an American. Abortion clinics for some time had been threatened with anthrax, had been bombed or burned, and their personnel had been subjected to terrorist activities ranging from threats and other harassment to actual assassination.

True humiliation came in foreign affairs. The Bush administration had deployed troops to Somalia for humanitarian reasons to counter a bloody civil war, and Clinton inherited the situation. As part of a United Nations peace-keeping mission, the forces were harassed with ambushed American troops wounded and killed. Images of the debacle flooded television. Clinton sent reinforcements but adopted more modest goals when Congress threatened to cut off funds.[7]

The greatest failure of the early Clinton presidency, however, was health care reform. Clinton had placed First Lady Hillary Rodham Clinton in charge of planning for the administration's new health initiative. She mastered the complicated details quickly, and working with a huge group of advisers created a complex proposal. At first, all sides agreed that because the need was so great, something would be done. As time progressed, the plan's complexity worked against it, and the opponents began to sense that they might be able to head off the program.

The president had insisted on universal coverage. The proposal provided it, but was built upon the traditional American approach to health care delivery. Instead of opting to utilize the government as a single payer, as the Canadian system does, the plan involved employer mandates. Employers would be required to provide insurance coverage, and would have received government subsidy if they were too small, or if the cost of coverage exceeded a certain level.

Public support for the program began to erode when opponents launched an unprecedented publicity campaign. Special interest lobbies such as the Health Insurance Association of America and the National Federation of Independent Business poured almost unlimited amounts into the campaign. Critics began to charge hysterically that Clinton was planning a "government health-care grab," and that he wanted to "socialize one-seventh of the U.S. economy." Such claims were preposterous. The Clinton administration had worked strenuously to ensure the continuation of private medicine, and to retain private insurance mechanisms.

Thus, their proposal had the virtue of avoiding radical solutions, but that meant also that it kept some of the most unsatisfactory features of America's health care delivery system — such as payment through notoriously inefficient private insurance, which had created part of the existing problem. It would have been a stronger proposal if there had been *greater* government involvement and control.[8] As it was, support dwindled and the proposal died without ever coming to a vote in Congress. All sides shared the blame for missing a rare opportunity, and one of America's most severe troubles continued — and still continues — to worsen.

The loss of health care weakened public confidence in the Clinton administration, and contributed to the Republican takeover of both houses of Congress after the 1994 elections. It was the first time that both the House and Senate had come under Republican control since January of 1955.

Clinton nemesis Newt Gingrich became the new House speaker. The new Republican majority proceeded as though the president were irrelevant. They overreached. Twice, in late 1995 and early 1996, they forced a government shutdown by sending Clinton appropriation measures that cut taxes, Medicare, and education — measures that he would not accept. He vetoed the measures, the Republicans refused to pass continuing resolutions to keep the government operating (some of the more extreme members had such anti-government attitudes that they assumed the country would be just as well off without a functioning government), and each time most government functions ground to a halt. The public saw the president as resolute and principled — instead of merely an opportunist as many had thought him to be — and saw his Republican opponents as rigid ideologues. Clinton's poll numbers soared.

One major factor — much mentioned but little recognized — shaped Bill Clinton's presidency. As *Washington Post* reporter John Harris put it, there was a "well-coordinated corps of aggrieved and methodical people who start[ed] each day looking for ways to expose and undermine" the new president.[9] Such a gang, he said, was lying in wait for Clinton in 1993:

> Conservative interest groups, commentators and congressional investigators waged a remorseless campaign that they hoped would make life miserable for Clinton and vault themselves to power. They succeeded in many ways. One of the most important was their ability to take all manner of presidential miscues, misjudgments or controversial decisions and exploit them for maximum effect. Stories like the travel office firings flamed for weeks instead of receding into yesterday's news. And they colored the prism through which many Americans, not just conservative ideologues, viewed Clinton.

Harris added that "the liberal equivalent of this conservative coterie does not exist.

It was elements of this "coterie," as Harris called it, that spread rumors that the suicide of Clinton aide and friend Vince Foster was actually a murder to keep him from "telling what he knew" about "Whitewater." Rush Limbaugh reported a rumor — complete nonsense — that Foster had died, not in the park where his body had been found, but in an apartment owned by Hillary Clinton. The more paranoid elements of the far-right fringe went even further, accusing the Clintons of a series of murders and of drug-running (some even accused former President Bush of being involved). Jerry Falwell hawked a videotape over television that portrayed Clinton as a multiple murderer.

The Travel Office firings should have been a simple matter, not a major scandal. The Travel Office in the White House arranges transportation for journalists who travel with the president, and its personnel are presidential employees who serve at the president's pleasure. Replacing them is, without question, within his authority. The special situation was that through the years the employees had ingratiated themselves with members of the press whom they served, the reporters reacted emotionally when their friends lost their positions, and the press therefore built up the episode into something that it was not.

National reporters and other Washington insiders form a smug, small, closely-knit, community; a "village," as some call it. The Clintons were interlopers who refused to play by their rules, and refused, as Eric Alterman observed, "to pay proper heed to their superior social grace and aristocratic breeding." He quoted the "dean" of Washington correspondents, David Broder, as saying to "famed Georgetown hostess and sometime reporter Sally Quinn," that Clinton "came in here and he trashed the place, and it's not his place." Equally on point were the comments of David Gergen, "editor at large at *U.S. News and World Report*," sometime highly visible conservative commentator on PBS and other "liberal" media who also had served in both the Reagan and Clinton administrations. "We all live together," Gergen said, "we have a sense of community, there's a small-town quality here. We all understand we do certain things, we make certain compromises," but a "cardinal rule of the village" was that one doesn't "foul the nest." Thus, as Alterman noted perceptively, "in a 'community' where everyone thinks pretty much the same thoughts, actual reporting is beside the point."[10]

To display their disdain for the Clintons reporters did even more with "Whitewater" than they did with the firings from the Travel Office. Whitewater was a small land deal in Arkansas years before, in which the Clintons were investors, and because of which they lost money.[11] Lurid allegations emerged that there was something sinister — no one specified exactly what it was, perhaps it was shady loans or inappropriate official influence, yet those in the press "knew" that it was there — and it ultimately led to the appointment of an independent counsel (a "special prosecutor") to investigate the Clintons' involvement.

The first independent counsel, Robert Fiske (a Republican), had investigated the Foster suicide thoroughly (as had the police) and found that it was just that, a tragic suicide. He also investigated Whitewater, but turned up nothing to damage the Clintons. In any case, Fiske was insufficiently dedicated to destroying the Clinton presidency. A three-judge panel replaced him with Kenneth Starr, who suffered no such disability.

Try as he might, Starr could find no evidence of any Clinton wrongdoing in Whitewater. He therefore requested permission to expand the scope of his inquiry. A woman from Arkansas, Paula Jones, had filed suit against Clinton, alleging that he had made advances to her in a Little Rock hotel room many years before when he was governor. She said she refused his advances, and departed. Nothing, she said, happened. Later, she decided to ask for damages. Clinton's opponents with extraordinary cynicism began to portray her suit as a "civil rights" case.

Starr received permission to expand his inquiry into Clinton's testimony in the Jones suit — a suit that had absolutely nothing to do with Whitewater. Ultimately, he discovered that Clinton had had a sexual encounter with a White House intern in her twenties, Monica Lewinsky — an encounter that had nothing to do with the Jones case, which had nothing to do with Whitewater, and that was in no way illegal.

Instead of investigating if there had been a crime and, if so, determining who was guilty, the Starr proceedings turned the function of the judicial system on its head. In true police-state fashion, Starr changed his investigation to center on a specific person to determine whether he might discover something damaging to that person, regardless of the existence of a crime. He made it clear that he no longer was seeking to uncover what happened regarding Whitewater, but that he was using the investigative power of the federal government, working closely with an opposition faction within Congress, to seek to destroy the President of the United States.

If the president had not committed a crime, perhaps Starr could cause him to commit one — to commit perjury in defending himself against questions that should never be asked, that is, about conduct that, although certainly embarrassing, was not illegal. Such was the media frenzy at the time that no reporter thought to point out the obvious danger: the misuse of governmental power. The misuse was not Clinton's feeble effort to avoid embarrassment but, rather, the misuse of investigative authority for partisan purposes. If such tactics can be brought to bear against the most powerful official in the world, they could be brought against any other person as well — and other persons have incomparably fewer resources with which to defend themselves.

When Starr ultimately released his report to Congress, the country was exposed to sexual detail and intrusive questioning that could appeal only to

the most prurient. The preoccupation with the sexual suggested the patho-
logical — not on the part of Clinton, but on the part of Starr and his inves-
tigators. It made the Clarence Thomas hearings appear discreet, and did the
Republican case against President Clinton no good.

As an example of the character of the actions against the Clinton administration, consider the prosecution of Clinton's first secretary of Housing and
Urban Development, Henry Cisneros. The prosecution was unrelated to
anything he did as a member of the administration. Instead, it centered upon
the information that Cisneros gave to the FBI when being investigated for
the cabinet appointment. At one time, he had had an affair. He admitted it.
He had paid his mistress to buy her silence, and had admitted that. The substance of the prosecution was that he had lied to the FBI, a federal crime,
because he misstated the *amount* of money he had paid her. That was all,
but it was sufficient to bring about his resignation, and ultimately his conviction.

Although the Republicans initially had assumed that Clinton would
lose the 1996 election, he won re-election handily. If not by a landslide, he
won certainly by a greater margin than his victory in 1992. He did not quite
receive a majority of the popular vote (he did take more than 49 percent,
but third-party candidate Ross Perot took over 8 percent). Republican candidate former Senator Robert Dole, however, received less than 41 percent.
Clinton received 379 electoral votes, more than 70 percent.[12] In 1998 during the off-year elections, the unthinkable happened. His party actually
gained seats in the House of Representatives. Off year elections usually bring
a loss of seats to the party of the president in power; for the president's party'
actually to gain seats in the *sixth year* of his presidency had not happened
since the two-party system had emerged.

Despite the Democratic gains in the house, the Republicans retained
control of both houses. After the election, a group of zealots in the House
of Representatives — including some who had been voted out of office — in
a lame duck session voted to impeach President Clinton. Some of those supporting impeachment had urged it since 1995, before the Monica Lewinsky
episode. Freshman Representative Robert Barr of Georgia had in fact before
that episode introduced an impeachment resolution.

Legislation passed in one house at the end of a congressional term but
not approved by the other house before the session ends, dies. The impeachment resolution should therefore have died with the end of the lame-duck
session, since it was too late for the Senate to deal with it. In 1999, however, the Republican-led Senate, in deference to its Republican colleagues
in the House, acted upon the impeachment resolution, and convened itself
on 7 January 1999 as a judicial body to consider the two articles of impeachment against President Clinton. On 12 January, the Senate acquitted the

president on both counts. On the first article, perjury, the vote for conviction was forty-five, all Republicans; on the second, obstruction of justice, fifty senators, all Republicans, voted for conviction. On the first article, ten Republicans voted with the Democrats for acquittal; on the second, five Republicans did so. Six days later, Clinton gave his State of the Union Address. It was a superb speech, and his popularity soared.

Evaluating such a complex presidency as that of Bill Clinton is challenging enough. Distilling it down to a place in a ranking is impossible. It had great strengths, and also great weaknesses. Assessing the weaknesses is different from those of any other presidency, because of the uniquely fierce opposition that Clinton faced from his political enemies and nearly all of the media.

In terms of civil liberties, the Clinton record was bad irrespective of attacks from his enemies. If he had an intellectual appreciation of traditional American freedoms, it did not shine through in his political positions. There were questions about his anti-terrorism bill (albeit nothing like those that could be levied against the "Patriot Act" under George W. Bush), and it should have been clear to him that the Communications Decency Act — designed to prohibit "indecency" (which is not a legal term) from the Internet — that he signed was unconstitutional (as the Court later declared). The same can be said with regard to Clinton's support for the "war on drugs" and the violations of civil liberties that it involves.

In terms of ethical standards, that most criticized feature of the Clinton administration, it actually appears that the administration fares better than those of other recent presidents, even disregarding Nixon's. "The total number of convictions experienced by the Reagan administration, which, like the Clinton administration, enjoyed two terms in office, was thirty-two, of which two were overturned on appeal. Fourteen of these were related to the Iran/Contra scandal; sixteen to the HUD housing scandals; and two to illegal lobbying of the Administration by ex-officials." In the first Bush administration, its one term saw indictments of seven officials. "Five were convicted and five officials were pardoned before they could be sentenced or convicted. For the Clinton administration, the sum of officials indicted is zero."[13] (There were two Clinton officials, Secretary of HUD Henry Cisneros and Assistant Attorney Webster Hubbell, who resigned and received convictions for actions committed before they took office. "Neither of these actions was taken while the person was in office or was in any way connected to his official duties.")[14]

On the environment, the picture is much brighter. Clinton was the most environmentally active president since Theodore Roosevelt. Carl Pope, executive director of the Sierra Club, said that Clinton will be remembered as one of the great defenders of the environment, "not only for everything the administration accomplished, but for all they things they stopped Congress from doing." The Wilderness Society declared him to be "one of the top conservation presidents of all time." He banned road building and most commercial logging on almost 60 million acres of public forests, "a patchwork of pristine woodlands that together would almost equal the size of Oregon." His clean-air standards were the "toughest in a generation." He created eleven new national monuments and increased the size of others. The list goes on and on. "However controversial, what the Clinton administration accomplished on the environmental front over eight years by all measures is significant in its scope, and in some cases, audacious." Much of what he accomplished he did on his own executive authority, using power granted to the president by the Antiquities Act of 1906 — an act that bore Theodore Roosevelt's signature. "He worked around a hostile Congress by brokering deals with state and local governments and industries; by rewriting and strengthening rules and regulations of existing laws; and by executive actions that did not require congressional involvement or approval."[15] No president since TR has been so active or so concerned regarding conservation.

On the economy, the picture also is bright. Despite claims from the left that Clinton abandoned the poor, those in the middle income groups and lower "made their biggest gains since" LBJ's Great Society. "According to Census Bureau figures, the gap between rich and poor remained virtually unchanged" during Clinton's presidency. "Given the enormous gains of families at the top during the 1990s, even holding inequality essentially stable has to be seen as a kind of triumph, for it required significant advances for workers on the economy's lower rungs as well."[16] Welfare reform was popular with the public, as was elimination of the deficit and the accumulation of a huge surplus.

With regard to foreign affairs, especially terrorism, Clinton reacted forcefully — and often faced resistance from Congress. He asked for legislation proposing "taggants — chemical markers in explosives that could help track terrorists," and Senator Orrin Hatch, Chairman of the Judiciary Committee, called it a "phony issue."[17] Despite predictions from such neo-conservatives as the frequently mistaken Jeane Kirkpatrick that the Clinton administration's involvement in Haiti would result in a "bloodbath," Clinton's policy there was quite successful. Regarding Iraq, as Steve Ricchetti, Clinton's former deputy chief of staff, put it, Iraq was far weaker in 2003 than it had been because of the Clinton administration's efforts. These included sanctions, enforcement of "no-fly" zones, and military action including air strikes. He cited terrorist plots stopped in and out of the country, a doubling of counterterrorism funding, the arrests of dozens of terrorist fugitives, and use of force against Osama bin Laden and Iraq — this, by the way, received much criticism as "grandstanding." Ricchetti pointed to

"America's successful efforts to stop ethnic cleansing and genocide in the Balkans," and the fact that the country was better able to handle "these challenges at the end of the Clinton administration than at the beginning."[18] The military that was so successful in Iraq in 2003, one should note, was the military that Clinton bequeathed to George W. Bush.

As one might expect of both Clinton and his critics, he left office to tremendous complaints, this time regarding a plethora of last-minute pardons. As noted previously, such pardons are far from unique. Overall, throughout his presidency Clinton issued 456 pardons, placing him somewhat ahead of Reagan's 406, far ahead of the first Bush's 77, somewhat behind Carter's 566, but far behind Eisenhower's 1157.[19] The only criticisms of any substance pertained to clemency for four Hasidic Jews in New York, and of financier Marc Rich. The Hasidic men had received convictions for "bilking the state and federal government of tens of millions of dollars."[20] There were speculations that the pardons were in return for their influence in persuading the Hasidic community to support Hillary Clinton in her race for the Senate. President George W. Bush's U.S. Attorney for the Southern District of New York investigated, and found nothing that would warrant prosecution. Regarding Rich, prominent Israeli leaders including Prime Minister Ehud Barak and Shimon Peres had urged the pardon, as had prominent Americans such as Elie Wiesel. In any case, as noted earlier, the power to pardon is absolute, even if the person receiving the pardon is George Steinbrenner, Armand Hammer, one of the Iran/Contra conspirators — or Marc Rich.

In evaluating Clinton's presidency, one should probably be lenient because of the enormous and unprecedented opposition that Clinton faced. In spite of the obstacles, he accomplished a great deal. One should also avoid the gratuitous comments that have become universal — condemning his "character," his moral example, and the like. It is not necessary to defend his lapses and his poor judgment, but one should remember that no other public official has ever been so exposed — none has ever had more than $70 million of public funds expended in an effort to bring him down and smear his record. Nor has any official had so many untrue allegations thrown at him to add to his actual conduct. "What is perhaps not adequately remembered is the utter baselessness of many of the charges that reasonable people took seriously at the time."[21] It is quite clear now, for example, *not* that there merely was "insufficient evidence to prosecute the Clintons," with regard to Whitewater, but, rather, that the Clintons in fact had done nothing wrong. If they had, certainly a determined prosecutor who had more than $70 million to spend would have been able to discover it. There has been no apology, however, from such paragons of journalistic integrity as the *Washington Post* and the *New York Times* that time and again blasted the

Clintons editorially and also in their news columns for their Whitewater "misdeeds," without a shred of valid evidence.[22]

Perhaps Clinton's greatest accomplishment may be that he saved the presidency. That may sound strange, because so many people argue that his efforts to defend himself *weakened* the presidency by bringing adverse court rulings, and the like. Nevertheless, impeachment was not the result of Monica Lewinsky, however much that episode may have given Clinton's opponents camouflage for their aims. "Well before the Lewinsky affair became public, a group of influential conservatives in the media had met to help Rep. Bob Barr (R. Ga.) on an impeachment resolution. The resolution lacked detail, referring only to a 'systematic abuse of office.' According to a *Wall Street Journal* editor who appeared supportive of impeachment, what was important was not the law or the Constitution but merely 'political will'."[23]

One president had already resigned the office. President Nixon had been forced to surrender his position in 1974, and for very good reasons. Roughly a quarter of a century later there was another effort to oust a president. In Nixon's case, his opponents were acting on sound constitutional principles, and were bipartisan. In Clinton's case, they were acting merely on "political will," were clearly partisan, and were acting on reasons that had nothing to do with Clinton's performance as president. If Clinton had been forced to resign, or had been removed from office — the second president in roughly a quarter of a century — there would then be a clear precedent for removals for political disagreements, regardless of the will of the voters.

Because of unwise Supreme Court decisions, a sitting president now can be forced to defend himself against a civil suit — anyone, of course, can sue anyone for anything — and a president's closest aides, even his bodyguards, can be forced to testify regarding their conversations with the president, conversations they may have overheard, or conduct that they may have seen. The political atmosphere in Washington during the last decade or two has become so poisoned that Republicans and Democrats no longer try to defeat one another on policy, but then set aside their differences and interact socially — they often attempt to destroy one another. Add to that the intrusive media that not only ferret out every possible bit of information, but that have become willing to publicize rumors and innuendo without basis in fact.

Given this mix of factors, if Clinton had left the office before his term was over, especially because of charges unrelated to his performance as president, it is quite likely that no president — except possibly the most innocuous — could ever again survive a full term. There would be no shortage of people trying to bring a president down, and no shortage of tools for them to accomplish their goal. The presidency is the key to the success of America's political system. Without a strong presidential office, it is doubtful that the system could continue — in any case, it would be vastly changed.

One thing is virtually certain. Without a strong president, there can be no hope for progressive policies in the United States. The odds are strongly against such policies in any case. Bill Clinton, then, for all his faults, should receive credit for the accomplishments of his administration, and for his personal strength, skill, and pure toughness that enabled him to beat back the powerful forces that were opposing not only the Clinton presidency but also the *American* presidency.

43

GEORGE W. BUSH

January 20, 2001–

Some distance from presidencies is necessary for the soundest evaluation. No doubt it is too close even to Clinton's administration to make the best of assessments. So, should one wait until George W. Bush is out of office to evaluate him? No. Evaluations of presidents in office are hazardous, but they are inevitable — even necessary. There will be no ranking, of course.

The election that put Bush in office did so only because it was so close as to be virtually a tie, making it possible for the institutions that were under Republican control to make the decision. Those institutions were Florida's legislature, Florida's secretary of state, Florida's governor (who was the brother of the chosen candidate), the U.S. House of Representatives, and the Supreme Court of the United States. It was the most tumultuous electoral situation since 1876. Only twice before had the electoral college selected the loser of the popular vote. It chose Benjamin Harrison in 1888 with little fanfare, and Rutherford B. Hayes in 1876 after much turmoil.

In no election in American history except for the Hayes victory did the electoral college choose a winner with a smaller majority than that of George W. Bush.[1] After the 1876 election, the delayed decision did not come until just before inauguration day in 1877. In that case, Congress appointed a committee to determine which of two sets of disputed electoral votes should be counted. The committee consisted of fifteen persons and all its decisions came along strict party lines. In 2000, it was the Supreme Court that made the decision — an even smaller group than the 1877 commission and one that was as thoroughly partisan. The Court's decision giving the election to Bush was five to four.

Bush had not only less than a majority, but also actually fewer popular votes than his opponent. Nevertheless, he began immediately to act as though he had won by a landslide. Despite this, there was little protest. Nor was there a massive public outcry about the failure of modern technology. "The lightning-fast technology of the twenty-first century proved unreliable in winning the campaign, predicting the election, or even counting the vote."[2] Florida, the key state, presented a bizarre mixture of election procedures that were confusing and incompetent and at the same time it was under the control of the winning candidate's brother and dominated by his political party. Even the revelation of such a banana-republic structure was insufficient to propel the country toward reform, except for a bit of posturing in Congress about updating electoral processes.

As always, of course, there were a few conspiracy theorists. The most fervent of these even drew dark connections between Bush's victory and the fact that his father at one time had headed the CIA. Regardless of the speculation surrounding the victory (all politicians "plot" to win, and some now and then certainly transgress the boundaries of good conduct), there was one clear and disturbing fact. Because the election was so close, despite the will of the people and no matter what the vote showed, the political institutions were arrayed so strongly against Democrat Al Gore that he had no possibility of becoming president. The Florida legislature made no secret of its "stop-at-nothing" fervor and openly declared its intention to guarantee that the Republican candidate would win. "In order to insure a victory for George Bush, the legislators threatened to choose the Florida electors themselves, regardless of the outcome of any court-ordered recounts."[3]

It did not have to come to that. The actual ballot count was still underway when the U.S. Supreme Court stepped into the state contest and decided the issue. It was "a bitter 5–4 division" that determined the outcome. "The choice of 104 million Americans depended on the voices of seven Republican and two Democratic lifetime appointees," said political scientist Gerald Pomper. There was, however, reason to celebrate. Bush's selection "resulted from confusing ballots, incompetent election administration, institutional flaws, and irreconcilable partisanship," but despite all that "the United States could take satisfaction in that it had chosen the most powerful leader in the world in relative calm and by constitutional means."[4]

Even though the public quickly turned its attention away from the way in which he became president, Bush did immediately face difficulties. The shaky election was less the cause than were two other factors. First, former President Bill Clinton still dominated the headlines even though he was out of office. If he and Bush gave talks the same day, Clinton's press coverage was likely to overwhelm Bush's — not from any media bias, but simply because of Clinton's penetrating intellect and his magnetic personality, and Bush's poor speaking ability.

Second, Bush had to contend with the widespread belief that he was inexperienced, poorly qualified, and probably not up to the job. Vice President Cheney's unusual visibility created the impression that he might really be the one in command. The worst of Bush's critics even questioned his mental capacity. Similar criticisms had circulated, of course, about Ronald Reagan. It had proven dangerous to underestimate either one, Bush or Reagan, as Pat Brown, Jimmy Carter, and Ann Richards no doubt would verify.

All this changed suddenly with the events of 9/11. Bush had been the country's leader in reality, but there was question whether the country accepted him as its symbol. The terrorist attacks brought him symbolic leadership as well. Vice President Cheney remained as active and visible as ever — even from his "undisclosed locations." Cheney remains the only vice president in history, even including Jefferson, who ever overshadowed the president — but no longer did the public question Bush's control. Bush no longer had to contend with Clinton for media coverage, even though Clinton still commanded attention from the press. When Bush's mid-term arrived, for example, not only did Clinton fail to overshadow him in the media, but also Bush's Republican Party triumphed in the congressional elections. There were a number of significant factors in this, including both congressional redistricting after 2000 and lackluster performance on the part of many Democrats, but Bush and his administration deserve substantial credit.

In response to the 9/11 crisis, Bush talked tough, ordered attacks on Afghanistan, and appeared firm and resolute. Of course, Bush did stay far from the capital until danger had passed, unlike James Madison, who had rallied residents personally when the British attacked Washington during the War of 1812. This brought Bush no negative publicity, though, and the media assured the public that his absence was justified. One explanation at the time was that there had been a threat to Air Force One (there was no reason given why Bush would have had to fly on Air Force One). Nevertheless, the public began to perceive Bush, much like Harry Truman, as one who seemed to have "grown in office."

Bush skillfully reassured a worried population. He exhorted it to maintain America's values and demonstrate its resolve to the world (one thing citizens could do would be to go shopping). No one paid attention to history, except to mention the obvious parallel with Pearl Harbor — the parallel was certainly real, although the Japanese attack had been much more devastating in a military sense. Perhaps it would have seemed in poor taste to point it out, but the obvious truth was that any president would have acted similarly in response to a direct attack on United States soil. There can be absolutely no doubt that Clinton, the first Bush, Reagan, Carter, Ford, Nixon, Johnson, Kennedy, Eisenhower, Truman, Franklin Roosevelt, or any other president would have been equally firm and resolute. It was Bush, though, who was in office.

Bush had without doubt grown to fill the symbolic presidency. Much as Reagan had done, he announced that America's enemies could run but not hide. Bush announced that capturing Osama bin Laden would be a measure of his success, and Americans quite justifiably invaded Afghanistan. Although Osama was able after all not only to run but also to hide, the odious Taliban regime fell from power in that unfortunate country. Bush received credit for that achievement, and he deserved that credit; Americans seemed to understand the obvious difficulties in capturing a well-financed fugitive who had an extensive organization. So, despite his comment, the public at least thus far has not held Bush accountable for Osama's escape.

The public similarly has not held Bush accountable for the failure to find the anthrax terrorist or terrorists. After a flurry of concern regarding the mailing of anthrax-laden letters and packages to officials (the recipients seem mostly to have been liberal Democrats, although postal workers tended to be the ones most frequently harmed), public attention appeared to have vanished. The responsible party is still at large.

Similarly, when Bush changed the subject from Osama and began instead to speak of invading Iraq, there were very few questions about such bait-and-switch tactics. Suddenly, it was as though Osama had morphed into Saddam Hussein. If we cannot find Osama, then Saddam, another Arab, will do. He is a murderous tyrant. We know he "aided terrorists" even if the most strenuous effort has failed to link him to 9/11.

Bush declared in his 2003 State of the Union message that Saddam Hussein had to go. More than any other reason was that he threatened the world with "weapons of mass destruction." The Americans did go into Iraq in a pre-emptive war (thereby setting a questionable precedent), and were quickly victorious. Hussein after a period of months did go.

As for weapons of mass destruction, the Bush administration in July 2003 admitted that Bush had cited forged evidence in his State of the Union message. The British government, too, conceded shortly thereafter that if weapons of mass destruction had been in Iraq, they would likely have been found already; therefore they probably never would be. Bush's excuse to the public when questioned about the use of doubtful evidence in one of the presidency's major addresses was that it had been the fault of the CIA. Harry Truman was known for saying, "the buck stops here." The Bush version is "the buck stops somewhere else — it's not my fault."

Initially, Bush benefited from low expectations. His actions immediately following 9/11 had been indisputably presidential. He deserved much credit for rallying the country, and helping restore its weakened morale. He also deserves credit for protecting the president's authority — authority that had been under assault from Congress and the courts during the Clinton administration.

Clinton had, of course, contributed to his own difficulties, but in no way had he created them. He deserves great credit for standing firm when a lesser person would have crumbled. By fending off the assaults, Clinton arguably saved the vital effectiveness of the American presidency. His employed his political skills to preserve the authority of the office against continuous legal attacks, a ferociously partisan impeachment, and adverse court rulings that often were no less partisan.

It is wise to give credit where it is due. President Bush should be commended for continuing to protect the office. That credit should be qualified, however, because his success results to a great extent from his relatively fortunate situation. His partisans are strong and in control; his opponents in no way have the passion to defeat — even to destroy — him regardless of the consequences that Clinton's did. Bush's opponents, in any case are wary of damaging the presidency in a way that Clinton's attackers were not.

Bush has so far succeeded in withholding information from Congress and the public that undoubtedly should be revealed. It is ironic that Congress and the courts insisted that Clinton make available all information — however trivial, however personal — even when it had no relation to the performance of presidential duties. Bush is attempting to withhold information that pertains not even to his, but to his *vice* president's advisers, and it is information related directly to the formation of the administration's energy policy. On 8 July 2003, the U.S. Court of Appeals for the District of Columbia ruled in a two-to-one decision that "the Bush administration must comply with a district court order to release the information,"[5] but, as of this writing, there has been no resolution.

It is clearly wrong for the Bush administration to attempt to withhold such relevant information, especially when compared to the Clinton precedents, but it does reflect an awareness of the need for presidential strength. Because a strong presidency is vital to the success of the American political system, both Presidents Clinton and Bush have made their contributions to the political stability of the United States — even though both may be justly criticized for actions that range from unwise to dangerous.

In the case of Bush, many of those actions may result from inexperience and limited background. Politically, in many ways he is highly skilled, but he seems to have little awareness of or interest in policy nuances. In Florida, he acted as if he were a clear winner when nothing was clear. Similarly, he entered the presidency acting as though he had won by a landslide. Initially, he had proposed a huge tax cut because of the large budget surplus. After he took office and the surplus turned into a deficit, he continued to push the tax cut, changing only his rationale. He has been equally intransigent with regard to many other policies. One of the most significant is Social Security. He was the first president ever to call openly from the White House for privatization. Initially, he justified privatization because of the booming stock market. After the stock market collapsed, he continued to call for privatization — when even many of its advocates have muted their support. In some ways he has been consistent, regardless of the circumstances. If he were better read, he might have been instructed by Emerson's admonition that a foolish consistency is the hobgoblin of little minds.

The Democrats for whatever reason have been ineffective in countering Bush's leadership. As indicated, Bush does deserve credit, but this credit, too, must be qualified. It was his petty arrogance early in his term that gave the Senate to the Democrats. His heavy-handed policy was the primary factor leading to the departure of Senator James Jeffords from the Republican Party. In a Senate that had been divided fifty-fifty, that was so arrogant as to be not only reckless, but also demonstrably foolish.

From the beginning, Bush's inexperience has been evident in his bluster that has antagonized other countries, and in his disregarding of the United Nations and of world opinion. He seemed for a time to be learning quickly, but then reverted to his tendency to act unilaterally if need be. His speech before the UN was excellent, despite his limited speaking abilities. When he urged the world body to act against Iraq, he said if it did not act the UN would be admitting that it would not enforce its own resolutions. The reaction to his speech — both in the United States and abroad — was favorable.

On the other hand, he did not receive UN support for military action, and refused to wait for the results of weapons inspections in Iraq. The British government of Tony Blair supported him, as did a few less significant states. Therefore, the invading troops came to be called the "coalition forces."

At times it has been difficult to distinguish whether Bush's actions reflect inexperience or simple petulance. He refused, for example, to congratulate German Chancellor Gerhard Schroeder following the chancellor's re-election in September 2002, because Schroeder had spoken against Bush's proposed invasion of Iraq. Bush reacted similarly with regard to France's opposition to his war plans. He thus not only violated international norms of courtesy, but succeeded in making the President of the United States seem petty. Schroeder, by way of contrast, announced to the Associated Press to a spokesman that he would congratulate Bush on the Republican victories in the mid-term elections.[6] When some American officials began referring to the American fast-food staple as "freedom fries," it only added to the impression, making the entire government appear petty.

CNN's Senior Correspondent, Sheila MacVicar, said that "in large parts of Europe they simply do not get George Bush. They do not understand his appeal," or his high approval ratings. They remember instead his election "perhaps under dubious claims of legitimacy," and see him as a "non-communicator" who does not listen to America's allies.[7]

Canada's Andrew Cohen said of the president, "for the incurious, untutored Mr. Bush, the least experienced and least distinguished president to take office since the 19th century, the last year has been the on-the-job training his critics had feared. The man who denounced the United Nations, rejected nation-building in Afghanistan, opposed campaign finance reform, and derided 'Washington' at every turn has learned much about coalitions, the obligations of a superpower, and the uses of government in domestic security." Bush now faces, continued Cohen, "the challenge of an unravelling economy: a falling stock market, weak job creation, and corporate malfeasance." He argued that if Bush had known of Theodore Roosevelt, "he would have understood how a president can contain big business." Because of his background, though, "he couldn't and didn't." His conclusion was that the post-9/11 Bush is what he always was: an accidental president.[8] Cohen wrote these words some three months before Bush's victories in the mid-term elections, but many of the challenges he cited remain.

Along the same lines, Thomas Friedman reported in the *New York Times* that Bush, should he choose to visit there, would likely be greeted in Germany with demonstrations requiring tear gas to control. Friedman said that this would not reflect anti–Americanism per se, because a month earlier former President Clinton visited Berlin to help unveil the refurbished Brandenburg Gate, and Germans "swarmed," him, clamoring "to see, hear or shake hands with" the former President of the United States. He attributed the difference to what he termed America's historic use of a combination of "hard power and soft power." That, he quoted a German official as saying, was what brought down the Soviet Union — not merely force, but also the soft side that reflects a naive optimism about human nature, and a commitment to the rule of law. In contrast, "when the Bush folks sneer at things like the World Court or Kyoto, and virtually every other treaty — without offering any alternatives but their own righteous power — they '"project an arrogance and obsession with power alone.'" Friedman was quoting a European political theorist, Yaron Ezrahi, who went on to say that "this undermines the American idealism that made Europe aspire to emancipate itself from the history that brought us World Wars I and II, it delegitimizes American power as an instrument of justice and international order and it makes it impossible for the rest of the world to stand up and say: 'I am a New Yorker.'" This, Friedman, wrote, is precisely what Al Queda's strategy encourages: the conversion of the United States into a "nation of pessimists."[9] The tragedy of all this is increased by the international good will for the United States that Bush's policies and attitudes have destroyed. Following 9/11, much of the world was sympathetic to the United States in its time of national trauma. Bush succeeded in squandering that good will so quickly and so dramatically that it warranted a front-page story titled, "Global Warmth for U.S. After 9/11 Turns to Frost."[10]

There are many other example of ill-considered policies. Civil liberties groups are up in arms about many of the restrictions that the Bush administration and its Attorney General, John Ashcroft, have adopted. Perhaps even more serious, the *New York Times* for 17 November 2002 reported that the Bush administration was considering resumption of nuclear testing. If this were to occur, it would be another instance of ignorance of the possible consequences, or possibly even of an arrogant lack of concern.

The presidency of George W. Bush has fallen short in many ways, despite Bush's apparently continuing popularity. This is not policy disagreement, which will always occur even among reasonable and well-informed people. Rather it is the indication that Bush has little clear understanding of the likely effects of his policies. Often, he seems to be acting with little or no true goal.

Bush's unilateral withdrawal from treaties with apparently little thought is an example. Yet another may be seen in his environmental policies. When the Environmental Protection Administration issued a report reflecting the strong consensus among scientists that global warming is a reality, and that human activities contribute considerably to it, President Bush dismissed the concern. He said that he had read "the report issued by the bureaucrats," as though that damned it. He gave no indication that he even recognized that they were his bureaucrats, that it was even his administration that issued the report.

At least as disturbing is the Bush tendency to make questionable, or even demonstrably false, assertions. In October 2002, in a nationally televised talk he warned that Saddam Hussein had an increasing fleet of unmanned aircraft potentially "for missions targeting the United States." He also said that October that objections from unions to a requirement that customs officers wear radiation detectors could delay implementing security policy "for a long time." The previous September, he said that there was a report from the International Atomic Energy Agency that Iraq was "six months away from developing a weapon." As Dana Milbank of the *Washington Post* said, "Further information revealed that the aircraft lack the range to reach the United States; there was no such report by the IAEA; and the customs dispute over the detectors was resolved long ago." Milbank quoted Brookings Institution scholar Stephen Hess as saying that such comments are "about public policy in the grandest sense, about potential wars and who is our enemy, and a president has a special obligation to getting it right." He was most worried, he said, that many such comments from Bush were not mistakes, but "appear to be with foresight."[11] The article contained a substantial list of untruths in Bush's statements. As of July 2003, there is national concern building that Bush used the existence of Iraqi weapons of mass destruction as his rationale for invading that country, asserting clearly that he had solid evidence when none existed. Former Nixon administration official and Watergate figure John Dean has even questioned whether "lying about the reason for war" is an impeachable offense.[12]

Even the cautious and courteous columnist David Broder has expressed concerns about Bush's policies and his capabilities. He has described "something both compelling and disturbing about his mental process." Bush, he wrote, has the capacity to take "even the most weighty presidential decisions and refine them down to the simplest terms." Regarding Iraq, for example, Bush repeated over and over his justification for going to war: "if Saddam must be disarmed, and he's not going to disarm, there's only one way to disarm him," and that is going to war. Bush has an "extraordinary capacity to reject any efforts to put this matter in any broader context," and simply keeps repeating the same simple formulation, Broder said. Regardless of the content of a question, Bush dismissed it "in a word, a phrase or a paragraph, after which the president reverted to a restatement of what he sees as the essentials of the situation: The threat is real and unacceptable; if Hussein does not disarm, he must be disarmed." When asked about North Korea and why he approached it differently, Bush said the same thing and reverted to Hussein. "As candidate and as president," Broder wrote with concern, "Bush often has demonstrated his belief that persuasion for him is often reduced to simple repetition."[13]

Under the presidency of George W. Bush, the great surplus that the Clinton administration bequeathed to its successor has vanished and has become an unprecedented deficit. Security lapses have been obvious. Osama bin Laden and the anthrax mailer are still at large. Unemployment surged, and the stock market first plummeted, and remains problematic.

The president pushed through Congress huge tax cuts that are openly calculated to benefit the most wealthy portion of society. His zeal for eliminating the estate tax that affects only the affluent and is designed to prevent the growing accumulation from generation to generation of tremendous fortunes, reflects Bush's priorities. Billionaires Bill Gates, Sr., Warren Buffett, and (to go back to the nineteenth century) even Andrew Carnegie all recognized the need for an estate tax in a democratic capitalist society.

The president and his attorney general are openly eroding the wall of separation between church and state, and eroding protections for individual liberties. They are continuing the recent Republican trend of politicizing the judiciary and orienting it away from individual rights. The clear policy is toward gutting environmental protections, while the president adamantly rejects any notion of global warming. Although a strong economy is important, it does not require the overwhelming bias in favor of industry that motivates the Bush administration, nor does it justify permitting industry officials to write public policy.

All administrations present a mixed picture. Bush has grown in office. His public presentations have improved. Few people any longer think of him as incompetent. Just as his administration squandered the international good will that benefited the United States following 9/11, though, Bush is in danger of sacrificing the improvement in his reputation for competence. When his excuse for using questionable material in the State of the Union address is that the CIA let him do it, it does not project an image that should inspire confidence.

Symbolism is important, and Bush has managed thus far to use symbolism quite effectively. His understanding of policy nevertheless remains in doubt. He therefore may face long-term difficulties with regard to his historical reputation.

Ultimately it is not only success in adopting policy that determines the success of an administration and of a president. Equally important is the quality and the effects of that policy. A president may be highly successful in pushing destructive policies through Congress. Such a president would be a failure.

NOTES

Introduction

1. *Life*, XXV (1 November 1948), pp. 65–66ff.

2. Arthur M. Schlesinger, Jr., "Rating the Presidents: Washington to Clinton," *Political Science Quarterly*, 112:2 (1997), p. 182.

3. *New York Times Magazine* (29 July 1962).

4. Thomas A. Bailey, *Presidential Greatness*, New York: Appleton-Century-Crofts, 1966.

5. Schlesinger, Jr., pp. 179–190; quotation on p. 181.

6. *Ibid.*, p. 181.

7. Gary M. Maranell, "The Evaluation of Presidents: An Extension of the Schlesinger Polls," *Journal of American History* 57 (June 1970), pp. 104–131.

8. See William Pederson and Ann McLaurin, eds., *The Rating Game in American Politics*, New York: Irving, 1987, p. 33.

9. Steve Neal, "Our Best and Worst Presidents," *Chicago Tribune Magazine* (10 January 1982), pp. 8–13ff.

10. See Robert K. Murray and Tim H. Blessing, *Greatness in the White House: Rating the Presidents Washington through Carter*, University Park: Pennsylvania State University Press, 1988.

11. William J. Ridings, Jr., and Stuart B. McIver, *Rating the Presidents*, rev. ed., New York: Citadel Press, 2000; the overall ranking is on p. xi, and the extensive list of participants is in the Appendix, pp. 284–297.

12. Schlesinger, Jr., p. 181.

13. Clinton Rossiter, *The American Presidency*, Baltimore: Johns Hopkins University Press, 1987; originally published 1956 (see the

excellent "New Introduction" by Michael Nelson).

14. James David Barber, *The Presidential Character: Predicting Performance in the White House*, 4th ed., Englewood Cliffs, NJ: Prentice-Hall, 1992; originally published 1972.

15. Charles F. and Richard B. Faber, *The American Presidents Ranked by Performance*, Jefferson, NC: McFarland, 2000.

16. Reported in "How Historians Rank the Presidents Now," in *The Washingtonian* (April 2000), p. 55.

17. Ridings and McIver, p. xi; 62–66.

18. Faber and Faber, p. 3.

19. *Ibid.*, p. 4.

20. *Ibid.*, p. 6.

21. *Ibid.*, p. 173.

22. Rossiter, p. 144.

23. Nothing in this discussion should lead one to conclude that systematic studies of presidential leadership necessarily are worthless; on the contrary, they may provide considerable insight. Worthwhile examples from the last decade or so include Marc Landy and Sidney Milkis, *Presidential Greatness*, Lawrence: University Press of Kansas, 2000; Philip Abbott, *Strong Presidents: A Theory of Leadership*, Knoxville: University of Tennessee Press, 1998; Erwin C. Hargrove, *The President as Leader*, Lawrence: University Press of Kansas, 1998; and Stephen Skowronek, *The Politics Presidents Make: Leadership from John Adams to Bill Clinton*, Cambridge, MA: Harvard University Press, 1997.

1. Washington

1. Douglas Southall Freeman, *George Washington*, 7 vols., New York: Scribner's, 1948–1957.

2. James Thomas Flexner, *George Washington: A Biography*, 4 vols., Boston: Little, Brown, 1965–1972.

3. Freeman, *Washington: An Abridgement in One Volume by Richard Harwell*, New York: Touchstone, 1995.

4. Flexner, *Washington: The Indispensable Man*, Boston: Little, Brown, 1974.

5. Forrest McDonald, *The Presidency of George Washington*, Lawrence: University Press of Kansas, 1974.

6. See, e.g., Richard M. Pious, *The Presidency*, Boston: Allyn and Bacon, 1996, p. 26; see also Michael A. Genovese, *The Power of the American Presidency: 1789–2000*, New York: Oxford University Press, 2001, p. 8.

7. Jack N. Rakove, "Origins of the Presidency," *National Forum*, 80:1 (Winter 2000), pp. 9–12; quotations on p. 9.

8. Alfred Steinberg, *The First Ten: The Founding Presidents and Their Administrations*, Garden City, NY: Doubleday, 1967, p. 15.

9. Sidney Milkis and Michael Nelson, *The American Presidency: 1776–1998*, 3rd ed., Washington, DC: Congressional Quarterly Press, 1999, p. 66.

10. *Ibid.*

11. *Ibid.*, p. 82.

12. Flexner, *Washington: The Indispensable Man*, p. 246.

13. *Ibid.*, p. 244.

14. Leonard White, *The Federalists: A Study in Administrative History*, New York: Macmillan, 1948, p. 258.

15. McDonald, p. 39.

16. See, e.g., James T. Flexner, *George Washington and the New Nation: 1783–1793*, Boston: Little Brown, 1970, p. 222.

17. *Ibid.*, pp. 215–218.

18. Freeman, *Washington*, p. 622.

19. See Michael Riccards, *The Ferocious Engine of Democracy: A History of the American Presidency*, I, Lanham, MD: Madison Books, 1997, p. 45.

20. McDonald, p. 167.

21. *Ibid.*, p. 173.

22. See Riccards, p. 44.

23. Stanley Elkins and Eric McKitrick, *The Age of Federalism*, New York: Oxford University Press, 1993, p. 528.

2. Adams

1. Richard Alan Ryerson, "John Adams and the Founding of the Republic: An Introduction," in Ryerson, ed., *John Adams and the Founding of the Republic*, Boston: Massachusetts Historical Society, 2001, p. 1.

2. Both quotations in Ralph Adams Brown, *The Presidency of John Adams*, Lawrence: University Press of Kansas, 1975, p. 7.

3. Ryerson, pp. 6–7.

4. Stanley Elkins and Eric McKitrick, *The Age of Federalism: The Early American Republic, 1788–1800*, New York: Oxford University Press, 1993, p. 529.

5. Quoted in David McCullough, *John Adams*, New York: Simon and Schuster, 2001, p. 476.

6. This does not mean, of course, that a president cannot have a rival from within the party as vice president. Both John Kennedy and Lyndon Johnson sought the presidency in 1960, for example, and the successful Kennedy chose Johnson as his running mate — Johnson served Kennedy loyally. It also does not mean that all vice presidents after the Twelfth Amendment were loyal to their presidents. Vice President John Nance Garner, for example, served two terms under President Franklin Roosevelt. He broke with FDR in their second term, and challenged him (to no avail) for the nomination. George Clinton, President Madison's first vice president, opposed administration policies and defeated the administration's attempt to re-charter the Bank of the United States by casting a tie-breaking vote in the Senate.

7. Arthur M. Schlesinger, "Our Presidents: A Rating by 75 Historians," *New York Times Magazine* (29 July 1962), pp. 12–13 ff.

8. Charles F. and Richard B. Faber, *The American Presidents Ranked by Performance*, Jefferson, NC: McFarland, 2000, p. 31.

9. The well-known "remember the laidies" exchange may lead modern observers to conclude that John was dismissing Abigail's views and "putting her in her place." On the contrary, their letters indicate a warm and respectful, flirtatious and even passionate, relationship that included humor — of which this exchange was an example. For instance, see Max J. Skidmore, *Legacy to the World: A Study of America's Political Ideas*, New York: Peter Lang, 1999, pp. 54–55 and 64–65.

10. A Federalist from Connecticut, Roger Griswold, insulted a Republican from Vermont, Matthew Lyon, who spat upon Griswold. The two then fought with fire tongs and a cane, and rolled on the floor until separated. See McCullough, p. 494.

11. *Ibid.*, p. 491.

12. Merrill D. Peterson, *Thomas Jefferson and the New Nation: A Biography*, London: Oxford University Press, 1970, p. 596

13. Elkins and McKitrick, p. 550.

14. Peterson, p. 596.

15. Elkins and McKitrick, p. 586.

16. McCullough, p.498.

17. See, eg., Peterson, p. 596.
18. Elkins and Mckitrick, p. 589.
19. McCullough, p. 501.
20. Quoted in Elkins and McKitrick, p. 554.
21. *Ibid.*, p. 590.
22. Quoted in Peterson, p. 605.
23. *Ibid.*, p. 592.
24. *Ibid.*, pp. 605–606.
25. Richard D. Brown, "The Disenchantment of a Radical Whig: John Adams Reckons with Free Speech," in Ryerson, p. 172.
26. *Ibid.*
27. Elkins and McKitrick, p. 591.
28. Garry Wills, *A Necessary Evil: A History of American Distrust of Government*, New York: Simon and Schuster, 1999, p. 134.
29. *Ibid.*, pp. 136–140.
30. See, e.g., Max J. Skidmore, *Legacy to the World: A Study of America's Political Ideas*, New York: Peter Lang, 1998, p. 67.
31. Wills, p. 134.
32. See Skidmore, pp. 106–107.
33. Elkins and McKitrick, p. 593.
34. McCullough, p. 518.
35. *Ibid.*, p. 510.
36. *Ibid.*, p. 507.
37. Alan Taylor, "John Adams," Alan Brinkley and Davis Dyer, eds., *Reader's Companion to the American Presidency*, Boston: Houghton Mifflin, 2000, p. 32.
38. McCullough pp. 503–504.
39. *Ibid.*
40. *Ibid.*, p. 512.
41. See, e.g., Elkins and McKitrick, pp. 635–641.
42. John Ferling, *John Adams: A Life*, Knoxville: University of Tennessee Press, 1992, p. 407.
43. Elkins and McKitrick, pp. 679–690.
44. McCullough, p. 518.
45. Joseph J. Ellis, *Passionate Sage: The Character and Legacy of John Adams*, New York: W. W. Norton, 1993, p. 23.
46. Elkins and McKitrick, pp. 737–739.
47. McCullough, p. 556.
48. Ferling, p. 412.

3. Jefferson

1. Charles F. and Richard Faber, *The American Presidents Ranked by Performance*, Jefferson, NC: McFarland and Co., 2000, p. 51.
2. Quoted in Michael Genovese, *The Power of the American Presidency*, New York: Oxford University Press, 2001, p. 43.
3. Marc Landy and Sidney Milkis, *Presidential Greatness*, Lawrence: University Press of Kansas, 2000, p. 71.
4. *Ibid.*, p. 51.
5. Ralph Ketcham, *James Madison: A Biography*, Charlottesville: University Press of Virginia, 1990, pp. 620–621.
6. *Ibid.*, p. 47.
7. James Thomas Flexner, *Washington: The Indispensable Man*, Boston: Little, Brown, 1974, p. 244.
8. Landy and Milkis, p. 47.
9. Leonard Levy, *Jefferson and Civil Liberties: The Darker Side*, Cambridge, MA: The Belknap Press of Harvard University Press, 1963.
10. Forrest McDonald, *The Presidency of Thomas Jefferson*, Lawrence: University Press of Kansas, 1976, pp. 30–31.
11. Joyce Appleby, "Thomas Jefferson: 1801–1809," in Alan Brinkley and Davis Dyer, eds., *Reader's Companion to the American Presidency*, Boston: Houghton Mifflin, 2000, p. 52.
12. On Jefferson's attitudes toward women, blacks, and America's native Indian population, see Max J. Skidmore, *Legacy to the World: A Study of America's Political Ideas*, New York: Peter Lang, 1998, pp. 98–101.
13. Stanley Elkins and Eric McKitrick, *The Age of Federalism*, New York: Oxford University Press, 1993, p. 205.
14. Garry Wills, *James Madison*, New York: Henry Holt, 2002, p. 45.
15. McDonald, p. 32.
16. *Ibid.*, 73.
17. Wills, p. 50.
18. Landy and Milkis, p. 61.
19. *Ibid.*, pp. 61–62.
20. McDonald, p. 34.
21. Landy and Milkis, p. 65.
22. Merrill D. Peterson, *Thomas Jefferson and the New Nation*, New York: Oxford, 1970, p. 686.
23. Landy and Milkis, p. 64.
24. McDonald, p. 50.
25. *Ibid.*, p. 51.
26. James F. Simon, *What Kind of Nation?*, New York: Simon and Schuster, 2002, pp. 193–197.
27. Peterson, pp. 795–796.
28. See McDonald, pp. 91–92.
29. Peterson, pp. 796–797.
30. McDonald, pp. 43–44.
31. *Ibid.* pp. 54–55.
32. *Ibid.*, p. 55.
33. Peterson, p. 759.
34. Wills, p. 51.
35. *Ibid.*, pp. 805–806.
36. *Ibid.*, p. 745.
37. Landy and Milkis, p. 72.
38. Wills, p. 54.

39. Landy and Milkis, pp. 72–74.
40. McDonald, p. 120.
41. *Ibid.*, p. 127; see also Peterson, pp. 841–852.
42. Appleby, p. 49.
43. See Peterson, p. 865.
44. *Ibid.*, pp. 869–870.
45. Simon, p. 258; on the Burr case, see pp. 220–259.
46. McDonald, p. 162.
47. Simon, p. 200.
48. McDonald, pp. 166–167.
49. Wills, pp. 59–60.
50. *Ibid.* pp. 60–61.
51. See Peterson, p. 918.

4. Madison

1. Garry Wills, *James Madison*, New York: Henry Holt, 2002, p. 1; see Jack N. Rakove, *James Madison and the Creation of the American Republic*, Glenview, IL: Scott Foresman, 1990.
2. Michael Genovese, *The Power of the American Presidency, 1789–2000*," New York: Oxford University Press, 2001, pp. 49–50.
3. Charles F. and Richard B. Faber, *The American Presidents Ranked by Performance*, Jefferson, NC: McFarland, 2000, p. 58.
4. Quoted by Vincent Buranelli, in "James Madison: The Nation Builder," in Michael Bechloss, ed., *History of the Presidents*, New York: Crown Publishers, 2000, p. 65.
5. Lester J. Cappon, ed., *Th Adams-Jefferson Letters*, Chapel Hill: University of North Carolina Press, 1959, vol. II, pp. 507–508.
6. Yanek Mieczkowski, *The Routledge Historical Atlas of Presidential Elections*, New York: Routledge, 2001, p. 24.
7. Rakove, p. 146.
8. Robert Rutland, quoted in Wills, p. 81.
9. Wills, p. 81.
10. Rakove, p. 146.
11. Robert A. Rutland, *James Madison: the Founding Father*, Columbia: University of Missouri Press, 1987, p. 206.
12. See *ibid.*, pp. 206–207.
13. Wills, pp. 64–65.
14. Rutland, pp. 220–221.
15. Wills, pp. 66–67.
16. Ralph Ketcham, *James Madison*, Charlottesville: University Press of Virginia, 1990, p. 492.
17. *Ibid.*, p. 481.
18. Wills, pp. 80–81.
19. Rutland, p. 209.
20. Wills, p. 82.
21. Ketcham, p. 424.
22. Wills, p. 83.
23. *Ibid.*, p. 62.
24. Rakove, p. 155.
25. Ketcham, p. 490.
26. Rakove, p. 156.
27. Wills, pp. 97–98.
28. *Ibid.*, pp. 108–109.
29. *Ibid.*, pp. 110–111.
30. *Ibid.*, p. 109.
31. Ketcham, p. 230.
32. *Ibid.*, p. 231.
33. Wills, p. 5.
34. *Ibid.*, pp. 132–136.
35. Ketcham, p. 596.
36. Wills, p. 153.
37. *Ibid.*, 154.
38. Quoted in *ibid.*, p. 157.
39. *Ibid.* pp. 155–156.
40. *Ibid.*
41. Quoted in Drew R. McCoy, *The Last of the Fathers: James Madison and the Republican Legacy*, Cambridge: Harvard University Press, 1989, p. 92.
42. See *ibid.*, pp. 92–105.

5. Monroe

1. See, e.g., Noble E. Cunningham, Jr., *The Presidency of James Monroe*, Lawrence: University Press of Kansas, 1996, p. 107.
2. John Ferling, *John Adams: A Life*, Knoxville: University of Tennessee Press, 1992, p. 437.
3. Cunningham, p. 31.
4. Genovese, p. 54
5. David Jacobs and Robert A. Rutland, James Monroe: The Era of Good Feelings," in Michael Beschloss, ed., *History of the Presidents*, New York: Crown Publishers, 2000, p. 77.
6. For an excellent general discussion, see Cunningham, pp. 137–147.
7. *Ibid.*, pp. 145–146.
8. *Ibid.*, p. 137.
9. Ralph Ketcham, *James Madison: A Biography*, Charlottesville: University of Virginia Press, 1990, pp. 630–631.
10. Cunningham, p. 159.
11. Genovese, pp. 54–55.
12. Cunningham, pp. 162–163.
13. See Robert V. Rimini, *Andrew Jackson*, New York: Harper Perennial, 1999, pp. 80–98.
14. Genovese, p. 52.
15. Cunningham, p. 187.
16. Ketcham, p. 621.
17. Michael A. Genovese, New York: Oxford University Press, 2001, p. 18.
18. Arthur M. Schlesinger, "Our Presidents: A Rating by 75 Historians," *New York Times Magazine* (29 July 1962), pp. 12–13ff.

19. Marc Landy and Sidney M. Milkis, *Presidential Greatness*, Lawrence: University Press of Kansas, 2000, p. 82.
20. Charles F. and Richard B. Faber, *The American Presidents Ranked by Performance*, Jefferson, NC: McFarland, 2000, pp. 32 and 59–64.

6. J.Q. Adams

1. Michael Genovese, *The Power of the American Presidency, 1789–2000*, New York: Oxford, 2001, p. 55.
2. See Mary Hargreaves, *The Presidency of John Quincy Adams*, Lawrence: University Press of Kansas, 1985.
3. Yanek Mieczkowski, *The Routledge Historical Atlas of Presidential Elections*, New York: Routledge, 2001, p. 29.
4. *Ibid.*, pp. 29–30.
5. Robert V. Remini, *John Quincy Adams*, New York: Henry Holt & Co., 2002, p. 67.
6. Paul C. Nagel, *John Quincy Adams: A Public Life, A Private Life*, Cambridge, MA: Harvard University Press, 1997, p. 293.
7. *Ibid.*, p. 292.
8. Mieczkowski, p. 31.
9. Nagel, p. 296.
10. Quoted in John Patrick Diggins, "John Quincy Adams," James McPherson, ed., *To the Best of My Ability: The American Presidents*, New York: Society of American Historians/Agincourt Press, 2001, p. 51.
11. Remini, pp. 78–79.
12. Nagel, pp. 301–302.
13. Diggins, p. 51.
14. Remini, p. 84.
15. Richard R. John, "John Quincy Adams," in Alan Brinkley and Davis Dyer, *The Reader's Companion to the American Presidency*, Boston: Houghton Mifflin, 2001, p. 88.
16. *Ibid.*, p. 90.
17. Diggins, p. 50.
18. Remini, *Martin Van Buren and the Democratic Party*, New York: Columbia University Press, 1959, p. 147.
19. Arthur M. Schlesinger, "Our Presidents: A Rating by 75 Historians," *New York Times Magazine* (29 July 1962), pp. 12–13ff.
20. Charles F. and Richard B. Faber, *The American Presidents Ranked by Performance*, Jefferson, NC: McFarland, 2000, p. 31.

7. Jackson

1. Robert V. Remini, *Andrew Jackson*, New York: Harper Perennial, 1999, p. 22.

2. Arthur M. Schlesinger, "Historians Rate Presidents," *Life*, XXV (1 November 1948), pp. 65–66ff.
3. Schlesinger, "Our Presidents: A Ranking by 75 Historians," *New York Times Magazine* (29 July 1962), pp. 12–13ff.
4. Arthur M. Schlesinger, Jr., "Rating the Presidents: Washington to Clinton," *Political Science Quarterly*, 112:2 (Summer 1997), p. 189.
5. Charles F. and Richard B. Faber, *The American Presidents Ranked by Performance*, Jefferson, NC: McFarland, 2000, pp. 71–76.
6. Marc Landy and Sidney M. Milkis, *Presidential Greatness*, Lawrence: University Press of Kansas, 2000, p. 80.
7. Remini, pp. 107–108.
8. Harry L. Watson, "Andrew Jackson," in Alan Brinkley and Davis Dyer, eds., *Reader's Companion to the American Presidency*, Boston: Houghton Mifflin, 2000, p. 101.
9. Robert V. Remini, *Martin Van Buren and the Democratic Party*, New York: Columbia University Press, 1959, p. 131.
10. See the history of the U.S. Postal Service at http://www.usps.com.
11. Landy and Milkis, p. 88; see also James Ceaser, *Presidential Selection*, Princeton: Princeton University Press, 1979, chapter 3.
12. Yanek Mieczkowski, *The Routledge Historical Atlas of Presidential Elections*, New York: Routledge, 2001, pp. 32–34; 150.
13. Remini, *Jackson*, pp. 20–22.
14. *Ibid.*, pp. 23–25.
15. *Ibid.*, p. 118.
16. Donald B. Cole, *The Presidency of Andrew Jackson*, Lawrence: University Press of Kansas, 1993, p. 29.
17. Remini, *Jackson*, pp. 124–125.
18. *Ibid.*, p. 126.
19. *Ibid.*, p. 128.
20. Landy and Milkis, pp. 95–96.
21. *Ibid.* p. 95.
22. Cole, pp. 39–41.
23. Remini, *Jackson*, pp. 123–124.
24. Cole, pp. 66–67.
25. Remini, *Jackson*, pp. 145–146.
26. *Ibid.*, p. 146.
27. *Ibid.*, p. 148.
28. Cole, p. 154.
29. See Kenneth M. Stampp, "The Concept of a Perpetual Union," *Journal of American History*, 65 (June 1978); see also Cole, pp. 160–161; Remini, *Jackson*, pp. 154–156.
30. Landy and Milkis, p. 113.
31. Schlesinger, Jr., p. 187.

8. Van Buren

1. For an excellent discussion of Van Buren's role in this regard, see Donald B. Cole, *Martin Van Buren and the American Political System*, Princeton: Princeton University Press, 1984.

2. See Robert V. Remini, *Martin Van Buren and the Making of the Democratic Party*, New York: Columbia University Press, 1959.

3. Arthur Schlesinger, "Rating the Presidents," *New York Times Magazine* (29 July 1962).

4. Charles F. and Richard B. Faber, *The American Presidents Ranked by Performance*, Jefferson, NC: McFarland, 2000, p. 82.

5. Michael A. Genovese, *The Power of the American Presidency, 1789–2000*, New York: Oxford, 2001, p. 16.

6. *Ibid.*, pp. 63–64.

7. See Major L. Wilson, *The Presidency of Martin Van Buren*, Lawrence: University Press of Kansas, 1984, pp. 187–188, for a discussion of Poinsett's plan; quotation on p. 188.

8. *Ibid.*, p. 188.

9. *Ibid.*, p. 189.

10. *Ibid.*

11. See Cole, pp. 330–360;

12. *Ibid.*, pp. 360–361.

13. Wilson, p. 210.

14. Cole, pp. 317–321.

15. *Ibid.*, pp. 328–330.

16. *Ibid.*, p. 329.

17. See Wilson, pp. 201–202.

18. Wilson, p. 209.

19. Cole, p. 376.

9. Harrison

1. See Max J. Skidmore, "Ranking and Evaluating Presidents: The Case of Theodore Roosevelt," *White House Studies*, 1:4 (2001), p. 496.

2. See Richard W. Waterman, *The Changing American Presidency*, Cincinnati: Atomic Dog Publishing, 2003, p. 71.

3. William J. Ridings, Jr., and Stuart B. McIver, *Rating the Presidents*, rev. ed., New York: Citadel, 2000, p. xi.

4. Norma Lois Peterson, *The Presidencies of William Henry Harrison and John Tyler*, Lawrence: University Press of Kansas, 1989, p. 19.

5. Yanek Mieczkowski, *The Routledge Historical Atlas of Presidential Elections*, New York: Routledge, 2001, pp. 40–41.

6. Peterson, p. 34.

7. *Ibid.*, p. 37.

8. *Ibid.*, p. 41; on the cabinet's role, see p. 40.

9. *Ibid.*, p. 43.

10. Quoted *ibid.*, p. 42.

10. Tyler

1. Richard M. Pious, "John Tyler: Tenth President, 1841–1845," in James M. McPherson, ed., *To the Best of my Ability*, New York: Society of American Historians/Agincourt Press, 2001, p. 80.

2. Norma Lois Peterson, *The Presidencies of William Henry Harrison and John Tyler*, Lawrence: University Press of Kansas, 1989, pp. 45–50.

3. Quoted in Michael A. Genovese, *The Power of the American Presidency, 1789–2000*, New York: Oxford University Press, 2001, p. 68.

4. William Lee Miller, *Arguing About Slavery*, New York: Knopf, 1996, p.386.

5. Arthur M. Schlesinger, "Our Presidents: A Rating by 75 Historians," *New York Times Magazine* (29 July 1962), pp. 12–13 ff.

6. Charles F. and Richard B. Faber, *The American Presidents Ranked by Performance*, Jefferson, NC: McFarland, 2000, p. 31.

7. Peterson, p. 56.

8. *Ibid.*, p. 56.

9. Margaret Truman, *First Ladies*, New York: Fawcett Columbine, 1995, p. 289.

10. Miller, p. 385

11. Truman, p. 290.

12. See Peterson, pp. 201–203.

13. See Truman, pp. 290–296 for a lively account, directed to a popular audience, of Julia Tyler as First Lady.

14. See Peterson, pp. 203–206.

15. Pious, p. 81.

16. Peterson, p. 211.

17. *Ibid.*, pp. 98–99.

18. See *ibid.*, pp. 212–223.

19. Quoted *ibid.*, p. 269.

20. Pious, p. 82.

11. Polk

1. See, e.g., Paul H. Bergeron, *The Presidency of James K. Polk*, Lawrence: University Press of Kansas, 1987, p. 16.

2. See, e.g., Thomas M. Leonard, *James K. Polk: A Clear and Unquestioned Destiny*, Wilmington, DE: Scholarly Resources, 2001, p. 37.

3. Clinton Rossiter, *The American Presidency*, 2nd ed., New York: Harcourt Brace and World, 1960, p. 106.

4. Michael Genovese, *"The Power of the American Presidency, 1789–2000,* New York: Oxford, 2001, pp. 68–70; see also Arthur M. Schlesinger, "Our Presidents: A Rating by 75 Historians," *New York Times Magazine,* (29 July 1962), pp. 12–13ff.

5. Charles F. and Richard B. Faber, *The American Presidents Ranked by Performance,* Jefferson, NC: McFarland, 2000, p. 32.

6. *Ibid.,* p. 96.

7. Sam W. Haynes, *James K. Polk and the Expansionist Impulse,* New York: Longman, 1997, p. 72.

8. Bergeron, p. 47.

9. Haynes, p. 76

10. Bergeron, p. 239.

11. See *ibid.,* pp. 24–25.

12. See *ibid.,* pp. 194–195.

13. *Ibid.,* pp. 73–74.

14. See, e.g., the history of the U.S. Postal Service at <http://www.usps.com>.

15. Quoted in Leonard, p. 189.

16. *Ibid.,* pp. 189–191.

12. Taylor

1. Paul H. Bergeron, *The Presidency of James K. Polk,* Lawrence: University Press of Kansas, 1987, p. 254.

2. Yanek Mieczkowski, *The Routledge Historical Atlas of Presidential Elections,* New York: Routledge, 2001, p. 46.

3. Mieczkowski, p. 45.

4. Elbert B. Smith, *The Presidencies of Zachary Taylor and Millard Fillmore,* Lawrence: University Press of Kansas, 1988, p. 50.

5. Bergeron, p. 257.

6. *Ibid.*

7. Smith, p. 57.

8. Arthur M. Schlesinger, "Our Presidents: A Rating by 75 Historians," *New York Times Magazine* (29 July 1962), pp. 12–13ff.

9. Michael A. Genovese, *The Power of the American Presidency, 1789–2000,* New York: Oxford, 2001, pp. 71–72.

10. *Ibid.,* p. 16.

11. Charles F. and Richard B. Faber, *The American Presidents Ranked by Performance,* Jefferson, NC: McFarland, 2000, p. 101.

12. *Ibid.,* p. 31.

13. Genovese, p. 71.

14. Smith, p. 70.

15. *Ibid.*

16. *Ibid.,* p. 85; see also pp. 74–85.

17. *Ibid,* pp. 91–92.

18. Gerald M. Capers, *John C. Calhoun: Opportunist,* Chicago: Quadrangle Books, 1969, p. 249.; see also Smith, p. 94.

19. Caper, *ibid.*

20. Smith, p. 191.

21. See Philip B. Kunhardt, Jr., Philip B. Kunhardt, III, and Peter Kunhardt, *The American President,* New York: Riverhead Books, 1999, pp. 140–147.

22. Smith, p. 263.

13. Fillmore

1. Jean Harvey Baker, "Millard Fillmore," in James M. McPherson ed., *To the Best of My Ability: The American Presidents,* New York: Society of American Historians/Agincourt Press, 2001, p. 98.

2. Arthur M. Schlesinger, "Our Presidents: A Rating by 75 Historians," *New York Times Magazine* (29 July 1962), pp. 12–13ff.

3. See Michael A. Genovese, *The Power of the American Presidency, 1789–2000,* New York: Oxford, 2001, p. 16 and p. 19.

4. Charles F. and Richard B. Faber, *The American Presidents Ranked by Performance,* Jefferson, NC: McFarland, 2000, p. 31.

5. Quoted in Genovese, p. 72.

6. Robert J. Rayback, *Millard Fillmore: Biography of a President,* Buffalo: Henry Stewart for the Buffalo Historical Society, 1959.

7. See Ralph E. Weber, ed., *Talking with Harry: Candid Conversations with President Harry S. Truman,* Wilmington, DE: Scholarly Resources, 2001, pp. 146–147.

8. Quoted in Baker, p. 101.

9. Elbert B. Smith, *The Presidencies of Zachary Taylor and Millard Fillmore,* Lawrence: University Press of Kansas, 1988, pp. 168–169.

10. *Ibid.,* p. 225.

11. *Ibid.,* pp. 225–226.

12. See Robert J. Scarry, *Millard Fillmore,* Jefferson, NC: McFarland, 2001, p. 208; also see Smith, pp. 226–227.

13. Smith, p. 227

14. See, e.g., *ibid.,* chapter 13, and Scarry, chapter 20.

15. Michael Holt, "Millard Fillmore," in Alan Brinkley and Davis Dyer, eds., *Reader's Companion to the American Presidency,* Boston: Houghton Mifflin, 2000, p. 163.

16. Baker, p. 100.

17. Smith, pp. 239–240.

18. Larry Gara, *The Presidency of Franklin Pierce,* Lawrence: University Press of Kansas, 1991, p. 22.

19. David C. Whitney, *The American Presidents,* Garden City, NY: Doubleday, 1969, p. 116.

20. Philip B Kunhardt, Jr., Philip B. Kunhardt, III, and Peter Kunhardt, *The American*

President, New York: Riverhead Books, 1999, p.221; this is the companion volume to the Public Television series on the presidents.

21. See Max J. Skidmore, "Abraham Lincoln: World Political Symbol for the Twenty-First Century," *White House Studies* 2:1 (2002), pp. 18–20.

22. Holt, p. 163.

23. David Jacobs and Robert Rutland, "Millard Fillmore," in Michael Bechloss, ed., *History of the Presidents*, New York: American Heritage, 2000, p. 166.

24. See, e.g., Rayback, p. 252.

25. Jacobs and Rutland, p. 169.

14. Pierce

1. Robert J. Scarry, *Millard Fillmore*, Jefferson, NC: McFarland, 2001, p. 344.

2. James A. Rawley, "Franklin Pierce," in James M. McPherson, ed., *To the Best of My Ability: The American Presidents*, New York: The Society of American Historians, 2001, p. 104.

3. Martin Luray and Robert Rutland, "Franklin Pierce: Overwhelmed by Events," in Michael Beschloss, ed., *History of the Presidents*, New York: American Heritage, 2000, p. 171.

4. Larry Gara, *The Presidency of Franklin Pierce*, Lawrence: University Press of Kansas, 1991, p. 180.

5. Arthur M. Schlesinger, "Our Presidents: A Rating by 75 Historians," *New York Times Magazine* (29 July 1962), pp. 12–13 ff.

6. Michael A. Genovese, *The Power of the American Presidency, 1789–2000*, New York: Oxford, 2001, p. 16.

7. Charles F. and Richard B. Faber, *The American Presidents Ranked by Performance*, Jefferson, NC: McFarland, 2000, p. 112.

8. Gara, p. xii.

9. *Ibid.*, pp. 30–31.

10. The text of his inaugural address is available at <http://www.bartleby.com/124/pres29.html>.

11. *Ibid.*, p. 54.

12. Gara, *p. 149.*

13. Roy Franklin Nichols, *Franklin Pierce: Young Hickory of the Granite Hills*, Philadelphia: University of Pennsylvania Press, 1931, pp. 257–258.

14. Max J. Skidmore, "Abraham Lincoln: World Political Symbol for the Twenty-First Century," *White House Studies*, 2:1 (2002), p. 21.

15. See Gara, pp. 112–120.

16. *Ibid*, p. 167.

17. *Ibid.*, p. 178.

18. *Ibid.*, p. 173.

15. Buchanan

1. Arthur M. Schlesinger, "Our Presidents: A Rating by 75 Historians," *New York Times Magazine* (29 July 1962), pp. 12–13ff.

2. Michael A. Genovese, *The Power of the American Presidency, 1789–2000*, New York: Oxford, 2001, p. 16.

3. Charles F. and Richard B. Faber, *The American Presidents Ranked by Performance*, Jefferson, NC: McFarland, 2000, p. 31 and pp. 113–118.

4. *Ibid.*, p. 116.

5. Jean Harvey Baker, "James Buchanan," in James M. McPherson, ed., *To the Best of My Ability*, New York: Society of American Historians/Agincourt, 2001, p. 116.

6. Philip Shriver Klein, *President James Buchanan: A Biography*, University Park: Pennsylvania State University Press, 1962, p. 202.

7. Elbert B. Smith, *The Presidency of James Buchanan*, Lawrence: University Press of Kansas, 1975, p. x.

8. *Ibid.*, p. 217.

9. *Ibid.*, p. x.

10. Quoted by William Gienapp, "James Buchanan," in Alan Brinkley and Davis Dyer, eds., *Reader's Companion to the American Presidency*, New York: Houghton Mifflin, 2000, p. 178.

11. Smith, pp. 24–29.

12. Gienapp, p. 182.

13. See Smith, pp. 196–197.

14. Klein, p. 340.

15. See, e.g., *ibid.*, p. 402; Smith, p. 190.

16. Smith, p. 196.

16. Lincoln

1. See Merrill D. Peterson, *Lincoln in American Memory*, New York: Oxford University Press, 1994; see also Max J. Skidmore, "Abraham Lincoln: World Political Symbol for the Twenty-First Century," *White House Studies*, 2:1 (2002), pp. 17–35.

2. J. G. Randall, *Lincoln: The Liberal Statesman*, New York: Dodd, Mead & Co., 1947, p. 93.

3. Brooks D. Simpson, *The Reconstruction Presidents*, Lawrence: The University Press of Kansas, 1998, p. 15.

4. A convenient source for Lincoln's inaugurals and many of his major speeches and writings is Paul M. Angle and Earl Schenck Miers, eds., *The Living Lincoln*, New York: Barnes and Noble, 1992; the First Inaugural is on pp. 381–389.

5. Quoted in Louis Auchincloss, *Theodore*

Roosevelt, New York: Times Books/Henry Holt, 2001, p. 104.

6. See, e.g., John Schaff, "The Domestic Lincoln: White House Lobbying of the Civil War Congresses," *White House Studies,* 2:1 (2002), pp. 37–50.

7. Steven Weisman, *The Great Tax Wars,* New York: Simon & Schuster, 2002, pp. 4–5 and p. 11.

8. *Ibid.,* p. 82.

9. LaWanda Cox, "Lincoln and Black Freedom," in Gabor S. Boritt, ed., *The Historian's Lincoln,"* Urbana: University of Illinois Press, 1996, p. 182.

10. Stephen Oates, "A Momentous Decree: Commentary on 'Lincoln and Black Freedom'," in Gabor S. Boritt, ed., *The Historian's Lincoln,* Urbana: University of Illinois Press, 1996, p. 198.

11. *Ibid.,,* p. 199.

12. *Ibid.,* p. 202.

13. See Max J. Skidmore, *Legacy to the World: A Study of America's Political Ideas,* New York: Peter Lang, 1998, pp. 203–206.

14. Garry Wills, *Lincoln at Gettysburg: The Words that Remade America,* New York: Simon and Schuster, 1992.

15. See, in addition to *ibid.,* Ronald C. White, Jr., *Lincoln's Greatest Speech: The Second Inaugural,* New York: Simon and Schuster, 2002.

16. Wills, p. 36.

17. *Ibid.,* pp. 25–26.

18. *Ibid.,* pp. 37–38.

19. *Ibid.,* pp. 38–39.

20. Arthur M. Schlesinger, Jr., *A Life in the 20th Century,* Boston, Houghton Mifflin, 2000, p. 452.

21. John Hope Franklin, "Lincoln and the Politics of War," in Ralph G. Newman, ed., *Lincoln for the Ages,* New York: Pyramid Books, 1960, p. 81.

22. Bruce Catton, *This Hallowed Ground,* New York: Washington Square Books, 1956, pp. 429–430.

23. Oates, "Commentary," p. 203.

24. Skidmore, "Abraham Lincoln," p. 32.

17. A. Johnson

1. Brooks D. Simpson, *The Reconstruction Presidents,* Lawrence: University Press of Kansas, 1998, p. 67.

2. Charles F. and Richard B. Faber, *The American Presidents Ranked by Performance,* Jefferson, NC: McFarland, 2000, pp. 31, and 125–130.

3. Clinton Rossiter, *The American Presi-*

dency, 2nd ed., New York: Harcourt Brace and World, 1960, p. 106.

4. Arthur M. Schlesinger, "Our Presidents: A Rating by 75 Historians," *New York Times Magazine* (29 July 1962), pp. 12–13 ff.

5. Michael A. Genovese, *The Power of the American Presidency, 1789–2000,* New York: Oxford University Press, 2001, p. 16.

6. Hans L. Trefousse, *Andrew Johnson,* New York: W. W. Norton, 1989, p. 196.

7. *Ibid.*

8. *Ibid.,* p. 197.

9. Simpson, p. 71.

10. Trefousse, p. 197.

11. Simpson, p. 72.

12. *Ibid.,* p. 91; see also pp. 86–90.

13. Quoted in Eric Foner, "Andrew Johnson," in Alan Brinkley and Davis Dyer, eds., *Reader's Companion to the American Presidency,* Boston: Houghton Mifflin, 2000, pp. 209–210.

14. See John J. Patrick, Richard M. Pious, and Donald A. Ritchie, *Oxford Essential Guide to the U. S. Government,* New York: Berkeley Books, 2000, p. 540.

15. Trefousse, pp. 241–242.

16. Simpson, p. 94.

17. Trefousse, p.273.

18. Ross and Trumbull quoted in Trefousse, pp. 330–331.

19. Simpson, p. 127.

20. Jean Edward Smith, *Grant,* New York: Touchstone/Simon and Schuster, 2001, p. 466.

21. Trefousse, p. 352.

22. Quoted in Simpson, p. 83.

23. Trefousse, p. 215.

18. Grant

1. Charles F. and Richard B. Faber, *The American Presidents Ranked by Performance,* Jefferson, NC: McFarland, 2000, p. 136; see also pp. 131–136.

2. Arthur M. Schlesinger, "Our Presidents: A Rating by 75 Historians," *New York Times Magazine* (29 July 1962), pp. 12–13 ff.

3. Michael A. Genovese, *The Power of the American Presidency, 1789–2000,* New York: Oxford, 2001, p. 16.

4. Arthur M. Schlesinger, Jr., "Rating the Presidents: Washington to Clinton," *Political Science Quarterly,* 112:2 (Summer 1997), p. 189.

5. *Ibid.,* p. 185.

6. *Ibid.,* p. 96.

7. Brooks D. Simpson, *The Reconstruction Presidents,* Lawrence: University Press of Kansas, 1998, p. 134.

8. Jean Edward Smith, *Grant,* New York: Touchstone/Simon and Schuster, 2001, p. 464.

9. *Ibid.*, p. 549.
10. Simpson, pp. 143–144.
11. Sidney M. Milkis and Michael Nelson, *The American Presidency*, 4 ed., Washington: CQ Press, 2003, pp. 174–175.
12. Smith, p. 479.
13. *Ibid.*, pp. 479–480.
14. Milkis and Nelson, p. 176.
15. *Ibid.*, pp. 176–177; it is interesting to compare the treatment of Grant in this edition with their discussion of Grant in their third edition (1999)_clearly, Milkis and Nelson have taken note of recent Grant scholarship and have added material, but they have not adequately revised their earlier treatment. They thus present a rather inconsistent view of the eighteenth president.
16. Smith, p. 489.
17. *Ibid.*, p. 490.
18. *Ibid.*, p. 687, n113.
19. *Ibid.*, p. 512.
20. *Ibid.*
21. *Ibid.*, p. 498.
22. *Ibid.*, p. 515.
23. See William McFeely, *Grant: A Biography*, New York: W.W. Norton, 1982.
24. Smith, pp. 542–545; 696 n11.
25. *Ibid.*, pp. 546–547.
26. See *ibid.*, pp. 562–568.
27. Simpson, p. 156.
28. Smith, pp. 585–586.
29. *Ibid*, p. 600.
30. Simpson, p. 135.
31. Jeffry D. Wert, "James Longstreet and the Lost Cause," in Carl Gallagher and Alan T. Nolan, eds., *The Myth of the Lost Cause and Civil War History*, Bloomington: Indiana University Press, 2000, pp. 129–130.
32. Douglas Southall Freeman, *R. E. Lee: A Biography*, 4 vols., New York: Charles Scribner's Sons, 1934–1935.
33. Quoted in Janny Scott, "History's Judgment of the 2 Civil War Generals is Changing," *New York Times on the Web* (30 September 2000).
34. Quoted in *ibid.*
35. See Lloyd A. Hunter, "The Immortal Confederacy: Another Look at Lost Cause Religion," in Gallagher and Nolan, pp. 205–206.
36. Brooks D. Simpson, "Continuous Hammering and Mere Attrition: Lost Cause Critics and the Military Reputation of Ulysses S. Grant," in Gallagher and Nolan, *The Myth of the Lost Cause*, p. 151.
37. Scott, "History's Judgment."
38. Quoted in *ibid.*
39. See Ulysses S. Grant, III, *Ulysses S. Grant: Warrior and Statesman*, New York: Morrow, 1968, pp. 269–270.
40. Brooks D. Simpson, *The Reconstruction Presidents*, p. 196; see also his *Ulysses S. Grant: Triumph Over Adversity, 1822–1865,* Boston: Houghton-Mifflin, 2000.
41. Scott, "History's Judgment."

19. Hayes

1. Ari Hoogenboom, *The Presidency of Rutherford B. Hayes*, Lawrence: University Press of Kansas, 1988, p. 24.
2. See Yanek Mieczkowski, *The Routledge Historical Atlas of Presidential Elections*, New York: Routledge, 2001, 63–64.
3. See Hans L. Trefousse, *Rutherford B. Hayes*, New York: Times Books/Henry Holt, 2002, pp. 82–83.
4. Brooks D. Simpson, *The Reconstruction Presidents*, Lawrence: University Press of Kansas, 1998, p. 208.
5. Hoogenboom, p. 69.
6. Simpson, p. 212.
7. Clinton Rossiter, *The American Presidency*, 2nd ed., New York: Harcourt Brace and World, 1960, p. 106.
8. Hoogenboom, p. 86.
9. Charles F. and Richard B. Faber, *The American Presidents Ranked by Performance*, Jefferson, NC: McFarland, 2000, p. 32; see also pp. 137–142.
10. Michael A. Genovese, *The Power of the American Presidency 1789–2000*, New York: Oxford University Press, 2001, p. 16.
11. *Ibid.*, p. 98.
12. Quoted in Hoogenboom, p. 68.
13. Justus D. Doenecke, *The Presidencies of James A. Garfield and Chester A. Arthur*, Lawrence: University Press of Kansas, 1981, p. 17.
14. Hoogenboom, p. 217.
15. *Ibid.*, p. 223.

20. Garfield

1. Justus Doenecke, *The Presidencies of James A. Garfield and Chester A. Arthur*, Lawrence: University Press of Kansas, 1981, p. 53.
2. *Ibid.*, p. 43; see also pp. 40–45.
3. Quoted *ibid.*, p. 44.

21. Arthur

1. Arthur M. Schlesinger, "Our Presidents: A Rating by 75 Historians," *New York Times Magazine* (29 July 1962), pp. 12–13ff.

2. Arthur M. Schlesinger, Jr., "Rating the Presidents: Washington to Clinton," *Political Science Quarterly*, 112:2 (Summer 1997), p. 189.

3. Charles F. and Richard B. Faber, *The American Presidents Ranked by Performance*, Jefferson, NC: McFarland, 2000, p. 32.

4. Michael A. Genovese, *The Power of the American Presidency, 1789–2000*, New York: Oxford University Press, 2001, p. 16.

5. Faber and Faber, p. 150.

6. See Thomas C. Reeves, *Gentleman Boss: The Life of Chester Alan Arthur*, New York: Knopf, 1975, p. 180.

7. Justus D. Doenecke, *The Presidencies of James A. Garfield and Chester A. Arthur*, Lawrence: University Press of Kansas, 1981, p. 75.

8. See *ibid.*, pp. 75–76.

9. *Ibid.*, p. 76.

10. *Ibid.*, p. 77.

11. Sidney M. Milkis and Michael Nelson, *The American Presidency*, 4th ed., Washington, DC: CQ Press, 2003, p. 186.

12. Doenecke, pp. 81–84.

13. *Ibid.*, p. 182.

14. *Ibid.*, p. 183.

11. *Ibid.*

12. *Ibid.*, p. 85.

13. See Lewis L. Gould, *The Presidency of William McKinley*, Lawrence: University Press of Kansas, 1980, p. 38; see also *ibid.*, p. 76.

14. See Sidney M. Milkis and Michael Nelson, *The American Presidency*, 4th ed., Washington, DC: CQ Press, 2003, pp. 187–188.

15. Rossiter, p. 106.

16. De Santis, p. 166.

17. Genovese, p. 102.

18. See Mieczkowski, pp. 71–72.

19. Homer E. Socolofsky and Allan B. Spetter, *The Presidency of Benjamin Harrison*, Lawrence: University Press of Kansas, 1987, p. 13.

20. Graff, pp. 96–97.

21. *Ibid.*, p. 97.

22. See Mieczkowski, pp. 73–74.

23. Graff, p. 114.

24. *Ibid.*, pp. 115–116.

25. *Ibid.*, p. 118.

26. See *ibid.*, pp. 119–120.

27. See Milkis and Nelson, pp. 193–194.

28. Graff, pp. 127–129.

22. Cleveland

1. Arthur M. Schlesinger, Sr., "Our Presidents: A Rating by 75 Historians," *New York Times Magazine* (29 July 1962), pp. 12–13ff.

2. Clinton Rossiter, *The American Presidency*, 2nd ed., New York: Harcourt Brace and World, 1960, p. 106.

3. Arthur M. Schlesinger, Jr., "Rating the Presidents: Washington to Clinton," *Political Science Quarterly*, 112:2 (Summer 1997), p. 189.

4. Michael A. Genovese, *The Power of the American Presidency, 1789–2000*, New York: Oxford University Press, 2001, p. 16.

5. Charles F. and Richard B. Faber, *The American Presidents Ranked by Performance*, Jefferson, NC: McFarland, 2000, p. 32; see also pp. 151–156.

6. Vincent P. De Santis, "Grover Cleveland," in James M. MacPherson, ed., *To the Best of My Ability*, New York: Agincourt/Society of American Historians, 2001, p. 160.

7. Henry F. Graff, *Grover Cleveland*, New York: Times Books/Henry Holt, 2002, p. 60.

8. See Yanek Mieczkowski, *The Routledge Historical Atlas of Presidential Elections*, New York: Routledge, 2001, pp. 68–70.

9. See Carole Chandler Waldrup, *The Vice Presidents*, Jefferson, NC: McFarland, 1996, pp. 125–129.

10. Graff, p. 77.

23. Harrison

1. Yanek Mieczkowski, *The Routledge Historical Atlas of Presidential Elections*, New York: Routlege, 2001, p. 72.

2. Quoted in Catherine Clinton, "Benjamin Harrison," in James M. McPherson, ed., *To the Best of My Ability*, New York: Agincourt/Society of American Historians, 2001, p. 172.

3. Homer E. Socolofsky and Allan B. Spetter, *The Presidency of Benjamin Harrison*, Lawrence: University Press of Kansas, 1987, p. 78.

4. Quoted in Clinton, p. 172.

5. Lewis L. Gould, *The Presidency of William McKinley*, Lawrence: University Press of Kansas, 1980, p. 38.

6. Louis W. Koenig, "Benjamin Harrison: Presidential Grandson," in Michael Beschloss, ed., *History of the Presidents*, New York: American Heritage, 2000, p. 303.

7. Arthur M. Schlesinger, Jr., "Rating the Presidents: Washington to Clinton," *Political Science Quarterly*, 112:2 (Summer 1997), p. 189.

8. Arthur M. Schlesinger, Sr., "Our Presidents: A Rating by 75 Historians," *New York Times Magazine* (29 July 1962), pp. 12–13ff.

9. Michael A. Genovese, *The Power of the American Presidency, 1789–2000*, New York: Oxford University Press, 2001, p. 105.

10. *Ibid.*, p. 106.

11. *Ibid.*, p. 16.
12. Charles F. and Richard B. Faber, *The American Presidents Ranked by Performance*, Jefferson, NC: McFarland, 2000, p. 31.
13. See *ibid.*, pp. 157–162.
14. Socolofsky and Spetter, p. 23.
15. See *ibid.*, pp. 110–111.
16. See *ibid.*, p. 130.
17. *Ibid.*, p. 123.
18. *Ibid.*, pp. 54–55.
19. *Ibid.*, pp. 189–190.
20. *Ibid.*, p. 186.
21. *Ibid.*, p. 187.
22. *Ibid.*, p. 48.

25. McKinley

1. Yanek Mieczkowski, *The Routledge Historical Atlas of Presidential Elections*, New York: Routledge, 2001, p. 77.
2. *Ibid.*, p. 78.
3. Lewis Gould, *The Presidency of William McKinley*, Lawrence: University Press of Kansas, 1980, p. 17.
4. *Ibid.*, pp. Vii, 152, etc.; chapter 10, in fact, bears the title: "The First Modern President."
5. *Ibid.*, p. 253.
6. Joseph M. Dixon, "Theodore Roosevelt," Typescript. Joseph Dixon papers, Series 55, Box 100, Folder 1, Archives of the University of Montana Library, Missoula, p. 40.
7. Gould, p. 37.
8. James Ford Rhodes, *the McKinley and Roosevelt Administrations: 1897–1909*, New York: Macmillan, 1922, p. 172.
9. Samuel Fallows, *Life of William McKinley: Our Martyred President,* Chicago: Regan Printing House, 1901, pp. 44–57.
10. Arthur M. Schlesinger, Sr., "Our Presidents: A Rating by 75 Historians," *New York Times Magazine* (29 July 1962), pp. 12–13 ff.
11. Arthur M. Schlesinger, Jr., "Rating the Presidents: Washington to Clinton," *Political Science Quarterly,* 112:2 (Summer 1997), p. 189.
12. Michael A. Genovese, *The Power of the American Presidency: 1789–2000,* New York: Oxford University Press, 2001, p. 16.
13. Charles F. and Richard B. Faber, *The American Presidents Ranked by Performance*, Jefferson, NC: McFarland, 2000, p. 168; see also pp. 163–167, and p. 31.
14. Rhodes, pp. 62–64.
15. Gould, pp. 88–89.
16. *Ibid., p.* 75.
17. *Ibid.*, p. 90.
18. *Ibid.*, pp. 91 and 121.

26. T. Roosevelt

1. William H. Harbaugh, *The Life and Times of Theodore Roosevelt*, rev. ed., New York: Oxford University Press, 1975, p. 434.
2. Kathleen Dalton, *Theodore Roosevelt: A Strenuous Life*, New York: Alfred A. Knopf, 2002, p. 268.
3. See Max J. Skidmore, "Ranking and Evaluating Presidents: The Case of Theodore Roosevelt," *White House Studies*, 1:4 (2001).
4. Henry F. Pringle, *Theodore Roosevelt A Biography*, New York: Harcourt Brace, 1931.
5. Arthur M. Schlesinger, Jr., *A Life in the 20th Century*, Boston: Houghton Mifflin, 2000, p. 264.
6. John Morton Blum, *The Republican Roosevelt*, New York: Atheneum, 1954.
7. Harbaugh, *op. cit.*
8. Edmund Morris, *Theodore Rex*, New York: Random House, 2001.
9. Nathan Miller, *Theodore Roosevelt: A Life*, New York: William Morrow, 1992.
10. Dalton, *op cit.*
11. Arthur M. Schlesinger, Sr., "Our Presidents: A Rating by 75 Historians," *New York Times Magazine* (29 July 1962), pp. 12–13ff.
12. Arthur M. Schlesinger, Jr., "Rating the Presidents: Washington to Clinton," *Political Science Quarterly*, 112:2 (Summer 1997), p. 189.
13. Michael A. Genovese, *The Power of the American Presidency: 1789–2000*, New York: Oxford University Press, 2001, p. 16.
14. Charles F. and Richard B. Faber, *The American Presidents Ranked by Performance*, Jefferson, NC: McFarland, 2000, pp. 2–5 and 169–173.
15. Results available from the Siena Research Institute at <http://www.siena.edu/sri/results/95%20Presidency%20Survey.htm.>
16. Wilfred Binkley, *The Power of the Presidency*, Garden City, NY: Doubleday, Doran, 1937, p. 267.
17. Clinton Rossiter, *The American Presidency*, rev. ed., New York: Harcourt Brace and World, 1960, pp. 143–144.
18. See Schlesinger, Jr., "Rating the Presidents," p. 187.
19. Eric F. Goldman, *The Tragedy of Lyndon Johnson*, New York: Knopf, 1969, p. 7.
20. Theodore Roosevelt, *Theodore Roosevelt: An Autobiography*, New York: Da Capo Press, 1985 [1913], pp. 371–372.
21. Dalton, pp. 215–217.
22. Louis Auchincloss, *Theodore Roosevelt*, New York: Times Books/Henry Holt, 2001, p. 63.
23. James Ford Rhodes, *The McKinley and Roosevelt Administrations: 1897–1909*, New York: Macmillan, 1922, p. 229.

24. Dalton, pp. 321–322.

25. Max J. Skidmore, "Theodore Roosevelt on Race and Gender," *Journal of American Culture*, 21:2 (Summer 1998), p. 43.

26. Roosevelt, p. 442.

27. See, e.g., Morris, pp. 91–92.

28. Roosevelt, p. 444.

29. See <http://www.Theodoreroosevelt.org/life/conservation.htm>.

30. Dalton, p. 244.

31. See Dalton's excellent discussion, *ibid.*, pp. 245–247; the quotations are hers.

32. Roosevelt, p. 483.

33. See Harbaugh, pp. 165–179; see also Roosevelt, pp. 479–493.

34. Dalton, p. 237.

35. John Milton Cooper, Jr., *The Warrior and the Priest*, Cambridge, MA: The Belknap Press of Harvard University Press, 1983, p. 73.

36. See Roosevelt, p. 526.

37. Pringle (Collector's Edition, Norwalk, CT: The Easton Press, 1988 [1931]), p. 285.

38. *Ibid.*, p. 286.

39. *Ibid.*, pp. 287–289.

40. Dalton, pp. 237–239.

41. Morris, pp. 177–210.

42. *Ibid.*, p. 210.

43. Roosevelt, p. 526.

44. *Ibid.*, pp. 541–542.

45. Dalton, pp. 281–282.

46. See *ibid.*, pp. 282–286.

47. *Ibid.*, p. 285.

48. Morris, p. 473.

49. *Ibid.*, p. 483.

50. See Dalton, pp. 280–281.

51. Roosevelt, p. 563; see pp. 563–574.

52. *Ibid.*, pp. 567–568.

53. Clinton Rossiter, *The American Presidency*, New York: Harcourt Brace and World, 1960, p. 103.

54. Dalton, p. 245.

55. Morris, pp. 485–487.

56. *Ibid.*; quotations are on p. 487.

57. Miller, p. 493.

58. Quoted *ibid.*

59. Cooper, pp. 86–88.

60. Quotations *ibid.*, pp. 87 & 88.

27. Taft

1. Paolo E. Coletta, *The Presidency of William Howard Taft*, Lawrence: University Press of Kansas, 1973, p. 19.

2. Michael A. Genovese, *The Power of the American Presidency, 1789–2000*, New York: Oxford University Press, 2001, p. 16.

3. *Ibid.*, pp. 115–117.

4. Arthur M. Schlesinger, Sr., "Our Presi-

dents: A Rating by 75 Historians," *New York Times Magazine*, (29 July 1962), pp. 12–13ff.

5. Arthur M. Schlesinger, Jr., "Rating the Presidents: Washington to Clinton," *Political Science Quarterly*, 112:2 (Summer 1997), p. 189.

6. Charles F. and Richard B. Faber, *The American Presidents Ranked by Performance*, Jefferson, NC: McFarland, 2000, p. 31.

7. *Ibid.*, p. 177.

8. See Theodore Roosevelt, *Theodore Roosevelt: An Autobiography*, New York: Da Capo Press, 1985 [1913], p. 412; see also Nathan Miller, *Theodore Roosevelt: A Life*, New York: William Morrow, 1992, pp. 477–478.

9. Miller, pp. 519–520.

10. Coletta, p. 67.

11. *Ibid.*, pp. 127–129.

12. Sidney M. Milkis and Michael Nelson, *The American Presidency*, 4th ed., Washington, DC: CQ Press, 2003, pp. 224–225.

13. Coletta, pp. 73–74.

14. *Ibid.*, p. 230.

15. Yanek Mieczkowski, *The Routledge Historical Atlas of Presidential Elections*, New York: Routledge, 2001, pp. 85–87.

16. Coletta, p. 251.

17. *Ibid.*, p. 259.

18. *Ibid.*, p. 258.

19. *Ibid.*, p. 247.

28. Wilson

1. Kendrick A. Clements, *Woodrow Wilson: World Statesman*, Boston: Twayne, 1987, p. 26.

2. Quoted in Kendrick Clements, *The Presidency of Woodrow Wilson*, Lawrence: University Press of Kansas, 1992, p. ix.

3. Arthur M. Schlesinger, Sr., "Our Presidents: A Rating by 75 Historians," *New York Times Magazine* (29 July 1962), pp. 12–13ff.

4. Arthur Schlesinger, Jr., "Rating the Presidents: Washington to Clinton," *Political Science Quarterly*, 112:2 (Summer 1997), p. 181; one should note that Clinton did teach law at the University of Arkansas Law School before becoming governor, but this of course was after Schlesinger's remark.

5. *Ibid.*, p. 189.

6. Michael A. Genovese, *The Power of the American Presidency, 1789–2000*, New York: Oxford University Press, p. 16.

7. Clinton Rossiter, *The American Presidency*, 2nd ed., New York: Harcourt Brace, 1960, pp. 104–105.

8. Charles F. and Richard B. Faber, *The American Presidents Ranked by Performance*, Jefferson, NC: McFarland, 2000.

9. Quoted in Schlesinger, Jr., p. 183.

10. Yanek Mieczkowski, *The Routledge Historical Atlas of Presidential Elections*, New York: Routledge, 2001, p. 86.

11. John Milton Cooper, Jr., *The Warrior and the Priest: Woodrow Wilson the Theodore Roosevelt*, Cambridge, MA: The Belknap Press of Harvard University Press, 1983, p. 229.

12. *Ibid.*, p. 230.

13. Paul F. Boller, Jr., *Presidential Inaugurations*, San Diego: Harcourt, 2001, p. 208.

14. John Morton Blum, *Woodrow Wilson and the Politics of Morality*, Boston: Little Brown, 1956, pp. 67–68.

15. See Eric F. Goldman, *The Tragedy of Lyndon Johnson*, New York: Knopf, 1969, p. 57.

16. Cooper, p. 235.

17. Daniel D. Stid, *The President as Statesman: Woodrow Wilson and the Constitution*, Lawrence: University Press of Kansas, 1998, p. 90.

18. Cooper, p. 232.

19. See Steven R. Weisman, *The Great Tax Wars*, New York: Simon and Schuster, 2002, pp. 268–284.

20. *Ibid.*, p. 284.

21. Blum, p. 82.

22. Cooper, p. 239.

23. Clements, *World Statesman*, p. 97.

24. Blum, pp. 111–112.

25. Clements, *World Statesman*, pp. 97–101.

26. Nathan Miller, *Theodore Roosevelt: A Life*, New York: William Morrow, 1992, p. 544.

27. Mieczkowski, pp. 88–89.

28. Blum, p. 88; emphasis added.

29. *Ibid.*, pp. 90–91; see also p. 93.

30. Miller, p. 556.

31. Kathleen Dalton, *Theodore Roosevelt: A Strenuous Life*, New York: Knopf, 2002, p. 487.

32. See Dalton, pp. 490–491.

33. See, e.g., Jeffrey K. Tulis, *The Rhetorical Presidency*, Princeton: Princeton University Press, 1987.

34. Blum, p. 191.

35. See Clements, *World Statesman*, pp. 216–217.

29. Harding

1. Arthur M. Schlesinger, Sr., "Our Presidents: A Rating by 75 Historians,' *New York Times Magazine* (29 July 1962), pp. 12–13ff.

2. Arthur M. Schlesinger, Jr., "Rating the Presidents: Washington to Clinton," *Political Science Quarterly*, 112:2 (Summer 1997), p. 189.

3. Margaret Truman, *First Ladies*, New York: Fawcett Columbine, 1995, p. 233.

4. *Ibid.*, pp. 233–243.

5. Charles F. and Richard B. Faber, *The American Presidents Ranked by Performance*, Jefferson, NC: McFarland, 2000, p. 32.

6. *Ibid.*, 193.

7. See Thomas A. Bailey, *Presidential Greatness*, New York: Appleton-Century-Crofts, 1966, pp. 312–315.

8. Joshua Hall, "Reassessing an Ohio President," a two-page essay on the Internet at <http://www.buckeyeinstitute.org/oped/reassessing.htm>.

9. Eugene P. Trani and David L. Wilson, *The Presidency of Warren G. Harding*, Lawrence: University Press of Kansas, 1977, p. 190; see also Robert K. Murray, *The Harding Era*, Minneapolis: University of Minnesota Press, 1969.

10. Trani and Wilson., pp. 190–191.

11. Carl Sferrazza Anthony, *Florence Harding*, New York: William Morrow, 1998.

12. See esp., Robert P. Watson, *The Presidents' Wives: Reassessing the Office of First Lady*, Boulder, CO: Lynne Rienner, 1999.

13. See Trani and Wilson, pp. 54–59.

14. *Ibid.*, pp. 141–142.

15. Sidney Milkis and Michael Nelson, *The American Presidency*, 4th ed., Washington, DC: CQ Press, 2003, pp. 254–255.

16. Trani and Wilson, p. 139.

17. *Ibid.*, pp. 101–102.

18. *Ibid.*, pp. 64–66.

19. *Ibid.*, pp. 103–105.

20. *Ibid.*, pp. 181–183.

21. See *ibid.*, pp. 178–185, which provided the basis for much of this discussion on the scandals of the Harding administration; quotation on p. 182.

22. *Ibid.*, pp. 106–107.

30. Coolidge

1. Robert H. Ferrell, *The Presidency of Calvin Coolidge*, Lawrence: University Press of Kansas, 1998, pp. 39–40.

2. See *ibid.*, pp. 19–23; quotations on p. 20.

3. Robert Sobel, *Coolidge: An American Dilemma*, Washington, DC: Regnery, 1998, p. 144.

4. Ferrell, p. 62.

5. Ferrell, pp. 40–41

6. Quoted in Sidney M. Milkis and Michael Nelson, *The American Presidency*, 4th ed., Washington, DC: CQ Press, 2003, p. 258.

7. *Ibid.*, p. 259.

8. *Ibid.*, pp. 259–261.

9. See Ferrell., pp. 21–22.

10. Arthur M. Schlesinger, Jr., "Our Presi-

dents: A Rating by 75 Historians," *New York Times Magazine* (29 July 1962), pp. 12–13ff.
11. Arthur M. Schlesinger, Jr., "Rating the Presidents: Washington to Clinton," *Political Science Quarterly*, 112:2 (Summer 1997), p. 189.
12. Charles F. and Richard B. Faber, *The American Presidents Ranked by Performance*, Jefferson, NC: McFarland, 2000, pp. 32, 194–199.
13. Milkis and Nelson, p. 258.
14. Ferrell, pp. 114–117.
15. Sobel, p. 269.
16. Ferrell, p. 170.
17. Ferrell, pp. 41–42.
18. *Ibid.*
19. Sobel, p. 317.
20. *Ibid.*, p. 318.
21. Ferrell, p. 192.
22. See *ibid.*, pp. 30–31.
23. Sobel, p. 401.
24. *Ibid.*
25. Ferrell, pp. 95–96.
26. Sobel, pp. 392–394.

31. Hoover

1. Arthur M. Schlesinger, "Our Presidents: A Rating by 75 Historians," *New York Times Magazine* (29 July 1962), pp. 12–13ff.
2. Arthur M. Schlesinger, Jr., "Rating the Presidents: Washington to Clinton," *Political Science Quarterly*, 112:2 (summer 1997), p. 189.
3. Michael A. Genovese, *The Power of the American Presidency, 1789–2000*, New York: Oxford University Press, 2001, p. 16.
4. Charles F. and Richard B. Faber, *The American Presidents Ranked by Performance*, Jefferson, NC: McFarland, 2000, p. 31.
5. Eugene Lyons, *Herbert Hoover*, New York: Doubleday, 1964.
6. *Ibid.*, p. 334.
7. See *ibid.*, chapters xvi and xvii, and *passim.*
8. See, e.g., William Appleman Williams, "What this Country Needs...," *New York Review of Books* (5 Nov. 1970).
9. Martin L. Fausold, *The Presidency of Herbert C. Hoover*, Lawrence: University Press of Kansas, 1985, pp. 49, 52.
10. *Ibid.*, p. 51.
11. Robert M. Eisinger, "Gauging Public Opinion in the Hoover White House: Understanding the Roots of Presidential Polling," *Presidential Studies Quarterly*, 30:4 (December 2000), pp. 643–661.
12. Fausold, p. 93.
13. *Ibid.*, p. 97.
14. *Ibid.*, pp. 88–89.

15. *Ibid.*, p. 129; see also pp. 125–129.
16. Dexter Perkins, *The New Age of Franklin Roosevelt*, Chicago: University of Chicago Press, 1964, p. 23.
17. Fausold, p. 136.
18. *Ibid*, pp. 199–203.
19. See *ibid.*, chapter 9.
20. Frank Freidel, *Franklin D. Roosevelt: A Rendezvous with Destiny*, Boston: Little, Brown, 1990, p. 212.
21. Sidney M. Milkis and Michael Nelson, *The American Presidency*, 4th ed., Washington, DC: CQ Press, 2003, p. 265.
22. See *ibid*, pp. 261–262.
23. Freidel, p. 82.
24. *Ibid.*, p. 83.
25. Fausold, pp. 238–240.
26. Robert Sobel, *Coolidge: An American Dilemma*, Washington, DC: Regnery, 1998, p. 412.
27. Lyons, p. 320.
28. Arthur M. Schlesinger, Jr., *A Life in the 20th Century*, Boston: Houghton Mifflin, 2000, p. 485.

32. F.D. Roosevelt

1. See Frank Freidel, *Franklin D. Roosevelt: A Rendezvous with Destiny*, Boston: Little, Brown, 1990, pp. 94–95.
2. *Ibid.*, p. 101.
3. *Ibid.*, p. 100.
4. *Ibid.*, p. 99.
5. Dexter Perkins, *The New Age of Franklin Roosevelt, 1932–1945*, Chicago: University of Chicago Press, 1964, p. 71.
6. James West (Carl Withers, pseudonym), *Plainville, U.S.A.*, New York: Columbia University Press, 1945, p. 216.
7. Perkins, p. 23.
8. Freidel, p. 97.
9. *Ibid.*, p. 95.
10. Eugene Lyons, *Herbert Hoover: A Biography*, Garden City, NY: Doubleday, 1964, p. 290.
11. See Max J. Skidmore, *Social Security and its Enemies*, Boulder, CO: Westview Press, 1999.
12. Freidel, p. 162.
13. Milkis and Nelson, p. 280.
14. *Ibid*, pp. 278–279.
15. See Perkins, pp. 96–102.
16. *Ibid.*, p. 111.
17. *Ibid.*, p. 112.
18. Freidel, p. 352; see also pp. 333–352.
19. *Ibid.*, pp. 359–361.
20. See *ibid.*, pp. 405–407.
21. *Ibid.*, p. 109.

22. Marc Landy and Sidney M. Milkis, *Presidential Greatness*, Lawrence: University Press of Kansas, 2000, pp. 192–193; the quotation is from Barry Karl.

23. Doris Kearns Goodwin, *No Ordinary Time: Franklin and Eleanor Roosevelt: The Home Front in World War II*, New York: Simon & Schuster, 1994, pp. 321–323.

24. *Ibid.*

25. See Michael Beschloss, *The Conquerors*, New York: Simon & Schuster, 2002, pp. 56–69; esp. p. 66.

26. *Ibid.*, p. 64.

27. *Ibid.*, p. 286.

28. *Ibid., passim.*

29. See Goodwin for the best study of Eleanor Roosevelt's role during the war and somewhat before; it also is the best study of domestic politics during the wartime Roosevelt administration.

30. Goodwin, pp. 323–326.

33. Truman

1. David McCullough, *Truman*, New York: Simon & Schuster, 1992.

2. See Arnold Offner, *Another Such Peace: President Truman and the Cold War, 1945–1953*, Palo Alto, CA: Stanford Nuclear Age Series, 2002.

3. Arthur M. Schlesinger, "Our Presidents: A Rating by 75 Historians," *New York Times Magazine* (29 July 1962), pp. 12–13ff.

4. Michael A. Genovese, *The Power of the American Presidency, 1789–2000*, New York: Oxford University Press, p. 16.

5. Arthur M. Schlesinger, Jr., "Rating the Presidents: Washington to Clinton," *Political Science Quarterly*, 112:2 (Summer 1997), p. 189.

6. Charles F. and Richard B. Faber, *The American Presidents Ranked by Performance*, Jefferson, NC: McFarland, 2000, p. 31.

7. Clinton Rossiter, *The American Presidency*, 2nd ed., New York: Harcourt Brace and World, 1960, p. 155.

8. *Ibid.*, pp. 157–158.

9. Donald R. McCoy, *The Presidency of Harry S. Truman*, Lawrence: University Press of Kansas, 1984, p. 15.

10. Michael Beschloss, *The Conquerors*, New York: Simon & Schuster, 2002; see pp. 226–292.

11. McCoy, p. 39.

12. Robert H. Ferrell, *Harry S. Truman: A Life*, Columbia: University of Missouri Press, 1994, p. 210.

13. McCoy, p. 23.

14. Ralph E. Weber, ed., *Talking with Harry*, Wilmington, DE: Scholarly Resources, 2001; Weber was referring to Frank's study, *Downfall: The End of the Imperial Japanese Empire*, and to Frank's conclusions therein.

15. Ferrell, p. 216.

16. McCoy, p. 39.

17. Sidney M. Milkis and Michael Nelson, *The American Presidency*, 4th ed., Washington, DC: CQ Press, 2003, pp. 296–298.

18. The exception is bizarre. The Twenty-Seventh Amendment prohibiting a salary increase from taking effect for members of Congress after they have voted one until after the passage of the next election, originally went out to the states for ratification along with the Bill of Rights. Failing to achieve support from the required three-fourths, it bounced around for two centuries_or more precisely lay dormant most of the time_until resuscitated and ratified on 7 May 1992 during a period of especially strong anti-congressional sentiment.

19. Rossiter, pp. 231–233.

20. Harry S. Truman, *Mr. Citizen*, New York: Bernard Geis & Associates, 1960, p. 225.

21. *Ibid.*, p. 226.

22. Ferrell, p. 218.

23. See McCoy, pp. 120–123.

24. *Ibid.*, pp. 137–139.

25. Ferrell, p. 297.

26. *Ibid.*, pp. 293–294.

27. Stephen A. Ambrose, *Eisenhower: Soldier and President*, New York: Simon and Schuster, 1990.

28. Ferrell, p. 268.

29. Ralph E. Weber, ed., *Talking with Harry: Candid Conversations with President Harry S. Truman*, Wilmington, DE: Scholarly Resources, 2001, p. 131.

30. Ferrell, p. 432, n. 2.

31. Harry S. Truman, "Harry S. Truman 1947 Diary," handwritten, entry for 25 July, p. 23; Harry S. Truman Library and Museum, online at <http://www.trumanlibrary.org/diary/page23.htm>.

32. See McCoy, pp. 292–293.

33. Milkis and Nelson, p. 292; see also their excellent discussion, pp. 291–294.

34. See Ferrell, pp. 330–336.

35. See McCoy, pp. 209–210.

36. *Ibid.*, p. 197.

37. *Ibid.*, p. 167.

38. *Ibid.*, p. 306.

39. *Ibid.*, pp. 307–309.

40. Ferrell, p. 379.

41. Harry S. Truman, *The Autobiography of Harry S. Truman*, Robert H. Ferrell, ed., Columbia: University of Missouri Press, 2002, p. 109.

42. See McCullough, pp. 550–552.

34. Eisenhower

1. Fred I. Greenstein, *The Hidden-Hand Presidency: Eisenhower as Leader*, New York: Basic Books, 1982.

2. Stephen A. Ambrose, *Eisenhower: Soldier and President*, New York: Simon & Schuster, 1990, p. 346.

3. Sidney M. Milkis and Michael Nelson, *The American Presidency*, 4th ed., Washington, DC: CQ Press, 2003, p. 298.

4. Arthur M. Schlesinger, Jr., "Rating the Presidents: Washington to Clinton," *Political Science Quarterly*, 112:2 (Summer 1997), pp. 179–180.

5. *Ibid.*, p. 181.

6. *Ibid.*

7. Arthur M. Schlesinger, Sr., "Our Presidents: A Rating by 75 Historians," *New York Times Magazine* (29 July 1962), pp. 12–13ff.

8. Schlesinger, Jr., p. 189.

9. Michael A. Genovese, *The Power of the American Presidency, 1789–2000*, New York: Oxford University Press, 2001, p. 16.

10. Charles F. and Richard B. Faber, *The American Presidents Ranked by Performance*, Jefferson, NC: McFarland, 2000, p. 31.

11. See Richard W. Waterman, *The Changing American Presidency*, Cincinnati: Atomic Dog Publishing, 2003, pp. 66–71.

12. Ambrose, p. 306.

13. Milkis and Nelson, pp. 299–300.

14. *Ibid.*, p. 303.

15. Ambrose, p. 306.

16. Chester Pach, Jr., and Elmo Richardson, *The Presidency of Dwight D. Eisenhower*, Lawrence: University Press of Kansas, 1991, p. 75.

17. *Ibid.*, p. 80.

18. Ambrose, p. 332.

19. *Ibid.*, p. 333; see also pp. 331–333.

20. *Ibid.*, p. 102.

21. *Ibid.* pp. 101–102.

22. *Ibid.*, pp. 102–103.

23. Pach and Richardson, pp. 126–135.

24. *Ibid.*, pp. 160–161.

25. Ambrose, p. 284; for a description of the incident, see pp. 282–285.

26. See Ambrose, pp. 307–308.

27. Milkis and Nelson, p. 300.

28. Ambrose, p. 307.

29. See *ibid*, p. 283.

30. Pach and Richardson, p. 137.

31. See Ambrose, p. 444; see also pp. 440–448.

32. *Ibid.*, p. 445.

33. Pach and Richardson, p. 60; see also pp. 61–62.

34. Milkis and Nelson, p. 304.

35. *Ibid.*

36. Tom Wicker, *Dwight D. Eisenhower*, New York: Times Books/Henry Holt, 2002, pp. 120–129.

37. Milkis and Nelson, pp. 302–303.

38. *Ibid.*, p. 426.

39. Pach and Richardson, p. 37.

40. Michael R. Beschloss, *Mayday: Eisenhower, Khrushchev, and the U-2 Affair*, New York: Harper and Row, 1986, p. 3; quoted in Milkis and Nelson, p. 344, n. 5.

41. Ambrose, p. 536.

42. *Ibid.*, p. 540.

35. Kennedy

1. Richard Reeves, *President Kennedy*, New York: Touchstone/Simon & Schuster, 1993, p. 36.

2. *Ibid.*, p. 24.

3. Yanek Mieczkowski, *The Routledge Historical Atlas of Presidential Elections*, New York: Routledge, 2001, pp. 115–117.

4. Seymour M. Hersh, *The Dark Side of Camelot*, Boston: Little, Brown, 1997, pp. 131–134.

5. Margaret Truman, *First Ladies*, New York: Fawcett Columbine, 1995, pp. 36–43; quotation on pp. 39–40.

6. See Reeves, pp. 475–476.

7. Allan Nevins and Henry Steele Commager with Jeffrey Morris, *A Pocket History of the United States*, 9th rev. ed., New York: Pocket Books, 1992, p. 550; note that this book was first published in 1942, and that the later editions are less reliable than the early ones.

8. *Ibid.*, pp. 37–38.

9. Garry Wills, *The Kennedy Imprisonment: A Meditation on Power*, Boston: Houghton Mifflin/Mariner Books edition, 2002 [revised from the original edition, 1981], pp. xiii–xiv.

10. Charles F. and Richard B. Faber, *The American Presidents Ranked by Performance*, Jefferson, NC: McFarland, 2000, p. 31.

11. Richard W. Waterman, *The Changing American Presidency*, Cincinnati: Atomic Dog Publishing, 2003, pp. 66 and 71.

12. Reeves, pp. 102–103.

13. Wills, pp. 222–223.

14. Reeves, p. 172.

15. See James N. Giglio, *The Presidency of John F. Kennedy*, Lawrence: University Press of Kansas, 1991, pp. 155–158.

16. *Ibid.*, pp. 234–236.

17. Stephen G. Rabe, ""John F. Kennedy and the World," in James N. Giglio and Stephen G. Rabe, *Debating the Kennedy Presidency*, Lanham, MD: Rowman and Littlefield, 2003, pp. 38–39; see also pp. 40–43.

18. See *Ibid.*, pp. 36–37.
19. Reeves, p. 121.
20. *Ibid.*, p. 552.
21. Rabe, p. 54.
22. *Ibid.*, p. 56.
23. *Ibid.*
24. Reeves, p. 39.
25. Giglio, p. 184.
26. See Max J. Skidmore, *Medicare and the American Rhetoric of Reconciliation*, Tuscaloosa: University of Alabama Press, 1970. See also Skidmore, *Social Security and its Enemies*, Boulder, CO: Westview Press, 1999; a transcript of Reagan's recorded comments is included as an Appendix.
27. Eric F. Goldman, *The Tragedy of Lyndon Johnson*, New York: Knopf, 1969, p. 13.
28. *Ibid.*, p. 14.

16. See Yanek Mieczkowski, *The Routledge Historical Atlas of Presidential Elections*, New York: Routledge, 2001, pp. 118–120.
17. See Dallek, p. 231.
18. Dallek, p. 114.
19. *Ibid.*, pp. 116–117.
20. *Ibid.*, p. 120.
21. *Ibid.*, p. 230.
22. For the tapes, see Michael Beschloss, ed., *Taking Charge*, New York: Simon & Schuster, 1997; and Beschloss, ed., *Reaching for Glory*, New York: Simon & Schuster, 2001.
23. Kearns, pp. 347–349.
24. Dallek, p.530.
25. For LBJ's discussion of the situation regarding the Court, see Johnson, pp. 543–547.
26. Dallek, p. 599.
27. Kearns, p. 352.

36. L.B. Johnson

1. Marc Landy and Sidney Milkis, *Presidential Greatness*, Lawrence: University Press of Kansas, 2000, p. 198.
2. *Ibid.*, p. 205.
3. Wilson Carey McWilliams, "Lyndon B. Johnson: The Last of the Great Presidents," in Marc Landy, ed., *Modern Presidents and the Presidency*, Lexington, MA: Lexington Books, 1985, pp. 163–182.
4. Arthur M. Schlesinger, Jr., "Rating the Presidents: Washington to Clinton," *Political Science Quarterly*, 112:2 (Summer 1997), p. 189.
5. See Richard W. Waterman, *The Changing American Presidency*, Cincinnati: Atomic Dog Publishing, 2003, pp. 64–72.
6. Schlesinger, p. 183.
7. Robert Dallek, *Flawed Giant: Lyndon Johnson and his Times, 1961–1973*, New York: Oxford University Press, 1998, p. 59.
8. See *ibid.*, p. 188.
9. Doris Kearns, *Lyndon Johnson and the American Dream*, New York: Harper and Row, 1976, p. 244.
10. See Lester A. Sobel, ed., *Presidential Succession: Ford, Rockefeller and the 25th Amendment*, New York: Facts on File, 1975, pp. 20–22.
11. See, e.g., Jeffrey K. Tulis, *The Rhetorical Presidency*, Princeton: Princeton University Press, 1987.
12. Goldman, p. 58.
13. See Robert A. Caro, *The Years of Lyndon Johnson: The Path to Power*, New York: Knopf, 1982.
14. Landy and Milkis, pp. 209–211.
15. Lyndon B. Johnson, *The Vantage Point: Perspectives of the Presidency, 1963–1969*, New York: Popular Library, 1971, p. 102.

37. Nixon

1. Forrest McDonald, *The American Presidency: An Intellectual History*, Lawrence, University Press of Kansas, 1994, p. 468.
2. Thomas P. O'Neill, Jr., *Man of the House: The Life and Political Memoirs of Speaker Tip O'Neill*, New York: Random House, 1987, p. 240.
3. See Richard W. Waterman, *The Changing American Presidency*, Cincinnati: Atomic Dog Publishing, 2003, pp. 63–72.
4. Arthur M. Schlesinger, Jr., "Rating the Presidents: Washington to Clinton," *Political Science Quarterly*, 112:2 (Summer 1997), p. 189.
5. Charles F. and Richard B. Faber, *The American Presidents Ranked by Performance*, Jefferson, NC: McFarland, 2000, p. 32.
6. Michael A. Genovese, *The Power of the American Presidency, 1789–2000*, New York: Oxford University Press, 2001, p. 16.
7. William J. Ridings, Jr., and Stuart B. McIver, *Rating the Presidents*, rev. ed., New York: Citadel Press, 2000, p. xi.
8. Schlesinger, p. 183.
9. Stephen E. Ambrose, *Nixon*, vol. II, *The Triumph of a Politician, 1962–1972*, New York: Simon & Schuster, 1989, p. 624.
10. *Ibid.*, p. 658.
11. Robert M. Dallek, *Flawed Giant: Lyndon Johnson and his Times, 1961–1973*, New York: Oxford University Press, 1998, pp. 618–619.
12. Ambrose, *Nixon*, pp. 315–316.
13. Ambrose, p. 337.
14. Richard M. Nixon, *RN: The Memoirs of Richard Nixon*, New York: Simon & Schuster, 1978, p. 415.
15. Tom Wicker, *One of Us: Richard Nixon*

and the American Dream, New York: Random House, 1991, p. 498.
16. Nixon, p. 423.
17. See *ibid.,* pp. 501–506; quotations on pp. 504 and 506.
18. Ambrose, p. 316.
19. George P. Shultz, "How a Republican Desegregated the South's Schools," *New York Times* (8 January 2003), p. A23.
20. Joseph A. Califano, Jr., "Race and the Party of Lincoln," letter to the editor, *New York Times* (10 January 2003), p. A22.
21. Wicker, p. 505.
22. David Firestone, "Billy Graham Responds to lingering Anger Over 1972 Remarks on Jews," *New York Times* (17 March 2002), Section 1, p. 29.
23. Ambrose, p. 350
24. *Ibid.,* p. 351.
25. See *ibid.,* pp. 641–646.
26. For detailed information, see Yanek Mieczkowski, *The Routledge Historical Atlas of Presidential Elections,* New York: Routledge, 2001, pp. 125–127.
27. Ambrose, p. 573.
28. *Ibid.,* pp. 573–574.
29. Genovese, p. 165.
30. Ambrose, pp. 465–466.
31. Genovese, pp. 165–166.

38. Ford

1. Gerald R. Ford, *A Time to Heal,* New York: Harper and Row, 1979, pp. 223–224.
2. See, e.g., Richard W. Waterman, *The Changing American Presidency,* Cincinnati: Atomic Dog Publishing, 2003, pp. 68–71.
3. Charles F. and Richard B. Faber, *The American Presidents Ranked by Performance,* Jefferson, NC: McFarland, 2000, pp. 31–32.
4. Mark J. Rozell, *The Press and the Ford Presidency,* Ann Arbor: University of Michigan Press, 1995, p. 52.
5. Ford included the photograph in his memoirs; see Gerald Ford, *A Time to Heal,* New York: Harper and Row, 1979, second page of photographs following p. 246.
6. See John Robert Greene, *The Presidency of Gerald R. Ford,* Lawrence: University of Kansas, 1995, 99. 42–52.
7. Stephen E. Ambrose, *Nixon: Volume Three, Ruin and Recovery, 1973–1990,* New York: Simon & Schuster, 1991, p. 461.
8. *Ibid.,* p. 462.
9. Ford, p. 197.
10. See Greene, p. 35.
11. *Ibid.,* p. 38.

12. *Ibid.,* pp. 39–42.
13. Greene, p. 75; on Ford's efforts to deal with the economy, see pp. 69–78.
14. See Ford, pp. 315–319.
15. *Ibid.,* pp. 319–332.
16. See Ford, pp. 275–284.
17. Greene, p. 151; see also pp. 143–151.
18. On the swine flu threat and Ford's actions, see the excellent study, Arthur Silverstein, *Pure Politics and Impure Science: The Swine Flu Affair,* Baltimore: Johns Hopkins University Press, 1981; see also "Swine Flu (Supplement), 317.0, The Case Program, Harvard University, John F. Kennedy School of Government, <http://www.ksgcase.harvard.edu/case.htm?PID=317>, and Paul Mickle, "1976: Fear of a Great Plague," <http:www.capitalcentury.com/1976.html> .
19. Margaret Truman, *First Ladies,* New York: Fawcett Columbine, 1995, p. 136.
20. *Ibid.,* p. 137.
21. *Ibid.,* pp. 137–143.
22. Greene, p. 185;
23. *Ibid.,* p. 186; on the debates, see also pp. 181–189.
24. Ford, p. 423.
25. Allan Nevins and Henry Steele Commager, with Jeffrey Morris, *A Pocket History of the United States,* New York: Pocket Books, 1992, p. 600; note that this book originally appeared in 1942; the more recent editions have added questionable interpretations.
26. James Cannon, *Time and Chance: Gerald Ford's Appointment with History,* Ann Arbor: University of Michigan Press, 1998, p. 416.
27. *Ibid.,* p. 415.

39. Carter

1. Erwin C. Hargrove, *Jimmy Carter as President: Leadership and the Politics of the Public Good,* Baton Rouge: Louisiana State University Press, 1988, p. 28.
2. See Richard W. Waterman, *The Changing American Presidency,* Cincinnati: Atomic Dog Press, 2003, pp. 306–308.
3. Burton I. Kaufman, *The Presidency of James Earl Carter,* Lawrence: University Press of Kansas, 1993, p. 66.
4. *Ibid.,* p. 112.
5. This discussion is based on, and all quotations come from, *ibid.,* p. 214.
6. For a listing of these polls, see Waterman, pp. 67–71.
7. William J. Ridings, Jr., and Stuart B. McIver, *Rating the Presidents,* New York: Citadel Press, 2000, p. xi.

8. Charles F. and Richard B. Faber, *The American Presidents Ranked by Performance*, Jefferson, NC: McFarland, 2000, p. 31.

9. Sidney M. Milkis and Michael Nelson, *The American Presidency*, 4th ed., Washington, DC: CQ Press, 2003, pp. 342–343.

10. Kaufman, p. 1.

11. *Ibid.*, pp. 1–2.

12. *Ibid.*, pp. 2–3.

13. For a study of this phase of the debate, see Max J. Skidmore, "Ronald Reagan and Operation Coffeecup: A Hidden Episode in American History," *Journal of American Culture*, 12:3 (Fall 1989); for a complete transcript of Reagan's attack on the Medicare proposal that he conducted on behalf of the American Medical Association, see Max J. Skidmore, *Social Security and its Enemies*, Boulder, CO: Westview Press, 1999, Appendix.

14. Kaufman, p. 211.

15. Douglas Brinkley, *The Unfinished Presidency*, New York: Penguin, 1999, p. 3.

40. Reagan

1. Yanek Mieczkowski, *The Routledge Historical Atlas of Presidential Elections*, New York: Routledge, 2001, pp. 131–133.

2. See Max J. Skidmore, "Ronald Reagan and 'Operation Coffeecup: A Hidden Episode in American Political History," *Journal of American Culture*, 12:3 (Fall 1989), pp. 89–96.

3. Lou Cannon, *President Reagan: The Role of a Lifetime*, New York: Public Affairs, 2000, pp. 48–49.

4. *Ibid.*, pp. 442–443.

5. For a detailed study of "The Speech," see Kurt Ritter, "Ronald Reagan and 'The Speech,': The Rhetoric of Public Relations Politics," *Western Speech*, XXXII:1 (Winter 1968); reprinted in Max J. Skidmore, *Word Politics: Essays on Language and Politics*, Palo Alto: James E. Freel and Associates, 1972, pp. 110–118 [page numbers cited hereafter are from this reprint].

6. For the complete text of the recording, see Max J. Skidmore, "Appendix," *Social Security and its Enemies: The Case for America's Most Efficient Insurance Program*, Boulder, CO: Westview Press, 1999, pp. 157–165.

7. Ritter, pp. 112–113.

8. Lawrence I. Barrett, *Gambling with History: Ronald Reagan in the White House*, Garden City, NY: Doubleday, 1983, p. 155.

9. *Ibid.*, p. 63.

10. Sidney M. Milkis and Michael Nelson, *The American Presidency*, 4th ed., Washington, DC: CQ Press, 2003, pp. 360–361.

11. *Ibid.*, pp. 360–361.

12. *Ibid.*, p. 361

13. Quoted *ibid.*, pp. 351–352.

14. Daniel P. Moynihan, "Reagan's Bankrupt Budget," *The New Republic* (21 December 1983); Moynihan's comments come from this article.

15. David A. Stockman, *The Triumph of Politics*, New York: Avon Books, 1987, *passim*; quotation is on p. 458.

16. Tom Wicker, "A Deliberate Deficit," *New York Times* (19 July 1985).

17. Milkis and Nelson, pp. 354–355.

18. Marlin Fitzwater, *Call the Briefing — A Memoir: Ten Years in the White House with Presidents Reagan and Bush*, no city: Xlibris Books, 2000, p. 308.

19. Cannon, p. 695.

20. *Ibid.*, p. 696.

21. Mieczkowski, pp. 134–136.

22. Cannon, pp. 566–567.

23. Arthur M. Schlesinger, Jr., "Rating the Presidents: Washington to Clinton," *Political Science Quarterly*, 112:2 (Summer 1997), p. 189.

24. Michael A. Genovese, *The Power of the American Presidency, 1789–2000*, New York: Oxford University Press, 2000, p. 16.

25. William J. Ridings, Jr., and Stuart B. McIver, *Rating the Presidents*, New York: Citadel press, 2000, p. xi.

26. In Richard W. Waterman, *The Changing American Presidency*, Cincinnati: Atomic Dog Publishing, 2003, p. 71.

27. Charles F. and Richard B. Faber, *The American Presidents Ranked by Performance*, Jefferson, NC: McFarland, 2000, p. 32.

28. See "Presidential Clemency Actions, 1789–2001," University of Pittsburgh School of Law, at <http://jurist.law.pitt.edu/pardonspres1.htm>.

29. Milkis and Nelson, pp. 352–353.

30. John L. Palmer and Isabel V. Sawhill, *The Reagan Record: An Urban Institute Study*, Cambridge, MA: Ballinger Publishing Co., 1984, pp. 15–16.

31. See Eric Alterman, *What Liberal Media?*, New York: Basic Books, 2003.

41. G.H.W. Bush

1. Herbert S. Parmet, *George Bush: The Life of a Lone-Star Yankee*, New York: Scribner's, 1997, pp. 344–348.

2. *Ibid.*, p. 349.

3. *Ibid.*, p. 436.

4. Yanek Mieczkowski, *The Routledge Historical Atlas of Presidential Elections*, New York: Routledge, 2001, pp. 133; 137–139.

5. Arthur M. Schlesinger, Jr., "Rating the

Presidents: Washington to Clinton," *Political Science Quarterly*, 112:2 (Summer 1997), p. 189.

6. See Richard W. Waterman, *The Changing American Presidency*, Cincinnati: Atomic Dog Publishing, 2003, p. 71.

7. Michael A. Genovese, *The Power of the American Presidency, 1789–2000*, New York: Oxford University Press, 2001, p. 16.

8. William A. Ridings, Jr., and Stuart McIver, *Rating the Presidents*, rev. ed., New York: Citadel Books, 2000, p. xi.

9. Charles F. and Richard B. Faber, *The American Presidents Ranked by Performance*, Jefferson, NC: McFarland, 2000, p. 31.

10. Parmet, p. 369.

11. Douglas Brinkley, *The Unfinished Presidency: Jimmy Carter's Journey Beyond the White House*, New York: Penguin, 1998, pp. 209–309; quotation on p. 309*l*

12. Lou Cannon, *President Reagan: The Role of a Lifetime*, New York: Public Affairs, 2000, p. 291.

13. See Sidney M. Milkis and Michael Nelson, *The American Presidency*, 4th ed., Washington, DC: CQ Press, 2003, pp. 370–371.

14. Parmet, pp. 477–485.

15. James Fallows, "Post President for Life," *The Atlantic Monthly* (March 2003), p. 67.

16. Mieczkowski, p. 143.

17. *Ibid.*, p. 97.

18. "Presidential Clemency Actions, 1789–2001," University of Pittsburgh School of Law, <http://jurist.law.pitt.edu/pardonspres1.htm>.

19. Peter Slevin and George Lardner, Jr., "Rush of Pardons Unusual in Scope, Lack of Scrutiny," *Washington Post* (10 March 2001); at <http://www.warroom.com/pardonme/unusualscope.htm>, p. 1.

20. Jonathan Alter, "Citizen Clinton Up Close," *Newsweek* (8 April 2002), p. 36.

21. Slevin and Lardner, p. 3.

22. Parmet, p. 510.

23. See Hillary Rodham Clinton, *Living History*, New York: Simon & Schuster, 2003, p. 320.

24. *Ibid.*, pp. 128–129.

25. *Ibid.*, p. 124.

26. Parmet, p. 510.

42. Clinton

1. See Sidney M. Milkis and Michael Nelson, *The American Presidency*, 4th ed., Washington, DC: CQ Press, 2003, p. 344, n. 5; John Eisenhower's comment originally reported in Michael R. Beschloss, *Mayday: Eisenhower, Khrushchev, and the U-2 Affair*, New York: Harper and Row, 1986, p. 3.

2. Michael A. Genovese, *The Power of the American Presidency, 1789–2000*, New York: Oxford University Press, 2001, p. 16.

3. See Richard W. Waterman, *The Changing American Presidency*, Cincinnati: Atomic Dog Publishing 2003, p. 71.

4. William J. Ridings, Jr., and Stuart B. McIver, *Rating the Presidents*, New York: Citadel Press, 2000, p. xi.

5. *Ibid.*, p. 283.

6. Charles F. and Richard B. Faber, *The American Presidents Ranked by Performance*, Jefferson, NC: McFarland, 2000, p. 31.

7. Milkis and Nelson, pp. 388–389.

8. See Max J. Skidmore, *Social Security and its Enemies*, Boulder, CO: Westview, 1999, chapter 8.

9. Quoted in Eric Alterman, *What Liberal Media?*, New York: Basic Books, 2003, p. 14.

10. *Ibid.*, p. 145.

11. For an interesting explanation of Whitewater from one who was intimately involved, see Susan McDougal, *The Woman Who Wouldn't Talk*, New York: Carroll and Graf, 2003.

12. Yanek Mieczkowski, *The Routledge Historical Atlas of Presidential Elections*, New York: Routledge, 2001, p. 146.

13. Alterman, p. 141.

14. *Ibid.*, p. 290, n. 7.

15. William Booth, "The Green President: By Circumventing Congress, Clinton Created an Environmental Legacy," *Washington Post National Weekly Edition* (22–28 January 2001), pp. 6–7.

16. Ronald Brownstein, "Clinton: The Untold Story," *The American Prospect* (25 February 2002), pp. 33–37.

17. "President Wants Senate to Hurry with New Anti-Terrorism Laws," *CNN Interactive* (30 July 1996) at <http://www.cnn.com/US/9607/30/clinton.terrorism/>.

18. Steve Ricchetti, "Don't Put the Blame on Clinton," *Washington Post* (22 February 2003), p. A25.

19. "Presidential Clemency Actions," University of Pittsburgh School of Law, at <http://jurist.law.pitt.edu/pardonspres1.htm>, pp. 3–4.

20. Randal C. Archibold, "Prosecutors Clear Clintons in Clemency of 4 Hasidic Men," *New York Times* (21 June 2002), p. A18.

21. Cass R. Sunstein, "The Warrior's Tale," *The American Prospect* (July/August 2003), p. 67.

22. See, e.g., Joe Conason, "Where's the Media Mea Culpa?," *Salon.com* (28 March 2002) at <http://www.salon.com/news/col/cona/2002/03/28/whitewater/index_np.html>.

23. Sunstein, p. 67.

43. G.W. Bush

1. Yanek Mieczkowski, *The Routledge Historical Atlas of Presidential Elections*, New York: Routledge, 2001, pp. 150–151.

2. Gerald M. Pomper, "The Presidential Election," in *The Election of 2000*, Gerald M. Pomper, ed., New York: Chatham House, 2001, p. 126.

3. *Ibid.* p. 130.

4. *Ibid.*, pp. 131–132.

5. "Court Backs Disclosure of Energy Advisers," *Kansas City Star* (9 July 2003), p. A9.

6. Quoted in a CNN report, "Europeans Fear a Bolder Bush," <http://www.cnn.com/2002/WORLD/europe/11/06/europe.us.reax/index.html> retrieved 6 November 2002.

7. *Ibid.*

8. Andrew Cohen, "Still the Accidental President," *Toronto Globe and Mail* (3 August 2002) p. A13.

9. Thomas L. Friedman, "The American Idol," *The New York Times* (6 November 2002).

10. Ellen Hale," Global Warmth for U.S. After 9/11 Turns to Frost: Military Plans Repulse Even European Allies," *USA Today* (14 August 2002), p. 1A.

11. Dana Milbank, "For Bush, Facts Are Malleable," *Washington Post* (22 October 2002), p. A01.

12. John W. Dean, "Missing Weapons of Mass Destruction: Is Lying About the Reason for War An Impeachable Offense?," *Findlaw* (6 June 2003), <http://writ.news.findlaw.com/dean/200330606.html>.

13. David Broder, "News Conference lays Bare Shortcomings," *Kansas City Star* (17 March 2003), p. B5.

BIBLIOGRAPHY

Abbott, Philip. *Strong Presidents: A Theory of Leadership.* Knoxville: University of Tennessee Press, 1998.

Alter, Jonathan. "Citizen Clinton Up Close." *Newsweek* (8 April 2002), p. 36.

Alterman, Eric. *What Liberal Media?* New York: Basic Books, 2003.

Ambrose, Stephen E. *Eisenhower: Soldier and President.* New York: Simon & Schuster, 1990.

_____. *Nixon.* Volume Two: *The Triumph of a Politician, 1962–1972.* New York: Simon and Schuster, 1989.

_____. *Nixon.* Volume Three: *Ruin and Recovery, 1973–1990.* New York: Simon & Schuster, 1991.

Angle, Paul M., and Earl Schenck Miers, eds. *The Living Lincoln.* New York: Barnes and Noble, 1992.

Anthony, Carl Sferrazza. *Florence Harding.* New York: William Morrow, 1998.

Appleby, Joyce. "Thomas Jefferson: 1801–1809." In Alan Brinkley and Davis Dyer, eds., *Reader's Companion to the American Presidency.* Boston: Houghton Mifflin, 2000.

Archibold, Randal C. "Prosecutors Clear Clintons in Clemency of 4 Hasidic Men." *New York Times* (21 June 2002), p. A18.

Auchincloss, Louis. *Theodore Roosevelt.* New York: Times Books/Henry Holt, 2001.

Bailey, Thomas A. "James Buchanan." In James M. McPherson, ed., *To the Best of My Ability: The American Presidents.* New York: Society of American Historians/Agincourt, 2001.

_____. "Millard Fillmore." In James M. McPherson, ed., *To the Best of My Ability: The American Presidents.* New York: Society of American Historians/Agincourt, 2001.

_____. *Presidential Greatness.* New York: Appleton-Century-Crofts, 1966.

Barber, James David. *The Presidential Character: Predicting Performance in the White House.* 4th ed. Englewood Cliffs, NJ: Prentice Hall, 1992; originally published 1972.

Barrett, Lawrence I. *Gambling with History: Ronald Reagan in the White House.* Garden City, NY: Doubleday, 1983.

Bergeron, Paul H. *The Presidency of James K. Polk.* Lawrence: University Press of Kansas, 1987.

Beschloss, Michael. *The Conquerors.* New York: Simon & Schuster, 2002.

_____. *Mayday: Eisenhower, Khrushchev, and the U-2 Affair.* New York: Harper and Row, 1986.

_____. *Reaching for Glory.* New York: Simon & Schuster, 2001.

_____. *Taking Charge.* New York: Simon & Schuster, 1997.

_____, ed. *History of the Presidents.* New York: Crown 2000.

Binkley, Wilfred. *The Power of the Presidency.* Garden City, NY: Doubleday, Doran, 1937.

Blum, John Morton. *The Republican Roosevelt.* New York: Atheneum, 1954.

_____. *Woodrow Wilson and the Politics of Morality.* Boston: Little, Brown, 1956.

Boller, Paul F., Jr. *Presidential Inaugurations: From Washington's Election to George W. Bush's Gala.* San Diego: Harcourt Brace, 2001.

Booth, William. "The Green President: By Circumventing Congress, Clinton Created an

Environmental Legacy." *Washington Post National Weekly Edition* (22–28 January 2001), pp. 6–7.

Boritt, Gabor S., ed. *The Historian's Lincoln.*" Urbana: University of Illinois Press, 1996.

Brinkley, Alan, and Davis Dyer, eds. *The Reader's Companion to the American Presidency* Boston: Houghton Mifflin, 2001.

Brinkley, Douglas. *The Unfinished Presidency: Jimmy Carter's Journey Beyond the White House.* New York: Penguin, 1998.

Brookhiser, Richard. *George Washington: Founding Father.* New York: The Free Press, 1996.

Brown, Ralph Adams. *The Presidency of John Adams.* Lawrence: University Press of Kansas, 1975.

Brown, Richard D. "The Disenchantment of a Radical Whig: John Adams Reckons with Free Speech." In Richard Alan Ryerson, ed., *John Adams and the Founding of the Republic.* Boston: Massachusetts Historical Society, 2001.

Brownstein, Ronald. "Clinton: The Untold Story." *The American Prospect* (25 February 2002), pp. 33–37.

Buranelli, Vincent. "James Madison: The Nation Builder." In Michael Beschloss, ed., *History of the Presidents.* New York: Crown, 2000.

Califano, Joseph A., Jr. "Race and the Party of Lincoln." Letter to the editor, *New York Times* (10 January 2003), p. A22.

Cannon, James. *Time and Chance: Gerald Ford's Appointment with History.* Ann Arbor: University of Michigan Press, 1998.

Cannon, Lou. *President Reagan: The Role of a Lifetime.* New York: Public Affairs, 2000.

Capers, Gerald M. *John C. Calhoun: Opportunist.* Chicago: Quadrangle, 1969.

Cappon, Lester J., ed., *The Adams-Jefferson Letters.* 2 vols. Chapel Hill: University of North Carolina Press, 1959.

Caro, Robert A. *The Years of Lyndon Johnson: Vol. 1. The Path to Power.* New York: Knopf, 1982.

Catton, Bruce. *This Hallowed Ground.* New York: Washington Square, 1956.

Clements, Kendrick. *The Presidency of Woodrow Wilson.* Lawrence: University Press of Kansas, 1992.

Clements, Kendrick A. *Woodrow Wilson: World Statesman.* Boston: Twayne, 1987.

Clinton, Catherine. "Benjamin Harrison." In James M. McPherson, ed., *To the Best of My Ability: The American Presidents.* New York: Society of American Historians Agincourt, 2001.

Clinton, Hillary Rodham. *Living History.* New York: Simon & Schuster, 2003.

Cohen, Andrew. "Still the Accidental President." *Toronto Globe and Mail* (3 August 2002), p. A13.

Cole, Donald B. *Martin Van Buren and the American Political System,* Princeton: Princeton University Press, 1984.

_____. *The Presidency of Andrew Jackson.* Lawrence: University Press of Kansas, 1993.

Coletta, Paolo E. *The Presidency of William Howard Taft.* Lawrence: University Press of Kansas, 1973.

Conason, Joe. "Where's the Media Mea Culpa?" *Salon.com* (28 March 2002) at http://www.salon.com/news/col/cona/2002/03/28/whitewater/index_np.html

Cooper, John Milton, Jr. *The Warrior and the Priest: Woodrow Wilson and Theodore Roosevelt.* Cambridge, MA: The Belknap Press of Harvard University Press, 1983.

"Court Backs Disclosure of Energy Advisers" *Kansas City Star* (9 July 2003), p. A9.

Cox, LaWanda. "Lincoln and Black Freedom" In Gabor S. Boritt, ed., *The Historian's Lincoln.*" Urbana: University of Illinois Press, 1996.

Cunningham, Noble E., Jr. *The Presidency of James Monroe.* Lawrence: University Press of Kansas, 1996.

Dallek, Robert. *Flawed Giant: Lyndon Johnson and his Times; 1961–1973.* New York: Oxford University Press, 1998.

Dalton, Kathleen. *Theodore Roosevelt: A Strenuous Life.* New York: Alfred A. Knopf, 2002.

Dean, John W. "Missing Weapons of Mass Destruction: Is Lying About the Reason for War an Impeachable Offense?" *Findlaw* (6 June 2003), http://writ.news.findlaw.com/dean/200330606.html.

De Santis, Vincent P. "Grover Cleveland." In James M. MacPherson, ed. *To the Best of My Ability: The American Presidents.* New York: Society of American Historians, Agincourt 2001.

Diggins, John Patrick. "John Quincy Adams." In James McPherson, ed., *To the Best of My Ability: The American Presidents*. New York: Society of American Historians/Agincourt, 2001.

Dixon, Joseph M. "Theodore Roosevelt." Typescript. Joseph Dixon papers, Series 55, Box 100, Folder 1, Archives of the University of Montana Library, Missoula.

Doenecke, Justus D. *The Presidencies of James A. Garfield and Chester A. Arthur.* Lawrence: University Press of Kansas, 1981.

Eisinger, Robert M. "Gauging Public Opinion in the Hoover White House: Understanding the Roots of Presidential Polling," *Presidential Studies Quarterly.* 30:4 (December 2000), pp. 643–661.

Elkins, Stanley, and Eric McKitrick, *The Age of Federalism.* New York: Oxford University Press, 1993.

Ellis, Joseph J. *Passionate Sage: The Character and Legacy of John Adams,* New York: W. W. Norton, 1993.

"Europeans Fear a Bolder Bush," CNN Report, http://www.cnn.com/2002/WORLD/europe/11/06/europe.us.reax/index.htl retrieved 6 November 2002.

Faber, Charles F., and Richard B. Faber. *The American Presidents Ranked by Performance,* Jefferson, NC: McFarland, 2000.

Fallows, James. "Post President for Life." *The Atlantic Monthly* (March 2003), p. 67.

Fallows, Samuel. *Life of William McKinley: Our Martyred President.* Chicago: Regan, 1901.

Fausold, Martin L. *The Presidency of Herbert C. Hoover.* Lawrence: University Press of Kansas, 1985.

Ferling, John. *Harry S. Truman: A Life.* Columbia: University of Missouri Press, 1994.

_____. *John Adams: A Life.* Knoxville: University of Tennessee Press, 1992.

Ferrell, Robert H. *The Presidency of Calvin Coolidge.* Lawrence: University Press of Kansas, 1998.

Firestone, David. "Billy Graham Responds to Lingering Anger Over 1972 Remarks on Jews." *New York Times* (17 March 2002), p. A 29.

Fitzwater, Marlin. *Call the Briefing A Memoir: Ten Years in the White House with Presidents Reagan and Bush.* No city: Xlibris, 2000.

Flexner, James T. *George Washington: A Biography.* 4 vols. Boston: Little, Brown, 1965–1972.

_____. *George Washington and the New Nation: 1783–1793.* Boston: Little, Brown, 1970.

_____. *Washington: The Indispensable Man.* Boston: Little, Brown, 1974.

Foner, Eric. "Andrew Johnson." In Alan Brinkley and Davis Dyer, eds., *Reader's Companion to the American Presidency.* Boston: Houghton Mifflin, 2000.

Ford, Gerald R. *A Time to Heal.* New York: Harper and Row, 1979.

Franklin, John Hope. "Lincoln and the Politics of War." In Ralph G. Newman, ed., *Lincoln for the Ages.* New York: Pyramid, 1960.

Freeman, Douglas Southall. *George Washington.* 7 vols. New York: Scribner's, 1948–1957.

_____. *R. E. Lee: A Biography.* 4 vols. New York: Scribner's, 1934–1935.

_____. *Washington: An Abridgement in One Volume by Richard Harwell.* New York: Touchstone, 1995.

Freidel, Frank. *Franklin D. Roosevelt: A Rendezvous with Destiny.* Boston: Little, Brown, 1990.

Friedman, Thomas L. "The American Idol." *The New York Times* (6 November 2002).

Gallagher, Carl, and Alan T. Nolan, eds. *The Myth of the Lost Cause and Civil War History.* Bloomington: Indiana University Press, 2000.

Gara, Larry. *The Presidency of Franklin Pierce.* Lawrence: University Press of Kansas, 1991.

Genovese, Michael A. *The Power of the American Presidency: 1789–2000.* New York: Oxford University Press, 2001.

Gienapp, William. "James Buchanan" In Alan Brinkley and Davis Dyer, eds., *Reader's Companion to the American Presidency.* New York: Houghton Mifflin, 2000. p. 178.

Giglio, James N. *The Presidency of John F. Kennedy.* Lawrence: The University Press of Kansas, 1991.

_____, and Stephen G. Rabe, eds. *Debating the Kennedy Presidency.* Lanham, MD: Rowman and Littlefield, 2003.

Goldman, Eric F. *The Tragedy of Lyndon Johnson.* New York: Alfred A. Knopf, 1969.

Goodwin, Doris Kearns. *No Ordinary Time: Franklin and Eleanor Roosevelt: The Home Front in World War II.* New York: Simon & Schuster, 1994.

Gould, Lewis L. *The Presidency of William McKinley.* Lawrence: University Press of Kansas, 1980.

Graff, Henry F. *Grover Cleveland.* New York: Times Books/Henry Holt, 2002.

Grant, Ulysses S., III. *Ulysses S. Grant: Warrior and Statesman* New York: Morrow, 1968.

Greene, John Robert. *The Presidency of Gerald R. Ford* Lawrence: University of Kansas, 1995.

Greenstein, Fred I. *The Hidden-Hand Presidency: Eisenhower as Leader.* New York: Basic, 1982.

Hale, Ellen. "Global Warmth for U.S. After 9/11 Turns to Frost: Military Plans Repulse Even European Allies." *USA Today* (14 August 2002), p. A 1.

Hall, Joshua. "Reassessing an Ohio President," a two-page essay on the Internet at http://www.buckeyeinstitute.org/oped/reassessing.htm

Harbaugh, William H. *The Life and Times of Theodore Roosevelt.* Rev. ed. New York: Oxford University Press, 1975.

Hargreaves, Mary. *The Presidency of John Quincy Adams.* Lawrence: University Press of Kansas, 1985.

Hargrove, Erwin C. *Jimmy Carter as President: Leadership and the Politics of the Public Good.* Baton Rouge: Louisiana State University Press, 1988.

_____. *The President as Leader.* Lawrence: University Press of Kansas, 1998.

Haynes, Sam W. *James K. Polk and the Expansionist Impulse,* New York: Longman, 1997.

Hersh, Seymour M. *The Dark Side of Camelot.* Boston: Little, Brown, 1997.

Holt, Michael. "Millard Fillmore." In Alan Brinkley and Davis Dyer, eds., *Reader's Companion to the American Presidency.* Boston: Houghton Mifflin, 2000.

Hoogenboom, Ari. *The Presidency of Rutherford B. Hayes.* Lawrence: University Press of Kansas, 1988.

"How Historians Rank the Presidents Now." *The Washingtonian* (April 2000), p. 55.

Hunter, Lloyd A. "The Immortal Confederacy: Another Look at Lost Cause Religion." In Carl Gallagher and Alan T. Nolan, eds., *The Myth of the Lost Cause and Civil War History.* Bloomington: Indiana University Press, 2000.

Jacobs, David, and Robert A. Rutland, "James Monroe: The Era of Good Feelings." In Michael Beschloss, ed., *History of the Presidents.* New York: Crown 2000.

_____, and _____. "Millard Fillmore." In Michael Beschloss, ed., *History of the Presidents.* New York: Crown, 2000.

John, Richard R. "John Quincy Adams." In Alan Brinkley and Davis Dyer, *The Reader's Companion to the American Presidency* Boston: Houghton Mifflin, 2001.

Johnson, Lyndon B. *The Vantage Point: Perspectives of the Presidency, 1963–1969.* New York: Popular Library, 1971.

Kaufman, Burton, I. *The Presidency of James Earl Carter.* Lawrence: University Press of Kansas, 1993.

Kearns, Doris. *Lyndon Johnson and the American Dream.* New York: Harper and Row, 1976.

Kennedy, Roger G. *Mr. Jefferson's Lost Cause: Land, Farmers, Slavery and the Louisiana Purchase.* New York: Oxford University Press, 2003.

Ketcham, Ralph. *James Madison: A Biography,* Charlottesville: University Press of Virginia, 1990.

Klein, Philip Shriver. *President James Buchanan: A Biography,* University Park: Pennsylvania State University Press, 1962.

Koenig, Louis W. "Benjamin Harrison: Presidential Grandson." In Michael Beschloss, ed., *History of the Presidents.* New York: Crown, 2000.

Kunhardt, Philip B., Jr. Philip B. Kunhardt III, and Peter Kunhardt. *The American President.* New York: Riverhead Books, 1999.

Landy, Marc, ed. *Modern Presidents and the Presidency.* Lexington, MA: Lexington Books, 1985.

_____, and Sidney Milkis. *Presidential Greatness.* Lawrence: University Press of Kansas, 2000.

Leonard, Thomas M. *James K. Polk: A Clear and Unquestionable Destiny,* Wilmington, DE: Scholarly Resources, 2001.

Levy, Leonard. *Jefferson and Civil Liberties: The Darker Side.* Cambridge, MA: Belknap Press of Harvard University Press, 1963.

Luray, Martin, and Robert Rutland, "Franklin Pierce: Overwhelmed by Events." In Michael Beschloss, ed. *History of the Presidents,* New York: Crown, 2000.

Lyons, Eugene. *Herbert Hoover.* New York: Doubleday, 1964.

Maranell, Gary M. "The Evaluation of Presidents: An Extension of the Schlesinger Polls." *Journal of American History* 57 (June 1970), pp. 104–131.

Marton, Kati. *Hidden Power: Presidential Marriages that Shaped Our History.* New York: Anchor, 2003.

McCoy, Drew R. *The Last of the Fathers: James Madison and the Republican Legacy.* Cambridge, MA: Harvard University Press, 1989.

McCoy, Donald R. *The Presidency of Harry S. Truman.* Lawrence: University Press of Kansas, 1984.

McCullough, David. *The American Presidency: An Intellectual History.* Lawrence, University Press of Kansas, 1994.

_____. *John Adams.* New York: Simon & Schuster, 2001.

_____. *The Presidency of George Washington.* Lawrence: University Press of Kansas, 1974.

_____. *The Presidency of Thomas Jefferson.* Lawrence: University Press of Kansas, 1976.

_____. *Truman.* New York: Simon & Schuster, 1992.

McDougal, Susan. *The Woman Who Wouldn't Talk.* New York: Carroll and Graf, 2003.

McFeely, William. *Grant: A Biography.* New York: W.W. Norton, 1982.

McPherson, James, ed. *To the Best of My Ability: The American Presidents.* New York: Society of American Historians/Agincourt, 2001.

McWilliams, Wilson Carey. "Lyndon B. Johnson: The Last of the Great Presidents" In Marc Landy, ed., *Modern Presidents and the Presidency,* Lexington, MA: Lexington, 1985, pp. 163–182.

Mickle, Paul. "1976: Fear of a Great Plague," Online at <http:www.capitalcentury.com/1976.html>.

Mieczkowski, Yanek. *The Routledge Historical Atlas of Presidential Elections,* New York: Routledge, 2001.

Milbank, Dana. "For Bush, Facts Are Malleable" *Washington Post* (22 October 2002), p. A01.

Milkis, Sidney, and Michael Nelson, *The American Presidency: 1776–1998.* 4th ed. Washington, DC: Congressional Quarterly Press, 2003.

Miller, Nathan. *Theodore Roosevelt: A Life.* New York: William Morrow, 1992.

Miller, William Lee. *Arguing About Slavery.* New York: Alfred A. Knopf, 1996.

Morris, Edmund. *Theodore Rex.* New York: Random House, 2001.

Moynihan, Daniel P. "Reagan's Bankrupt Budget." *The New Republic* (21 December 1983).

Murray, Robert K. *The Harding Era.* Minneapolis: University of Minnesota Press, 1969.

_____, and Tim H. Blessing, *Greatness in the White House: Rating the Presidents Washington through Carter.* University Park: Pennsylvania State University Press, 1988.

Nagel, Paul C. *John Quincy Adams: A Public Life, A Private Life.* Cambridge, MA: Harvard University Press, 1997.

Neal, Steve. "Our Best and Worst Presidents" *Chicago Tribune Magazine* (10 January 1982), pp. 8–13ff.

Nevins, Allan, and Henry Steele Commager with Jeffrey Morris. *A Pocket History of the United States.* 9th rev. ed. New York: Pocket, 1992.

Newman, Ralph G. ed. *Lincoln for the Ages.* New York: Pyramid, 1960.

Nichols, Roy Franklin. *Franklin Pierce: Young Hickory of the Granite Hills.* Philadelphia: University of Pennsylvania Press, 1931.

Nixon, Richard M. *RN: The Memoirs of Richard Nixon.* New York: Simon & Schuster, 1978.

Oates, Stephen. "A Momentous Decree: Commentary on 'Lincoln and Black Freedom,'" In Gabor S. Boritt, ed., *The Historian's Lincoln.* Urbana: University of Illinois Press, 1996.

Offner, Arnold. *Another Such Peace: President Truman and the Cold War, 1945–1953.* Palo Alto, CA: Stanford Nuclear Age Series, 2002.

O'Neill, Thomas P., Jr. *Man of the House: The Life and Political Memoirs of Speaker Tip O'Neill.* New York: Random House, 1987.

Pach, Chester, Jr., and Elmo Richardson, *The Presidency of Dwight D. Eisenhower.* Lawrence: University Press of Kansas, 1991.

Palmer John L., and Isabel V. Sawhill. *The Reagan Record: An Urban Institute Study,* Cambridge, MA: Ballinger, 1984.

Parmet, Herbert S. *George Bush: The Life of a Lone-Star Yankee.* New York: Scribner's, 1997.

Patrick, John J., Richard M. Pious, and Donald A. Ritchie, *Oxford Essential Guide to the U.S. Government.* New York: Berkeley Books, 2000.

Pederson, William, and Ann McLaurin, eds. *The Rating Game in American Politics*. New York: Irving, 1987. p. 33.

Perkins, Dexter. *The New Age of Franklin Roosevelt, 1932–1945*. Chicago: University of Chicago Press, 1964.

Peterson, Merrill D. *Lincoln in American Memory*. New York: Oxford University Press, 1994.

_____. *Thomas Jefferson and the New Nation: A Biography*. London: Oxford University Press, 1970.

Peterson, Norma Lois. *The Presidencies of William Henry Harrison and John Tyler*. Lawrence: University Press of Kansas, 1989.

Pious, Richard M. "John Tyler: Tenth President, 1841–1845." In James M. McPherson, ed., *To the Best of my Ability: The American Presidents* New York: Society of American Historians/Agincourt, 2001.

_____. *The Presidency*. Boston: Allyn and Bacon, 1996.

Pomper, Gerald M. "The Presidential Election." In Gerald M. Pomper, ed., *The Election of 2000*. New York: Chatham House, 2001.

"President Wants Senate to Hurry with New Anti-Terrorism Laws." *CNN Interactive* (30 July 1996). Online at http://www.cnn.com/US/9607/30/clinton.terrorism/.

Presidential Clemency Actions, 1789–2001." University of Pittsburgh School of Law. Online at http://jurist.law.pitt.edu/pardonspres1.htm.

Pringle, Henry F. *Theodore Roosevelt A Biography*. New York: Harcourt Brace, 1931.

Rabe, Stephen G. "John F. Kennedy and the World." In James N. Giglio and Stephen G. Rabe, eds., *Debating the Kennedy Presidency* Lanham, MD: Rowman and Littlefield, 2003.

Rakove, Jack N. *James Madison and the Creation of the American Republic*. Glenview, Il: Scott Foresman, 1990.

_____. "Origins of the Presidency." *National Forum* 80:1 (Winter 2000).

Randall, J. G. *Lincoln: The Liberal Statesman*. New York: Dodd, Mead, 1947.

Randall, Willard Sterne. *George Washington*. New York: Henry Holt, 1997.

Rawley, James A. "Franklin Pierce." In James M. McPherson, ed., *To the Best of My Ability: The American Presidents*. New York: The Society of American Historians/Agincourt, 2001.

Rayback, Robert J. *Millard Fillmore: Biography of a President*. Buffalo, NY: Henry Stewart for the Buffalo Historical Society, 1959.

Reeves, Richard. *President Kennedy*. New York: Touchstone/Simon & Schuster, 1993.

Reeves, Thomas C. *Gentleman Boss: The Life of Chester Alan Arthur*. New York: Alfred A. Knopf, 1975.

Remini, Robert V. *Andrew Jackson*. New York: HarperPerennial, 1999.

_____. *John Quincy Adams*. New York: Henry Holt 2002.

_____. *Martin Van Buren and the Making of the Democratic Party*. New York: Columbia University Press, 1959.

Rhodes, James Ford. *The McKinley and Roosevelt Administrations: 1897–1909*. New York: Macmillan, 1922.

Riccards, Michael. *The Ferocious Engine of Democracy: A History of the American Presidency*. 2 vols. Lanham, MD: Madison, 1997.

Ridings, William J., Jr., and Stuart B. McIver. *Rating the Presidents*. Rev. ed. New York: Citadel, 2000.

Ritter, Kurt. "Ronald Reagan and 'The Speech,': The Rhetoric of Public Relations Politics" *Western Speech* 32:1 (Winter 1968). Reprinted in Max J. Skidmore, ed., *Word Politics: Essays on Language and Politics*. Palo Alto, CA: James E. Freel, 1972. pp. 110–118.

Roosevelt, Theodore. *Theodore Roosevelt: An Autobiography* New York: Da Capo Press, 1985 [1913].

Rossiter, Clinton. *The American Presidency*. Baltimore: Johns Hopkins University Press, 1987 [1956].

Rozell, Mark J. *The Press and the Ford Presidency*. Ann Arbor: University of Michigan Press, 1995.

Rutland, Robert A. *James Madison: The Founding Father*. Columbia: University of Missouri Press, 1987.

Ryerson, Richard Alan, ed. *John Adams and the Founding of the Republic*. Boston: Massachusetts Historical Society, 2001.

Scarry, Robert J. *Millard Fillmore.* Jefferson, NC: McFarland, 2001.

Schaff, John. "The Domestic Lincoln: White House Lobbying of the Civil War Congresses." *White House Studies* 2:1 (2002), pp. 37–50.

_____. *A Life in the Twentieth Century.* Boston: Houghton Mifflin, 2000.

Schlesinger, Arthur M., Jr. "Rating the Presidents: Washington to Clinton." *Political Science Quarterly.* 112:2 (1997), p. 182.

Schlesinger, Arthur M., Sr. "Historians Rate U. S. Presidents." *Life Magazine* (1 November 1948), pp. 65–66ff.

_____. "Our Presidents: A Rating by 75 Historians," *New York Times Magazine* (29 July 1962), pp. 12–13ff.

Scott, Janny. "History's Judgment of the 2 Civil War Generals Is Changing." *New York Times on the Web* (30 September 2000).

Shultz, George P. "How a Republican Desegregated the South's Schools." *New York Times* (8 January 2003), p. A23.

Silverstein, Arthur. *Pure Politics and Impure Science: The Swine Flu Affair.* Baltimore: Johns Hopkins University Press, 1981.

Simon, James F. *What Kind of Nation?* New York: Simon & Schuster, 2002.

Simpson, Brooks D. "Continuous Hammering and Mere Attrition: Lost Cause Critics and the Military Reputation of Ulysses S. Grant" In Carl Gallagher and Alan T. Nolan, eds., *The Myth of the Lost Cause and Civil War History.* Bloomington: Indiana University Press, 2000.

_____. *The Reconstruction Presidents.* Lawrence University Press of Kansas, 1998.

_____. *Ulysses S. Grant: Triumph Over Adversity, 1822–1865.* Boston: Houghton Mifflin, 2000.

Skidmore, Max J. "Abraham Lincoln: World Political Symbol for the Twenty-First Century." *White House Studies* 2:1 (2002), pp. 17–35.

_____. *Legacy to the World: A Study of America's Political Ideas.* New York: Peter Lang, 1999.

_____. *Medicare and the American Rhetoric of Reconciliation.* Tuscaloosa: University of Alabama Press, 1970.

_____. "Ranking and Evaluating Presidents: The Case of Theodore Roosevelt." *White House Studies,* 1:4 (2001).

_____. "Ronald Reagan and Operation Coffeecup: A Hidden Episode in American History." *Journal of American Culture* 12:3 (fall 1989).

_____. *Social Security and its Enemies* Boulder, CO: Westview, 1999.

_____. "Theodore Roosevelt on Race and Gender." *Journal of American Culture* 21:2 (Summer 1998).

_____, ed. *Word Politics: Essays on Language and Politics.* Palo Alto, CA: James E. Freel, 1972.

Skowronek, Stephen. *The Politics Presidents Make: Leadership from John Adams to George Bush.* Cambridge, MA: Harvard University Press, 1993.

Slevin, Peter, and George Lardner, Jr. "Rush of Pardons Unusual in Scope, Lack of Scrutiny." *Washington Post* (10 March 2001); online at http://www.warroom.com/pardonme/unusualscope.htm, p. 1.

Smith, Elbert B. *The Presidencies of Zachary Taylor and Millard Fillmore.* Lawrence: University Press of Kansas, 1988.

_____. *The Presidency of James Buchanan.* Lawrence: University Press of Kansas, 1975.

Smith, Jean Edward. *Grant.* New York: Touchstone/Simon & Schuster, 2001.

Smith, Richard Norton. *Patriarch: George Washington and the New American Nation* Boston: Houghton Mifflin, 1993.

Sobel, Lester A., ed. *Presidential Succession: Ford, Rockefeller and the 25th Amendment* New York: Facts on File, 1975.

Sobel, Robert. *Coolidge: An American Dilemma.* Washington, DC: Regnery, 1998.

Socolofsky, Homer E., and Allan B. Spetter. *The Presidency of Benjamin Harrison.* Lawrence: University Press of Kansas, 1987.

Stampp, Kenneth M. "The Concept of a Perpetual Union." *Journal of American History.* 65 (June 1978).

Steinberg, Alfred. *The First Ten: The Founding Presidents and Their Administrations.* Garden City, NY: Doubleday, 1967.

Stid, Daniel D. *The President as Statesman: Woodrow Wilson and the Constitution.* Lawrence: University Press of Kansas, 1998.

Stockman, David A. *The Triumph of Politics*. New York: Avon Books, 1987.
Sunstein, Cass R. "The Warrior's Tale." *The American Prospect*. (July/August 2003.
"Swine Flu (Supplement)," 317.0. The Case Program. Harvard University, John F. Kennedy School of Government. Online at http://www.ksgcase.harvard.edu/case.htm?PID=317
Taylor, Alan. "John Adams." In Alan Brinkley and Davis Dyer, eds., *Reader's Companion to the American Presidency*. Boston: Houghton Mifflin, 2000.
Trani, Eugene P., and David L. Wilson, *The Presidency of Warren G. Harding*. Lawrence: University Press of Kansas, 1977.
Trefousse, Hans L. *Andrew Johnson*. New York: W. W. Norton, 1989. p. 196.
_____. *Rutherford B. Hayes*. New York: Times Books/Henry Holt, 2002.
Truman, Harry S. *The Autobiography of Harry S Truman*. Robert H. Ferrell, ed. Columbia: University of Missouri Press, 2002.
_____. "Harry S Truman 1947 Diary." Handwritten. Harry S. Truman Library and Museum. Online at http://www.trumanlibrary.org/diary/page23.htm.
_____. *Mr. Citizen*. New York: Bernard Geis, 1960.
Truman, Margaret. *First Ladies*. New York: Fawcett Columbine, 1995.
Tulis, Jeffrey K. *The Rhetorical Presidency*. Princeton: Princeton University Press, 1987.
Waldrup, Carole Chandler. *The Vice Presidents*. Jefferson, NC: McFarland, 1996.
Waterman, Richard W. *The Changing American Presidency*. Cincinnati: Atomic Dog, 2003.
Watson, Harry L. "Andrew Jackson" In Alan Brinkley and Davis Dyer, eds., *Reader's Companion to the American Presidency*. Boston: Houghton Mifflin, 2000.
Watson, Robert P. *The Presidents' Wives: Reassessing the Office of First Lady*. Boulder, CO: Lynne Rienner, 2000.
_____, and Ann Gordon, eds., *Anticipating Madam President*. Boulder, CO: Lynne Rienner, 2003.
Weber, Ralph E., ed., *Talking with Harry*. Wilmington, DE: Scholarly Resources, 2001.
Weisman, Steven. *The Great Tax Wars*. New York: Simon & Schuster, 2002.
Wert, Jeffry D. "James Longstreet and the Lost Cause" In Carl Gallagher and Alan T. Nolan, eds, *The Myth of the Lost Cause and Civil War History*. Bloomington: Indiana University Press, 2000.
West, James (Carl Withers, pseudonym). *Plainville, U.S.A.* New York: Columbia University Press, 1945.
White, Leonard. *The Federalists: A Study in Administrative History*. New York: Macmillan, 1948.
White, Ronald C., Jr. *Lincoln's Greatest Speech: The Second Inaugural*. New York: Simon & Schuster, 2002.
Whitney, David C. *The American Presidents* Garden City, NY: Doubleday, 1969.
Wicker, Tom. "A Deliberate Deficit" *New York Times* (19 July 1985).
_____. *Dwight D. Eisenhower*. New York: Times Books/Henry Holt, 2002.
_____. *One of Us: Richard Nixon and the American Dream*. New York: Random House, 1991.
Williams, William Appleman. "What this Country Needs...." *New York Review of Books* (5 Nov. 1970).
Wills, Garry. *James Madison*. New York: Henry Holt, 2002.
_____. *The Kennedy Imprisonment: A Meditation on Power*. Rev. ed. Boston: Houghton Mifflin/Mariner, 2002.
_____. *Lincoln at Gettysburg: The Words that Remade America*. New York: Simon & Schuster, 1992.
_____. *A Necessary Evil: A History of American Distrust of Government*. New York: Simon & Schuster, 1999.
Wilson, Major L. *The Presidency of Martin Van Buren*. Lawrence: University Press of Kansas, 1984.

INDEX